THE UNIVERSITY OF CALIFORNIA
LIBRARY AT BERKELEY

1900–1945

THE UNIVERSITY OF CALIFORNIA
LIBRARY AT BERKELEY

1900–1945

BY

KENNETH G. PETERSON

UNIVERSITY OF CALIFORNIA PRESS
BERKELEY · LOS ANGELES · LONDON
1970

University of California Publications
LIBRARIANSHIP: 8

Approved for publication November 21, 1969
Issued September 28, 1970
Price $6.00

University of California Press
Berkeley and Los Angeles

◇

University of California Press, Ltd.
London, England

ISBN: 0-520-09211-2

Library of Congress Catalog Card No.: 71-629639
© 1970 by the Regents of the University of California
Printed in the United States of America

CONTENTS

PREFACE

THE PURPOSE of this account of the University of California library at Berkeley from 1900 to 1945 is twofold. First, it traces the growth of one of the nation's great research libraries during the most crucial years of its development. In that period the book collection increased from approximately 80,000 to over 1,250,000 volumes; annual expenditures for materials rose from about $7,000 to $80,000 (1941/42); and the scholarly value and comprehensiveness of the library's holdings became widely recognized. Second, it contributes a significant amount of data and knowledge which, along with similar studies about other institutions, will provide an understanding of academic library developments in the United States. Since there is no single comprehensive history on this subject for the years after 1800, the accounts of individual college and university libraries will serve as a valuable basis from which a larger history may eventually be written.

The scope of this study has necessarily been limited. In 1930, Dora Smith wrote (for the Master of Arts in Librarianship degree at California) a thesis entitled "The History of the University of California Library to 1900." On the basis of time, therefore, the period here covered extends from 1900, where the Smith thesis concluded, to 1945, when the Leupp administration ended and the library was on the threshold of a new period of post-war development. Events prior to 1900, however, have been reviewed in many instances to provide helpful background information. Consideration has also been restricted primarily to the General Library and those branches on the Berkeley campus that were under the jurisdiction of the University librarian during those years. Thus, the Bancroft Library, departmental libraries, and other smaller collections that were administered separately from the General Library are only discussed briefly.

A topical arrangement has been used for presenting information. Subjects have been broadly grouped into eight chapters: two dealing with collection development, two with the people responsible for library growth, one with buildings and facilities, one with administrative organization and finances, one with organization and distribution of materials, and a final one with public services provided by the library. Within these chapters arrangement has sometimes been subtopical and sometimes chronological, depending upon the nature of the subjects covered. The introduction briefly describes the State of California and its University as the setting for the library, and the conclusion draws attention to those aspects of the library's development that were most significant. Tables and other relevant supplementary data have been included in the appendixes.

Primary source materials related to the University and the library are abundantly available and have been heavily used. These include the reports of the regents' secretary, the University president, the librarian, and the Library Committee; they also include the minutes of the Board of Regents, the Academic Senate, the Library Committee, the Library Staff Council, and the Library Staff Association. In addition, Rowell's Letter Books, manuscripts, and other papers; very complete office files for the entire Leupp period; and the files of the University president were indispensable. Oral interviews were held with seventeen people, including staff and faculty members who were associated with the library before 1945, and members of the Leupp family; information gathered from these people proved exceptionally helpful. Finally, supporting secondary materials pertaining to California, the University, American higher education, and academic librarianship were also consulted.

Acknowledgments are in order for many individuals who offered information, suggestions, encouragement, and help in the preparation of this work for publication. From the University of California they include: Ray E. Held, J. Periam Danton, and Raynard C. Swank of the School of Librarianship; Donald Coney, University librarian (1945–1968); Thomas R. McConnell of the Center for the Study of Higher Education; James R. K. Kantor, University archivist; John Barr Tompkins and other members of the Bancroft Library staff; Verne A. Stadtman, editor of *The Centennial Record of the University of California;* Bette Eriskin, secretary to the University librarian; and the secretaries in the Office of the Regents' Secretary and the Office of the Academic Senate. From the University of Virginia they include: Donald Jackson, editor of the Papers of George Washington; Ray W. Frantz, Jr., University librarian; and Martha Gunter, who prepared the final typescript. Gratitude is especially expressed to the people who were available for interviews; their enthusiasm for the writing of this account added personal meaning to the endeavor. Finally, the patience, understanding, and moral support of my wife and children have been the most valuable of all.

KENNETH G. PETERSON

INTRODUCTION

As a state, California was especially well endowed to develop a University destined to achieve national distinction. Its abundance of natural resources and favorable climatic conditions attracted people of great diversity from all sections of the United States and many foreign lands to become its citizens. California's population of 1,500,000 in 1900 accounted for slightly under 2 percent of the national total; by 1945 its 9,000,000 residents represented over 6 percent of the nation's population. Although agriculture and mining primarily formed the basis of the state's early economy, a wide variety of industries developed in the twentieth century vastly increased California's commercial activities and financial resources.

California's cultural attainments provided a favorable setting for the University's development. The state won literary recognition for the works of Frank Norris, Jack London, Kathleen Norris, Edwin Markham, John Steinbeck, and Henry Miller; at the same time the national conscience was stirred by the writings of Ambrose Bierce, Robinson Jeffers, Lincoln Steffens, and Upton Sinclair. Although widespread attention was drawn to the motion picture industry in southern California, in the fields of music and the theater San Francisco had gained a reputation rivaling that of the East's largest cities. Hardly less significant were the state's art and museum collections, which ranked among the nation's finest. California had become a haven for artists and musicians who established colonies at Carmel, Santa Barbara, and other communities along the Pacific.

Interest in public education was expressed by California's constitution of 1849, which called for establishment of a system of common schools and a state university. At the beginning of the twentieth century 17 percent of the state's annual expenditure was used to support elementary and secondary schools; by 1945 this budget item had increased to 23 percent. California benefitted not only from its publicly supported university system and many junior and four-year colleges, but also from a significant number of private institutions of higher education. Several of these, including Stanford University, California Institute of Technology, and the University of Southern California, had gained national prominence. Having created a state library in 1850, California also passed legislation to authorize establishing tax-supported city libraries in 1878 and county library systems in 1909. Notable privately developed collections, such as the Hubert Howe Bancroft Library at Berkeley, the William Andrews Clark Library at Los Angeles, the Henry E. Huntington Library at San Marino, and the Hoover Library of War, Revolution and Peace at Stanford, further evidenced the value of California's educational and cultural resources.

The history of the University of California, which was established in 1868, divides into three general periods. The earliest period, spanning the last third of the nineteenth century, saw the University through the years of its founding and consolidation as an institution of higher learning. The latest period, which began at the close of World War II, has been one of tremendous growth and expansion. Between these two periods occurred the most crucial phase in the University's development: in that time the character of the institution as a first-rate center for education and research was molded. According to Clark Kerr, "During the administration of President Benjamin Ide Wheeler, the University of California became a university in fact as well as in name; during the administration of Robert Gordon Sproul, it became one of the most eminent universities in the nation."[1]

By 1900 the University had reached an enrollment of 3,337 students with 188 faculty members, and was approaching an annual income of $500,000. Among the twelve universities in the United States with over 2,500 students (California, Chicago, Columbia, Cornell, Harvard, Illinois, Michigan, Minnesota, Northwestern, Pennsylvania, Wisconsin, and Yale), California ranked fifth in total enrollment, sixth in number of graduate students, eighth in total income, and eleventh in faculty size. Compared with the five state-supported universities in that group (California, Illinois, Michigan, Minnesota, and Wisconsin), California's standing was first in number of graduate students, third in total number of students and amount of income, and fourth in faculty size.[2]

From 1900 to 1945 the University grew tremendously as enrollments multiplied, new campuses were developed, and educational programs expanded far beyond earlier conceptions. Benjamin Ide Wheeler, who served as president from 1899 to 1919, brought to that position strong personal qualities of scholarship, leadership, and administrative skill. During his years in office several new academic departments, the schools of architecture, education, and jurisprudence, and the graduate division were established, and a large number of new buildings were constructed. Under Wheeler's influence the faculty was strengthened, student government was encouraged, and several "branches" for special activities were created beyond Berkeley.

---

[1]Clark Kerr, "Foreword," in George A. Pettitt, *Twenty-eight Years in the Life of a University President* (Berkeley: University of California, 1966), p. iii.

[2] *Report of the Commissioner of Education,* U. S. Bureau of Education (Washington: 1900–01), II, 1652–71, 1688–1704.

In the 1920's the presidency of the University passed successively to two noted scholars drawn from the California faculty, David Prescott Barrows (1919–23) and William Wallace Campbell (1923–30). Rising post-war student enrollments, the "faculty revolt" against the vestige of Wheeler's administrative authority, and the pressing needs for additional facilities at Berkeley and expanded educational services in other parts of the state challenged the fortitude of these men. Both Barrows and Campbell were determined in the face of these problems not to compromise academic excellence. Fortunately, sufficient funds were provided to maintain the quality of the faculty, construct new buildings, develop a "southern branch" which became the University of California at Los Angeles in 1927, and encourage research activities.

California and the nation were on the threshold of the great depression when Robert Gordon Sproul became University president in 1930. With deft administrative ability and dedicated concern for public higher education, Sproul successfully brought the University through a difficult period when financial support was seriously limited. During World War II, when much needed building construction was postponed and many students and faculty members were called for military service, Sproul again mobilized the University's resources to meet new challenges in education and research. Although groomed as an administrator rather than a scholar, Sproul won the respect of the academic community and led the University to a position of national distinction.

Evaluations of its faculty gave several indications of the University's academic strength. In 1934 the American Council on Education rated California's teaching staff as distinguished or adequate in thirty-one fields. No other American university was ranked higher. In the number of distinguished departments, according to the same report, the University placed second only to Harvard. An analysis of the scholars listed in *American Men of Science* (1938), made by Stephen S. Visher of Indiana University, showed that while the University of California ranked after Harvard, the University of Chicago, and Columbia in total number of names included, California's gain since the similar previous study (1927) was the greatest.[3] When Ernest O. Lawrence received the Nobel prize in 1939 for developing the cyclotron, California was the first state university to have a faculty member so honored.

In terms of its graduates also, the University made a favorable showing during Sproul's presidency. In 1940, when Kunkel and Prentice analyzed

[3] Stephen S. Visher, "Education of the Younger Starred Scientists," *Journal of Higher Education*, X (1939), 124–32. (References from pp. 128–9.)

the achievements of American university graduates, as indicated by a survey of names included in *Who's Who in America* during the preceding decade, California ranked second highest among all institutions. A survey of the recipients of Guggenheim Foundation fellowships awarded from 1925 to 1942 showed that graduates from California outnumbered those from any other university.[4]

Rebounding from the effects of the war years, the University's statewide enrollment rose to over 40,000 students by 1946, making it the nation's largest institution of higher education. Berkeley's 22,000 students ranked that campus alone in fourth place (after Columbia, Minnesota, and Illinois) among American universities. California's total income of $24,000,000 at that time was exceeded only by that of Michigan, Illinois, and Harvard.[5] The University of California was ready to embark upon a new and even more distinguished period of service.

Within the context provided by California and its University, and through the efforts of determined and influential men, the library at Berkeley developed with strength during the years from 1900 to 1945 and served as an indispensable asset to the scholarly community.

[4] *Report of President Robert Gordon Sproul to the Regents of the University of California, September 18, 1942* (mimeographed), 2 pp.

[5] *American Universities and Colleges* (5th ed.; Washington: American Council on Education, 1948), 1054 pp.

CHAPTER I

A LIBRARY FOR HIGHER SCHOLARSHIP

WHEN THE UNIVERSITY OF CALIFORNIA was chartered in 1868, it received the 1,036-volume library collection of the College of California. During the period before 1900 some funds were provided by the University for the purchase of additional library books, but these were generally quite meager. On several occasions the state legislature voted special appropriations for the University library. The largest of these, in 1885, amounted to $10,000. For a considerable share of its growth the library was dependent upon gifts. Despite financial limitations the book collection grew steadily. By 1900 it contained 80,224 volumes.[1] About that time, Joseph C. Rowell, University librarian, wrote the following description of the library: "While the University of California stands in the front rank of American institutions in respect to endowment, ability of its teachers, courses of instruction, and students, its library has not advanced with the same degree of rapidity; but the appropriation of its book funds in a certain fixed ratio, for different departments of knowledge represented in the faculty, annually for many years, has resulted in a fairly symmetric growth. Limitation in amounts of money for expenditure has one advantage (?)—only the best books are purchased."[2]

GROWTH AND FINANCIAL SUPPORT

After 1900 the library grew much more rapidly. By 1945 it contained 1,260,504 volumes,[3] an increase of 15.7 times. The rate of this growth can be seen in two ways: first, the book collection doubled four times during this period; second, the average increase in number of volumes every half decade from 1900 to 1945 was 36.8 percent.

---

[1] *Reports of the Librarian,* University of California (1900–44). Unless otherwise noted, statistics on the library's size have been derived from this source, hereinafter cited as *Librarian's Reports.* The *Librarian's Reports* for the years 1900–30 were included, sometimes with deletions, in the printed annual and biennial *Reports of the President,* and also printed separately in full form for most years after 1910; unless otherwise noted, citations have been made from the separately printed copies. From 1931 through 1944 the *Librarian's Reports* were not printed; citations for those years have been made from typewritten copies included in the bound volume, *Reports of the Librarian, 1931–1944.*

[2] Joseph C. Rowell, "The University of California Library," *Public Libraries,* IV (1899), 212–3.

[3] *Volumes in the Libraries of the University of California, 1 July 1945.* (mimeographed; February 1946), 1 p., hereinafter cited as *Volumes in the Libraries . . . 1945.*

In 1945 the total number of library volumes on the Berkeley campus was distributed as follows: General Library, 945,006; Biology Library, 80,489; Lange Library of Education, 7,440; Boalt Hall (School of Jurisprudence) library, 82,649; Engineering Library, 10,766; Giannini Foundation (agricultural economics) library, 5,503; Bancroft Library, 79,415; Bureau of Public Administration library, 521; and 85 departmental libraries, 48,715.[4]

The University of California library's growth may be compared with that of other major American universities from 1900 to 1947 (appendix A, table 1). Among all college and university libraries in 1900, California was tied with Georgetown University for thirteenth place in the size of its collection. By 1947, California ranked seventh. During that period, among American universities that by 1947 enrolled 5,000 or more students and had libraries containing over one million volumes, California's rate of library growth at Berkeley was exceeded only by that of the Universities of Illinois and Minnesota.

Spanning the years from 1910 through 1940, an average of 70.7 percent of the volumes added to the California library were acquired by purchases, 22.3 percent by gifts, and 7 percent through exchange arrangements with other institutions. Since the value of books sent through the exchange program was not deducted from the library's budget, books received by exchange constituted no charge against the book funds. The receipt of exchange books plus those acquired as gifts together accounted for almost 30 percent of the library collection's growth.

The amount of funds available for the purchase of library books increased from $7,000 in 1899/1900 to $61,000 in 1944/45 (appendix A, table 2). For those years an average of 13.5 percent of the total amounts came from gift and designated funds, and 86.5 percent from the general fund. This strong upward trend reflected not only the overall growth patterns of California and the University but also the University's distinctive movement toward greater emphasis on graduate programs and research which required richer library resources.

Several events during that period accounted for the book fund's development. An increase from $7,000 in 1899/1900 to over $21,000 in 1904/05 resulted from President Wheeler's great concern for the library. In his first annual report to the regents he pressed for an increase in library funds. This resulted in an appropriation of $15,000 for books and periodicals in the budget for the 1901/02 fiscal year. During the twenty years of Wheeler's

---

[4] Ibid. The Biology Library and Lange Library of Education were branches of the General Library and administratively under the jurisdiction of the University librarian on the Berkeley campus.

presidency annual library book funds multiplied over four times. During the 1920's the library's book budget rose 150 percent. The prosperous economic conditions of that decade along with an ever-increasing interest in graduate study and research projects at the University were responsible for this spectacular growth. The depression of the thirties, however, caused a marked decline in library appropriations. By the fiscal year 1933/34 the book fund had dipped to $50,083. Fortunately this trend was reversed within a few years. The library budget provided $75,000 for books by 1939/40, and $80,000 for each of the fiscal years 1940/41 and 1941/42. The effects of World War II, which brought adjustments in the University's budget and the closing of many overseas sources for the purchase of books and periodicals, caused the library's book funds to decline once again. By 1944/45 the amount appropriated was $61,000.

Financial support for the University of California library at Berkeley may be compared with that of other major universities from 1919/20 through 1939/40 (appendix A, table 3). Considering expenditures (exclusive of salaries) for university libraries containing over one million volumes by 1943/44, California ranked ninth in 1919/20, eighth in 1924/25, seventh in 1929/30, eighth in 1934/35, and seventh in 1939/40. Thus, California's support was consistent when compared with other similar institutions. Moreover, in terms of financial resources California's rank was comparable with its rank for collection size.

The University of California was fortunate in receiving special gift funds to provide books for the library. In most cases this income was set apart for purchases in special subject fields. In some instances, however, it was used to supplement the general book funds. Several sizeable gift funds were received between the 1870's and the 1920's. Of the two largest, one came near the beginning and the other near the end of this period. In 1879, $50,000 was received as a bequest from Michael Reese, a highly successful San Francisco businessman, to purchase books in the arts, sciences, and literature. By 1945 the Reese Fund had provided total income of over $200,000, which was added to the general book funds. One hundred thousand dollars was received in 1919 from the estate of General Horace W. Carpentier of New York City. In keeping with Carpentier's interests President Wheeler designated the income from this fund "for the purchasing of books and other material of instruction and research relating to the five great areas of Asiatic civilization, particularly China, Japan, India, Arabia and Babylon."[5] In 1900 President Wheeler reported a gift of $25,000 from

[5] *Financial Statement,* University of California Academic Senate, Library Committee (1920/21), p. 3; 43 annual reports in one volume, hereinafter cited as *Financial Statements.*

Jane K. Sather, with $15,000 designated for the Law Library, and $10,000 for the General Library; income from the latter sum was used for materials in the fields of classical philology and archaeology. Subsequent additional gifts from Mrs. Sather increased the total amount of these funds to almost $35,000, and history was added as a subject for library book purchases.

On several occasions James K. Moffitt contributed to an endowment fund which amounted to over $5,000 by the early 1920's. In 1928 May T. Morrison gave $25,000, the income of which was used to purchase additional books for the Alexander F. Morrison Memorial Library. Other designated endowments for the library included a fund originally established by Regent E. A. Denicke in 1899, which grew through subsequent additions to $2,500 by 1923; the Eugene Meyer, Jr., fund of $2,000, received as a bequest in 1911; and the Horace Davis fund of $10,000, bequeathed to the University in 1917. No large designated gift funds were established during the 1930's because of the effects of the depression. The library did receive $1,900 in 1942 from the estate of Edmund C. Sanford to purchase books in the classics, and $5,000 in 1944 from Pauline A. Dworzek for books in the field of education.

In addition to endowment funds, the California library received numerous sums of money for specific purchases, plus book collections and private libraries as gifts or bequests. Although the specific value of these items cannot accurately be calculated, when added to the resources provided by the state, they enabled the library over a forty-five year period to develop an outstanding research collection.

Book Selection and the Development of Collecting Policies

Between 1900 and 1945, the faculty played the dominant role in the selection of library books at the University of California. This fact was not accidental but stemmed from the Orders of the Board of Regents. As early as 1884, according to the *Regents' Manual,* professors and instructors were directed to present lists of books to the Library Committee at least once a year as suggestions for purchase.[6] These lists were reviewed and adopted or revised by the committee after the librarian had been consulted regarding the prices and bibliographical verification of all items. This policy was reaffirmed in principle and its procedure described with considerable detail in the 1904 edition of the *Regents' Manual*. The essential change that had occurred was the transfer of review jurisdiction over the book-suggestion lists from the Library Committee to the librarian and the president of the University.

------

[6] "Orders of the Board," Article 478, *Regents' Manual,* University of California (1884,) p. 220.

When the regents' Orders relating to the library were revised in 1925, no reference was made to the regents' Library Committee or the president; responsibility for book selection was delegated to the faculty, the librarian, and the Library Committee of the Academic Senate. By 1938 the regents' *By-laws and Standing Orders* were shortened and only stated: "The University Library shall be administered in accordance with regulations to be prescribed by the President acting with the advice of the Academic Senate."[7]

After the Library Committee of the faculty was established and began meeting regularly in 1901, one of its major responsibilities was the allocation of the library's book funds.[8] The committee's minutes through the years show that its members took this responsibility very seriously. The book funds were held in two general categories. Designated funds from special gifts or endowments were used to purchase materials recommended either by the instructional departments of the University in whose subject fields they belonged or by the Library Committee itself. All nondesignated funds were considered part of the library's general book fund and subject to allocation by the committee.

The general funds were handled in two ways. Each year certain amounts were first set aside for specified types of materials, determined either by their form of publication or the nature of their usefulness to the book collection. Included here were periodicals and some serial publications, reference and general interest books, and materials in subject fields of particular importance. In most cases subcommittees were appointed to recommend purchases in each of these areas. The balance of the general fund was then distributed among the instructional departments. In order to make this distribution as equitable as possible, an allotment system was devised whereby the total amount of undesignated funds was divided each year into units. Although a distribution formula was never adopted, the standing of each department was considered by the committee in the assignment of units. Commenting on this method, University Librarian Harold L. Leupp wrote in 1923: "The Library Committee endeavors to arrive at some sort of idea of the relative book needs of the various departments by comparison of such information as the individual members of the Committee may have, by consideration of the courses given, by reference to any special plea that any department may have preferred, and by

---

[7] "Libraries and University Press," [Article] 1 (c), *By-laws and Standing Orders,* University of California Board of Regents (1938), p. 60.

[8] The Library Committee of the faculty, which was separate from the regents' Committee on Library and Museum, was first under the jurisdiction of the Graduate Council, later of the Academic Council, and finally of the Academic Senate; these changes are described in Chapter IV.

reference to the previous book expenditures of each department. . . . When the Committee has satisfied itself and has made a tentative allotment of units to each department, the sum available is divided by the total number of units allotted, giving the value of the individual unit."[9]

Once the funds had been allocated, each department was able to request the purchase of library materials to the limit of its allotment. Occasionally faculty members or departments complained about the unit assignment system. In response to one complaint a subcommittee appointed to review the matter reported in 1939 that "the system seems fairly responsive to changing requirements"[10] and recommended that it be retained. Thus, from 1900 to 1945 the method of allocating books funds remained essentially the same.

California's system of distributing book funds was not atypical of the practices followed at many other universities. Regarding this procedure Ralph E. Ellsworth, director of libraries at the University of Colorado, wrote in 1942: "In recent years it has usually been assumed that the funds would be divided, with a general sum left in the hands of the librarian."[11] Donald Coney, while librarian at the University of Texas in 1942, also wrote: "It is common practice for a university to assign the responsibility for selecting its library books to members of the faculty as a panel of experts."[12] Both Ellsworth and Coney went on to point out, however, that the real problem was to arrive at a satisfactory standard or formula on which the apportionment could be based. In analyzing the replies from an inquiry sent to fourteen university libraries, one of the conclusions stated by Robert Vosper, of the University of California at Los Angeles, in 1948 was: "Division of funds among fields should be made with as much objectivity as possible, but common sense is probably more useful in this task than any presently known statistical formula."[13] Vosper's statement well described the general practice that had evolved at Berkeley.

After units had been assigned to each department all faculty members were eligible to recommend titles for purchase. Although department chair-

[9] Harold L. Leupp to Dr. Guy S. Millberry, Dean, University of California College of Dentistry, San Francisco, Dec. 12, 1923, *Correspondence and Papers* (CU-12, Carton 8), University of California Archives, Berkeley.

[10] *Minutes,* University of California Academic Senate, Library Committee, Minute Book no. 3 (1921–45), Mar. 24, 1939, hereinafter cited as *Library Committee Minutes.*

[11] Ralph E. Ellsworth, "Some Aspects of the Problem of Allocating Book Funds Among Departments in Universities," *Library Quarterly,* XII (1942), 486.

[12] Donald Coney, "An Experimental Index for Apportioning Departmental Book Funds for a University Library," *Library Quarterly,* XII (1942), 422.

[13] Robert G. Vosper, "Allocation of the Book Budget: Experience at UCLA," *College and Research Libraries,* X (1949), 216.

men were to sign all order requests, the Library Committee had stated as early as 1908 that "this is not to be construed as implying that the right, or the responsibility, of ordering books rests exclusively with Heads of Departments."[14] Concern was expressed at times that in some departments the chairman or certain faculty members were doing most of the book selecting. In response to one such complaint, Professor A. C. Lawson, who served as committee chairman for many years, affirmed in 1912 that "other members of the department have a perfect right to nominate books for new purchase."[15]

Although the faculty played a major role in book selection from 1900 to 1945, the University librarian also participated actively in the selection process. Recognizing the important contribution the librarian could make, and perhaps aware of some faculty members' tendencies to press their own interests in selecting books, President Wheeler directed that "in the annual appropriation of the book fund a considerable part should be set apart for expenditure by the Librarian himself."[16] To comply with the president's wishes, the Library Committee annually designated a sum for purchases recommended by the librarian, and called the "Librarian's Fund." Although varying considerably in size during the course of years, this amount generally ranged between 2 and 5 percent of the total general book budget. In addition, the librarian was able to recommend purchases from the "General Interest Fund" as well as designated funds in specific areas. As secretary of the Library Committee and a member of several subcommittees, the librarian was also able to express freely his opinions concerning book selection and the overall development of the collection.

The participation of other library staff members in selecting books was limited. On several occasions attempts were made to open this activity to the professional staff. A plan was adopted by the Staff Council in 1912 appointing five members to serve on a book selection committee; each member was assigned to read book reviews in specific periodicals, from which recommendations for purchase were to be made.[17] The following year it was decided that members of the Reference Department should check second-hand and remainder catalogs as time allowed to make selec-

---

[14] *Library Committee Minutes,* Minute Book no. 1 (1901–10), Sept. 14, 1908.

[15] Andrew C. Lawson, University of California, Berkeley, to Harold L. Leupp, undated (written at bottom of Leupp letter to Lawson, Nov. 1, 1912), *Lawson Correspondence and Papers* (C-B 602), Bancroft Library, Berkeley.

[16] *Report of the President,* University of California (1898–1900), p. 29, hereinafter cited as *President's Report.*

[17] *Minutes,* University of California Library Staff Council (1911–38), Feb. 15, 1912, hereinafter cited as *Library Staff Council Minutes.*

tions for purchase.[18] Both of these activities continued for several years, but insufficient time devoted to them by the staff gradually led to their discontinuation. In 1929 the Serials and Exchange Division reported that its members were systematically checking the lists of official publications of foreign governments,[19] and a similar checking for United States government publications was reported by the Reference Department in 1931.[20] A General Interest Committee, made up of library staff members, was appointed by the Staff Council in 1936 to make recommendations for book purchases based upon reviews published in general interest periodicals. Neither the council's minutes nor the librarian's reports indicate any productive results from this action. Thus, by the thirties and early forties, aside from the work of the Gifts and Exchange Division and the development of the "sets" collection program under the direction of the Library Committee, the principal activity of book selection within the library was carried on by the librarian who largely concentrated this activity in his own office.

During the years 1900–45, both de facto and specifically developed selection policies were in operation at the University of California. Sometimes they operated fairly distinctly from each other, while on occasion their lines crossed. The philosophy which underlay all selection activities and policies throughout that period was expressed by University Librarian Joseph C. Rowell, who in 1906 wrote: "In purchasing books the chief end in view has been the building up of a complete library of reference and research for higher scholarship."[21]

In the de facto category the most important selection policy developed at California pertained to completing important files of periodical literature, filling gaps in published sets and monograph series, and purchasing new sets. Credit for this policy during the library's early years was due to the bibliothecal interest and foresight of Rowell. As early as 1885 he wrote: "The best foundation for an extensive reference library, such as that at Berkeley is rapidly becoming, consists in complete sets of periodical literature, of transactions and memoirs of learned bodies, literary or philological, scientific or technical."[22] For that year alone Rowell reported having been able to acquire or complete forty sets of publications.

On many occasions in the decades after 1900 need was expressed within

[18] Ibid., Feb. 13, 1913.

[19] Ibid., Oct. 4, 1929.

[20] Ibid., Feb. 6, 1931.

[21] "Librarian's Report," in *President's Report* (1904–06), p. 101.

[22] Joseph C. Rowell, "The University Library" (unpublished; 1885), 4 leaves, in his *Writings* (1880–1920), vol. III, no. 3, University of California Archives, Berkeley.

the Library Committee to concentrate efforts on filling gaps in the library's incomplete files of serial publications, and to appropriate sums specifically for the purchase of important sets of volumes. In the book budget for 1902/03, $1,000 was appropriated as a special designation to secure necessary items to complete sets.[23] In 1911 the Library Committee adopted a plan, proposed by Professor Frederick J. Teggart, allowing for an annual allotment of $5,000 for eight years to fill gaps in serial sets and purchase new sets; faculty members were asked to compile desiderata lists for this purpose. The designation of funds to meet these special needs was continued throughout the librarianship of both Rowell and Leupp. So important had this practice become, in fact, that it was incorporated into the library's major selection policy, formulated in 1931, and became an integral part of the acquisition program. The amount appropriated annually to fill gaps and purchase sets increased steadily until, by 1931/32, it reached $15,000, which was equivalent to almost 23 percent of the total book budget. Although this sum was reduced considerably when the book budget declined in the thirties, it began to assume renewed importance immediately preceding World War II, when it increased to $8,000 annually.

The acquisition of periodical literature was closely related to the policy of filling gaps and acquiring sets of publications. In 1900, $1,440 of California's $7,000 book budget was being spent for periodical subscriptions; that year Librarian Rowell recommended that the appropriation be increased 25 percent.[24] By 1904/05, the subscriptions fund was raised to $4,200. It continued to increase steadily until it reached $20,000 in 1934/35. This level was maintained until the closing of many foreign markets during World War II reduced the amount necessary and allowed a reserve fund to accumulate for post-war purchases. As the result of strong financial support the number of current periodicals received at California rose to 18,313 by 1940.[25]

During most of this period the subscriptions allotment was kept as a separate budget designation. In 1913, however, a plan was proposed and adopted to distribute a portion of the periodicals funds along with unit allotments to each department. Subscriptions in related subject fields were thus charged to departmental library funds. This arrangement continued until 1927 when, in response to complaints by the departments that more than half of their allotments were being spent to meet periodical costs and

---

[23] *Financial Statement* (1902/03), p. 1.

[24] Librarian's Report," in *President's Report* (1898–1900), p. 87.

[25] Harold L. Leupp to George A. Pettitt, Assistant to the President, University of California, Dec. 28, 1939, *Correspondence and Papers* (CU-12, Carton 28), University of California Archives, Berkeley.

not enough money was available for current book selections, the Library Committee rescinded its earlier action and reestablished a separate periodicals fund.

The overall policy at California regarding periodical subscriptions was based on several important decisions. Recognizing the great need for complete files, the Library Committee decided in 1911 that no subscriptions could be discontinued by the librarian or any department without the committee's consent. Librarian Leupp later commented: "This ruling was made necessary by the habit developed by certain departments of carrying a subscription for a year or two, dropping it in order to utilize the funds for something else, and then picking it up later on, leaving a gap in the file."[26] The committee's policy remained in effect throughout Leupp's administration. The continuing importance of uninterrupted subscriptions was especially recognized in the 1930's when, despite the effects of reduced budgets, both the Library Committee and Leupp stood firmly against any decrease in funds for periodicals. This was the wisest decision made concerning the California collection in the period 1900–45, for it assured ongoing support in an area where the library was already strong and in which its continued strength was indispensable to the research activities of the University. Although some subscriptions were cancelled, these were mainly for titles duplicated between the General Library and departmental collections, and where the effects were not detrimental to the needs of scholarship. In 1934, the Library Committee reported to the Academic Senate that "the serial continuations, constituting the basic element of the collections, should not be interrupted."[27] The next year this policy was formally stated in the committee's minutes: "The Library Committee has adopted the policy of maintaining the periodical files, even at the expense of other important and legitimate demands upon the book fund. This policy has been carefully considered, and accords with that of . . . the great majority of libraries of the scholarly type."[28]

Another decision that helped assure unbroken periodical files was made in response to the effects of World Wars I and II. During both those periods, when the flow of materials from overseas was disrupted, the library arranged for foreign dealers to store its periodicals until the end of hostilities. In these endeavors California cooperated with other univer-

---

[26] Harold L. Leupp to Miss Harriet E. Boss, Librarian, College of the Pacific, San Jose, California, Nov. 21, 1923, *Correspondence and Papers* (CU-12, Carton 12), University of California Archives, Berkeley.

[27] *Report of the Library Committee for the Year 1934/35,* University of California Academic Senate, Library Committee, p. 8, hereinafter cited as *Library Committee Reports.*

[28] *Library Committee Minutes,* Minute Book no. 3 (1921–45), April 29, 1935.

sity libraries and government agencies. The outcome was not completely successful, however, especially during World War II, since some of the stored materials were destroyed in the fighting. Yet through their actions Librarians Rowell and Leupp and members of the Library Committee sought to uphold the library's basic policy regarding a strong periodical collection.

Collecting Californiana was another important aspect of the library's selection policies. As a public trust a state university library ought to show particular interest in the literary products of its own area; at California it was especially true for several reasons. Rowell's personal interest in gathering such materials laid the foundations for the collection. Rowell was an avid collector. Whenever possible he personally contacted California authors and publishers, as well as persons who wrote about the state, requesting copies of their works for the library. This activity continued not only until Rowell retired in 1919 but also while he served the University as librarian emeritus and archivist until his death in 1938. Rowell did not limit his collecting to published materials but sought with great effort to obtain the personal papers and manuscripts of many notable persons on the California literary scene. The University was fortunate, moreover, in securing two very valuable Californiana collections: the libraries of Robert E. Cowan and Hubert Howe Bancroft. The strength of the University's history department and the interest of its faculty also favored the library's collecting of Californiana. In response to a survey showing that no other library in the state was systematically collecting these materials, the University library in 1941 reaffirmed its policy to collect "books by prolific California authors, or books published in California."[29]

Finally, the allocation of library book funds to instructional departments directed selection mainly along subject lines. Some exceptions did develop, such as collecting the complete works of noted authors, procuring theses from German universities, extensively acquiring both United States and foreign government documents, and adding materials to strengthen special collections already in the library. Provision was also made for purchasing reference and general interest books, largely at the recommendation of the librarian. Not until the collection was surveyed in the 1930's and a formal policy statement drawn up was there a shift away from selection mainly according to subject fields parallel with the departments of instruction. The broadening and overlapping of traditional scholarly disciplines, as well as the growing international interests of the academic community during that period, was mainly responsible for this change.

---

[29] *Library Staff Council Minutes* (1939–45), Feb. 7, 1941.

The library's de facto policies were formalized to the extent that they were described in the annual *Financial Statements* issued by the Library Committee from 1902/03 through 1944/45. As early as 1903 it was indicated that "a suitable portion of the funds . . . should be set apart annually for the purchase of books in fields of learning that seem properly entitled to representation in the library even though they do not fall within the boundaries of the regularly organized departments of instruction at present provided by the University." For many years, however, purchase recommendations had to be submitted through department chairmen, and it was difficult in practice for book selection to cross subject lines. During the twenties and thirties the committee became increasingly receptive to suggestions that many faculty members made directly to it. By 1942 the committee indicated in its *Financial Statement* that "Recommendations for purchase . . . will be received from any member of the faculty, and all officers of instruction . . . are urged to give the Library Committee the benefit of their suggestions."

In 1930 a plan was adopted by the Library Committee to survey the collection to determine its basic needs. A special Survey Committee was appointed with Professor Robert J. Kerner as chairman. Recognizing the need to clarify the library's aims and objectives in collection development, Kerner's committee studied the situation carefully and drew up a detailed and comprehensive policy statement. After review and some revision by the Library Committee, this statement was submitted to the Academic Senate where it was officially approved in November, 1931. This action not only provided California with its most completely formulated policy statement on book selection up to that time, but also launched the library on a proposed ten-year acquisition program purposely planned to strengthen the collection to meet the growing research interests of the University.

Entitled "Special Report of the Library Committee on the Aims of the University Library based upon the Survey of the Collection," this statement set forth three primary objectives: "first, to build up the collection of books and documents more systematically; second, to avoid duplication of special collections, and to reduce the price-raising competition among libraries west of the Rockies by an inter-library agreement as to special aims; third, to offer Friends of the University Library a concrete program for their support."[30] These proposals were not intended to eliminate existing book-selection activities, but to supplement the more routine requests submitted by the departments, faculty members, and the librarian.

---

[30] *Library Committee Minutes,* Minute Book no. 3 (1921–45), 3 pp., mimeographed copy tipped in after minutes for Dec. 2, 1931.

Collection development needs were then presented and outlined in three main sections. The first one, "Basic Immediate Needs of the University Library in All Fields," stressed the indispensable value of published sets as "the fundamental sources of human knowledge in all its branches." Building upon an earlier informal policy for filling gaps, it sought to engage the library in a systematic and thorough program, with supplementary finances and staff, to acquire "(1) publications of the leading academies and learned societies; (2) the most important periodicals, especially those of older date; (3) documents, newspapers, pamphlets and maps . . . especially indispensable for the Social Sciences"; it also gave greater recognition to acquiring "(4) important editions and translations in literature, as well as other materials indispensable for research in the Humanities, Arts, and Sciences." The value to research of collecting in depth was thus formally recognized. Although not completely new, these collection aims were now officially set forth and soon also related to a definite program for implementation.

The statement's second section dealt with "Special Aims of the University Library." Recognizing the unique strengths the library had already attained, and mindful of areas of knowledge of primary concern to the University, the report proposed collecting to national preeminence in some fields and in others to preeminence on the Pacific Coast. The fields for national preeminence were: "(1) The Pacific Basin; (2) History of Science; (3) Applied Social Sciences; (4) Semi-Arid and Sub-Tropical Agriculture; (5) Agricultural economics." Preeminence on the Pacific Coast was to be achieved for: "(1) Engineering and Technology; (2) Americana (exclusive of first editions and rarities understood to be the special province of the Huntington Library); (3) The History and Literature of Southwestern America, Latin America and Spain; (4) History of Modern Europe; (5) Russian Language and Literature and general history of Russia; (6) Italian Literature and History; (7) Classical Archaeology; (8) The British Empire." Departing from the practice of selecting library materials primarily according to subjects, this section established collecting interests along the lines of geographical area basis and became widely recognized among research libraries after World War II, especially through the development of the Farmington Plan. Yet the designation of specific areas within these two groups showed that at California as early as 1931 a regional approach to collecting was already recognized as important.

In its last section the report considered "Relatively Undeveloped Fields" in which the library had "few or almost no materials." In some of these the University was offering courses, whereas others represented "kindred or related fields" in which instruction might eventually be given. In either case, "energetic support" was called for so that the library might overcome its serious deficiencies. The fields included in this group, selected on the basis of consultations with faculty members, were: "(1) Music and History of Music; (2) The Arts and History of the Arts; (3) Dutch Language, Literature and History; (4) Scandinavian Languages, Literatures and History; (5) Languages, Literatures and History of the Minor Slavic Peoples; (6) Languages, Literatures and History of the Near East, including the Ancient Near East and Byzantine Period; (7) Languages, Literatures and History of the Middle East, including especially Persia and India; (8) Expansion of Europe; (9) Malayan Languages and Literatures; (10) Celtic Language and Literature."

California's overall development of book-selection policies may be considered in the light of several statements by other university librarians. William Warner Bishop of the University of Michigan wrote in 1940 that there were four types of materials needed for research: "specialized periodicals in the various subjects of study; ... transactions, memoirs, bulletins, reports and other printed materials issued by academies, specialized societies, universities, museums, observatories and other institutions; ... publications of governments, including laws and reports of court decisions; [and] ... the immense number of printed books ... [that are] the staple of libraries."[31] Bishop's recommendations, written nine years after California's 1931 policy statement was adopted, parallel very closely the "basic immediate needs" which that statement presents. In 1953 Herman H. Fussler of the University of Chicago wrote: "All libraries have acquisition policies, whether they are recognized or not, and whether the policies are stated or not.... The extent to which a library fails to recognize the kinds of policies which it is following may possibly be a measure of the potential inadequacies of its collections over a long period of time."[32] California was not distinguished from other university libraries by the fact that it had, during a period of years, evolved book-selection policies. Rather, it was the recognition of those policies and the adoption in 1931 of a formal statement of selection aims and objectives that led California further to develop a collection of sufficient strength to support research work. Finally, Robert G. Vosper, while librarian of the University of Kansas in 1953, observed also that "an acquisition policy need not be a limiting factor full of 'Thou

[31] William Warner Bishop, "The Responsibility of American Libraries for the Acquisition of the Materials for Research," in William E. Randall, ed., *The Acquisition and Cataloging of Books* (Chicago: University of Chicago Press, 1940), pp. 39, 41.

[32] Herman H. Fussler, "Acquisition Policy: A Symposium; the Larger University Library," *College and Research Libraries,* XIV (1953), 363.

shalt not'; it may be quite the opposite, a statement of hopes and plans."[33] At California this was indeed true, for the development of collection policies culminating in the 1931 statement was followed by a program aimed not only at overcoming the library's weaknesses, but also at improving its position in those areas in which it was already strong.

Although California's collection was still relatively small in 1900, its foundations were laid and a pattern for its development had begun to emerge. The successful expansion that occurred during the next forty-five years was due largely to the provisions by the Board of Regents and the presidents of financial support commensurate with the University's growth, as well as their delegation of primary responsibility to the faculty for the collection's development. In terms of the kinds of materials selected, the library benefited from the high academic quality and ever-broadening scholarly interests of the faculty, and the constant attention and bibliothecal interest of the librarians. These elements working together made it possible, as Rowell suggested many years earlier, for California to build a library "for higher scholarship."

---

[33] Robert G. Vosper, "Acquisition Policy—Fact or Fancy?" *College and Research Libraries,* XIV (1953), 368.

CHAPTER II

AMASSING A RESEARCH COLLECTION

THE DEVELOPMENT of an outstanding library collection at the University of California required much time and effort. Along with selecting materials and particularly in connection with specialized collecting activities, a well-organized and capably staffed acquisition department was essential. Moreover, the value of thoughtful planning for the library's growth, based upon developing specialized collecting programs, was recognized. As a result, by 1945 California's library not only supported the demanding research activities of the University but also had won widespread acclaim within the American academic community.

THE ORDER AND ACCESSIONS DEPARTMENT

Before 1900, when the library staff numbered only a few persons and there was no formal organization into departments, the work of acquisition was carried on mainly by Librarian Rowell himself. An Order Department was established when Arthur B. Smith was appointed to the staff in November 1902.[1] Working alone in the capacity of order librarian, for nine years Smith handled all purchases for the General Library and department libraries. Sydney B. Mitchell joined the staff in August 1911 and, upon Smith's resignation later in the year, took charge of acquisitions work. At that time the department's name was changed to Accessions Department, which it was called until after 1945. The number of staff members in the department gradually increased during those years as the library's acquisitions grew. Mitchell continued to supervise the department until 1922 when, because of his responsibilities as associate librarian and chairman of the Department of Library Science, he was succeeded by Frank M. Bumstead. Following Bumstead, the position of department head was held from 1939 to 1942 by Frank A. Lundy, and beginning in 1942 by Dorothy B. Keller.

The activities of the Accessions Department were described by Librarian Leupp in 1929.[2] It was responsible for "the preparation and handling of book orders and periodical subscriptions for the General Library and all

---

[1] "Librarian's Report," in *President's Report* (1902–04), p. 98.
[2] Harold L. Leupp to Edward A. Henry, Director, University of Cincinnati Libraries, Cincinnati, Ohio, Feb. 25, 1929, *Correspondence and Papers* (CU-12, Carton 12), University of California Archives, Berkeley.

department libraries in Berkeley." In addition it performed various biblio-graphical tasks such as "preparation of desiderata lists, checking dealers' catalogs and order cards with the library catalog and other records; han-dling and acknowledging gifts; [and] handling exchanges." Some pro-cessing activities were also performed by the department, including "re-cording, stamping and distribution of serials, preparation and handling of binding orders for the General Library and some department libraries; repairing books; packing or wrapping books for shipment and unpacking shipments received; keeping accounts for approximately 200 library funds; cutting leaves in books and periodicals; [and] perforating, plating and pocketing books." Subsequently, some of these activities were made the responsibility of the Division of Serials and Exchanges and its successors, the Division of Gifts and Exchanges and the Serials Division.

SPECIAL ASPECTS OF BOOK ACQUISITION AND COLLECTION DEVELOPMENT

At California special acquisition activities proved indispensable in build-ing the University's research collection. Supplementing routine purchases, the "sets" program, book buying abroad by faculty members, and acquiring large quantities of materials enbloc added richly to the library's resources. Regular appropriations for binding and an aggressive exchange program likewise greatly strengthened the collection from 1900 through 1945.

THE "SETS" PROGRAM

The need to fill gaps in important sets and series publications had been recognized at California before 1900, and faculty members were encouraged to order materials wherever possible to meet these needs. Following appoint-ment of the Survey Committee in 1930, its chairman, Professor Kerner, pro-posed that a qualified bibliographer be appointed to the library staff to locate gaps in the collection and submit orders to fill them. This proposal stemmed from a growing realization by faculty members that time pre-vented them from engaging in sufficient bibliographical work for this ac-tivity. Morever, the faculty was coming to recognize that increasing num-bers of librarians possessed skill and training in this area, and could make valuable contributions by working full-time at book selection. Kerner's suggestion was favorably received by the Library Committee, and with financial support provided by the University administration, Frank A. Lundy was appointed in September 1931 as bibliographer. The special "sets" program was largely independent of routine library activities. Although Lundy worked as a member of the library staff under the jurisdiction of Leupp, his activities were mostly directed by Kerner. Checking standard reference works, bibliographies, and publication records from scientific and learned societies throughout the world, Lundy drew up extensive lists that were checked against the library's holdings. He also worked closely with Ivander MacIver, head of the Division of Serials and Exchanges, giving her many suggestions that further developed the library's exchange program. The sets program also focused attention on the geographical and subject areas designated in the 1931 policy statement as special collecting fields, and on implementing the aims of that statement. As a result the library's acquisition of materials from the Dutch East Indies, Australia, New Zealand, and the areas comprising the Pacific Basin increased considerably. Unfortunately, the effects of the depression prevented the continuation of Lundy's services as bibliographer, and in July 1933 he was transferred to regular service in the Accessions Department. Although the Division of Serials and Exchanges and the Library Committee sought to perpetuate this aspect of collection development, the effectiveness of the sets program declined in subsequent years.

In its report for 1945/46 the Library Committee indicated a need to shift more of the responsibility for book selection from the faculty to the library. Regarding university libraries and book selection, J. Periam Danton wrote in 1963: "There is unmistakable evidence, when one reviews the current situation and the history of this century, of a trend not only toward greater library-staff participation in book selection, but also toward greater assumption by the library of over-all responsibility both for selection and for general collection building."[3] By delegating major responsibility for book selection to a member of the library staff, the appointment in 1931 of a bibliographer for acquisitions and collection development was a precursor of the Library Committee's expressed need and of Danton's observation. This decision was a positive step not only in building California's research library but also in recognizing the value of a trained librarian specifically engaged in a systematic book-selection program.

FACULTY PURCHASING FOR THE LIBRARY

Valuable contributions to the acquisition program were made on numerous occasions by faculty members who purchased books for the University library while travelling abroad. In 1907 Professor Samuel A. Chambers was authorized to use the Spanish department's book fund during a visit to Spain to buy library materials. The Library Committee in 1910 allowed Professor Lucien Foulet a portion of the French department's

---

[3] J. Periam Danton, *Book Selection and Collections: A Comparison of German and American University Libraries* (New York: Columbia University Press, 1963), p. 79.

allotment to purchase library books in Paris. At the close of World War I, the committee responded favorably to an offer from George Clark, Stanford University's librarian who had earlier been assistant librarian at California, to purchase books for the library while travelling in the Orient buying materials also for Stanford.

According to the committee's minutes, purchases were also subsequently made by Professors H. E. Bolton, G. H. Guttridge, and R. J. Kerner, in history; B. H. Bronson, in English; F. D. Lessing, in Oriental languages; A. Torres-Rioseco, in Spanish; and A. H. Rowbotham, in French. In the case of Professor Lessing, $3,000 was appropriated for him to spend while in China and Japan in 1936. This resulted in the acquisition of a notable collection of Chinese Buddhist writings (including a T'aisho edition of the "Tripitaka," the canon law of Buddhism) essential for research in Oriental literature and religion. These purchases by faculty members were valuable because they were based on the actual inspection of books by individuals with special knowledge of their subjects; moreover, they allowed the library to have more direct contact with foreign book markets than would otherwise be possible. This aspect of book selection and acquisition added significant strength to the University of California library.

EN BLOC ACQUISITIONS

Numerous individual collections acquired en bloc added great strength to the library's resources. Some were received as gifts, others were purchased. California was fortunate in securing collections en bloc for several reasons. The Board of Regents and the presidents recognized the value of such materials and on various occasions made supplementary financial appropriations for their purchase. Faculty members were frequently aware of the availability of special collections and pressed for their acquisition. Moreover, many professors and other friends who were interested in the library's development donated research materials which they either already owned or bought for this purpose.

The importance of en bloc acquisitions had been recognized at California well before 1900. In 1870, shortly after the University took over the small library of the College of California, $500 was paid for the library of Alexander S. Taylor. Reflecting Taylor's interests as a nineteenth-century California author and bibliographer, the collection consisted of 300 volumes, mostly Californiana. Michael Reese's gift of $2,000 in 1873 allowed the library to purchase the 3,000-volume collection, notable in the fields of political science and economics, of Columbia University's Professor Francis Lieber. That same year through the bequest of a wealthy San Francisco banker, F. A. Pioche, the University received his library of 1,500 volumes in French literature and linguistics. In the remaining years of the nineteenth century several other collections of considerable value were acquired en bloc. The most outstanding among these was the private library of the noted California bibliographer and book collector, Robert E. Cowan, which was purchased in 1897 by Collis P. Huntington for $3,000 and given to the University. Among libraries pertaining to California and Spanish America, this collection, consisting of 600 bound volumes, 3,300 pamphlets, and over 12,000 manuscripts, was considered second in importance only to the Bancroft Library.

From 1900 to 1945 few years passed in which the University did not receive some notable en bloc library acquisitions. In 1901, the late Regent Andrew S. Hallidie's private library of 2,500 volumes in the field of technology was given by his widow to the University. The following year, after Professor Joseph Le Conte's death, Mrs. Le Conte gave his 2,000-volume collection to the library. Through the generosity of industrialist John D. Spreckels of San Francisco, $7,000 was received in 1904 to purchase the private library of the University of Berlin's deceased professor, Karl Weinhold. This outstanding collection of some 8,500 books and pamphlets in the fields of German linguistics, literature, and folklore, claimed by California's Professor Hugo K. Schilling to be the largest and most distinguished German scholarly library brought to the United States up to that time, formed the basis of the German department's seminar collection for many years.

The high point in California's acquisition of special collections came in 1905, when it obtained the Hubert Howe Bancroft Library. In regard to size and its indispensable value for research in California and western American history, the Bancroft Library was literally priceless. Commenting on this collection, President Wheeler wrote: "The acquisition in November, 1905, of the Bancroft library as a body of independent and original documents, relating to the history of California and, indeed, other parts of the new world, has been an event of the highest significance for the department of history. The library, aside from its meaning for the state whose birth certificates it contains, will become a laboratory for graduate work in the department of history."[4]

Acquisition of the Bancroft Library had been considered as early as 1898, when Bancroft expressed willingness to part with the collection. At that time he offered to sell it to the Library of Congress for $500,000, but, according to Librarian Ainsworth R. Spofford, "the Library Committee could not

---

[4] *President's Report* (1904–06), p. 23.

consider its purchase, as they regarded the valuation prohibitory."[5] John Shaw Billings also indicated that the Bancroft Library had been offered to the New York Public Library, of which he was the director; Billings stated that in his personal opinion the collection might be worth about $150,000.[6] The collection remained unsold until 1905 when Bancroft offered it to the University of California for $250,000. Several people, including Reuben Gold Thwaites, librarian of the Wisconsin State Historical Society, had already been consulted by the University and asked to appraise it. A careful study of the materials led Thwaites to suggest a value between $250,-000 and $300,000. After some months of negotiations, Bancroft offered $100,000 as his personal contribution toward the purchase price, and agreed to accept payment of the remaining $150,000 over a three-year period at the rate of $50,000 per year. Upon President Wheeler's recommendation the regents quickly accepted the offer, and the sale was concluded on November 24, 1905. At the time California's Professor Henry Morse Stephens wrote, "All credit for the acquisition of the Bancroft belongs to the Regents of the University of California and to President Wheeler. The latter said that it ought to be done and it was done."[7]

The Bancroft Library was not moved from San Francisco to Berkeley until May 1906, but fortunately it escaped damage from the San Francisco earthquake and fire which occurred a month earlier. At the time of its sale the Bancroft collection contained 60,000 bound volumes plus 10,000 manuscripts; it included newspaper files, periodicals, transactions of political bodies, early western imprints and rare books, all related primarily to California, the West, and Spanish America.

Also in 1906, but overshadowed by the Bancroft acquisition, the University received as a permanent deposit from the San Francisco Microscopical Society its library of 2,500 volumes on the subject of microscopy.

The development of California's extensive holdings in Oriental literature, which led after World War II to the creation of the East Asiatic Library at Berkeley, resulted largely from the receipt of several notable private collections. The first of these was the Kiang Chinese library. Stemming from the ancient Chou dynasty, the Kiang clan in Peking had gathered over many

---

[5] Ainsworth R. Spofford, Librarian of Congress, Washington, D. C., to Joseph C. Rowell, July 30, 1898, *Correspondence and Papers* (C-B 419), Bancroft Library, Berkeley.

[6] John Shaw Billings, Director, New York Public Library, to Joseph C. Rowell, Sept. 30, 1898, *Correspondence and Papers* (C-B 419), Bancroft Library, Berkeley.

[7] Henry Morse Stephens, *The Bancroft Library; Remarks by Professor H. Morse Stephens before the California Library Association, Feb. 27, 1906* (unpublished; 1906), p. 1; typescript copy of address included in the Henry Morse Stephens papers, Bancroft Library, file series no. 926, Berkeley.

years a collection of about 50,000 volumes; unfortunately, much of the collection was destroyed in the Boxer Rebellion. Because of the 1910 revolution in China, S. C. Kiang Kang-Hu, a member of the clan, was exiled. He came to Berkeley and eventually became a member of the University faculty. With the help of the United States legation, Professor Kiang arranged for shipment of the remainder of the family library from China; he presented it to the University in 1916. Although the collection, then about one-fourth its original size, had many broken sets, it did contain over 2,000 works which were complete and in good condition. In his article, "Chinese Books and Libraries," Walter T. Swingle judged the Kiang library at that time to be the third largest Chinese collection in the United States, exceeded in size only by those at the Library of Congress and Chicago's Newberry Library. The Kiang Library, as he described it, contained many rare items and was especially rich in belles lettres.[8]

Another major acquisition in the field of Oriental literature was the collection of Professor John Fryer, bequeathed to the University in 1928. Having served at California since 1895 as Agassiz Professor of Oriental Languages, Fryer had built up a considerable library of Chinese and Japanese works which included 1,500 volumes and 5,000 lantern slides. In 1930 the University received the collection of Professor E. T. Williams, who also had been a member of the Department of Oriental Languages and Literature, and whose books were primarily related to Chinese literature and culture. California's Oriental collection was further strengthened in 1935 when the Chinese government gave 400 volumes of facsimile reproductions of works from the Emperor Chien Lung's library. Then, in 1942, the University acquired the library of the late Professor Y. S. Kuno, who had served as chairman of the Department of Oriental Languages and Literature, and whose collection contained over 1,000 volumes, mostly in Japanese, on the social, political, and economic history of Japan. The combined strength of these private libraries provided an unusually rich collection of Orientalia to support the University's teaching and research activities.

Another en bloc acquisition that attracted considerable attention was the Library of French Thought. After it was received in 1917 this 2,500-volume collection was described as "covering all fields of French literature, philosophy, and science, originally assembled for exhibition in the French Pavilion at the Panama-Pacific International Exposition, and presented by the French government, at the close of the exposition, to the University

---

[8] Walter T. Swingle, "Chinese Books and Libraries," *American Library Association Bulletin,* XI (1917), 121–4.

of California, under the patronage of the Friends of France."[9] Housed in a separate room that was dedicated to it, this special library was open fifteen hours a week and supervised by Théodora Livingstone, who served as curator from 1917 to 1920. After Miss Livingstone's resignation, in view of the rather limited use made of it, the Library of French Thought was placed under the care of the French department and used as a seminar collection.

In 1918 Mrs. G. H. Howison presented over 1,200 volumes from her late husband's library to the University. Having served for many years as a professor and also chairman of California's philosophy department, Howison had developed a valuable collection which included several incunabula and numerous choice editions of ancient and modern philosophers. Following Mrs. Howison's death in 1931, the balance of this collection was received from her estate, thus adding substantially to the University's resources in philosophy.

Notable also among the libraries received from University faculty members was that of Professor Henry Morse Stephens. Stephens had distinguished himself both as an historian and teacher. During his long career at Cornell and the University of California he had gathered a collection of over 12,000 volumes, which was bequeathed to the library upon his death in 1919. In reporting this notable acquisition Librarian Leupp wrote: "Its most valuable portion is the extensive collection relating to the British in India, containing many items of considerable rarity and some that are unique. The Kipling and Omar Khayyam collections were Professor Stephens' two great hobbies; the former in particular is valuable as containing every edition of the author's collected works known to Professor Stephens, every obtainable significant edition of the individual books, and innumerable periodical articles and newspaper clippings. The collection relating to the French Revolution and Napoleon is fairly extensive and the greater part of it is not now represented in the University Library."[10]

The University also received in 1919 the collection of the late Rabbi Jacob Voorsanger of San Francisco, containing 1,800 volumes in the field of Semitics. Voorsanger had served as professor of Semitic languages and literatures at California from 1894 until 1908, when he had developed much of his personal library.

California continued to acquire several notable collections en bloc during the 1920's. In 1923 the library of the late Professor August Fournier, who had taught at the University of Vienna, was purchased. This 4,000-

---

[9] *The Dedication of the Library of French Thought ... at the University of California* (Berkeley: 1918), p. 6.

[10] "Librarian's Report," in *President's Report* (1919–20), p. 127.

volume collection in the field of history included a number of rare German works from the Napoleonic period. The following year the library of the late Professor Alvin Putzker was presented to the University by his son. Putzker, a world-famous linguist, was a member of California's German department for forty-three years. His library contained 4,000 volumes published in many languages and included many rare scholarly works which added great strength to the University's book resources.

The development of a valuable Italian collection at California began in 1924 when the University was given the Commendatore Mark J. Fontana Library. Upon accepting this gift of over 700 volumes President Campbell described it as "representative of the best thought and the highest material achievement of the Italian race ... designated to set before the students of the University the contribution of Italy to the advancement of civilization."[11] Added to this was the acquisition in the years 1930–32 of the Trevisani library. Tracing its development from the private libraries of Francesco Maria Trevisani, minister of Ferdinand IV, king of Naples, and of the Reverend Father G. Trevisani, a member of the Theatine Order, this collection was especially rich in Italian literature from the sixteenth through eighteenth centuries, and included several incunabula. Part of the library, consisting of 2,700 volumes, was acquired in 1930 when its $6,000 purchase price was underwritten by a group of San Francisco citizens of Italian descent. Two years later the remaining 2,300 volumes were also acquired at a price reduced from $3,700 to $2,500.[12] A gift of 300 volumes from the Italian government in 1934 further strengthened the University's resources in Italian literature and culture. Finally, in 1939 California was able to purchase from Harvard University almost 6,000 volumes from the Henry Nelson Gay library of Italian risorgimento, which were duplicates of books already in the Harvard collection.

A valuable collection of old books, many of them rare, in the fields of mathematics and probability theory was given in 1926 by Julius Wangenheim, the University Alumni Association's president. Notable items in this gift included a first edition of Euclid's *Elements* (1482) from the Ratdolt Press at Venice, copies of the earliest Greek (1553) and English language (1570) editions of Euclid, and several first editions of works by Sir Isaac Newton.

The largest book collection received by the University during the 1920's was the private library of the late San Francisco Attorney Alexander F.

---

[11] *Presentation of the Commendatore M. J. Fontana Library to the University of California* (Berkeley: 1924), p. 2.
[12] *Library Committee Minutes,* Minute Book no. 3 (1921–45), Jan. 20, 1932.

Morrison, given by his widow, May T. Morrison. Receipt of the Morrison library stemmed from a desire on the part of Librarian Leupp and other members of the University community to establish a recreational reading room for students. When it became known that Mrs. Morrison had considered giving her husband's books to the University, Julius Wangenheim and Robert Gordon Sproul approached her with the plan of creating a special reading room and using Morrison's library as the nucleus of its collection. Thus, the University received 15,000 volumes for the Alexander F. Morrison Memorial Library, which was dedicated in 1928. This collection was strongest in history, biography, travel, English literature, sociology, economics, and political science. It also included some excellent items in the fields of fine arts and music. Although not acquired for subject specialists, the Morrison books formed an important contribution to California's literary and cultural resources for students.

The importance of acquiring en bloc additions by purchase as well as by gift continued to be recognized at the University. In response to a suggestion by Leupp that a revolving fund be established for this special purpose, the Library Committee voted in the twenties and reaffirmed in the thirties to endorse "as a matter of prime importance the addition to the Library budget of a certain sum for bloc purchases."[13] It was hoped that prospective donors would thereby be encouraged to make contributions and that the library would have funds readily available to negotiate purchases of desired collections as soon as they became available.

Despite the depression of the thirties (or perhaps because of it), California acquired several notable collections during that decade. In 1930, the scholarly private library of Professor Paul Miliukov was purchased for $10,000. In addition to $5,000 appropriated by the Library Committee, the regents voted upon President Campbell's recommendation to use $4,000 from the President's Emergency Fund for this purchase; the balance was contributed by "an alumnus."[14] Professor Miliukov, who had taught at the Universities of Moscow and Sofia, was devoted to the cause of constitutional government in Czarist Russia; he served as minister of foreign affairs in the Kerensky government, but after its overthrow he was forced into exile. His library was secretly removed from Russia to Finland in 1921 and eventually to the United States, where it was stored at Stanford

---

[13] Ibid., Mar. 26, 1923; reaffirmed Jan. 20, 1932.

[14] *Minutes,* University of California Board of Regents, vol. XXVI (1929–31), Nov. 22, 1929, p. 105, hereinafter cited as *Regents' Minutes;* also, William Wallace Campbell to James K. Moffitt, San Francisco, California, Nov. 18, 1929, and Campbell to Harold L. Leupp, Nov. 26, 1929, *Correspondence and Papers* (CU-5: 1929, folder no. 1692), University of California Archives, Berkeley.

University. When acquired by the University of California, it was described by Professor R. J. Kerner as "one of the best private collections of Russian history and civilization outside Slavic Europe."[15] It contained 4,000 books and periodical volumes, plus large numbers of pamphlets and manuscripts. Although the greater part of this was in Russian, Bulgarian, Serbian, and other Cyrillic-alphabet languages, there were 1,200 works in English, French, German, and other western European languages.[16] The Miliukov library gave California the nucleus of a strong Slavic collection suitable for graduate and research work.

Several important collections were received from University faculty members during the early 1930's. The late Professor W. D. Matthew's library in the field of vertebrate paleontology, containing 300 books, 5,000 pamphlets and reprints of learned society publications, plus several valuable periodical files, was received in 1930. This gave the University library almost complete coverage of developments on that subject for the previous thirty years. In 1931, following the death of California's longtime history professor, Bernard Moses, the University received his private library. It consisted of 3,500 volumes and much unbound material on political science and history, primarily as related to the Philippine Islands, Spanish America, and the Scandinavian countries. Also received in 1931 was the private library of the late Professor Florian Cajori, who had been a member of the mathematics department. His collection, pertaining largely to the history of science and mathematics, added 1,750 volumes and large amounts of unbound materials to the library. The University was fortunate that same year in receiving botany Professor W. A. Setchell's collection of books on tobacco, which included some of the earliest known works written on that subject. In 1933 the library of the late E. C. Hills, professor of romance philology, was given to the University; it contained 1,200 books,

---

[15] *News Notes of California Libraries*, XXV (1930), 27–8.

[16] An interesting sidelight to the acquisition of the Miliukov library was the story of the Miliukov "trunk." When the collection was shipped to the United States and stored at Stanford, it was packed in twenty-six boxes plus Miliukov's trunk. Apparently the trunk was separated from the rest of the collection, and when the materials were received and checked at the University of California, it was assumed that some of the original items had been lost in shipment. On May 2, 1944, however, H. H. Fisher, Acting Chairman of Directors at Stanford's Hoover Library of War, Revolution and Peace, wrote to Librarian Leupp reporting that a trunk containing Russian materials had been found in the basement and was apparently part of the Miliukov collection. Thus, fourteen years after its purchase, the California library received the supposedly "lost" items of the Miliukov library. See: H. H. Fisher, Acting Chairman of Directors, Hoover Library of War, Revolution and Peace, Stanford, California, to Harold L. Leupp, May 2, 1944, and Leupp to Fisher, May 26, 1944, *Correspondence and Papers* (CU-12, Carton 43), University of California Archives, Berkeley.

500 unbound volumes, and much pamphlet, reprint, and periodical material in the field of philology.

During the mid-thirties, two important newspaper collections were purchased en bloc. The first was a long run of the *London Gazette,* which was acquired in 1934 and, except for some gaps totalling twenty-four years, give the University a continuous file from 1665. The next year the library purchased the Léon Clerbois collection of newspapers; although priced at $15,000, its value had been estimated at twice that sum. Upon the Library Committee's recommendation for purchase, President Sproul requested a special appropriation from the regents to cover the cost.[17] The Clerbois collection contained "examples of journals from the first news-letters and broadsides of the sixteenth century to the modern newspaper."[18] It also included newspapers primarily from France, Belgium, and other western European countries for the period from the French Revolution to the Franco-Prussian War; largely drawn from the smaller cities and towns, they provided "a very unusual crosssection of public opinion at several critical periods in recent European history."[19] Three hundred volumes on the history of the press were also contained in the Clerbois collection, thus adding to its value. In 1941 the purchase of a complete file of the *Boston Evening Transcript* extending from July 1830 to date added a third important acquisition to California's newspaper collection.

During the late thirties the University library was considerably enhanced by the en bloc purchase of several foreign private libraries. The most notable one was the Burdach-Bremer collection acquired in 1938 for $20,000. It consisted of the private libraries of two German professors highly regarded for their scholarship, Konrad Burdach and Otto Bremer. The Burdach library contained 19,300 volumes on the history and literature of Europe, especially Germany, from the late Middle Ages to the Renaissance; the Bremer collection, containing close to 10,000 volumes, pertained largely to German linguistics and literature since 1600. In view of the price, the unwillingness of the German agents handling the sale to divide the collections, and the extent of duplication with books already at Berkeley, it was decided, in consultation with President Sproul and library representatives from the University of California at Los Angeles, that the purchase would be made for the whole University. In addition to $12,600 appropriated from book funds at Berkeley and $6,000 from those at Los Angeles,

---

[17] *Library Committee Minutes,* Minute Book no. 3 (1921–45), Feb. 15 and Sept. 13, 1935.

[18] *Librarian's Report* (1936), p. 2.

[19] Harold L. Leupp to Robert Gordon Sproul, President, University of California, Feb. 19, 1935, *Correspondence and Papers* (CU-12, Carton 21), University of California Archives, Berkeley.

Sproul provided $2,000 from special funds for this purchase.[20] After the collection was received, 40 percent was retained at Berkeley, 36 percent sent to Los Angeles, and the remainder sold to other libraries. After acquiring the Burdach-Bremer collection, California was again fortunate in purchasing the 900-volume Scandinavian philology library of the late Professor Verner Dahlerup of the University of Copenhagen. Negotiations were also begun to purchase in Prague the Masaryk-Beneš library, containing about 2,000 items related to the lives and careers of two notable Czechoslovakian statesmen. The outbreak of hostilities, however, delayed acquisition of the collection until after World War II.

California continued to acquire en bloc several special collections during the 1940's. Over 10,000 volumes were received in 1941 through the bequest of C. A. Kofoid, noted professor of zoology at the University for many years and especially remembered for his proclivity for book collecting. The Kofoid collection made a substantial addition to the University's Biology Library. In 1942 the private library of California's late Professor James Westfall Thompson was purchased for $5,000 by an anonymous donor and given to the University. This collection of over 2,000 volumes represented Thompson's interests in the study of European history. Duplicate copies of books already at Berkeley, amounting to over one-half of the collection, were given to the library at Los Angeles.

California's most outstanding en bloc acquisition of rare books and works on the history of printing was the John Henry Nash library. Nash had established himself in 1918 as a printer of fine books in San Francisco. In conjunction with his work and also from personal interest he had gathered a large collection estimated to have cost about $60,000. In 1943 the Nash library was purchased by the University of California for $12,500, of which $7,500 was donated by Milton S. Ray of San Francisco and $5,000 added from the legacy of Albert M. Bender. The collection contained over 3,000 books and pamphlets and almost 1,700 broadsides. Especially valuable were 19 incunabula and 208 incunabula leaves; 23 books from the sixteenth, 24 from the seventeenth, and 53 from the eighteenth centuries; a complete set of Nash's own printed works; examples of fine printing from the presses of John Baskerville, William Morris, and many other well-known English and American printers; a complete set of the Limited Editions Club publications; and Nash's own typographical collection.

---

[20] *Library Committee Minutes,* Minute Book no. 3 (1921–45), Oct. 27, 1937; also, Jens Nyholm to Harold L. Leupp, Aug. 11, 1943, and Leupp to John E. Goodwin, Librarian, University of California at Los Angeles, Aug. 17, 1943, *Correspondence and Papers* (CU-12, Carton 37), University of California Archives, Berkeley.

In 1944 the University was given the library of the late Professor C. E. Rugh, formerly of the education department, containing 1,200 volumes largely in the fields of education, psychology, and philosophy. During the same year the library of A. A. Boehtlingk, a Russian-born chemist and noted petroleum specialist, was purchased. In addition to Russian works on petroleum engineering and technology, this collection contained several valuable files of Russian patent specifications and abridgements for many of the years from 1875 to 1941. The acquisition of the Leo Newmark collection in 1945 brought to the California library 400 volumes in the field of Near Eastern languages and literature, as well as several miscellaneous rarities in the field of religion.

Thus, for seventy-five years, and especially from 1900 through 1945, the acquisition en bloc of valuable private and special collections was one of the most significant aspects of the University's library development. Although their monetary value was incalculable, these materials were indispensable to the quality of graduate studies and research activities for which California had become distinguished.

BINDING

Since subscriptions to periodicals and other serial publications formed a major part of library acquisitions, California's early adoption of a continuous binding program added greatly to the value of its collection. According to the librarian's report in 1900, the library's periodicals had been quite completely bound up to that time. The binding of government documents, university publications, transactions of societies, and much other miscellaneous unbound material, however, had not been kept up at the same rate.

Until after the turn of the century the library's materials were bound at a commercial establishment in San Francisco. The rising costs of binding work, however, led Librarian Rowell and the Library Committee to propose in 1902 that a bindery be established at the University. The destruction of about 1,000 of the library's volumes in a San Francisco bindery during the earthquake and fire of 1906 finally led the regents to take favorable action, and in 1908 binding operations were begun on the Berkeley campus. At first the bindery was considered a department of the library, but its operation was soon transferred to the jurisdiction of the University Printing Office.

In 1908/09, 3,685 library volumes were bound at a cost of slightly less than $4,000.[21] As the rate of library acquisitions increased, the annual bind-

---

[21] "Librarian's Report," in *President's Report* (1908–10), p. 102.

ing appropriations grew, although not always proportionately. From 1911/ 12 through 1926/27 the amounts for binding were equal to almost 25 percent of total funds spent for books (appendix A, table 4). On several occasions Librarian Leupp reported that library binding was falling behind, and several times the binding appropriations were increased by the University to try to catch up with accumulated binding arrears. In 1942 Leupp summarized the library's binding record for the preceding ten years (appendix A, table 5). The average amount spent for binding during that period was equal to 22 percent of the amount spent for books.

On the basis of his observations regarding binding appropriations, Maurice Tauber stated in 1954, "It is sometimes difficult to determine how much a library spends for binding, since the funds are often included in the totals for the purchase of books and periodicals. However, few libraries have the funds to provide the best possible care for all the materials which they acquire."[22] Statistics for the growth of California's book collection do not state separately the number of volumes added by binding as distinguished from purchased books. Yet the annual reports and financial appropriations provide clear indications that the library's binding needs were taken seriously, thereby preserving periodicals and other kinds of literature indispensable for research at the University.

THE EXCHANGE PROGRAM

The University of California library benefitted greatly from the successful development of an active exchange program. One phase of this activity consisted of trading duplicate volumes from the California collection for needed items from other libraries. Far more significant, however, were the agreements established with learned societies, scientific institutions, and other universities whereby series and other publications issued by these agencies were exchanged for those of the University of California.

Initial efforts toward an exchange program were made in 1884 by Librarian Rowell, who sent ninety-eight letters to learned societies and universities in the United States and abroad proposing establishment of exchange relationships with the California library. Only thirty-five favorable replies were received.[23] Rowell was not discouraged, but continued to pursue efforts in this direction. In 1893 the University's first two series publications appeared, in the fields of geology and education. These helped

[22] Maurice F. Tauber and Associates, *Technical Services in Libraries* (New York: Columbia University Press, 1954), pp. 314–5.

[23] Joseph C. Rowell, *The Beginnings of a Great Library: Reminiscences by Joseph C. Rowell* (unpublished; 1938), p. 13, University of California Archives, Berkeley, hereinafter cited as Rowell, *Beginnings*.

considerably to foster the exchange plan. For the fiscal year 1902/03 Rowell reported 101 books received by exchange and commented that, "The enlarged output of the University Press has resulted in a great increase in the number of society publications received by this Library."[24] In 1909/10, 2,008 volumes were received by exchange; at that time University publications were being sent to 932 other institutions.[25] The manager of the University Press, Albert H. Allen, attributed the program's success to the active interest of faculty members who promoted it through their personal ties with people at other institutions. Allen added: "With the continued growth of the University's publications, greater assurance can be felt in requesting exchange privileges from the leading institutions and learned societies of the world."[26]

As the volume of publishing increased, the exchange program came to be handled by the University Press under the guidance of its Editorial Committee. By 1912, however, lack of coordination between the Press and the library was evident and the Editorial Committee suggested transferring exchange activities to the library. The Library Committee, already concerned about the increasing number of broken sets of exchange publications, had also suggested that the library establish a Collection and Exchange Department "to collect national, state and municipal documents in this country and abroad, the publications of academies and learned societies, etc., using for the purpose the exchange facilities of the University Press."[27] The president approved the plan to transfer exchange activities, but because of administrative difficulties it was not accomplished until 1914. The Exchange Division was established as part of the library's Accessions Department, and Evelyn A. Steele was appointed to head its operation. The number of institutions on the exchange list by then had grown to 1,200.[28]

During World War I, exchanges with many European universities and societies were temporarily disrupted. California thus sought new directions for developing exchange relations. Working through state and municipal libraries in the United States, the library obtained greater numbers of documents published by state and city governments. Exchange agreements with private institutions and government agencies in Japan, India, South Africa, and several countries of Central and South America were also established. Despite these efforts, by 1919 the effects of the war had caused

[24] "Librarian's Report," in *President's Report* (1902–04), p. 98.
[25] "Report of the Manager of the University Press," in *President's Report* (1908–10), p. 116.
[26] Ibid., p. 113.
[27] *Library Committee Minutes,* Minute Book no. 2 (1910–21), Mar. 11, 1912.
[28] *Librarian's Report* (1915), p. 20.

the number of volumes annually received by exchange to decrease nearly 50 percent.[29]

During the twenties the exchange program increased again. In 1922, at the Library Committee's suggestion, President Barrows established the Committee to Promote Exchange Relations, with Professor C. A. Kofoid as chairman. Its purpose was to advise and assist the librarian in establishing additional exchange agreements. Within the decade the exchange program not only recovered from the disruptions of World War I but was also adding new titles at the rate of 250 per year and regularly exchanging publications with over 2,000 institutions and agencies.

The increased volume of work as well as the vitality of the exchange program made apparent the need to coordinate it with the activities of the library's Periodical Service, which was established in 1928. Responsibility for handling periodical and exchange materials was thus completely separated from the Accessions Department in 1929 when the Division of Serials and Exchanges was created. Organized as part of the "Readers Department," which had been initiated in 1928, the new division was administered by Ivander MacIver. Her service for many years and the wide range of new relationships she established not only strengthened California's exchange program but also led to its widespread recognition as a model for this library activity.[30]

By the mid-thirties California was receiving by exchange over 4,000 serial titles annually from seventy-seven foreign countries. The annual valuation of those acquisitions, exclusive of nonserial publications, was estimated by Miss MacIver at over $9,000.[31] The faculty's interest and cooperation was constantly sought in suggesting additional exchanges and using its offices to initiate new exchange agreements. Shipping and receiving services provided by the Smithsonian Institution in Washington, D.C., were also used for about 20 percent of these items. As branches of the University grew in the 1930's and also wanted to participate in this program, the division at Berkeley began to handle exchanges for the libraries of all California's campuses and was allowed to draw upon the University Press to supply its

---

[29] Ibid. (1919), p. 4.

[30] The University of California librarian's correspondence and papers during the period 1930–45 contain numerous letters from other university librarians, including Louis R. Wilson, inquiring about the Division of Serials and Exchanges. Miss MacIver's published articles (listed in the bibliography) attest to her knowledge and skill in the area of exchanges. Also, a copy of the organization chart of California's Gift and Exchange Department was included in Louis R. Wilson and Maurice F. Tauber, *The University Library* (2d ed.; New York: Columbia University Press, 1956), p. 171.

[31] Ivander MacIver to Harold L. Leupp, Jan. 1934 (specific date not given), *Correspondence and Papers* (CU-12, Carton 19), University of California Archives, Berkeley.

publications (except those which were specially subsidized) to any extent needed. Although a bookkeeping record of their value was kept by the University Accounting Department, the cost of these items was not charged against the library's book funds.

In order to group the total range of acquisitions activities more logically, the Division of Serials and Exchanges became the Division of Gifts and Exchanges in 1940. Responsibility for all nonpurchased items was centralized in this division, whereas purchased periodicals and serials were handled by the Accessions Department. Miss MacIver continued in charge of the reorganized division, but in connection with other changes in the library's administration about that time, Gifts and Exchanges came under the general supervision of the assistant librarian for technical processes.

The outbreak of World War II again disrupted exchanges with many European countries and led California to develop exchange agreements with Latin American countries. By 1943, 635 serials were being received from the Spanish-speaking countries of South America, 100 from Brazil, 130 from Mexico, and 40 from Central America.[32] Meanwhile, the University reserved copies of its publications to send after the war in exchange for materials also stored in foreign countries where shipping had been suspended. Several shipments from Russia sent via Siberia and the Pacific Ocean, however, were received during that period. Within months after hostilities ended in 1945, many exchanges disrupted by the war were again resumed.

California was successful in developing an exchange program for several reasons. The scholarly interests of the faculty stimulated acquisition of materials issued by other universities and learned societies. Recognizing the value of its faculty's research activities, the University also supported an extensive publication program. The elements of need and a supply of available materials were both present and conducive to promoting exchange arrangements. Moreover, the active interest and diligence with which librarians and faculty members pursued opportunities for establishing exchange agreements were indispensable to this activitiy.

In his study of book selection and collecting, Danton stated, "The vigorous prosecution of an exchange program is obviously much to the library's advantage in view of the quality of the materials received and the savings to the book budget."[33] Although California participated in some duplicate book exchanges, by far the greater share of its program was directed toward exchanging serial publications with other universities and learned societies.

[32] *Daily Californian,* Aug. 30, 1943, p. 3.
[33] Danton, op. cit., p. 130.

Its "vigorous prosecution" of this activity proved highly beneficial in developing a scholarly library collection.

EVALUATION OF THE LIBRARY'S RESOURCES

Before the Survey Committee was appointed in 1930, no systematic attempt had been made at California to evaluate the library. The general condition of the collection was often discussed in meetings of the Library Committee, particularly when the book fund allotments were decided. Aside from recognizing special areas where additional strength was needed, the committee issued no statements assessing the collection except for occasional references included in its annual reports to the Academic Senate. Several times in their reports Librarians Rowell and Leupp expressed their views regarding certain aspects of the collection, but these were not offered as comprehensive evaluation. A kind of de facto evaluation had occurred insofar as faculty members judged the library's needs while ordering new materials. These efforts were directed mainly toward book selection, however, and did not result in any formalized appraisals of the library's resources.

When the Survey Committee began its study of the collection in 1930, it sought the advice and opinions of faculty members. The committee's findings were expressed in the "Special Report of the Library Committee on the Aims of the University Based upon the Survey of the Collection," presented to the Academic Senate in 1931. The results of this evaluation helped the library by defining the basis for book-collecting activities in the thirties and also making faculty members of the University and the academic community at large more aware of the overall scope and particular specialties of the library's resources. A poll of the English department taken by Homer Halvorson in 1934 revealed that most of its faculty members felt the Survey Committee's evaluation had been very beneficial. From the opinions stated, Halvorson concluded that "the collection of English and American literature in the library is more than adequate for the needs of all undergraduate instruction in all fields, and that as far as graduate work is concerned the collection is quite fair."[34]

In 1942 the results of a study sponsored by the Board on Resources of American Libraries of the American Library Association were published.[35] The aim of the study, directed by Robert B. Downs, was to answer the

---

[34] Homer Halvorson, *A Study of the Library Needs of the English Department of the University of California* (M.S. thesis, University of California, 1934), p. 3.

[35] Robert B. Downs, "Leading American Library Collections," *Library Quarterly,* XII (1942), 457–73. Although the article states that 75 subject fields were investigated, 76 were actually listed when the results were reported.

question, "Where are the leading collections for advanced study and research in American libraries?" The investigation sought the opinions of 500 authorities in the United States, mostly professors, librarians, and persons engaged in research at many institutions, and ranging over seventy-six subject fields. Each individual consulted was asked where the best American library collections in his field of interest were located. When the replies were received, the libraries cited were asked to provide data to support the opinions of the persons polled, thus verifying the conclusions. The results of the inquiry, in which 250 libraries were each named in at least one field, showed that in numbers of fields cited the University of California at Berkeley ranked in third place behind Harvard and the Library of Congress. California was included in fifty-four of the seventy-six subject fields actually listed (appendix B). Moreover, it ranked first among the libraries of all state universities and was the only library west of Chicago included among the first ten in the nation.[36] The value of this survey was greater for libraries where subject coverage was broadly inclusive than for those with highly specialized collecting areas. Thus, California's standing in the results of Downs' investigation attested to the high quality of its library collection.

Three library-evaluation studies more limited in scope were undertaken in the mid-forties. The first, entitled "Indispensable Monographs in Medieval and Renaissance Studies," was directed by S. Harrison Thomson of the University of Colorado. Professor Thomson, who edited the journal *Progress of Medieval and Renaissance Studies in the United States and Canada,* complied a list of 400 titles necessary for research in that field. These were checked by eighty libraries in the United States. From the results California ranked fourth in the group considered.[37] The second study, reported by Librarian Leupp, was conducted by the library of Iowa State College of Agriculture and Mechanic Arts. Thirty university and college libraries were asked to check their holdings against a list of 102 periodicals most often referred to in the journals of chemistry. In the results the University of California ranked in fourth place.[38] The third study was carried out by Charles H. Brown for the Association of Research Libraries. It measured the holdings of scientific journals in five specific fields by fifty-five American re-

---

[36] Of other western libraries listed, Stanford ranked 14th, University of Washington 23rd, and the Henry E. Huntington Library 28th. The 76 subject fields, with a designation of those in which the University of California was or was not included, are listed in appendix B.

[37] S. Harrison Thomson, "Monographic Holdings of American Libraries in the Medieval and Renaissance Field," *Progress of Medieval and Renaissance Studies in the United States and Canada,* Bulletin no. 18 (June 1944), 28–52; rating given on pp. 47–9.

[38] *Librarian's Report* (1944), p. 11. The specific source for this information is not cited in the *Report.*

search libraries, as shown in the *Union List of Serials in the United States and Canada* (2d ed., 1943). The conclusions rated California first in terms of overall holdings in all five fields. In the ranking by individual fields, the library was first in physics and botany, second in physiology, third in chemistry, and seventh in mathematics.[39]

Following upon these studies the University of California undertook an extensive survey of its libraries in 1945–46. The suggestion for a library study was first made to President Sproul in 1942, a few months after the results of the Downs survey were published. Since the effects of World War II had curtailed the acquisition of much research material from overseas, it was thought that a comprehensive study would provide the basis for planning the collection's post-war growth. With the endorsement of Librarian Leupp at Berkeley and Librarian Lawrence C. Powell of the University of California at Los Angeles, President Sproul presented the proposal to the board of regents, where it was approved in December 1944. Dr. Fulmer Mood, formerly librarian at the University of Redlands and later assistant professor in the University of California School of Librarianship, was appointed special assistant to the President "to make a survey of the libraries on the eight campuses of the institution and to develop a buying program to be put into effect when conditions became normal."[40]

Covering libraries on all campuses, Mood collected data from January 1945 through December 1946. The methods he used included asking librarians and other staff members for their opinions of the library resources; interviewing faculty members and holding conferences within instructional departments to gain the views of those using the collections for teaching and research purposes; consulting library records, accession files, shelf-lists, and the public catalogs, and checking these against scholarly bibliographies; studying records of items borrowed through interlibrary loans to determine materials lacking from the collections; reviewing existing descriptions of the collections from department and library records, bibliographies, and special catalogs; and examining many library materials on the shelves. Mood first surveyed the resources at Berkeley, where the largest percentage of his activity was concentrated, and then moved in turn to the other campuses.

Mood's survey was extensive both in scope and detail. Regarding library

---

[39] Louis R. Wilson and others, *Report of a Survey of the Libraries of Cornell University . . . October 1947–February 1948* (Ithaca: Cornell University, 1948), pp. 131–3. The authors acknowledge that information was derived from an unpublished study made by Charles H. Brown and used with his permission.

[40] Fulmer Mood, *A Survey of the Library Resources of the University of California* (Berkeley: Library Photographic Service, 1950), p. ii, photocopy of typescript.

resources on the Berkeley campus he found consistently strong periodical files in almost all subject fields. This observation was supported by faculty members who generally considered California's periodical holdings to be the backbone of the collection. Mood found the collection strong in all major areas of knowledge. Weaknesses uncovered were generally in specialized aspects of subject fields and in particular languages or periods. Examples of this were in sociology, where Mood cited a lack of census publications for a number of foreign countries; in geography, where the literature of travel and demography was limited; and in Near Eastern studies, where the collections in Aramaic, Syriac, and Sanskrit were not well developed. He reported predominantly favorable comments from faculty members about the library's resources, however, and quoted some of these in his report. Finally, although strong in many areas, Mood reported that the greatest general uniformity of strength was in the physical and biological sciences as contrasted with the social sciences, humanities, and arts.

Thus, the results of several outside studies as well as the Mood survey indicated that library resources on the Berkeley campus were among the strongest in the United States, and that with a few exceptions they were adequate to support the kinds of teaching and research programs which the University had undertaken. An added value of the Mood report was that it uncovered those areas where the collections were weak, thus directing attention to them and their need for improvement.

At California the development of a strong acquisition program from 1900 to 1945 depended largely upon the organization and capable staffing of the Accessions Department. The acquisitions program was amplified by developing the "sets" program, providing for faculty assistance in overseas book purchasing, working to acquire notable en bloc collections, attending to the library's binding needs, and establishing a successful exchange program. In these efforts the library benefited from the skill and faithful service of the librarians and their staff, the strong interest of the faculty (especially those members who served on the Library Committee), and the encouragement and support of the men who held the office of University president. The interaction of these qualities, combined with the insights gained from evaluations of the library's holdings, enabled California to amass a valuable research collection.

CHAPTER III

LIBRARIANS AND THEIR STAFFS

THE DEVELOPMENT of the University of California's library staff up to 1945 can best be understood in the light of three important facts. First, for the seventy-year period from 1875 to 1945, the library was administered by two men. Joseph C. Rowell served as librarian (1875–1919) and as librarian emeritus and University archivist (1919–38); Harold L. Leupp served as associate librarian (1910–19), and as librarian (1919–45). The personalities, interests, and administrative activities of these men had decisive effects upon the library's growth.

Second, the major growth in the size of the library staff came in the years 1900–45, and especially after 1910. In 1900 there were four persons serving on the staff, exclusive of part-time help for evening hours. According to the librarian's report, six full-time and one half-time members were appointed to the staff in 1910 (including Leupp as associate librarian), and ten people were appointed in 1911 (including Carleton B. Joeckel as assistant reference librarian, Sydney B. Mitchell as head of the Accessions Department, and Edith M. Coulter as senior assistant). Although there were also several resignations during that period, the overall gain was substantial. In 1920 there were 28 members on the regular staff of the library; by 1945 the library was budgeted for 84 staff positions (exclusive of the Bancroft Library).[1]

Finally, the library set consistently high standards in terms both of qualifications and performance for its staff members. For example, when Fannie Bonté was hired by the regents in 1897 and given the title assistant librarian, Rowell protested the professional implications of this appointment on the ground that she was not trained for library work.[2] With the development of summer library courses (1902), the Department of Library Science (1922), and eventually the School of Librarianship (1926), the general staffing policy was to appoint to professional positions only college grad-

---

[1] Figures cited from: *Report of the Secretary to the Board of Regents,* University of California (1900), p. 57, hereinafter cited as *Secretary's Report;* "Librarian's Report," in *President's Report* (1910–12), pp. 87–8, and (1919–20), p. 107; and *Budget,* University of California (1944–45), pp. 177–80. For all figures cited, no separate designation is given for professional and nonprofessional staff members except insofar as names of individuals are listed.

[2] Joseph C. Rowell to Samuel T. Black, Chairman, Committee on Library and Museum, University of California Board of Regents, July 26, 1897, in Rowell's *Letter Book* (1896–97), p. 253.

uates who had completed a course in library instruction. Moreover, a considerable number of people who served on the California staff went on to important library administration and teaching positions in other institutions after leaving the Berkeley campus.

JOSEPH CUMMINGS ROWELL

Rowell came to the University of California as a student in 1870. His association with the University continued for sixty-eight years, until his death in 1938. Born in Panama, Rowell was reared in San Francisco and attended the public schools there. His undergraduate years at the University were occupied with thoughts of entering the consular service, but upon graduation in 1874 he accepted appointment at the University as lecturer in English history, recorder of the faculty, and secretary to President Daniel Coit Gilman. When Edward Rowland Sill resigned as professor of English and University librarian in 1875, Rowell was appointed California's first full-time librarian. In order to prepare for his new responsibilities, Rowell embarked upon a ten-week trip, visiting important libraries in the East and conferring with their librarians. He kept a careful record of his visits, including diagrams of the floor plans of libraries, descriptions of various library practices and methods, and notes concerning important ideas and insights that he had gained. Reflecting upon what he had seen and learned, Rowell wrote: "An ignorant young man from western wilds, armed with not a single letter of introduction, but only a card bearing his own name and title, barged into the sanctums of librarians of high and low degree, was welcomed with cordiality everywhere, and was given every possible facility and help in his investigations. How proud I am to be admitted to the ranks of a profession officered by such scholars and—gentlemen! Freely have I received; freely must I give."[3]

When Rowell became University librarian, the collection contained 13,000 volumes and was housed in South Hall on the Berkeley campus. His first major undertaking was cataloging the library's books.[4] Rowell approached this task with two firm convictions based on what he had learned on his eastern trip: books should be arranged according to relative rather than fixed locations, and a card catalog should replace the older book catalogs. By 1879 he had completed a short-title analytical author catalog and

---

[3] Rowell, *Beginnings*, p. 7.

[4] Information pertaining to Rowell's library activities and career, as well as development of the University library before 1900, has been derived primarily from his "Some Notes on the Professional Life and Work of Joseph C. Rowell," in *Library Historical and Descriptive Documents* (unpublished; [1875–1935]), no. 2, 6 leaves, University of California Archives, Berkeley, hereinafter cited as Rowell, "Professional Life and Work;" also his *Beginnings*.

a full-title subject catalog for the library. In the process of cataloging, Rowell devised his own classification scheme which was completed in 1892 and published in 1894.[5] It was used as the sole basis for classifying books at California until the Library of Congress classification was adopted in 1913. Rowell next turned his interests to compiling a list of the periodical holdings of nine libraries in the San Francisco Bay area; this was published in 1880, with subsequent enlarged editions in 1892 and 1902.[6] In addition, feeling the need for a subject approach to the growing volume of periodical literature, Rowell began to compile his own periodical index. It was kept in file form and arranged according to the subject headings found in the printed catalog of the Quincy, Massachusetts, Public Library. Although Rowell also contributed to the periodical index which was being compiled by William Frederick Poole, he continued his own indexing project until 1900.

Rowell's concern with establishing methods and devices for bibliographical control did not overshadow his great personal appreciation for books. Symbolic of this interest was the special exhibition which he arranged in 1884. Many book rarities from private collectors and other libraries were borrowed to display with the University's own volumes of unique interest, and a printed catalog was compiled describing all items included in the exhibit.[7] Rowell made his most lasting contribution to the California library in the area of book collecting. It was largely through his interests and efforts that the library's Californiana collection was begun, the exchange program was initiated, and strong emphasis was placed on the acquisition of periodicals and sets. The University's documents collection was begun under Rowell's guidance as the library began receiving British government publications in 1880 and became a depository library for United States documents in 1884. Rowell kept in close contact with the book market by attending auctions and developing friendships with local bookdealers. His concern for acquiring especially wanted volumes was so great that occasionally he purchased them himself for the library lest they be sold before an order could be sent by the regents' secretary. When it became known in the 1890's that the Bancroft Library was for sale, Rowell urged its acqui-

---

[5] Joseph C. Rowell, *Classification of Books in the Library [of the University of California]*, University of California Library Bulletin, no. 12 (Berkeley: 1894), 49 pp.; (2d ed.; 1915), [109], 46 pp.

[6] *Cooperative List of Periodical Literature [in Libraries of Central California]*, University of California Library Bulletin, no. 1 (Berkeley: 1880), 29 pp.; (2d ed.; 1892), 54 pp.; (3d ed.; 1902), 130 pp.

[7] *Catalogue of the Loan Book Exhibition Held at the University of California, Berkeley, May 26–31, 1884*, University of California Library Bulletin, no. 5 (Sacramento: 1884), 96 pp.

sition by the University. He personally sought the opinions of noted American scholars and librarians concerning the collection's value and solicited the help of influential University faculty members in persuading the regents to make the purchase. He made similar efforts to acquire the Sutro Library and was disappointed when the University failed to secure it. During Rowell's tenure the California library grew significantly; when he retired as librarian in 1919, the collection contained over 392,000 volumes.

Rowell was responsible for several other important developments related to the library. He participated in planning for the construction of two library buildings: the Bacon Library and Art Museum (completed in 1881) and the Doe Library (completed in its initial stage in 1911). As early as 1886 he sought permission to engage in interlibrary loan activities. This was approved in successive degrees by the regents during the years 1894–98. Through Rowell's efforts a summer training course in library methods was introduced at the University in 1902, and was successfully repeated several times in later years. Having watched the University grow over a period of almost thirty years, and anticipating its future development under President Wheeler, Rowell recognized the library's need to adapt to the increased demands facing it. Thus, he wrote to Harvard Librarian W. C. Lane in 1899: "This library is (as I firmly believe) on the eve of important and large development, and I am trying to plan in advance for a corresponding change in its organization and administration."[8]

The personal associations Rowell established during his trip to the East in 1875 led him early in his career to appreciate the importance of cooperation and the sharing of common interests among librarians. Although his participation in the American Library Association was limited by his location on the Pacific Coast, Rowell did serve as Association vice-president in 1891. His interest in promoting cooperation among libraries in California led him to work with Librarian George T. Clark of Stanford (who had earlier served as Rowell's assistant) toward organizing the Library Association of Central California (later to become the California Library Association) in 1895. Rowell was elected president of the new Association and served in that position through 1897.

Having benefited greatly from his visits to eastern libraries twenty-five years earlier, Rowell used an eight-month leave of absence, granted to him in 1900 partly for health reasons, to travel in Europe. He saw over 100 libraries during that time, and made careful inspection of about twenty, including the British Museum, the Bibliothèque Nationale, and the notable

---

[8] Joseph C. Rowell to W. C. Lane, Librarian, Harvard University, Nov. 3, 1899, in Rowell's *Letter Book* (1899–1900), p. 134.

libraries in Munich, Leipzig, and Florence. Upon his return to the United States, Rowell stopped at several university libraries in the East before returning to California. He noted various changes that had taken place since his earlier visits, such as the considerable growth in the sizes of collections and the amounts of money provided for books, as well as the expansion of library service activities. He also observed, however, that the universities appeared to be growing at a faster rate than their libraries, that the libraries were generally inadequate for the increasing needs of students and teachers, and that prevailing crowded conditions reflected pressing needs for larger and better-planned library buildings. After his return he published two articles describing the observations made on his trip: "Impressions of a Philobib Pilgrim," and "A Peep into the Vatican Library."[9]

After 1900, Rowell did not engage in any new bibliographical ventures but devoted himself largely to helping plan the new Doe Library building, to book collecting, and to his personal interests in writing. With the steady growth of the library staff in the decade 1900–10, Rowell was prepared to have new people take over many responsibilities that earlier he had fulfilled with little assistance. It must be remembered that while six men had served in the office of University president and numerous changes in the faculty had occurred during the last quarter of the nineteenth century, Rowell had been the only University librarian during that time. The value of his contribution to the library in those years cannot be questioned. He labored within the limitations of inadequate financial support for books and even greater handicaps in terms of staff. The library's functioning had depended upon his direct participation in all phases of its operation, hardly a situation for the development of administrative leadership. Moreover, Rowell had received no formal education in librarianship. Although he later referred to his trip to the East in 1875 as "the first summer session in library science on record,"[10] it allowed him but an acquaintance with other libraries. His real training came on the job and through his own experience. From these facts and the circumstances of the University's growth under President Wheeler's dynamic leadership, it became apparent that the library demands were becoming greater than Rowell could fulfill. Thus, in 1910, as construction of the initial part of the new Doe building was nearing completion and plans were being made to occupy it, the position of associate librarian was created to provide for greater administrative leadership. From that time until his retirement in 1919, Rowell's primary activity was in

---

[9] Joseph C. Rowell, "Impressions of a Philobib Pilgrim," *University of California Magazine*, VII (Feb. 1901), 1–10; and "A Peep into the Vatican Library," *Impressions,* I (1901), 264–5.
[10] Rowell, "Professional Life and Work," leaf 1.

the area of book selection and collection development, and especially in building up the University archives and the library's Californiana collection. He continued to meet with the Library Committee, although he no longer served as its secretary. He still participated in making policy decisions, but the main responsibility for executing them and administering the library generally became the function of his associate.

Rowell was appointed librarian emeritus and University archivist in 1919. He continued to maintain an office at the library and regularly worked there three half-days a week, devoting his energies to the collection of California authors, the archives, and matters related to the University's history. Failing health in the spring and summer of 1938 prevented Rowell from going to the campus. His death in November of that year ended a lifetime of service to his beloved alma mater.

Beyond the record of a man's accomplishments lie his own views toward his profession and the personal attitudes governing his relations with other people. Joseph C. Rowell was a modest man, although not self-effacing. By nature he was gentle and mild-mannered, endowed with a strong personal sense of integrity and dedication to his work. Although he had scholarly interests and a natural proclivity toward writing, he made no pretentions of being a scholar. He accepted his role as a librarian with great respect, regarding himself mainly as a bibliographer and book collector. He was both sensitive and sympathetic, and possessed a deep sense of human understanding.

The portraiture that best fitted Rowell was the one he used to describe librarians in an address to the Library Association of Central California in 1896:

> He [a librarian] is a person of stern integrity, whose word is equal to another man's bond. He has high impulse, energy, earnestness, and a confidence in himself based on training and on the experience of others. He doesn't dream of his bank account; he is unselfishly devoted to his work. While not a genius, his enthusiasm takes the place of great talent....
>
> Our librarian is a positive, aggressive person. Neat, orderly, and punctual, he expects similar qualities in his assistants. He heeds petty details, but, Wellington-like, is not over-mastered by them. Of administrative ability, he plans improvements in the service, and is always "short on" red tape. He is loyal to his co-workers, alleviates their toils, takes personal interest in their welfare, and they in turn are loyal to him....
>
> Our ideal librarian, paradoxically as it may appear, is a scholar. He does not know everything; he isn't a perambulating cyclopaedia; but he has received a broad, thorough education, and has acquired mental power to tackle problems from which less bold spirits shrink.... He is a book-lover and delights in bril-

liant proofs, in lustrous, wide margins and dainty bindings, though his private cupboard contains never a one.[11]

The contrasting traits of Rowell's personality are apparent from some of his letters and other writings. When occasion warranted it, Rowell was capable of expressing a sense of righteous indignation. For instance, in response to the slovenly way in which a foreign bookdealer followed his addressing and shipping directions Rowell wrote: "We cannot too severely condemn such inexcusable carelessness on the part of your shipping clerk, which we trust will never occur again."[12] To a student who was dilatory about returning library books he wrote: "An immediate explanation for non-return of books over-due and repeatedly requested, is due from you to me personally. Pending such explanation, I have given orders not to issue books to you."[13] By contrast, when Rowell learned that one of his staff members was afflicted with a fatal illness, he wrote: "I have lost an intelligent, faithful and lovable helper."[14]

Rowell combined his sense of humor and interest in writing in the following piece which he posted in the library alcove containing works of Latin authors:

Fastidious Horace in a Pig-pen.

To Horatius, Greeting:—

I have seen thy unquiet shade of late flitting sadly in alcove F. I have seen the mournful look in thy dark-fringed eyes; and that painful sigh from thy ghostly lips has smitten my very soul.

These scavengers in Latin 3x do most shamefully toss about and illtreat, —swine-like amid linguistic roots, the beloved tomes of thy charming lyrics.

Rest thee, Horatius. And this foul doing cease not, By Hecate! I will convey thy sweet numbers down to my innermost sanctuary, where no profaning hand shall touch.

Thy friend
Bibliothecarius.[15]

Again later, in response to President Sproul's notification that the University wished to confer on him the honorary degree Doctor of Laws at Charter Day exercises in 1935, Rowell's modesty was expressed with an element of humor in his reply: "I am not conscious of any achievement attained which merits the honor proposed. Possibly I am singled out, as

---

[11] Joseph C. Rowell, "Standards of Success," *Library Journal,* XXI (1896), 110.

[12] Joseph C. Rowell to Gustav Fock, Leipzig, Germany, May 4, 1903, in Rowell's *Letter Book* (1902–03), opp. p. 234.

[13] Joseph C. Rowell to L. E. Stern, Berkeley, California, Feb. 20, 1903, in Rowell's *Letter Book* (1902–03), p. 149.

[14] Joseph C. Rowell to Banjamin Ide Wheeler, President, University of California, Feb. 14, 1903, in Rowell's *Letter Book* (1902–03), p. 143.

[15] Joseph C. Rowell, "Fastidious Horace in a Pig-pen" (unpublished; 1 leaf), in his *Writings* (Berkeley: 1880–1920), vol. 3, no. 20, University of California Archives, Berkeley.

the most persistent, and pestiferous, beggar (in behalf of the University) on the records."[16]

Rowell's statements regarding the University library and problems re-lated to librarianship provide clues to his professional opinions. Concern-ing the library's need for more adequate support he wrote in 1897: "No library can make a symmetric, well-rounded growth which depends to a great extent upon donations of books, especially a library connected with an educational institution like the University. However desirable and wel-come book gifts may be, the fact remains that the book *most* wanted, the *new* book, fresh from the press, is only to be had upon payment of hard cash.... An endowment of $1,000,000 would not be any too large to meet the just needs of a university library"[17]

His philosophy of developing a library collection was summed up in the following excerpt from an address given at the American Library Asso-ciation convention in 1905: "Frankly abandon the idea of building up a 'well balanced standard' collection; I have heard of such libraries, but have never seen one. Indeed, disproportion of books tends toward distinc-tiveness, and later on distinction.... Specialization attracts other books of the same kind; encourages specific endowments, and thus relieves tension on funds."[18]

Of equal importance in assessing a man's professional accomplishments are the views which others hold of him. Rowell was described several times by his associate and successor in the librarian's position, Harold L. Leupp:

> In the days of small beginnings Mr. Rowell laid solidly and well the founda-tions upon which in later years he built one of the important university li-braries of the country. The record of what he accomplished under the handicaps of an attenuated book fund, insufficient assistance, and inadequate housing for the Library, is little short of astonishing.[19]
>
> Nothing will ever replace the kindly interest and courteous personal service which those earlier readers received from the man who made the library.... Only those who know the story can realize the devotion to duty, the patient drudgery and unsparing attention to detail directed through so many years to the same end.[20]

---

[16] Joseph C. Rowell to Robert Gordon Sproul, President, University of California, Feb. 12, 1935, *Correspondence and Papers* (C–B 419), Bancroft Library, Berkeley.

[17] Joseph C. Rowell, "The Library of Our State University," *Merchants' Association Review* (March 1897), p. 4; copy in his *Writings* (Berkeley: 1880–1920), vol. 1, no. 15, University of California Archives, Berkeley.

[18] Joseph C. Rowell, "On the Distribution of Income in the College Library" (unpublished), pp. 3–4, in his *Writings* (Berkeley: 1880–1920), vol. 3, no. 8, University of California Archives, Berkeley.

[19] Harold L. Leupp, "Joseph Cummings Rowell," *Library Journal*, LXIV (1939), 286.

[20] *Librarian's Report* (1919), p. 5.

In conferring the honorary Doctor of Laws degree upon Rowell, President Sproul paid him the following tribute:

Son of this University's youth; her patient and faithful servant during two generations; transformer of a college library into a great University collection; exemplar of selfless devotion to the cause of higher education in California; a modest man who speaks ill of no one.[21]

HAROLD LEWIS LEUPP

Leupp was born in New York City in 1877, the son of an author-journalist who also served in governmental positions and as United States Commissioner of Indian Affairs. His early professional aspirations for a military career led him to seek entrance to the United States Military Academy at West Point. Commenting on this later he wrote: "I applied all right, and succeeded in securing appointment as alternate; but as my principal passed the entrance examinations I turned my attention to more peaceful pursuits."[22] Leupp received the Bachelor of Arts degree from Cornell University in 1902 and went on to the New York State Library School at Albany, 1902–04. Although he completed the course work, Leupp did not submit the thesis required for a degree. During the years at Albany he developed lasting friendships with other future librarians, among whom were Charles H. Brown (later librarian of Iowa State College of Agriculture and Mechanic Arts) and Sydney B. Mitchell (later Leupp's associate at California and first director of its School of Librarianship). He then also met Beulah L. Cross, whom he married in 1906. Leupp spent the years 1904–10 in Chicago, serving successively as assistant reference librarian at the John Crerar Library (1904–06), superintendent of the retail and library departments of the University of Chicago Press (1906–09), and librarian of the University of Chicago's history group library (1909–10).

In 1910 Leupp went to the University of California and began a thirty-five year professional relationship, first as associate librarian (1910–19) and then as librarian (1919–45). His appointment to the position at Berkeley was in part due to the influence of Professor Henry Morse Stephens. Leupp had been one of Stephens' students at Cornell. Stephens' close friendship

---

[21] Harold L. Leupp to George A. Pettitt, Assistant to the President, University of California, Nov. 28, 1938, *Correspondence and Papers* (CU-12, Carton 25), University of California Archives, Berkeley.

[22] Harold L. Leupp to Leon M. Solis-Cohen, New Rochelle, N. Y., April 22, 1937, *Correspondence and Papers* (CU-12, Carton 24), University of California Archives, Berkeley. Biographical data and general information pertaining to Leupp's career have been derived primarily from his letters contained in *Correspondence and Papers* (1911–45; CU-12), University of California Archives, Berkeley; additional information has been obtained from Mrs. Harold L. Leupp and Graham M. Leupp, a son, who were interviewed by the author.

at California with President Wheeler gave him the opportunity to recommend Leupp when an associate librarian was being sought.

Leupp's administrative ability soon impressed President Wheeler and led him to turn over to the new associate librarian, within the first year after his arrival, the major responsibility for the library's operation.[23] He was given charge of the library's public services, staff relations, finances, and matters related to the building. He also supervised the work of acquisition and cataloging, although Rowell continued active in book selection and collection development.

The shuffling of administrative responsibilities could very easily have led to strained relations between Rowell and Leupp; this was not the case, however. Rowell, in true gentlemanly fashion, accepted Leupp as an equal and insisted that his title be "associate librarian" rather than "assistant."[24] Rowell recognized and respected Leupp's capabilities in areas where the library needed them, and thus welcomed him as a colleague. Likewise, Leupp was mindful of Rowell's accomplishments in laying the library's foundations. Commenting on this in an address to the library staff in 1935, Leupp said: "At a very early date my respect for my predecessor took a lively upturn as I came to realize what he had accomplished with inadequate means and little assistance."[25] Although Leupp was by nature much more aggressive than Rowell, and more interested in the daily problems of administration, the common bond of their mutual sense of integrity and dedication to the library enabled the two men to work well together.

When Leupp arrived on the Berkeley campus he immediately became involved in a wide range of library activities. Initial construction of the Doe Library building was nearing completion, and he took charge of planning and supervising the moving of the book collection from Bacon Hall to its new quarters. Of equal importance was his recruiting of additional staff members. Leupp was fortunate in securing Sydney B. Mitchell from Stanford to head the Accessions Department, Carleton B. Joeckel from the St. Louis Public Library and Edith M. Coulter from Stanford to work in the

---

[23] The accounts of Professor Stephens' influence in Leupp's appointment and President Wheeler's action in delegating the library's main administrative authority to Leupp are reported by Sydney B. Mitchell in his autobiography. See *Mitchell of California*, ed. by Lawrence C. Powell (Berkeley: California Library Association, 1960), pp. 206–7. Both these accounts have been confirmed by the author in personal conversations with Mrs. Harold L. Leupp.

[24] Joseph C. Rowell to Benjamin Ide Wheeler, President, University of California, May 3, 1910, *Correspondence and Papers* (CU-5; 1910–11, folder no. 52), University of California Archives, Berkeley.

[25] Harold L. Leupp, "My 25 Years in the 'New Building,'" in *Staff Association Celebration of Library Silver Jubilee, 1910–1935,* University of California Library Staff Association (unpublished; 1935), p. 7, *Correspondence and Papers* (C-B 419), Bancroft Library, Berkeley.

Reference Department, and Dr. Edwin Wiley, Nella J. Martin, and Philena R. Sheldon, all from the Library of Congress, and Anne S. Pratt from Yale, to work in the Catalog Department. The addition of these people early in Leupp's administration added considerable strength to the staff and enabled the library to meet the challenges which both his leadership and moving into the Doe building brought. Another area of major activity for which Leupp was responsible during those early years was the result of the decision, wisely made in 1913, to reclassify the library collection from the Rowell scheme to that of the Library of Congress. In 1912 Leupp was instrumental in activating the summer courses in librarianship, which had lapsed after 1907. This action later led to establishment of the Department of Library Science in the College of Letters and Science, and eventually to creation of the School of Librarianship. During most of the years until he became librarian in 1919 Leupp directed the program and personally taught several of its courses.

Although unsuccessful in pursuing his earlier plans for a military career, after the entry of the United States into World War I Leupp was granted a leave of absence for service in the army. He was commissioned a second lieutenant in the infantry in August 1917, served with the 166th Depot Brigade at Camp Lewis, Washington, and was discharged in December 1918 with the rank of major. He then entered the second phase of his career in the California Library. Upon Rowell's retirement in 1919, Leupp was appointed to the position of University librarian. Even though he had already been the library's main administrator for several years, Leupp at last officially bore the title as well as the responsibilities of that office.

Recovering from the disruptions of the war years, the library during the 1920's experienced considerable growth, both in the size of the book collection and in the total amount of library expenditures. Several developments which had lasting significance occurred in those years. The reserve book room, first opened in 1918, grew greatly both in the size of its collection and in circulation. In conjunction with the reserve book room a book rental service was also established in 1929. In 1924 the Lange Library of Education was opened in Haviland Hall as the first branch library under the jurisdiction of the General Library. Within a few years, as construction of the Life Sciences building was begun, plans were also made for the Biology Library, the second branch library on the Berkeley campus; it was opened in 1930. Leupp's desire for a recreational reading room for students was also realized in 1928 when the Alexander F. Morrison Memorial Library was dedicated and opened in the Doe Library building. In the field of library education, although the main responsibility had been turned over to Mitchell, Leupp gave active support to the establishment of the School of Librarianship in 1926. During Mitchell's absence in 1926–27, Leupp directed the program of the school for its first year of operation.

In the period 1930–45 the library faced many problems occasioned by the depression of the thirties and the effects of World War II. With the exceptions of the Photographic Service and the Documents Division, the library was unable to expand its services during that time. Plans which were made for a third branch library in the fields of engineering had to be postponed until after the war. Despite lower budgets, Leupp tried to administer the library without reducing its effectiveness. The problems of inadequate space in the Doe Library building, which had already arisen in the twenties, were growing in intensity. Although rooms were rearranged and services relocated, such solutions were only temporary. The need for an annex or a new library building was very apparent, but there was no immediate hope for its realization. Leupp continued personally to function with a sense of dedication and pressed his staff members in the performance of their tasks, but both he and his assistants were limited by circumstances beyond their control. For this reason, the later years of his librarianship lacked the kinds of exciting developments that had occurred in the first two decades of his service at the University. Leupp retired as University librarian in 1945, at the age of sixty-eight.

Leupp's personality expressed itself in many and varied ways which at times operated in opposition to each other. Consequently he was not as easily understood by his fellow-workers as his more relaxed predecessor had been. He displayed the gentlemanly qualities of kindness, sympathy, loyalty, and graciousness on many occasions toward those who worked with him. Excerpts from several letters he wrote display these qualities. When Frank Bumstead, head of the Accessions Department, was forced by illness to take an extended leave of absence in 1936 (from which he never returned), Leupp closed a letter to him with the following paragraph: "Now you had better settle down to a good loaf, and not only get rid of this thing but build up some reserve, as we shall find plenty to keep you busy when you get back. The best of luck, and for the love of Mike *don't worry*. Worry has killed more people than tuberculosis ever has."[26]

During the time of Bumstead's illness Leupp went directly to President Sproul on Bumstead's behalf to request that his leave of absence, already extended, be extended again. Two years later, when Rowell was in his

---

[26] Harold L. Leupp to Frank M. Bumstead, Berkeley, California, July 30, 1936, *Correspondence and Papers* (CU-12, Carton 21), University of California Archives, Berkeley.

final illness, Leupp wrote to him: "I shall look in on you again in a few days and hope to find you greatly improved. . . . Take good care of yourself, so that we may have you back with us soon."[27] In 1940 Leupp wrote Inez Colby, a staff member in the Catalog Department, in regard to her husband's illness: "As I said in my telegram, I want you to take such time as you may need to look after Mr. Colby. . . . Should matters take a turn which creates any difficulties or embarrassments for you in which I can be of any service to you, please have no hesitation in calling upon me. It would be a genuine satisfaction to me to be able to express in some personal and practical way my very deep appreciation of your long period of faithful and effective service to the library."[28]

Leupp's personal quality of concern did not pass unnoticed by his staff. After eleven years of service at the library, one former employee wrote to express appreciation for "the kindness, wisdom and guiding hand of its Chief . . . [who showed] interest, encouragement, and special capacity for that difficult duality,—critical yet inspiring consideration of one's work."[29] These excerpts reveal a somewhat paternal quality in Leupp's relationship with his staff members; and among themselves many of the library's employees referred to him as "father."

On the other hand, Leupp also had a very stern and harsh side to his personality which caused difficulty for his associates. By nature he was a perfectionist and had an astonishing memory for details. He strove for efficiency in getting work accomplished quickly and accurately. He became impatient and on occasions gave vent to outbursts of temper when he came upon situations which, by his standards, revealed inefficiency. In this regard he always kept in close touch with all that was going on in the library. In 1923 he wrote to a fellow librarian: "In our library the heads of departments are given a pretty free hand and are held responsible for results in their own fields; but the days are few and far between when I am not in every department at least once, and for a long enough time to make my own observations."[30] Staff members were very much aware of his

[27] Harold L. Leupp to Joseph C. Rowell, Oakland, California, April 25, 1938, *Correspondence and Papers* (CU-12, Carton 26), University of California Archives, Berkeley.

[28] Harold L. Leupp to Mrs. Inez S. Colby, Olympia, Washington, July 19, 1940, *Correspondence and Papers* (CU-12, Carton 29), University of California Archives, Berkeley.

[29] Amy Wood Nyholm, Berkeley, California, to Robert Gordon Sproul, President, University of California, Dec. 13, 1943, *Correspondence and Papers* (CU-12, Carton 37), University of California Archives, Berkeley.

[30] Harold L. Leupp to Charles H. Brown, Librarian, Iowa State College of Agriculture and Mechanic Arts, Ames, Iowa, March 16, 1923, *Correspondence and Papers* (CU-12, Carton 8), University of California Archives, Berkeley.

presence throughout the library and conscious of the fact that they were often under his watchful eyes.

Moreover, Leupp possessed a Puritan-like belief in the virtues of hard work and strict discipline. He insisted that staff members arrive promptly at their desks, that they not engage in conversations extraneous to their tasks during working hours, and even that their dress and grooming be such that they not attract undue attention. Men were to wear coats at all times while at work, and women were to refrain from wearing bright-colored dresses and heavy perfumes. It must be said on his behalf, however, that the standards he set for others were no higher than those he set for himself. He worked long hours, coming early to the library and leaving late; likewise in his own conservative dress he sought to set an example for what he considered proper appearance for the library's employees.

With regard to student infractions of library regulations, Leupp was a martinet. In 1941, concerning a report of stolen and mutilated library books, he wrote: "I quite agree that regardless of the monetary value of the volume stolen or mutilated, penalty for theft or mutilation should be severe. . . . If this thing is to be broken up, the first steps must be the imposition of severe penalties and the publicizing of the names of the offenders."[31]

These contrasting and at times conflicting qualities of Leupp's personality accounted for both the strengths and the weaknesses of his administration. Mitchell's comments about Leupp revealed the tension which some people felt in working with him. Mitchell wrote: "He once told me just before his retirement that his drawback as an administrator was that he was never able to keep his fingers out of every department. But if you had the guts to stand up to him (he had no use for doormats or carpets, and he would trample on you if you were a softie), you could work with him and have more opportunity to get your ideas adopted than with most of the administrators of his time. It was a tough job of course to carry on under these conditions, and he naturally came in for a good deal of criticism, particularly from the old staff of the library which had been used to Mr. Rowell's easier and gentler administration."[32]

Leupp's professional interests were not circumscribed by his responsibilities at the California library. He recognized the value of keeping in contact with other librarians and participating in the activities of professional associations. In 1915 he was elected president of the California Library

---

[31] Harold L. Leupp to Edwin C. Voorhies, Professor, University of California, Feb. 13, 1941, *Correspondence and Papers* (CU-12, Carton 33), University of California Archives, Berkeley.
[32] *Mitchell of California,* op. cit., pp. 207–8.

Association. He served the American Library Association as a member of the Council (to which he was elected in 1923), chairman of the College and Reference Section (1930), and as a member of the Commission on Classification of Library Personnel (also known as the Telford Commission; 1928). When the Association of Research Libraries was organized in 1932, Leupp was elected to serve on its Advisory Committee along with J. Christian Bay, James T. Gerould, C. C. Williamson, Phineas L. Windsor, and Donald B. Gilchrist. In 1941, at the request of the Association of Research Libraries, he and M. L. Raney of the University of Chicago library made a critical and constructive examination of the H. W. Wilson Company's system of pricing its bibliographical and indexing services. The resulting report provided valuable information that was beneficial to libraries dependent upon the Wilson publications.

In the course of these activities Leupp won the respect and confidence of other librarians, who regarded him as a person of sound, practical judgment and frank opinion. As his correspondence files reveal, Leupp frequently exchanged ideas with such men as Bishop of Michigan, Gilchrist of Rochester, Gerould of Princeton, Windsor of Illinois, and especially Charles H. Brown of Iowa. Late in his career Leupp continued to be held in high regard among librarians in the United States. In 1942 he was appointed by Archibald MacLeish, Librarian of Congress, to serve on that library's Advisory Council.

In addition to attending American Library Association conventions frequently, Leupp made several trips to the East, visiting other university libraries in order to study their methods for dealing with common administrative and service problems. In 1929 he was granted a three-month leave of absence to travel in Europe to visit libraries and bookdealers, and to attend meetings of the first World's Library and Bibliographical Congress at Rome and Venice as well as the Conference on Adult Education at Cambridge, England.

Leupp was personally very much interested in book collecting. Among his activities as librarian, the one he considered his special responsibility and which he enjoyed most was reading the catalogs and lists received from publishers and from used-book and remainder dealers. His own interests in book selection were not on the same scholarly plane as those of faculty members who regularly taught and engaged in research, but he did select many works of a general and more current nature which he felt had a place in the collection. In addition to pursuing this interest for the library, Leupp personally bought many books, especially in the fields of history, literature, and travel. His own private collection included over 4,000 volumes, most of which were sold after his death to the University of California library on the Davis campus. Leupp was also interested in fine printing and was for many years a member of the Folio and Roxburghe Clubs of San Francisco. It was partly through those associations that he developed friendships with James K. Moffitt and Albert M. Bender, who generously contributed many fine gifts to the University library.

With regard to the operation of the library, Leupp was a very practical person. When he arrived on the Berkeley campus, the library's administrative organization was relatively undeveloped. During the next thirty-five years he created a system of departments and divisions to which the various activities of the library were assigned. Although the organizational structure was not as refined and sophisticated as in large university libraries of more recent years, it was comparable to that of other similar institutions before World War II. Leupp's greatest strength as an administrator was his ability to select very able people to work on his staff. However, as already indicated by Mitchell's statement above, his chief weakness lay in not relinquishing authority completely to those to whom he had delegated it. In addition, he relied too much for the library's administration upon his secretary, Elinor Hand Hickox, who later was appointed assistant to the librarian.

Leupp was a progressive librarian in his time. On the basis of his experience with the monumental-style Doe Library building, Leupp learned that future library structures should sacrifice ornate design in order to achieve functional arrangements and adaptability to changing needs. He was confronted with the problems of directing library operations that were becoming increasingly centralized and, with the construction of additional buildings on the campus, farther removed from the areas of instruction and faculty activity. In light of this situation, and because many small departmental collections had developed that were difficult to administer, Leupp responded to the opportunity of establishing the Biology Library in 1930, which set a pattern for California's branch library system. This new library, located in the recently completed Life Sciences building, successfully brought together many small departmental collections and placed them under the administrative control of the University librarian. Also, as early as the 1930's, Leupp advocated establishment of undergraduate libraries on university campuses to serve the needs of college students separately from the needs of faculty members and students engaged in research. Believing firmly that a library should serve its users, Leupp established a Readers' Department in 1928, through which reference and circulation activities were coordinated. In the 1940's these activities were designated as "public services" and placed under the jurisdiction of the associate librarian. Leupp tried several plans for arranging reserve books and establishing browsing collections, in order to minimize restrictions on the use of such materials. He also espoused the cause of greater cooperation among university libraries in both the acquisition and circulation of books. In 1944, following a meeting of the Association of Research Libraries, he wrote: "Convinced as I am that such cooperation is the only answer to the enormous problems which the not-distant future holds for the Universities of the country and for their libraries... it is a most cheering thought that we seem to have set certain definite goals and to have made a beginning of planning how we are to achieve them."[33]

Leupp evoked a variety of reactions and opinions from those who came into contact with him. To a student in 1915, for instance, he appeared as "the tall, sombrero-ed, unsmiling, very efficient-looking man who strides out of the office at the west end of the loan room, says what he thinks and strides back again."[34] Some members of his staff regarded him as a "fatherly" type of person who, while stern and demanding, was kind and sympathetic with their problems. Others remembered him as autocratic in nature, harsh in his judgments, and severe in his rebukes. He appeared to members of the faculty as a person of great energy with a keen sense of order and dignity, with high professional standards, and as one whose apparent formal bearing was tempered by a wry wit.[35] To fellow librarians in California Leupp was a man who spent "thirty-five years of untiring concentration on the tremendous job of keeping a library abreast of a rapidly growing university."[36] Leupp's longtime friend and fellow librarian, Charles H. Brown, described him "primarily as an administrator... [with] an exceptionally clear understanding of research," who was direct and incisive, "not an appeaser... [nor] a publicist," and a true gentleman.[37] In a tribute to him, Lawrence S. Thompson wrote in 1952: "Mr. Leupp distinguished himself not only as an administrator but also as a torchbearer of the humane tradition of librarianship.... Future academic librarians will speak with conviction of the twenties and thirties as the age

---

[33] Harold L. Leupp to Paul North Rice, Chief, Reference Department, New York Public Library, March 17, 1944, *Corespondence and Papers* (CU-12, Carton 39), University of California Archives, Berkeley.

[34] "Behind the Scenes: the Library," *Daily Californian*, Aug. 24, 1915, p. 4.

[35] "Harold L. Leupp," *In Memoriam*, University of California (Berkeley: 1957), pp. 83–4.

[36] "Harold L. Leupp and the University of California Library," *California Library Association Bulletin*, VII (1945–46), 28.

[37] Charles H. Brown, "Harold L. Leupp, Administrator," *College and Research Libraries*, VI (1945), 353–4.

of the Bishops, the Putnams, the Browns, the Wilsons, the Mitchells, and the Leupps."[38]

LIBRARY STAFF MEMBERS

The position of assistant librarian was created at California in 1886. It was first held by George T. Clark (1886–87), who later served as librarian of the San Francisco Public Library and subsequently for twenty years as Stanford University librarian. William J. C. Variel succeeded Clark at California (1887–88) and was followed by Joseph D. Layman (1888–1907). The assistant librarian performed a variety of tasks, mostly related to the daily operation of the library. Since the staff at that time was very small, the administrative nature of this position remained quite undeveloped. During Librarian Rowell's eight-months leave of absence in 1900, Layman was given charge of the library. In 1907 he resigned his position to accept appointment as librarian of the University of Nevada, and for the next three years the responsibilities formerly assigned to the assistant librarian were distributed among several other members of the staff.

It was not until Leupp served as associate librarian (1910–19) that the position of "second in command" really became significant in the library. The circumstances of his appointment and the extent of administrative authority given to him were unusual; while Rowell remained titular librarian, Leupp had become the library's main administrator. When Leupp succeeded Rowell as librarian in 1919, the associate librarian's position was continued, but with more limited responsibilities.

Sydney B. Mitchell was appointed associate librarian in 1919. He was not a newcomer to the California staff at that time, having come to the library in 1911 from Stanford at Leupp's personal request to head the Accessions Department. During Leupp's leave of absence for military service in 1917–18, Mitchell was appointed by President Wheeler to serve as acting associate librarian. Since Mitchell had developed a strong interest in education for librarianship and Leupp was primarily concerned with matters of administration, responsibility for the library training courses was turned over to Mitchell when he became the associate librarian. The duties of this position continued to include serving as head of the Accessions Department. With the creation of the Department of Library Science in 1922, Mitchell became an associate professor of the University while continuing as associate librarian, but he was then relieved of responsibility for the Accessions Department. In 1926 he relinquished the associate li-

---

[38] Lawrence S. Thompson, "Necrology: Harold L. Leupp," *College and Research Libraries,* XIII (1952), 271.

brarianship and took a leave of absence as associate professor in order to teach for one year at the University of Michigan. Returning to California in 1927, Mitchell devoted full time to serving as director (later dean) of the School of Librarianship.

Mitchell contributed much to the California library and its staff during his fifteen years of service. He was a scholarly person as well as a capable librarian who possessed a strong positive outlook toward his work. He was shrewd in dealing with difficult situations, yet his sensitivity and kindness and the warmth of his personality endeared him to many fellow workers and students. Commenting about him, one staff member said: "As a taskmaster he was severe to the degree that he demanded—and got—good work and constant devotion to the job, but his subordinates were rewarded with the pleasure of good conversation . . . in moments of lesser pressure and in having an understanding superior officer. He never 'stood on his dignity'. . . . The *esprit de corps* in the Order Department in those old days was therefore excellent."[39]

The library was without an assistant or associate librarian from the time of Mitchell's resignation until 1929 when John S. Richards was appointed to the reestablished assistant librarian's position. Richards, who was a graduate of the New York State Library School, had served as librarian of the Washington State Normal School. He joined the California staff in 1926 as superintendent of circulation, became head of the newly created Readers' Department in 1928, and was advanced to assistant librarian in 1929. Leupp described Richards as "thoroughly reliable, conscientious, has initiative . . . deals well with people, a good organizer."[40] But Richards was not given administrative authority commensurate with his position. In 1934 he resigned from the California staff to become the executive assistant and subsequently associate librarian at the University of Washington. Later in his career Richards served as head of the Seattle Public Library system, and was also elected president of the American Library Association (1955/56).

Peyton Hurt followed Richards as assistant librarian and served from January 1935 until June 1937. Having received the Ph.D. degree from the University of California in 1931 and a Certificate in Librarianship in 1933, Hurt brought to his new position strong interests in scholarship and research which caused him to be well accepted among the faculty members.

[39] Cora R. Brandt, "Sydney B. Mitchell, Dean of Horticulture in California," in *Mitchell of California*, op. cit., pp. 229–30.

[40] Harold L. Leupp to Frederick M. Hunter, Chancellor, University of Denver, May 20, 1932, *Correspondence and Papers* (CU-12, Carton 15), University of California Archives, Berkeley.

He also won Leupp's admiration and great respect, as shown by the following excerpts from letters which Leupp wrote:

Hurt's great assets, which have made him highly valuable to me, are his ability to analyze a situation, to take a new idea and think it through to a definite program, and to get results. While he did not always avoid stepping on toes in the process, he was never discouraged by opposition, but if he found one path blocked, took another to the same goal; and like a good military commander, always had an alternative method for reaching his objective.[41]

Hurt is a human dynamo. . . . He has more ideas to the square inch than most people, and displays more ingenuity in translating them into action. . . . He is quite open minded and is always ready to examine criticism of himself and his ways and to admit error as soon as he is convinced that it exists.[42]

During his years at California Hurt was particularly interested in the use of the library by various groups of students, and with the encouragement of Leupp and the University administration he made several studies in this field. Hurt's appointment to the librarianship at Williams College prompted his resignation from the California staff in 1937.

For the next eight years Jerome K. Wilcox served at California, first as assistant librarian (1937–40) and then as associate (1940–45). A graduate of the University of Illinois Library School, Wilcox had served as assistant and associate reference librarian at Chicago's John Crerar Library (1928–35) and as head of Duke University library's Acquisition Department (1935–37). Wilcox's greatest interests and contributions as a librarian were in the fields of bibliography and government documents. His main task at the University of California was developing the library's newly created Documents Division and building the collection in that field. While he also served as interim head of the Accessions Department during his early years on the California staff, his responsibilities shifted to the area of public services after he became associate librarian in 1940. Concerning Wilcox, Leupp wrote:

He is able, a tremendous worker, and possesses the personal qualifications which have made many friends for him among both faculty and students.[43]

He has been most helpful in devising ways and means to meet the numerous

[41] Harold L. Leupp to Carleton B. Joeckel, Professor, University of Chicago, Jan. 5, 1937, *Correspondence and Papers* (CU-12, Carton 23), University of California Archives, Berkeley.

[42] Harold L. Leupp to Theodore W. Koch, Librarian, Northwestern University, Evanston, Illinois, Oct. 31, 1940, *Correspondence and Papers* (CU-12, Carton 30), University of California Archives, Berkeley.

[43] Harold L. Leupp to Carl M. White, Director, University of Illinois Library, Urbana, Illinois, Aug. 20, 1941, *Correspondence and Papers* (CU-12, Carton 33), University of California Archives, Berkeley.

problems, both of public service and internal administration, resulting from war conditions, and I have found him always a loyal, reliable, and efficient worker.[44]

Wilcox left California in 1945 to become librarian of the City College of New York. He published several works in the fields of bibliography and documents, and also served for several years as chairman of the Committee on Public Documents of the American Library Association. His particular ability as a specialist in the field of government publications was recognized when he was appointed documents analyst and consultant for the United Nations Library in 1949.

In 1939 Jens Nyholm was appointed as an assistant librarian on the California staff. Although Nyholm's original training for librarianship had been in Denmark, he was also graduated from Columbia University's School of Library Service in 1928. He had served as a cataloger at the Library of Congress (1928–37) and as head of the Catalog Department at the University of California at Los Angeles. At Berkeley he was given charge of the library's technical processes, and was especially made responsible for coordinating the activities of the Accessions and Catalog Departments. Nyholm possessed qualities which suited him uniquely for his position. He was both a linguist and a bookman. In addition, he possessed a thorough knowledge of cataloging and a natural ability for systematizing library activities. Even though he remained somewhat out of touch with the library's administrative problems in areas other than those for which he was responsible, Nyholm was regarded by his colleagues as a very capable librarian. Leupp had great respect for his abilities and described him as follows:

> He is a highly educated, excellently trained man, careful and responsible, who has shown good judgment in handling the technical questions which have come before him.... His tastes and interests, while scholarly, have not taken him out of touch with common people. Among the faculty I have found no one that did not like him ... and respect him.[45]

> He has background, excellent training and experience in cataloging, and with it a very detached viewpoint and an ability to view the matters at issue from the standpoint of the user of the library.[46]

[44] Harold L. Leupp to Frank N. Freeman, Dean, University of California, Berkeley, Oct. 13, 1943, *Correspondence and Papers* (CU-12, Carton 36), University of California Archives, Berkeley.

[45] Harold L. Leupp to Carl H. Milam, Executive Secretary, American Library Association, Chicago, Illinois, Aug. 3, 1944, *Correspondence and Papers* (CU-12, Carton 42), University of California Archives, Berkeley.

[46] Harold L. Leupp to Charles H. Brown, Librarian, Iowa State College of Agriculture and Mechanic Arts, Ames, Iowa, Sept. 22, 1944, *Correspondence and Papers* (CU-12, Carton 31), University of California Archives, Berkeley.

Nyholm left the California staff in 1944 to become librarian at Northwestern University. During his career he participated in a wide range of professional activities, mainly through the American Library Association, and served for many years on the Board of Directors and the Executive Committee of the Midwest Inter-Library Center.

In addition to those who served as assistant or associate librarians at California, many other people distinguished themselves through the length of time they served and the important positions they held on the library staff before 1945. With the exceptions of Librarians Rowell and Leupp, no one served with more devotion than Frank M. Bumstead. Educated for library service at the University of Illinois, he joined the California staff in 1906. Bumstead's most important positions were superintendent of circulation (1919–23) and head of the Accessions Department (1923–37). Forced by severe illness to take an extended leave of absence, he died in 1938, after a thirty-two year association with the library. Bumstead was an able and intelligent worker who in his shy and behind-the-scenes way contributed much to the library's development.

Pauline Gunthorp served as head of the Catalog Department (1907–26) during the period when reclassification of the collection was begun. Miss Gunthorp was considered by younger members of her staff as a librarian of the "old school" who was strict in administering the department. Despite her stern appearance and businesslike manner she was a kind and thoughtful supervisor who inspired many of her staff members to high standards of work. Agnes M. Cole, who had served with Miss Gunthorp since 1916, succeeded her as head of the department (1926–36). Miss Cole's major responsibility for recataloging activities had given her a thorough knowledge of the Library of Congress classification. This fact, plus easy rapport with her subordinates, were the major strengths during her years of administration. Leadership of the department passed from Miss Cole to Antoinette H. Goetz (1936–40) whose strict attention to detail in cataloging and insistence on the importance of revision made a lasting impression on those who were supervised by her. Jens Nyholm directed the department's activities until 1944, when Doris Higgins was appointed head cataloger.

Edith M. Coulter, who began working at the library in 1911, held the position of reference librarian (1915–28) until she was appointed as assistant professor in the School of Librarianship. Miss Coulter participated actively in the California Library Association, of which she was elected secretary-treasurer in 1915, and read papers at several of its meetings. She was also a longtime member of the American Library Association and attended many of its conventions. As a librarian and teacher Miss Coulter had a distinguished career; she has been remembered by many of her former students and colleagues as a person who had a passionate love for the detective work of reference service as well as a scholarly knowledge of California history and geography. Bess Lowry was appointed reference librarian in 1932 and held that position until after 1945. Under her direction the Reference Department rendered especially valuable service to defense industries and government agencies in the West during World War II. Ivander MacIver's long career at the California library (1920–58) was particularly distinguished after her appointment in 1930 as chief of the Division of Serials and Exchanges, later Gifts and Exchanges, where she made a notable contribution to the collection's development.

Important services were likewise performed by those who were in charge of the two branch libraries on the Berkeley campus. From 1924 until after 1945 Mabel Coulter served first as assistant and later as head of the Lange Library of Education. M. Jessamine Abbott served from 1930 until after 1945 as head of the Biology Library and through the quality of service she developed was largely responsible for drawing several science department collections into that new facility.

Although not a professional member of the staff, Elinor Hand Hickox served as the librarian's secretary (1920–39) and administrative assistant to the librarian (1939–45). She was an efficient manager, so that in time control of personnel, finances, building, and equipment all came to be centered in her office. In the course of handling many administrative activities for the librarian Mrs. Hickox came to wield considerable influence over the library's internal affairs. Many of the professional staff members were unhappy and indignant about the fact that Leupp allowed her to carry out many of the duties of his position. Mrs. Hickox was regarded as an ambitious woman who was intrigued by the power she had gained within the library. In addition to her duties as administrative assistant she was also responsible for organizing and supervising the operation of the library's Photographic Service.

The library also had on its staff during the period 1900–45 a number of persons who, on leaving the Berkeley campus, went on in other places to important careers in librarianship. After almost ten years as a cataloger and head of the Order Department, Arthur B. Smith left the staff in 1912 to become librarian of Kansas State Agricultural College at Manhattan, Kansas. Carleton B. Joeckel served at the University of California (1911–14) as assistant reference librarian and then as superintendent of circulation, when he was appointed librarian of the Berkeley, California, Public Library. He later became a distinguished teacher and writer in the field of librarianship at the Universities of Michigan, Chicago (where he also served as dean of the Graduate Library School) and California. Rudolph H. Gjelsness held the position of senior bibliographer in the Accessions Department at California (1922–24); later in his career Gjelsness became librarian at the University of Arizona and professor of library science (later chairman of the department) at the University of Michigan.

Herman H. Henkle's career in librarianship began as junior librarian in the Biology Library at Berkeley (1930–35). After leaving California he taught librarianship at the University of Illinois and Simmons College, served as director of the Library of Congress' Processing Department, and finally became librarian (later director) of the John Crerar Library. Neal Harlow, later assistant librarian at the University of California at Los Angeles, librarian of the University of British Columbia, and dean of Rutgers University's Graduate School of Library Service, also began his career on the staff of California's Bancroft Library (1934–38). Frank A. Lundy entered upon a long career as librarian of the University of Nebraska after having served at two different times at the California library, first as bibliographer for the "sets" program and assistant head of the Accessions Department (1931–36), and again as acting head cataloger and head of the Accessions Department (1939–42). Robert G. Vosper served as a junior librarian in the Reference Department at Berkeley (1940–42); he later became director of the University of Kansas libraries and subsequently librarian and professor of library science at the University of California at Los Angeles.

Several conclusions may be drawn from this account of California's librarians and their staffs. Aware of the library's importance to the academic community, the regents and the men who served as University president early recognized that full-time administrative leadership for the library was necessary. By the appointment of capable librarians and the delegation of authority, they took the necessary steps to meet that need. Moreover, the men who administered the library were diligent in performing their tasks, resourceful in responding to the demands placed upon them, and skillful in appointing qualified people to assist them. Although Rowell and Leupp possessed distinct differences in personality, professional interests, and preparation for the librarian's position, they both were committed wholeheartedly to the purposes of the University and the library. Finally, the people who served on the staff displayed a high degree of ability, initiative, and loyalty in fulfilling their professional responsibilities. In addition to those who have been named and whose careers have been described, there were also many others who served capably and with devotion in their respective positions. Thus, it was the combined efforts of the librarians and their staffs, supported by the officers and regents of the University, that accounted largely for the success of the library's growth and operation from 1900 to 1945.

Chapter IV

REGENTS, PRESIDENTS, FACULTY MEMBERS, AND FRIENDS

WITHIN the University community, in addition to the librarians and their staffs, responsibility for California's library development was shared by the regents, the men who held the office of president, and members of the faculty. In addition, various friends of the library contributed to its growth through their interest and gifts. Complementing one another, these people fulfilled significant roles in the library's history.

THE REGENTS

Authority for the organization and government of the University of California at the time it was founded in 1868 was entrusted to the Board of Regents. Although its size and makeup were modified in later years, the board retained overall responsibility for the operation of the University. Ten standing committees were created when the regents began functioning. One of these committees was on the library and consisted of three members appointed annually by the president. The size of the committee was subsequently increased to five members, and provision was made to include faculty members among them. When the Bacon Library and Art Museum was opened in 1881, the title of the committee was officially designated as Standing Committee on Library and Museum.[1]

The Orders of the board in 1884 defined the responsibilities of its committees by stating: "The standing committees are specially charged with the immediate care and supervision of the subject-matters indicated respectively by their title."[2] The duties of the Committee on Library and Museum were further to include revising and adopting lists of books suggested by professors for purchase.[3] Minutes of the committee kept from 1881 until

---

[1] Information pertaining to the Regents' Library Committee has been derived from the *Minutes,* University of California Board of Regents, Committee on Library and Museum (1881–1906), and Committee on Library, Research and Publications (1920–22), and from the *Annual Reports of the Secretary to the Board of Regents* (1875–1938/39), University of California Archives, Berkeley.

[2] "Orders of the Board," Article 376, *Regents' Manual,* University of California (1884), p. 195.

[3] Ibid., Article 478, p. 220, Article 481, p. 221.

1906 show that its major activities, in addition to acting on recommendations for book and periodical purchases, consisted of approving bills for payment, discussing the library's building problems and making recommendations for their solution, determining the hours during which the library would be open, and generally establishing policies for the library's administration.

After 1900 the importance of the regents' Committee on Library and Museum declined. This was due to the creation in 1898 of the Advisory Committee on Library, made up of faculty members, which met regularly beginning 1901 as the Library Committee of the Graduate Council, and to which the regents delegated some of the authority earlier exercised by the Committee on Library and Museum. Moreover, after the arrival of President Wheeler in 1899, there was a considerable shifting of responsibilities for the University's administration from the Board of Regents and its various committees to the office of the president, as well as to the faculty and its committees. Members continued to be appointed annually to the Committee on Library and Museum through 1908/09, but in 1909 the Board of Regents altered the designation of its standing committees and the Committee on Library and Museum was discontinued. (See appendix C for names of members who served on the Committee on Library and Museum, 1900–09.)

In 1919 the provision for standing committees was again changed by the regents, and the Committee on Library was re-established. The following year the scope of its responsibilities was enlarged and its name changed to Committee on Library, Research and Publications. The concerns of the committee were general in nature and pertained more to matters of financial provision for the library than to its administration. The committee kept minutes of its meetings for the years 1920–22. Although it continued to be appointed annually thereafter, it rarely functioned, and most of its duties were fulfilled by the Library Committee of the Academic Senate (known before 1911 as the Library Committee of the Graduate Council.) Finally, when the regents' Standing Orders regarding committees were changed in 1938, the Committee on Library, Research and Publications was eliminated. (See appendix D for names of members who served on the Library Committee, 1919–20, and the Committee on Library, Research and Publications, 1920–38.)

Thus, the regents exercised authority quite directly in matters affecting the library's administration before 1900; after that time, however, their role became mainly one of making financial appropriations and confirming staff appointments. Authority for the library's administration increasingly came to be vested in the librarian, and responsibilities for determining library policies and allocating book funds were carried out by the Library Committee of the Academic Senate.

THE PRESIDENTS

In the early years of the University's history the president was concerned mainly with academic affairs, whereas major business and administrative functions were performed by the Board of Regents through its secretary and standing committees. Despite attempts in the 1890's to establish more clearly the president's role as the University's chief executive and to restrict the activities of the regents primarily to determining policies, appropriating funds, and confirming appointments, these goals were not realized until Wheeler became president. During his administration and again later under Robert Gordon Sproul, the president clearly became the University's chief executive with "full authority and responsibility for the administration of academic and student affairs," administering "such business and fiscal operations as are not specifically the responsibility of the secretary, treasurer, or general council of the Regents."[4] Thus, through his authority over fiscal and personnel matters, the president more than any other officer of the University determined the library's development from 1900 to 1945. For that reason the interests and attitudes of the four men who held that office during those years had tremendous bearing upon the history of the California library.

BENJAMIN IDE WHEELER

When Wheeler became president in 1899, California gained a man who was a scholar in the finest academic traditions of his day. He had been graduated from Brown University, studied in Germany at the Universities of Leipzig, Jena, Berlin, and Heidelberg (where he earned the Ph.D. degree), and taught classical philosophy at Cornell for thirteen years before accepting the California appointment. No one could have been more interested in the development of the University library than Wheeler. In his inaugural address on October 25, 1899, he said:

Among the demands for the internal development of the University, none ranks in my estimation with those of the library. The present collection has been made with great skill and sobriety. But it is far too small and incomplete in any department to serve the purposes of advanced study and research....

[4] *The Centennial Record of the University of California*, ed. by Verne A. Stadtman (Berkeley: University of California, 1967), p. 9, hereinafter cited as *Centennial Record*. General information pertaining to the University presidents has been derived from this source and from the *President's Reports* (1900–42.)

Instead of seventy-five thousand volumes there ought to be today three hundred thousand; instead of an income for purchases of four thousand dollars there ought to be thirty thousand. The library force is seriously overworked, the building is overcrowded. A fireproof building, equipped with seminary rooms on the most generous scale, must be provided within the next three or four years.[5]

In his reports to the Board of Regents and in other public statements Wheeler reiterated his concern for the library and pressed for its greater support and development. In 1900 he wrote: "The isolation of California from the centers where great collections have accumulated makes it peculiarly incumbent that here a great library should be founded and maintained as a citadel and refuge for the creative scholarship of the Pacific Coast. With it we can have here a university and maintain the national standard of scholarship; without it we cannot.... We need $25,000 a year for the purchase of books. This means the income of $500,000."[3]

Wheeler had two assets of great value, in addition to his standing as a scholar, on which he was able to draw for the benefit of the library: he had secured from the regents, as a condititon for his accepting the presidency, greater authority for the University's administration than any of his predecessors in that office had received; and he was "remarkably successful in drawing together private gifts for the University."[7] It was through Wheeler's efforts that Charles Franklin Doe was persuaded to bequeath funds to the University in 1904 to be used toward construction of a new library building and also that the second stage (with the exception of some sections of the book stacks) was completed in 1917. Annual appropriations for library books (exclusive of binding) were increased from $4,000 when he took office in 1899 to $25,000 when he retired in 1919. It was primarily Wheeler's influence that led the regents to appropriate funds to purchase the Bancroft Library. Several other very valuable private collections were also acquired by the library during that period.

At the time of his retirement, justified tribute was paid to President Wheeler both as a person and for his accomplishments on behalf of the University by Regent Charles Stetson Wheeler (no relative to President Wheeler), who said:

[5] Benjamin Ide Wheeler, "Inaugural Address," in his *The Abundant Life,* ed. by Monroe E. Deutsch (Berkeley: University of California, 1926), pp. 32–3.

[6] *President's Report* (1898–1900), p. 28.

[7] Ralph P. Merritt, *After Me Cometh a Builder: the Recollections of Ralph Palmer Merritt* (Berkeley: University of California, 1962), p. 33, typescript based on tape-recorded interviews conducted by the Regional Cultural History Project, Bancroft Library, Berkeley, and used by permission.

The plain solemn truth is that a great man in the fulness of his power took hold of our institution at the psychological moment, proved himself adequate to the great task that was before him; and, aided only by such sympathetic assistance as this board could give, perfected an organization and established an institution second to none today. He has placed the University of California in a position of strength and power and has made it a factor for tremendous good. He has won and earned every laurel that an educator and great administrator can earn.[8]

Among the most notable accomplishments of Wheeler's administration was the development of the University library which, as Leupp wrote, received his "unfailing support."[9]

DAVID PRESCOTT BARROWS

Barrows was appointed and took office as University president in December 1919. A graduate of Pomona College in 1894, he had pursued studies in the fields of anthropology and political science at the University of California and Columbia University before earning the Ph.D. degree at the University of Chicago in 1897. His career as a teacher and academic administrator included two years on the faculty of San Diego State College, nine years as superintendent of schools in Manila, Philippine Islands, and thirty-three years as a professor of the University of California. At Berkeley, in addition to teaching, Barrows served as dean of the Graduate School and of the faculties, as well as acting president while Wheeler was on leave in 1913. Through the publication of several books and numerous articles, he had distinguished himself as a scholar. During World War I Barrows served in Belgium with Herbert Hoover on the American Relief Commission; he was later commissioned a major in the United States Army.

Barrows came to the University presidency at a difficult time. He had both to follow Wheeler in that office, which of itself was not an easy task, and to lead the University at a time when it was destined for new growth and challenging demands in the years after World War I. Amid the many claims for his interest and attention Barrows was not unmindful of the library's importance. In his *Report* to the regents in 1923 he wrote: "It [the library] is the heart of the university and the center of its most serious work. It is rapidly becoming one of the great libraries of this country."[10] After serving four years as president, Barrows resigned in order to return to full-time teaching and research activities. By 1922/23, the last year of his ad-

---

[8] "Regent Wheeler Pays Tribute to Retiring Executive at Meeting," *Daily Californian*, Feb. 12, 1919, p. 1.

[9] Harold L. Leupp, "The Library the Heart of the University," *Library Journal*, XLIX (1924), 619.

[10] *President's Report* (1922–23), p. 2.

ministration, the annual appropriation for library books and periodicals (exclusive of binding) had increased to almost $35,000 (out of a total library budget of over $168,000) and the size of the collection had passed the 500,000 volume level.

WILLIAM WALLACE CAMPBELL

The appointment of Campbell as University president in 1923 brought to that position another person whose scholarly reputation was widely acclaimed. A graduate of the University of Michigan, Campbell taught at the University of Colorado and at Michigan before beginning work at the University of California's Lick Observatory in 1891. His distinction as an astronomer led to his appointment as the Observatory's director in 1900, a position that he continued to hold even while serving as president from 1923 to 1930.

Campbell's background as a scientist led him to approach the University's administrative problems by methods of observation and analysis. After gathering the factual data and seeking advice on a particular matter, he would study it thoroughly and then make a decision. Campbell was generally conservative in his judgments as an administrator, dedicated to running the University efficiently and economically. The years of his administration were described at the time of his retirement as "a period of tranquillity and healthy growth such as few universities have enjoyed."[11]

Annual appropriations for library books and periodicals (exclusive of binding) during Campbell's tenure increased from $37,000 (out of a total library budget of $170,000) in 1923/24 to almost $70,000 (out of $237,000 for the total library budget) for 1929/30.[12] During that seven-year period the collection added over 240,000 volumes. Moreover, it was through the special financial appropriation that Campbell was able to arrange that the Miliukov collection was purchased. In his *Report* to the regents in 1924, Campbell commented that "the University Library is the center and soul of the institution. It is in dire need of greatly enlarged resources for the purchase of books and bookstacks."[13] He further observed, however, concerning the library's use that "entirely too many of our students go to the University Library building in search of warmth and quiet, where they may study their own notes and textbooks, rather than to draw books from the Library shelves. This abnormal use of reading-room space in the Library is to be regretted."[14]

---

[11] "William Wallace Campbell," *In Memoriam,* University of California (Berkeley: 1938), p. 6.

[12] *Librarian's Report* (1924), p. 9; (1930), p. 10.

[13] *President's Report* (1923–24), p. 12.

[14] Ibid., p. 2.

Tensions developed between President Campbell and Librarian Leupp because Campbell felt that library personnel costs were too high (65 percent of the library budget in 1925/26.) In 1926, therefore, Campbell ordered that the number of "senior assistant" positions at the library not be increased. That order remained in effect until after Campbell's retirement, despite both the library's growth in expenditures for books and Leupp's protests about this arbitrary staff limitation.[15] (By 1929/30, personnel costs accounted for 58 percent of the library's budget.) In this regard Campbell held an autocratic view of the powers of his office and disregarded the opinion and advice of the librarian. Overlooking that situation, the regents paid tribute to President Campbell upon his retirement with the following statement: "In the midst of complex external problems and great material development, he has never lost sight of the main purposes of a university: the advancement of teaching and learning and the increase of usefulness to its students and to the state."[16]

ROBERT GORDON SPROUL

When Sproul became president in 1930 he brought to that office background and experience considerably different from those of his three immediate predecessors. After receiving the Bachelor of Science degree at California in 1913, Sproul had returned to the Berkeley campus in 1914, where he held several administrative positions for the next sixteen years. Although he was not a teacher and had not gained a scholar's reputation, Sproul was highly regarded as a gifted administrator and spokesman for the University throughout the state. By natural intellectual ability as well as temperament he proved to be eminently well qualified for the president's office.

Despite the financial limitations imposed by the depression during the 1930's and the restricting effects which World War II had upon the University, Sproul was keenly interested in the library's development. Addressing the American Library Association's conference in 1930 at Los Angeles, he said: "The library is the heart of the university. No other division of the university articulates with all departments of instruction and research on the educational side, and certainly no department can rank with the library, which conserves and makes available the thought, and capitalizes

[15] Harold L. Leupp to Charles H. Brown, Librarian, Iowa State College of Agriculture and Mechanic Arts, Ames, Iowa, Nov. 19, 1928, *Correspondence and Papers* (CU-12, Carton 11); and Harold L. Leupp to Robert Gordon Sproul, President, University of California, Nov. 16, 1931, *Correspondence and Papers* (CU-12, Carton 14), University of California Archives, Berkeley.

[16] *President's Report* (1928–29 and 1929–30), p. 804.

the experience of all mankind.... The intellectual growth and vitality of every school and every division, of every professor and every student depends on the vitality of the library."[17]

In the early years of Sproul's administration appropriations for books and periodicals (exclusive of binding) increased from $69,000 in 1930/31 to $77,000 in 1932/33. This amount decreased to $50,000 the following year, but thereafter began to rise again. By 1941/42 it had increased to $80,000, the highest level of the pre-1945 period.[18] The size of the book collection reached one million volumes in 1938, and by 1945 had increased an additional 260,000. In addition, Sproul was instrumental in securing special financial appropriations for the purchase of several en bloc collections. These accomplishments would not have been possible without his continued interest in the library. In his *President's Report* for 1936–38, he wrote: "Libraries are the reservoirs in which the experiences of the world are caught and placed ready to the hand of the student who seeks to contribute his bit to that which we call progress. The books that they contain are teachers without whose aid any program of instruction above the simplest handicrafts could scarcely be conducted. In the last analysis the strength of a university's library is a measure of the richness of its curriculum."[19]

Although the University presidents did not administer the library themselves, they exerted tremendous influence over its development through the appointment of staff members to whom administrative authority was delegated, and over the recommendation of financial appropriations for the library's operation. California was fortunate in having presidents during the period 1900–45 who, as scholars and administrators, quite consistently recognized the indispensable value of a strong library to the University. Without that recognition the library could not have developed as it did, and the greatness of the University would have been seriously impaired.

The Faculty and the Library Committee

At the University of California, faculty members played an important role in the library's development from 1900 to 1945. Although not responsible for appropriating funds, appointing personnel, or administering the library, they were given authority to select books as well as to determine acquisi-

---

[17] Robert Gordon Sproul, "The Place of the Library in Higher Education," *American Library Association Bulletin*, XXIV (1930), 333.

[18] *Financial Statements* (1902/03–1944/45).

[19] *President's Report* (1936–38), p. 29.

tion policies, allocate the library's book funds, and advise the librarian regarding the library's services. It was largely through the direct acquaintance of particular faculty members, for instance, that many of the valuable en bloc collections were acquired.

Although the regents had provided in 1875 for faculty members to serve on the board's Standing Committee on the Library, not until 1898 was there a library committee composed exclusively of teaching personnel. In September of that year, at the suggestion of Librarian Rowell, three members were chosen from the Graduate Council to serve on an Advisory Committee on Library.[20] Rowell reported in 1899 that "two conferences with the Librarian have been held for the discussion of free access to shelves and the annual allotment of money for book purchases."[21] The committee did not function very long thereafter, however, for in February 1901 Rowell wrote to Professor Merrill suggesting the desirability of establishing a Library Committee in order that the library and faculty could be in closer touch with each other.[22] Rowell also wrote to President Wheeler suggesting that the Academic Senate's concern for the library be committed to the Graduate Council, a standing committee of the senate, and that the president appoint a Library Committee, subject to the approval of the council.[23] A committee was appointed as a standing committee of the Graduate Council and given authority to advise the librarian regarding library policies and expenditure of funds. The new Library Committee first met on September 23, 1901, and continued meeting regularly thereafter. Its size increased from five members at the time it was established to ten by 1945. The librarian at first was an ex officio member and served as committee secretary; in later years he continued as secretary but ceased to be a voting member.

For several years after its creation neither the status nor the jurisdiction of the Library Committee was clearly defined. Until 1911 it was regarded at various times as a standing committee both of the Graduate Council and of the Academic Senate. Regarding its jurisdiction the committee's minutes in 1903 stated that "while he [the president] was somewhat in doubt as to the powers of the Committee, the Committee might assume jurisdiction over such matters as should naturally come before it for consideration."[24]

---

[20] Reference to the "Advisory Committee on Library" was made by Rowell in his *Letter Book* (1899–1900), p. 112; Professors Bacon, Merrill, and Slate were chosen as members.

[21] "Librarian's Report," in *President's Report* (1898–1900), p. 87.

[22] Joseph C. Rowell to William A. Merrill, Professor, University of California, Feb. 16, 1901, in Rowell's *Letter Book* (1900–01), p. 116.

[23] Joseph C. Rowell to Benjamin Ide Wheeler, President, University of California, Feb. 19, 1901, in Rowell's *Letter Book* (1900–01), p. 120.

[24] *Library Committee Minutes*, Minute Book no. 1 (1901–10), Sept. 14, 1903.

According to the Orders of the Board of Regents, published in 1904, authority was delegated to the Academic Senate, subject to the regents' Committee on Library and Museum, to "allot the funds available for the purchase of books; and, in general, direct the policy of the Library and advise the Librarian in its administration."[25] These responsibilities of the Senate were carried out by the Library Committee, as its minutes and annual reports for many years indicated.

The Committee's status and jurisdiction were clarified after the Graduate Council was discontinued in 1911. Upon the recommendation of its Committee on Regulations, the Academic Senate adopted the following standing rule in January, 1913:

> There shall be a standing committee on the University Library. It shall be the duty of this committee to assist in the administration of the Library, in accordance with the orders of the Board of Regents, and to perform such other duties relative to the Library as may be committed to the Senate by proper authority. The committee shall report its proceedings regularly to the Senate.[26]

Although the above rule did not refer to the allocation of book funds, this responsibility continued to be fulfilled by the committee, as its minutes showed. The committee's functions were described in its report to the Academic Senate for 1920/21: "The Library Committee acts in a dual capacity. On the one hand it allocates the book funds of the General Library; on the other, it directs the policy of the Library and advises the Librarian in its administration."[27] These functions were officially confirmed in the "Orders Relating to the Library" adopted by the regents in 1925, which read:

> A Committee of the Academic Senate, to be known as the Library Committee, shall allot the funds available for the purchase of books and periodicals and shall advise the Librarian in the administration of the Library.
> The Library Committee shall in general direct the policy of the Library, subject to the approval of the Academic Senate.[28]

Despite some changes in the wording of the Academic Senate's bylaws and the regents' Orders pertaining to the committee, its status and jurisdiction remained essentially the same throughout the period from the 1920's through 1945. The committee confined its activities to allocating book funds, approving book purchases other than those routinely recommended

---

[25] "Orders of the Board," Article 107, *Regents' Manual,* University of California (1904), p. 302.

[26] *Library Committee Minutes,* Minute Book no. 2 (1910–21), Jan. 31, 1913.

[27] *Library Committee Report* (1920/21), p. 1.

[28] Orders Relating to the Library," [Article] 2, *Regents' Minutes,* vol. XXIV (1925–27), May 12, 1925, pp. 81–2.

by faculty members, and considering questions of general policy in the library's operation. It exercised no authority over the staff, funds appropriated for maintenance, or matters strictly administrative in nature. Members of the committee were eleced by the Senate, upon nomination by its Committee on Committees. The Senate also designated the chairman. Much of the Library Committee's business was transacted by various subcommittees appointed by the chairman at the beginning of each academic year. Its greatest period of activity came each fall, when the annual allocation of book funds was made. The committee's jurisdiction was limited to the General Library and its branches on the Berkeley campus, and did not include any departmental or special libraries.

More than 100 faculty members served on the Library Committee between 1900 and 1945 (appendix E). The men who served as chairman made particularly important contributions to the committee's effective services.[29] Edward B. Clapp, the first appointed chairman, held the position at two different times (1901–02, 1911–12). As a professor and later chairman of the Latin department, he represented the fields of classical languages and the humanities generally. Andrew C. Lawson, noted geologist at Berkeley and at one time also dean of the College of Mining, served a total of fifteen years as Library Committee chairman (1902–06, 1910–11, 1912–18, 1919–23). The stimulating and at times provocative nature of his personality made its influence felt in committee meetings. Lawson was keenly interested in the library's efforts to collect scientific periodicals and sets of publications. Adolph C. Miller also served on the committee for many years, and as its chairman (1906–10). He brought to that position his background and knowledge as professor and chairman of the Department of Economics.

With the exception of two years, Henry Morse Stephens was a member of the Library Committee continuously from 1902 until his death in 1919. He also held the chairman's office (1918–19). Greatly beloved as a teacher and highly esteemed as a scholar, Stephens was able to represent the interests of both students and faculty in the library. Having also held office as director of University Extension, dean of the College of Letters and Science, and a member of the Council of Deans, as well as having been a personal friend and adviser to President Wheeler, Stephens' advice and counsel were of great benefit to the library. After Stephens' death his term

---

[29] Information pertaining to faculty members who served as chairmen of the Library Committee has been derived primarily from the *Centennial Record,* and from *Correspondence and Papers,* University of California Library (1878–1945; CU-12), University of California Archives, Berkeley.

as committee chairman was completed by Leon J. Richardson, professor of Latin.

The committee chairmanship changed more frequently from 1923 until 1945. During the twenties, following Lawson's term, it was held by Samuel J. Holmes (1923–25), professor of zoology and noted geneticist, and by J. Franklin Daniel (1925–30), also a professor and later chairman of the zoology department. Benjamin H. Lehman, professor of English and chairman of the Department of Dramatic Art, served as chairman (1930–32, 1933–34) and was primarily responsible, along with Robert J. Kerner, for initiating the collection survey in 1930 and developing the library's "sets" program. George P. Adams, a longtime committee member and former dean of the College of Letters and Science, was also a chairman (1932–33, 1934–35). Having succeeded George H. Howison as Mills Professor of Mental and Moral Philosophy and Civil Polity at the University, Adams represented the strong interests of the humanities in the library. He was followed by Alva R. Davis (1935–38), professor and chairman of the botany department, and subsequently by Charles L. Camp (1938–45), chairman of the Department of Paleontology and director of the University's Paleontology Museum. In addition to being full professors, most of the men who served as Library Committee chairman also held offices as chairmen of instructional departments at Berkeley.

Although they did not serve as chairman, professors Frederick J. Teggart and Charles A. Kofoid made valuable contributions to the committee. Teggert had been assistant and acting librarian at Stanford (1893–98) and librarian of the Mechanics Institute library in San Francisco (1898–1907) before coming to the University of California. At Berkeley he was honorary custodian and curator of the Bancroft Library (1906–16) as well as a member of the faculty (1921–40). His knowledge of West Coast history and bibliography were very beneficial to the library; he also was chairman of the Carpentier Fund subcommittee for several years and a member of the librarian's Advisory Committee. Kofoid rendered especially valuable service to the library when the Division of Serials and Exchanges was established in 1930. As a professor and later chairman of the zoology department, and as a world traveller with a notable scholarly reputation, he helped the library to establish agreements for publication exchanges with many scientific societies in foreign countries. Moreover, as a great book collector (his personal library contained over 30,000 volumes) Kofoid's knowledge of the book market, especially the availability of important individual titles and collections, made his membership on the committee highly beneficial to the library.

In representing the University's instructional and research interests the Library Committee channeled the resources provided by the president and the regents into a strong library collection. The committee also helped to determine the policies by which the librarians and library staff made these resources available for use. Through the interest and activities of its members the faculty Library Committee strongly contributed to the development of the library at Berkeley.

FRIENDS OF THE UNIVERSITY LIBRARY

The University of California had received many gifts and bequests from alumni and other persons, but before 1930 it did not have an organization to encourage public philanthropic interests in the library. In that year Professor B. H. Lehman, chairman of the Library Committee, proposed that a "Friends of the University Library" group be organized to encourage the interests of outside sources in giving to the library.[30] In conjunction with this it was suggested that a "Treasure Room" be established to house rare items and special memorial gifts. A friends group was established in 1931; and within a year, through its efforts the library received $2,500 in gifts. A room was set aside in the Doe Library building where the library's incunabula, limited editions, and literary curiosities were placed, along with unique and valuable items given by friends. The depression, however, made solicitation for gifts increasingly difficult. Interest in the friends group declined, and by the mid-thirties it ceased to exist.

The University owes much to the people who, although not members of any organization for that purpose, gave generously to the library. Both the Bacon and Doe Library buildings were erected primarily with funds received as bequests from Henry Douglas Bacon and Charles Franklin Doe. The descriptions of designated funds and special gifts, as well as of many private collections that were given provide the names of many people who were the library's friends in the years before 1945. Three individuals especially stand out, however, for the unique nature and the length of time involved in their giving. They were James K. Moffitt, Juan C. Cebrián, and Albert M. Bender.

Moffitt was a "lifelong benefactor of [the] University Library."[31] A California graduate (Class of 1886), he held office as president of the Alumni Association (1909–12) and served thirty-seven years as a regent (1911–48). Having gained considerable wealth from a family business as well as from his own career in banking, Moffitt began making financial gifts to the

---

[30] *Library Committee Minutes,* Minute Book no. 3 (1921–45), March 7, 1930.
[31] *Centennial Record* p. 62.

library in the 1890's. A modest man, he preferred to give anonymously, as several of his letters indicated. In 1901 Moffitt wrote to Rowell: "I will be obliged if you can keep notice of this small matter out of public print."[32] Again in 1906 Rowell was instructed by Moffitt: "Please make no note of the matter in the public prints."[33] The gifts from Moffitt, which consisted of individual volumes, book collections, and substantial sums of money, were listed in the records as from "An Alumnus." Hardly a year passed during the first half of the twentieth century when that designation did not appear among the reports of library gifts. Through the years both Librarians Rowell and Leupp knew that Moffitt could be relied upon for financial assistance whenever special library needs or unusual opportunities arose. In 1936 Leupp wrote to Moffitt: "I am very keenly appreciative of your constant interest in the Library and your generosity in adding to the collection. . . . The research collections in many of the sciences, as well as in accounting and in other fields, owe a great deal to you."[34] In addition to the value of books donated, Moffitt's monetary gifts to the library for the years 1897 through 1947 amounted to over $30,000 out of approximately $135,000 that he contributed to the University during that period.[35]

Juan C. Cebrián was also a benefactor of the University library for many years. A native of Spain, Cebrián had come to San Francisco in 1870, where he established a prosperous construction business. Wanting to promote knowledge of Spain and Spanish culture in his adopted country, in 1912 Cebrián began giving books in that field to the California library. The size of his gifts annually ranged between 300 and 1,000 volumes; they included works of literature and philology, history, economics, science, and the arts. On several occasions when Cebrián travelled in Europe he collected books and sent them to the University library. In 1921 he wrote Leupp: "My endeavor is to make for the University of California the largest, richest, and most valuable collection of Spanish books in America."[36] During the course of twenty years Cebrián gave over 10,000 volumes. In addition, he subsidized the publication of a two-volume work: *Spain and Spanish America in the Libraries of the University of California.* The first volume, compiled by Alice I. Lyser, a member of the library staff, was

[32] James K. Moffitt, San Francisco, California, to Joseph C. Rowell, May 9, 1901, *Correspondence and Papers* (C-B 419), Bancroft Library, Berkeley.

[33] Ibid., July 27, 1906.

[34] Harold L. Leupp to James K. Moffitt, San Francisco, California, July 3, 1936, *Correspondence and Papers* (CU-12, Carton 22), University of California Archives, Berkeley.

[35] *Record of Donations Received by the University of California,* University of California, Office of the Controller [Part I] 1868–1940 (comp. 1941), 3 vols.; [Part II] 1940–50 (comp. 1952), 3 vols.

[36] *Librarian's Report* (1921), p. 14.

issued in 1928. It listed all titles in that field held by the General Library. The second volume, compiled by Eleanor Ashby, assistant to the Bancroft Library director, was completed in 1930. It included all works on Spain and Spanish America in the Bancroft collection. Following Cebrián's death in 1935, the library received a $400 bequest from his estate designated "to be used and expended for the purchase of such books pertaining to Spanish history and literature as will be to the best advantage [of the University]."[37]

From 1925 until his death in 1941, Albert F. Bender was a generous University benefactor. A highly successful insurance agent in San Francisco, Bender was also a lover of fine books and bindings; to him they expressed man's creative spirit combined with an appreciation for beauty. About 1920 he began giving works of fine printing to libraries. Mills College, Occidental College, Trinity College (Dublin), the Library of Congress, the California School of Fine Arts, and Stanford University, as well as the University of California, were recipients of his gifts. At California, Bender was interested in establishing a collection of works of modern fine printers and binders. His initial gift of books, in 1925, was made in connection with an exhibit of such works displayed at the library for eight months. Bender also encouraged his personal friends who were lovers and collectors of fine books to contribute many items to the University library. Through his efforts the Book Club of California also presented in 1925 a complete set of its publications, and four specially designed wooden display cases were given by Walter S. Heller, Eugene Meyer, Jr., E. S. Heller, and Mrs. Sidney M. Ehrman. During the next fifteen years the "Albert M. Bender and Friends" collection grew as numerous gifts were annually added. In addition to giving books, on several occasions Bender made generous financial contributions to the library. Wanting to provide future gifts also, in 1940 he gave the University a paid-up life insurance policy, valued at over $4,500, to be used after his death for purchasing fine books, manuscripts, and prints. Bender's legacy was used toward purchasing the John Henry Nash collection for the library in 1943.

The contributions of Moffitt, Cebrián, and Bender, as well as those of many other interested individuals and faculty members, all enriched the University library at Berkeley. Had the collection been dependent for its growth solely upon the books purchased with appropriated funds, it would have been considerably smaller and its strength far less than it was in 1945.

---

[37] Harold L. Leupp to Sylvanus G. Morley, Professor, University of California, March 17, 1937, *Correspondence and Papers* (CU-12, Carton 24), University of California Archives, Berkeley.

From 1900 to 1945 the University of California had officials who recognized the library's indispensable value and who provided financially for its support and administration. In addition, the high level of interest sustained by the faculty and the participation of alumni and friends in the library's development proved to be indispensable assets. The unique combination of stability and vision which these people represented largely accounted for the successful standing of the library after more than seventy-five years of service to the University.

CHAPTER V

COMMON MEETING GROUND OF ALL DEPARTMENTS

AT THE UNIVERSITY OF CALIFORNIA, as at many similar institutions, provisions made for library buildings and facilities showed considerable variety during the period from its founding in 1868 until 1945. No single or continuous pattern of planning and construction was present. Instead, library quarters developed in stages and in response to the changing conditions which the University's growing needs produced. In the course of its development, however, one fact was clear: the library on the Berkeley campus came strongly to be regarded as the "common meeting ground of all departments."[1]

THE BACON LIBRARY BUILDING

Before moving into the Bacon Library building in 1881, the library had been temporarily housed in two other locations. From 1869 to 1873, while the University was operating in the buildings of the former College of California in Oakland, the book collection occupied quarters on the top floor of Brayton Hall. Although the University transferred its activities to the Berkeley campus in the fall of 1873, the library was not moved there until the following spring. Lack of funds delayed construction of the library building which had been planned. Consequently, a room on the first floor at the north end of South Hall was assigned to the library, and the collection was installed there. According to a description given by Librarian Rowell, the room measured thirty-six by fifty feet and contained two tables and thirty chairs, black walnut bookcases along the walls, and some paintings as well as five bronze busts for decoration.[2] Crowded conditions in these limited quarters soon developed. Despite the opening of a reading room for students in the basement of North Hall and the provision of additional space in the basement of South Hall for book storage, library

[1] Herbert Putnam, "Addresses at the Dedication of the Doe Library Building: Address of the Librarian of Congress," in *Dedication of the Library*, University of California (Berkeley: 1912), p. 25.

[2] Joseph C. Rowell, "The Library of Bacon Hall Days," in *Staff Association Celebration of Library Silver Jubilee, 1910–1935*, University of California Library Staff Association (unpublished; 1935), p. 4, *Correspondence and Papers* (C-B 419), Bancroft Library, Berkeley, hereinafter cited as Rowell, "Bacon Hall Days"; information pertaining to physical accommodations for the California library prior to 1900 has also been derived from Rowell's *Beginnings*.

accommodations were far from satisfactory. By the late 1870's the need for a new library building had become imperative.

In 1877 Henry Douglas Bacon of Oakland offered to donate, in addition to his personal library and art collection, $25,000, to be used toward construction of a library and art museum building. Bacon's offer was conditional upon the state's providing an equal amount for this purpose. This sum was appropriated by the legislature the following year. Plans were prepared by architect John A. Remer for a building variously described as "modern gothic" and "renaissance" in style, and construction was begun in 1880. Reminiscing in later years about the Bacon Library and Art Museum building, Rowell wrote: "Here at last was a commodious and beautiful structure, with oceans of room for books and readers, cream tinted walls adorned with paintings and portraits, iron work, shining with new gilt, and six portraits delineated by Narjot on the ceiling of the rotunda. It was completed just in time for the reception of new books purchased with the first Reese fund income."[3]

The Bacon Library, a frame structure with brick exterior, was located near the center of the campus and in close proximity to the buildings in which classroom and laboratory facilities were located for many years. The rectangular front section, 86½ feet wide and 38 feet deep, was four stories high and surmounted by a central tower that rose to an elevation of 102 feet. This part of the building contained several work and consultation rooms at the ground level and three reading rooms on the first floor. The art museum occupied the entire area of the second floor, and a tower room above the museum was used to house additional works of art and collections of antiques.

The back section of the building, forming the main part of the library, was a rotunda, 69 feet wide and 54 feet to the rear wall. The outer part of the main floor and the two open galleries above were divided by bookcases into 20 small alcoves. Sliding doors on the main floor allowed the rotunda area to be opened to the three reading rooms along the front of the building. Likewise, a balcony with doors opening from the art museum allowed the entire rotunda to be visible from that section. The building was equipped with an elevator that had a lifting capacity of two tons and extended from the basement level to the second floor. When completed, the Bacon Library cost over $54,000, and had a book storage capacity of 90,000 volumes.[4]

---

[3] Rowell, *Beginnings,* p. 10.

[4] *Secretary's Report* (1881), p. 27. Very detailed descriptive information concerning the Bacon Library was provided by John A. Remer, "Description of the Bacon Art and Library

The original plans for the Bacon Library had included providing gas lines and fixtures for artificial lighting. Because of insufficient funds, these items were not installed at the time of construction. Shortly after the building's completion the architect recommended that "Gas fixtures must be provided throughout."[5] By 1896, however, his suggestion had not yet been adopted, for Rowell wrote to Regent J. B. Reinstein, "This University Library has never been opened at night for lack of lighting facilities."[6] That year the gift of $1,000 contributed by Levi Straus, Louis Sloss, J. L. Flood, and G. W. McNear, interested friends of the University, made possible the installation of electric wiring and lighting fixtures. These facilities allowed the library for the first time to remain open during evening hours. As the size of the student body and the number of volumes continued to grow, the limitations of the Bacon Library's size and general arrangement became increasingly apparent. Thus, when the University was engaged in developing a master plan for the Berkeley campus in 1896–97, Librarian Rowell suggested that a new library building be anticipated.

Although the architectural plan for the campus, including Rowell's suggestions, was adopted, funds were lacking for the construction of the proposed new library building. Meanwhile, problems of overcrowding and inconvenient arrangements in the Bacon Library reached a point requiring remedial measures. In 1900, the art museum area was converted to an additional reading room, and shelves were installed in the basement for storing books. An addition to the building was constructed in 1902, consisting of a basement and two floors extending 20 feet around the circumference of the rotunda. Six seminar rooms and accommodation for about 80,000 volumes were provided, thereby almost doubling the book capacity as well as considerably increasing the utility of the structure. The addition to the Bacon Library cost over $24,000, which was appropriated from University funds. The library's building problems were solved, but only temporarily. In 1904, President Wheeler reported that the new space would be fully occupied within three years, and he stressed the urgency of preparing plans for a new library building.[7]

The Bacon building continued to be used as the library until 1911,

Building," in [Joseph C. Rowell, comp.], *Notes on Library Progress and Description of the Bacon Art and Library Building,* University of California Library Bulletin, no. 2 (n.p.: 1881), 8 pp.

[5] Remer, op. cit., p. 8.

[6] Joseph C. Rowell to J. B. Reinstein, Regent, University of California, Jan. 10, 1896, in Rowell's *Letter Book* (1893–96), p. 470.

[7] *President's Report* (1904), p. 49.

although various adaptations in the use of available space had to be made. Reading rooms on the main floor eventually were used for ordering and cataloging activities. The art museum, already converted to a reading room and subsequently used also for seminar purposes, finally became the periodical and map room. Additional shelving was provided in the basement under the rotunda area to increase the book storage capacity. Despite these supplementary facilities, crowded conditions resulted in frequent shifting of books as the collection passed the 200,000-volume mark in 1910, the last year the library occupied the Bacon building.

In several respects the Bacon Library and Art Museum symbolized a stage in the development of both the University and its library. The building's construction in 1880–81, seven years after the University had moved from Oakland, represented an important phase in the consolidation of activities on the Berkeley campus. In its architecture as well as its very presence this structure denoted a growing sense of stability and purpose. In terms of design the Bacon Library marked that era before the concept of planned campus development at Berkeley emerged. The library's location, in close proximity to the sites of teaching and experimental work, bespoke the integral way in which it was related to the Universiy's most essential activities. Although the appointment of Benjamin Ide Wheeler as president in 1899 and the adoption the following year of the Hearst Architectural Plan for campus and building development marked more dramatically the beginnings of a new stage in the University's growth, the fact that the library had outgrown the Bacon building about that time also represented just as significantly the passing of one era and the emergence of another.

For thirty years the Bacon Library and Art Museum had served as the University library. When, in 1911, the collection was transferred to the Doe Library, the older building was remodeled and renamed Bacon Hall. It was used by the geology and geography departments until 1961, when it was demolished.

THE DOE LIBRARY BUILDING

When the campus architectural plan was in its early stages of development in 1898, Librarian Rowell's proposal for a new library building included several specific suggestions. The structure should accommodate 800,000 volumes and provide facilities for 1,000 readers, and should be designed with ample space and adaptability for future expansion. Moreover, he felt the library should be located in the center of the campus, that all its rooms should be rectangular, and that it "should be planned primarily with regard to its use and contents, and not purely architectural and decorative effects."[8]

While travelling in the East and in Europe in 1900, Rowell studied the arrangements and architectural design of the many libraries he visited. He sought the opinions of other librarians in order to formulate his own ideas regarding the new building at California, and also made several sketches showing possible room arrangements. His basic idea was that the stack area should form the central core of the library, and that reading and seminar rooms as well as staff workrooms should extend around the outside area. According to Rowell's plan, the central area would have been enclosed by other portions of the building only on three sides, thereby allowing for future expansion of the stacks to the rear.[9]

Although the site directly west of North Hall was approved for the new library in 1903 when the regents adopted the revision of the Hearst Architectural Plan, funds for construction had yet to be secured. In 1904, through the efforts of President Wheeler, the University received from Charles Franklin Doe of San Francisco a bequest of 24 percent of his estate to be used for the new library building. At the time it was expected the amount would exceed $600,000.[10]

The original plans for the library had been prepared by John Galen Howard, the University architect, in 1901–02. As designed, it was to contain four blocks, or units, costing about one million dollars each, which could be constructed in successive stages. Approval was not given to Howard's original proposals, and in 1904 he submitted new ones calling for a slightly smaller structure which had a more unified overall design. These plans generally followed Rowell's earlier suggestions except that the building was to be entirely enclosed on all four sides, thereby limiting future stack expansion to the central core area.

Members of the faculty Library Committee and the regents carefully studied Howard's new plans. They were also sent to a number of highly

---

[8] Joseph C. Rowell to J. B. Reinstein, Regent, University of California, Nov. 16, 1898, in Rowell's *Letter Book* (1897–98), p. 228.

[9] [Joseph C. Rowell], *Tentative Plan Proposed for a New Library Building for the University of California,* University of California Library Bulletin, no. 14 (Berkeley: 1901), [4] p., plus 4 diagrams.

[10] *President's Report* (1904), p. 115. Rowell reported in later years that estimates of the amount to be received from the Doe bequest varied, with some figures as high as one million dollars or more. Before the estate was settled, however, much of the Doe property was destroyed by the San Francisco fire in 1906. The University actually received $595,492.99 from the original bequest, and an additional sum of $148,957.91 from the Doe estate in 1911. See Rowell, "Bacon Hall Days," p. 6; also his "Red Letter Annals of the Library," in *Dedication of the Library,* University of California (Berkeley: 1912), pp. 12–21.

respected librarians at other institutions, whose opinions were sought and from whom generally very favorable comments were received.[11] Upon recommendation of its Committee on Library and Museum, which acted in concurrence with the faculty Library Committee, the regents officially adopted the general arrangement and design for the new library in October 1905 and authorized the architect "to proceed with plans for construction not to exceed $700,000."[12]

Meanwhile, anticipating that a considerable length of time would be required for the large amount of excavating, ground was broken at the Doe Library site on August 3, 1905. During the next two years the librarian, members of the faculty Library Committee, and the regents devoted much time with the architect to working out details of the final construction plans. When it was realized late in 1906 that the income from the initial Doe bequest would not exceed $600,000, the plans were modified in order to scale down costs. Priority was given to providing the main reading room, the loan hall, sufficient stack facilities to accommodate 300,000 volumes, and the seminar rooms, all of which would comprise about three-fifths of the total structure. The remaining sections would be completed as soon as sufficient funds were available. The revised building plans were adopted by the regents, and in April 1907 the Committee on Grounds and Buildings was "authorized to proceed with construction of the first floor as planned, and as much as possible of the north portion of the building, expenditures not to exceed $575,000."[13]

Work on the foundations was thus begun and progressed to completion the following year. On November 26, 1908, Thanksgiving Day, students, faculty members, and friends of the University gathered for a special cornerstone-laying ceremony. At that occasion, Librarian Rowell first spoke of the library's universal role within the university not only to supply research materials, but also to "counsel, comfort, stimulate, and inspire."[14] Following Rowell's address, tribute was paid to Charles Franklin Doe,

---

[11] The library's files contain copies of letters sent to and received from the following librarians: Frederick J. Teggart (Mechanics Institute, San Francisco), W. I. Fletcher (Amherst College), C. W. Andrews (John Crerar Library, Chicago), Herbert Putnam (Library of Congress), W. C. Lane (Harvard University), Walter M. Smith (University of Wisconsin), James H. Canfield (Columbia University), J. C. Schwab (Yale University), Theodore W. Koch (University of Michigan), and Anderson H. Hopkins (Carnegie Library, Pittsburgh, Pa.), *Correspondence and Papers* (CU-12, Carton 5), University of California Archives, Berkeley.

[12] *Secretary's Report* (1906), p. 29.

[13] Ibid. (1908), p. 21.

[14] Joseph C. Rowell, "Laying the Corner-stone of the Doe Memorial Library: Address by the Librarian," *University of California Chronicle*, XI (1909), 47.

and then in a moment of solemnity President Wheeler addressed the cornerstone:

Stand here square and true throughout the generations to serve the life of man; to encourage and confirm the true; to defeat malice and the lie; to shelter those zeals which conserve, upbuild, unfold; to restrain the hands of such as would destroy, pervert, or waste the stored-up substance and experience of the ages; to make men understand each other by learning one of the other; to dissolve the barriers of prejudice between nations, bloods, and creeds, and bring men to sit down together as the sons of God.[15]

Construction of the Doe Library continued for the next two and one-half years. During that time many details concerning the building underwent further planning, requiring numerous consultations between the architect and the librarian, Library Committee members, and the regents' secretary. One of the major considerations was the possibility of installing pneumatic tubes and book conveyors between the loan desk and the stack area. Both the librarian and committee members strongly favored such installations. The proposed costs, according to estimates submitted to the architect, were $2,800 for the pneumatic tubes and $7,760 for the conveyor system.[16] In view of economies considered necessary at that time, however, these mechanical facilities were not provided. As the library's problems in paging books and general circulation work later showed, this was a shortsighted decision and proved to be a very serious mistake.

Another decision of somewhat temporary although considerable importance related to the library staff's workrooms. As originally planned, these quarters were to be located on the west side of the second floor in fairly close proximity to the public catalog, the loan hall, and the reference collection. When it became necessary to reduce the size of initial construction, thus eliminating that part of the building housing the workrooms, it was planned that the staff be located in several seminar rooms on the ground floor until the remainder of the building was completed. Recognizing the problems that would result from this arrangement, Rowell proposed an alternate plan. Consequently, arrangements were made to construct tem-

---

[15] Benjamin Ide Wheeler, "Laying the Corner-stone of the Doe Memorial Library: President's Address to the Cornerstone," *University of California Chronicle,* XI (1909), 50.

[16] C. T. Cutting, District Manager for the Lamson Consolidated Store Service Co., San Francisco, to John Galen Howard, May 4, 1910 (2 letters, same dates), in "Correspondence relating to plans for the Doe Library, 1902–11," *Correspondence and Papers* (CU-12, Carton 3), University of California Archives, Berkeley.

porary staff workrooms on the second floor in the location where part of the permanent staff quarters were eventually to be built.[17]

Following his appointment as associate librarian in 1910, Leupp became directly involved in decisions concerning the final stages of building construction. Several matters, such as the shelving for the main reading room and seminars, arrangements pertaining to the loan desk and placement of catalog cabinets in the loan hall, and the provision for linoleum floor coverings in many areas of the building, were then decided. Although the general design of library furnishings had been worked out between Rowell and the Library Committee in the fall of 1909, Leupp consulted with the regents' Committee on Grounds and Buildings regarding specific furnishing needs, for which contracts were awarded. Finally, in May 1911, the initial portion of the Doe Library building was completed at a total cost of $870,000,[18] and plans were made to move the collection from Bacon Library to its new quarters.

The basic arrangement and design of the new building were not altered by the fact that the entire structure as planned was not constructed at one time. The dominating feature of the building was the housing of the book collection, the heart of the library, in centrally located stacks. A court area 100 feet square was created, which was eventually to accommodate two main stack blocks of nine tiers each; light wells were also planned, extending from east to west on either side and between each of the stack blocks. The court area was to be covered by a four-sided pitched roof with a large center skylight. In the initial construction phase, only the first five tiers of the north stack, enclosed with a temporary roof and rear wall, were provided. The remainder of the court area was left open for future development according to the plan. The entire stack capacity was planned to accommodate over one million volumes; the amount completed in 1911 was sufficient to house about 300,000.

---

[17] *Library Committee Minutes,* Minute Book no. 1 (1901–10), Jan. 31, 1908 and following; also "Correspondence relating to plans for the Doe Library, 1902–11," *Correspondence and Papers* (CU-12, Carton 5), University of California Archives, Berkeley. Included among these papers is a sketch, dated Jan. 8, 1910, which Rowell made for the proposed temporary staff workrooms.

[18] This figure, which included costs of construction, furnishings, and equipment, was given by the University on March 15, 1912, in a press release entitled, "$870,000 Doe Library to Be Dedicated" (mimeographed), 3, p.; copy in *University Library, Bacon + Doe Library, Historical Materials* (box containing miscellaneous uncataloged programs, papers, clippings, etc.) University of California Archives, Berkeley. The actual cost of building construction wa $698,278.16, according to John Galen Howard as reported in his "The Library," in *Dedication of the Library,* University of California (Berkeley: 1912), p. 11. The contract for the five tiers of steel stacks, awarded in April, 1910, to the Library Bureau, amounted to $73,000

The part of the structure surrounding the central stack-court area was rectangular, extending 224½ feet along the north and south sides and 262 feet along the east and west.[19] The north side, constituting the building's front section, was entirely completed in the initial construction stage. The main entrance, centrally located here, opened to a spacious columned foyer, at the rear of which was a divided marble staircase leading to the second floor. On either side of the entrance-foyer were two large reading rooms with alcoves and a balcony extending along their south walls; these rooms were planned to accommodate about 125 readers and 15,000 volumes each. The Bancroft Library, which had been located in California Hall since 1906, was housed in the east room, and the one extending to the west became the periodical room.

The main reading room, the loan hall, and the librarian's office occupied the second floor of the front section. The reading room was the dominant feature in this area. Extending the complete length from east to west along the library's north side, it was 210 by 53 feet and rose 45 feet from the floor to an arched ceiling directly beneath the roof. A bank of windows on the north wall, great arched windows at the ends, and three large skylights provided an abundance of natural light. This room, lined with bookcases sufficient for about 25,000 volumes, was planned to accommodate 276 people. Two years after the building was completed, however, seating capacity was increased to 420. Above the black marble casing inside the room's main entrance was inscribed a text from the Latin Bible: SAPIENTA AEDIFICAVIT SIBI DOMUM: VENITE COMEDITE PENEM MEUM ET BIBITE VINUM QUOD MISCUI VOBIS ("Wisdom hath built herself a house. Come and eat my bread and drink the wine that I have mixed for you."—Proverbs 9:1a, 5).

The loan hall occupied the central area between the main reading room and the stack court. It was also spacious and extended two stories to a skylighted ceiling. The loan desk was located in the center along the south wall of the room, and passageways provided direct access from the book circulation area to the stacks. The loan hall also contained the card catalog and exhibit cases. A smaller room directly west of the loan hall served as the library's administrative office.

The remaining three sides of the building's outer area were planned for seminar and additional reading rooms as well as staff work quarters. In the initial stage of construction, the first floor of these areas was completed and provided accommodations mainly for seminars (and library training

---

[19] Descriptive information for the Doe Library has been derived primarily from Howard, "The Library," op. cit., pp. 3–11.

classes, when they were held). Additional space on the second floor, adjacent to the associate librarian's office, was subsequently enclosed as an interim measure to provide rooms for the Accessions and Catalog Departments.

Metal, stone, and glass were the principal materials used in the Doe Library. The building was constructed on a reinforced steel frame, sheathed on the exterior with white California granite. The roof consisted of concrete slabs over which red "mission" tiles were laid, with copper used on the skylights and ornamental cornices. All sash, doors, and trim were metal, and plate glass went into the reading room windows. The relation between the stacks and the outer parts of the building was that of one structure built within the area of another, with light wells providing varying degrees of physical separation on the four sides. By reason of its materials and overall arrangement the building was planned to be fireproof as well as highly earthquake-resistant. The exterior architecture was Corinthian, with imposing half-columns on the front facade, and Ionic for the remaining sections. Symbolic of the library's importance to the academic community, a bronze statue of the head of Athena was ensconced above the main entrance on the building's exterior.

The process of moving the University library from the Bacon to the Doe building took place from May 29 to June 8, 1911.[20] At that time the collection contained over 210,000 volumes. Bids had been received from several commercial firms for this work, but they were considered too high to accept.[21] Thus, plans were made to use the men of the library staff plus nine hired students, along with a wagon and team of horses, for the moving operation. Runways and loading platforms were constructed, additional book trucks and other small equipment acquired, and the labelling of sections of the collection was carried out in advance. When the work was completed, the total moving cost (aside from the salaries of the regular staff members) amounted to $454.

Dedication of the Doe Library was held in conjunction with the University's annual Charter Day observance on March 23, 1912. Herbert Putnam, Librarian of Congress, delivered the morning Charter Day address, and also spoke later at the library dedication. Calling attention to the national interest in libraries, he described the library of the University by saying: "It is, indeed, no mere department, but the common meeting

[20] A very detailed account of this activity was written by Harold L. Leupp, "Moving the University of California Library," *Library Journal,* XXXVI (1911), 458–60.

[21] Bids received, as reported by Leupp, ranged from $1,038 to $1,780. Harold L. Leupp to V. H. Henderson, Secretary of the Board of Regents, March 15 and 21, 1911, *Correspondence and Papers* (CU-12, Carton 6), University of California Archives, Berkeley.

ground of all departments, and a unifying influence among them."[22] In the fall of 1914, two and one-half years after the dedication, a commemorative bronze tablet was placed on the west wall of the library's vestibule inscribed with these words written by President Wheeler:

CHARLES FRANKLIN DOE

Born August 13, 1833, in Parsonsfield, Maine
Died January 16, 1904, in San Francisco
Son of Colonel Barlett Doe and Mary Sanborn Doe
Grandson of Deacon John Doe

He was a quiet man of simple tastes and orderly life. Diligent in business, he dealt honourably with all men. Charity for divergent views and a gentle tolerance toward the beliefs of others tempered the native sternness of his convictions. Shrinking from the social turmoil, he found through books abundant converse with the best who have thought and recorded; and now that he has yielded the stewardship of his goods, his last desire opens the companionships he loved to the use of all the recurring generations of the young.[23]

The growth pattern of the University as well as the library made it apparent when the Doe building was occupied that it would soon be crowded with readers and filled with books. In 1911 space for approximately 500 people had been provided, although there were more than 4,000 students at the University. The stacks and reading rooms combined could accommodate about 350,000 volumes; already the book collection filled two-thirds that capacity. Within two years, additional seating was installed in the main reading room, and by 1914 the president reported that the stacks were full. Likewise, the temporary staff workrooms were seriously overcrowded, and various adjustments were made in the allotment of space to accommodate the steadily growing numbers of readers and books.

Discussions between the librarians, committee members, and the architect, looking toward drawing plans for the second stage of construction, began in 1914. These plans, completed the following year, called for the erection of four additional tiers of stacks, thus completing the north stack block. The entire stack-court area was also to be covered by a permanent roof and large center skylight. In addition, the second through fourth floors in the outer sections of the building's east, south, and west sides were to be constructed, thereby providing a second large reading room, permanent staff quarters, additional seminar as well as special-purpose rooms, and

[22] Herbert Putnam, "Address at the Dedication of the Doe Library Building," in *Dedication of the Library,* University of California (Berkeley: 1912), p. 25.
[23] Memorial tablet, Doe Library Building vestibule (west wall); copy of text printed also in *Librarian's Report* (1915), p. 7.

faculty offices. The anticipated cost for this project was $400,000.[24] In November 1914 a $1,800,000 bond issue for University building needs was authorized by a state election thereby enabling the regents to proceed with construction plans for the library as well as several other buildings on the Berkeley campus. In February 1916 contracts for the library addition were approved; building costs actually amounted to $525,000, plus $22,000 for furnishings.[25]

Construction work was completed in the summer of 1917, and with the addition of equipment, the library was able to occupy its new quarters in August that year. The new stacks about doubled the previous storage capacity; since almost the entire collection had to be rearranged, a considerable amount of time and work was required to move books.

The most imposing feature of the new addition was the east reading room. Located on the second floor, it was 135 feet long, 45 feet wide, and two stories high. Architecturally, this room was dominated by an impressively ornate paneled and carved ceiling of Italian design; large windows opened along the east wall. The main entrance from the north was decorated with two large pillars, and inscribed in the marble casing above this doorway were the words: BENE LEGERE SAECLE VINCERE ("To read well is to vanquish the centuries"). Planned to accommodate 240 readers, and with bookcases lining its walls, the east room became the library's new periodical room. The library's reference desk was located in a smaller room that connected the periodical room at a right angle to the loan hall and also opened to the north reading room.[26]

In the other sections of the new addition rooms were provided on the second floor along the west side for the Accessions and Catalog Departments, and along the south side for binding and preparation activities and library instruction classes. The south and west sides of the third floor were mainly occupied by seminar rooms; in addition, the specially designed and furnished room for the Library of French Thought was located there, along with rooms for maps and special collections (later called the Treasure Room). Faculty studies and additional seminars were provided along the east, south, and west sides of the fourth floor. A rear entrance near the west end at the basement level was constructed, the south side of the first floor was remodeled to provide larger seminar rooms, and two public elevators were installed at either end of the west side of the building.

[24] "Secretarys' Report," in *President's Report* (1915), p. 222.

[25] *Regents' Minutes,* vol. XIX (1916–17), Feb. 8, 1916, p. 13; and *President's Report* (1916), p. 14.

[26] In the early 1950's the former periodical (east) reading room was remodeled to serve as the library's loan hall.

Changes in the location of several library departments and services were made both at the time the new addition was completed and in subsequent years. The reserve book collection, formerly housed in the main reading room on the second floor, was transferred to the reading room previously used for periodicals and located on the first floor west of the foyer. Within three years after the new facilities were opened, both the growth in reserve book services and crowded conditions in the reading rooms led Librarian Leupp to propose the provision of a new reading room on the first floor by removing partitions between the existing seminar rooms on the east side of the building. He further suggested removal of the Bancroft Library to the east side of the fourth floor where it would have adjacent stack space on tiers eight and nine. The former Bancroft room, connecting with the proposed new reading room on the first floor, would thus become the new reserve book room. This plan was endorsed by the Library Committee in September of that year and presented the following month to the regents. Authorization for these changes was given and thus the Bancroft Library was moved to the fourth floor in the fall of 1922. The former Bancroft quarters as well as the converted seminar rooms along the east side of the first floor were then used for reserve books. When the L-shaped reserve book room on the east and south sides was finally completed in the summer of 1926, the new facilities increased the combined capacity of the library's first-floor reading rooms from 250 to 600 people.

The continued growth of the book collection and library use led to further proposals during the 1920's, the most important of which concerned erection of the south stack block. Recommendations were made by the librarian and the president as early as 1922 for the construction of additional stack facilities. In 1925, $120,000 was appropriated by the state legislature for additional stacks. When completed in November 1927, 50 percent more storage capacity had been added to the stack area. A rear stairway, connecting the basement with the first floor, was also constructed. Although recommended by the librarian, no provision was made for installing pneumatic tube and book-conveyor facilities at that time.

Several other changes, mostly in the location of collections and library services, were made in the late 1920's. In 1926 the current periodicals collection was moved to the main reading room on the second floor so that the east reading room on that level could be used exclusively by graduate students. This plan did not prove satisfactory, however, and in 1930 the periodicals were returned to the east room. Space was also sectioned off at the west end of the main reading room as a separate study area for graduate students, and the reference desk previously located in the small room east of

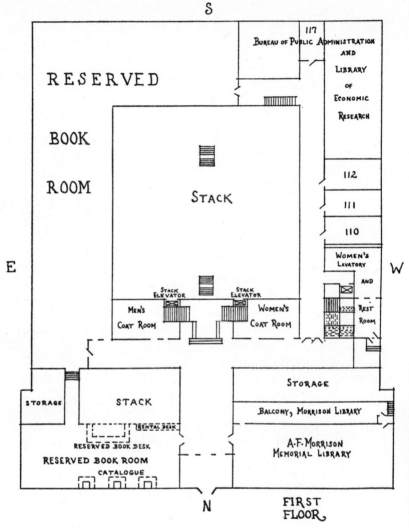

Fig. 1. Doe Library, first (ground) floor plan, showing arrangement of rooms and services in 1936. (Courtesy of the University of California Archives, Berkeley.)

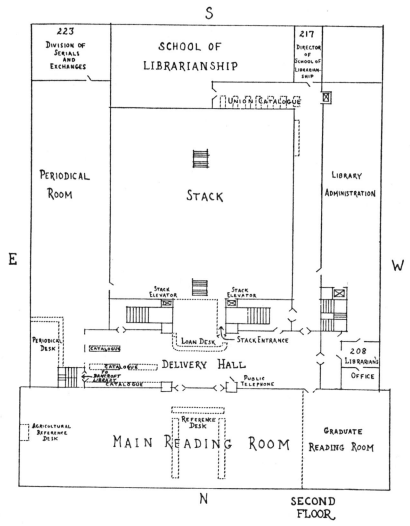

Fig. 2. Doe Library, second (main) floor plan, showing arrangement of rooms and services in 1936. (Courtesy of the University of California Archives, Berkeley.)

the loan hall was moved to the center of the main reading room directly inside the doorway from the loan hall. The agricultural reference service desk was also placed in the main reading room at the east end.

Meanwhile, when the University received the Morrison collection in 1927, the first-floor reading room west of the main entrance, which had served originally as the periodical and later as the reserve book room, was extensively remodeled and suitably furnished for recreational reading purposes. The Alexander F. Morrison Memorial Library was dedicated in 1928. In 1931, when efforts were made to organize a Friends of the Library group, a room on the third floor was set aside and officially designated as the Treasure Room. The library's rare book, Californiana, and other valuable collections were brought together in that location.

The general arrangement of library space and location of services remained essentially the same from about 1930 to 1945. Some minor changes were made in provisions for reserve books, and alterations were also worked out for the library administrative offices and staff workrooms. As book circulation steadily increased (from about 640,000 in 1929/30 to about 1,320,-000 in 1939/40), serious problems of congestion developed in the area of the loan desk. Lack of sufficient funds, however, again prevented the installation of mechanical facilities to remedy this situation. The crowding of the stacks necessitated the completion of the remaining section in the southwest quarter of that area. Flooring and shelves for three tiers were added during the summer of 1938, and the remaining tiers in 1940. Librarian Leupp proposed that stack facilities be installed in the center light well in order to use that area for additional book storage, but the intervention of World War II delayed these improvements until after 1945.

Despite the additions and changes that were made between 1911 and 1945, toward the close of that period it was evident that the Doe Library was inadequate for the University's increasing needs. In 1904, when the initial phase of construction was being planned, President Wheeler predicted that this first portion would "serve the purposes of the next fifteen or twenty years."[27] Yet within five years after the building was dedicated, the second stage of construction was in progress. Storage capacity in the stacks had been planned for slightly over one million volumes; the collection reached that size in 1938. By the 1930's, reading room accommodations had been expanded to provide for over 1,450 people.[28] Enrollments at

---

[27] *President's Report* (1904), p. 24.

[28] Harold L. Leupp to Thomas B. Steel, Registrar, University of California, July 21, 1933, *Correspondence and Papers* (CU-12, Carton 17), University of California Archives, Berkeley. Leupp reported total seating capacity in reading rooms of the Doe Library and the two branch libraries at 1,773; according to figures previously stated by Leupp, seating in the Doe Library was as follows: 550 in the main reading room, 264 in the periodical (east) reading room, and 650 in the first floor reading rooms, or a total of 1,464.

Joseph Cummings Rowell, ca. 1919. (Courtesy of the University of California Archives, Berkeley.)

Harold Lewis Leupp, ca. 1940. (Courtesy of the University of California Archives, Berkeley.)

Bacon Library and Art Museum, west facade, ca. 1900. (Courtesy of the University of California Archives, Berkeley.)

Bacon Library, interior of rotunda, ca. 1900. (Courtesy of the University of California Archives, Berkeley.)

Doe Library, north (front) and east (side) facades, ca. 1920. (Courtesy of the University of California Archives, Berkeley.)

Doe Library, main (north) reading room, ca. 1916. (Courtesy of the University of California Archives, Berkeley.)

Doe Library, loan hall (facing west), ca. 1915. (Courtesy of the University of California Archives, Berkeley.)

Doe Library, periodical (east) reading room, ca. 1928, when used as a graduate reading room. (Courtesy of the University of California Archives, Berkeley.)

Berkeley ranged from slightly over 12,000 students in the early thirties to over 17,000 by 1940. Thus, seating was available in the Doe Library's reading rooms for approximately one-eighth to one-eleventh of the students during that period. This was considerably less than the standards suggested in the forties, that seating be provided for 25 to 30 percent of the student enrollment.[29] The opening of branch libraries for education (1924) and biology (1930) did provide some relief for the crowded conditions in the central library and also indicated a new direction for future library development. However, these additional facilities did not eliminate the need to consider seriously the future of the Doe building and provision for the main library collection.

As early as 1931, the Library Committee had requested the president to reserve the area east of the Doe Library (where North Hall had been earlier located), as well as the areas occupied by South and Wheeler Halls, as possible sites for a future library annex. Thought was also given to the feasibility of eventually constructing a new library in the sunken garden area north of the Doe building. Because of the depression, no action was taken regarding either new construction or the later suggestions that the Bancroft Library and the reserve book service be relocated in other buildings. In 1939, a Committee on Library Needs, subsequently called the Administrative Committee on the University Library, was appointed by the president. In the early stages of its work this committee favored planning for a new building to be constructed on a unit basis with ample space provided to accommodate undergraduate needs and the Bancroft Library, plus a large stack area.[30] The committee realized after further study, however, that the Doe Library was well located on the campus and contained facilities that were still very usable. These facts, combined with the availability of adjacent land for expansion and uncertainty as to whether sufficient funds would be available in the post-World War II years to undertake a new long-range project, led the committee to alter its opinion. In 1944, therefore, it proposed that an annex be constructed on the east side of the Doe building. This recommendation was accepted by the regents, and architect Arthur Brown was authorized to proceed with building plans. It

[29] Louis R. Wilson and others, *Report of a Survey of the Libraries of Cornell University . . . October 1947–February 1948* (Ithaca: Cornell University, 1948), p. 163; this report suggested a ratio of "one seat for every four students." Also Louis R. Wilson and Raynard C. Swank, *Report of a Survey of the Library of Stanford University . . . November 1946–March 1947* (Chicago: American Library Association, 1947), p. 183; the authors stated, "Thirty per cent was generally accepted as adequate in the recent past."

[30] *Report,* University of California, Administrative Committee on the University Library (typewritten), July 22, 1943, *Correspondence and Papers* (CU-12, Carton 38), University of California Archives, Berkeley.

was anticipated that the annex would provide stack accommodations equal to seven-ninths of the Doe stacks, plus two large reading rooms, quarters for the reserve book and rental services, and about thirty faculty offices.

When it was built, the Doe Library contained many commendable features. By locating the book collection in a central stack area and arranging the service departments relatively close to one another, administrative control over the library's operation was facilitated. Moreover, space for book storage, readers, and administration was planned to allow for future expansion. The building was very sturdily constructed and, apart from routine maintenance, required little repair work. It was architecturally well proportioned and handsomely impressive in design.

From the vantage point of later years, however, several deficiencies became apparent. The space provided for readers could have accommodated considerably more people had the building not been dominated by reading rooms of monumental sizes, with excessively high ceilings. Although more practically proportioned additional reading areas were later constructed, the library suffered a lasting handicap from the amount of wasted space in the rooms originally planned. The enclosure of the stack-court area on all four sides restricted future expansion for book storage. Had the south side of the building's outer section been omitted, as Rowell had originally proposed, additional stack blocks could have been constructed and the east and west sides extended. Furthermore, when the building was planned, a considerable number of rooms were allocated for seminars and faculty offices, thereby limiting the amount of space available for library purposes. Even though the regents' Committee on Library, Research and Publications recommended in 1922 that the library's needs be given primary consideration in the use of the Doe building, part of the first and most of the third and fourth floors continued to be used by instructional departments despite the overcrowded conditions in reading rooms and staff workrooms. Barring from consideration the improvements which later developed in the field of library planning and construction, these basic changes at the time it was designed would have appreciably increased the building's total future usefulness.

At the University of California the Doe Library reveals at least three salient facts which had significance for other rapidly growing universities also. First, the length of time for which long-range library planning remained valid steadily decreased as the University's size increased. The life expectancy of the Doe Library as originally planned was for some fifty or more years; yet long before that period of time elapsed, its adequacy had diminished. Moreover, the library's functional use was limited by its ornamental architectural style and rigid rather than flexible construction. Finally, it became increasingly apparent during the period ending in 1945 that the concept of a large, centrally located general library was in need of modification. This was true for both the physical location of library facilities and the special subject interests to be served. Even though the decision was made about that time to construct an annex to the Doe Library, two branch libraries located in other buildings on the campus had already been established, and plans were being made for additional ones.

The Doe Library was a prototype for many notable university library buildings in the United States from 1911 to 1935. William Warner Bishop commented that it had "great influence on the planning of subsequent libraries" and noted in particular that the "location of the reading-room on the second-floor front with delivery desk behind it is repeated at Harvard, Michigan, Minnesota, North Carolina, Illinois and other university libraries."[81] Except at Harvard, the library building at each of those universities, plus Northwestern (Deering Library, 1932). followed overall arrangements similar to California's except that the stack area was not enclosed by a rear section. The plan at Columbia (Butler Library, 1934) did enclose the central stack on all four sides, thereby even more closely resembling the California pattern.

Library construction declined during the depression of the thirties and ceased during World War II. When new library planning was resumed following that period, it was apparent that the day of the rigidly constructed, highly styled, monumental building had largely passed. Thus, by 1945 the Doe Library was outgrown not only in size but also in adaptability to changing concepts of library service. It had served well for many purposes, however, and even with the planning of supplemental library facilities on the Berkeley campus would continue to be used for many more years.

Throughout the period 1900–45, the need for adequate library facilities was recognized. The library's changing building needs reflected changes that were occurring within the University. Moreover, the situation at Berkeley reflected general developments among academic libraries in the United States during those years. Both the men who served as librarian

---

[81] William Warner Bishop, "The Historic Development of Library Buildings," in Herman H. Fussler, ed., *Library Buildings for Library Service; Papers Presented before the Library Institute of the University of Chicago, August 5–10, 1946* (Chicago: American Library Association, 1947), p. 6. The library buildings referred to were constructed in the following years: Harvard (Widener Library), 1915; Michigan, 1919; Minnesota, 1924; Illinois, 1926; and North Carolina, 1929.

and the members of the Library Committee at California revealed progressive attitudes in considering and accepting changes regarding building arrangements that held promise of improving the quality of library service. Likewise, the regents and those who served as University president recognized the need for improvements and were ready to provide for them whenever circumstances permitted.

Chapter VI

PLANNING, ORGANIZING, STAFFING, AND FINANCING

Library administration was relatively simple at California before 1900. The collection was small, requiring the services of only a few people for its maintenance and use. From 1900 to 1945, however, the rapid growth of the University and its book collection required a considerable expansion and development of library administration. This fact was reflected in the provisions that were made for library government, internal organization, staffing, and financial support.

Library Government

The governmental basis for the University of California library was derived from the Board of Regents. The "Orders of the Board," first printed as part of the *Regents' Manual* in 1884, contained a chapter entitled "Management of the Library." According to it, the library was to be "general in its character, and shall include judiciously selected works pertaining to Literature, Science and the Arts."[1] It also describes the responsibilities of the faculty, Library Committee members, and the librarian regarding the ordering of new books, and set forth policies concerning books not returned to the library and items received as gifts. These Orders made no provisions for any other aspects of the library's administration.

In 1887, upon recommendation of the Committee on Library and Museum, the regents adopted a code of regulations drafted by Librarian Rowell and entitled *Library Rules of the University of California*. It provided specific regulations concerning library hours, conduct of readers, circulation procedures, privileges and duties of library users, fines, and authorization for the board's secretary to sign library orders during the president's absence. In the section pertaining to the librarian's responsibilities, in addition to enumerating his routine duties, the rules stated: "Under the direction of the Committee on Library and Museum the Librarian shall have custody and administration of the Library, and shall

---

[1] "Orders of the Board," Article 477, *Regents' Manual*, University of California (1884), p. 220. Subsequent revisions of the *Regents' Manual* were issued in 1904, 1907, and 1911; copies of the *By-laws and Standing Orders of the Regents of the University of California* were issued in 1938, and 1940.

annually present to the President of the University a report on its conditions, growth, losses, wants, etc."[2] Although it was "under the direction of the Committee," the librarian was thereby given more inclusive authority than had been provided by the board's Orders in 1884.

Provisions for the library's government and administration were further elaborated in 1904 when a revised edition of the *Regents' Manual* was issued. Regarding the librarian these Orders stated:

> The Librarian shall be entrusted with the custody and administration of the general library of the University and shall present to the Board, though the President of the University, annual, or other, reports upon its condition, growth, and needs.
>
> He shall enforce rules relating to the Library promulgated by the Board.
>
> He shall collect fines for the undue detention of books and for damage to or loss of the same, and shall pay over all moneys so collected to the Secretary.[3]

In general, the board's Orders closely regulated the library's administration rather than providing broad policy statements and delegating authority to the librarian to work out the details of their implementation. In matters such as library expenditures, circulation of books and interlibrary lending, and rules concerning the conduct of the library, the regents had set forth very detailed provisions. Likewise, in each of these activities the duties of the librarian were closely prescribed. He was given authority in consultation with the Library Committee, however, to determine the library's hours of service, rules for the deportment of users, and selection of materials to be bound.

Although the *Regents' Manual* was reissued with some additional Orders in 1907 and 1911, no changes pertaining to the library were made. The matter that needed greater clarification was the relationship between the librarian and the Library Committee. During the period 1901 to 1911, as the minutes showed, the committee shared the library's administration to the extent that the librarian was serving more as its "executive secretary" than as a university officer. After Leupp became associate librarian that situation changed. In 1911, when President Wheeler gave him administrative authority for the library, Leupp was also appointed to replace Rowell as secretary of the Library Committee (although Rowell maintained committee membership until 1919). A special meeting of the committee was called in March to consider its relation to the library's administration. After lengthy discussion it was concluded that the committee was to act in an

---

[2] *Library Rules of the University of California,* University of California Board of Regents (Sacramento: 1887), p. 5.

[3] "Orders of the Board," Article 108, *Regents' Manual* (1904), pp. 302–3.

advisory capacity and "matters of purely internal administration should be handled by the librarian and not by the Committee."[4] The committee's action was significant because it represented acceptance of the president's decision that the library's administration was primarily the responsibility of the librarian.

In 1913, and again in 1920, the Library Committee studied the regents' Orders concerning the library. Proposals were drafted that were intended to free the librarian from the minor restrictions earlier prescribed by the board, thus giving him greater discretion to act within the framework of general policies. When favorable action was finally taken in 1925, the regents' secretary reported: "The orders relating to the government of the University Library were amended in particulars designed to bring them into harmony with present day library practice."[5]

General provisions for the government and administration of the library as they had evolved up to the late twenties show that the librarian had been given authority for the custody and administration of the General Library and the branch Education Library located in Haviland Hall. Departmental libraries, however, were under the jurisdiction of the various department heads. The librarian reported directly to the president, and was responsible for preparing the General Library's proposed budget. Although the librarian had no official relationship to libraries on University of California campuses outside Berkeley, he acted as purchasing agent for some of them as well as for all departmental collections in Berkeley. He also served as secretary of the Library Committee, and was ex officio a member of its subcommittees. The Library Committee of the Academic Senate was charged with authority to allot the book funds, determine policies other than those pertaining to the internal administration of the library, and advise the librarian regarding library services.

During the thirties a situation developed which threatened to upset the equilibrium between the librarian's administrative authority and the advisory function of the Library Committee. In 1933 it was brought to the attention of President Sproul that some faculty members were dissatisfied with the library, feeling that the person in charge should be a scholar rather than an administrator.[6] Sproul appointed a committee, consisting of Professors George P. Adams (chairman), Frederick J. Teggart, George D.

[4] *Library Committee Minutes,* Minute Book no. 2 (1910–21), March 22, 1911.

[5] "Standing Orders of the Board," in *President's Report* (1924–26), p. 148.

[6] Monroe E. Deutsch, Provost, to Robert Gordon Sproul, President, University of California, Sept. 11, 1933, *Correspondence and Papers* (CU-5:1933, folder no. 93), University of California Archives, Berkeley. Deutsch did not express an opinion in this matter, but merely reported the information to Sproul.

Louderback, Benjamin H. Lehman, and James W. Thompson, to study the organization of the University Library.

The committee submitted a lengthy report in March 1934, charging that the existing library organization was no longer adequate for the University's needs, and that the details of administration were absorbing too much of the librarian's time and attention.[7] It recommended the creation of an Administrative Board, made up of three faculty members appointed by and directly responsible to the president, with authority for investigating all matters affecting the General Library and special collections on the Berkeley campus and other campuses of the University in northern California. The librarian on the Berkeley campus would be the executive officer responsible for carrying out the board's policies as well as directing the technical activities of the General Library. All matters concerning staff appointments, expenditures, and the use of space in the library building would require the board's approval. In matters concerning collection development, the board was to be advised by the Academic Senate's Library Committee, which was to be representative of the instructional departments of the University. The committee summarized its plan, stating: "It concentrates in the office of the Librarian the responsibility for administrating the technical work of the General Library, and for the carrying out of policies. It makes the Senate Library Committee the nucleus of faculty groups concerned with building up the collections in the various fields of knowledge, and it provides a medium for the voicing of faculty opinion with respect to the conduct of the Library."[8] The results of these changes would have been far more extensive than this summary suggested, for they would have stripped the librarian of his authority as a university officer, and left him to serve as an advisor to the board and a supervisor of the library's operation.

Reactions to the proposal were forthcoming from several quarters. Provost Deutsch wrote to Sproul, "I am not sure how successful a board of three will be and whether we will not have to come to the directorship of the Library of which we have spoken at times."[9] In response to President Sproul's request for his comments, Librarian Leupp stated: "It [the Board] would prevent the direct access to the President now enjoyed by an officer charged with the administration of an important department of the Uni-

[7] George P. Adams and others, "Report of Sub-committee on Organization of the University Library," submitted to Robert Gordon Sproul, President, University of California, March 19, 1934, 6 pp.; *Correspondence and Papers* (CU-5: 1934, folder no. 80), University of California Archives, Berkeley.

[8] Ibid., p. 1.

[9] Monroe E. Deutsch to Robert Gordon Sproul, March 30, 1934, *Correspondence and Papers* (CU-5: 1934, folder no. 80), University of California Archives, Berkeley.

versity, and . . . would assume control of Library personnel and of administrative sections of the Library budget now exercised by the Librarian."[10] Leupp favored "unifying and coordinating direction and control of the libraries on the Berkeley campus." He believed this could best be accomplished through a library director, however, because the delegation of authority to a board or committee would be "administratively unsound and unfair to the responsible officer." Leupp added, "Selection of personnel must remain with the librarian as a condition of his functioning as a responsible administrative officer." Sydney B. Mitchell, director of the School of Librarianship at Berkeley, was also asked to comment on the proposal. He expressed the opinion that administration of the library by a committee or board would create an impossible situation, and he cited Columbia University's experience with such an arrangement (beginning in 1914) as an example of failure. Mitchell wrote, "there is danger of this committee confusing advice and administration and seeking to acquire control of the machinery to carry out its policies." Furthermore, he stated, "faculty control of library administration would result in only a second rate librarian caring for that position."[11]

During the summer of 1934 no action was taken on the special committee's report. In September, Professor Lehman wrote to Sproul, asking him to clarify the authority of the Library Committee and of the librarian with respect to the library's administration. Answering this inquiry for the president, Provost Deutsch cited the provisions of the regents' Standing Orders and the bylaws of the Academic Senate regarding the library.[12] In response to a further inquiry by Lehman, questioning the extent of the Library Committee's authority to determine policies and the librarian's responsibility to carry them out, Deutsch again replied: "In as much as the Library Committee is to direct the policy, it should formulate one that will best serve the needs of the University community. The details of administration and the supervision of the carrying out of this policy must be in the hands of the librarian."[13]

Several underlying reasons were responsible for the expression of dis-

---

[10] Harold L. Leupp to Robert Gordon Sproul, April 5, 1934, *Correspondence and Papers* (CU-5: 1934, folder no. 80), University of California Archives, Berkeley.

[11] Sydney B. Mitchell, Director, University of California School of Librarianship, to Robert Gordon Sproul, June 16, 1934, *Correspondence and Papers* (CU-5: 1934, folder no. 80), University of California Archives, Berkeley.

[12] Monroe E. Deutsch to Benjamin H. Lehman, Professor, University of California, Sept. 27, 1934, *Correspondence and Papers* (CU-5: 1934, folder no. 80), University of California Archives, Berkeley.

[13] Monroe E. Deutsch to Benjamin H. Lehman, Dec. 26, 1934, *Correspondence and Papers* (CU-5: 1934, folder no. 80), University of California Archives, Berkeley.

content with the library and the resulting proposal concerning its administration. Tensions had developed between Leupp and some faculty members based upon conflicts of interest as well as personality. In administering the library Leupp adhered closely to an organizational structure and a method of operation that were intended to achieve maximum efficiency. Rules and regulations were strictly to be followed. Thus, he became impatient with professors who, in his opinion, sacrificed the common good of the academic community when it interfered with their own interests in using library materials. Likewise, he resented the intrusions by certain individuals who entered the technical departments of the library with demands concerning book orders and processing, thereby intimidating various staff members.

Some of the faculty were equally resentful because they did not consider Leupp to represent fully or primarily the interests of scholarship. Although many notable collections had been acquired during his tenure, Leupp had not made any notable contributions in the field of research. Despite his interests in book collecting, he was not generally regarded by the faculty as a bookman. Moreover, Leupp was a strong-willed man who held firmly to his opinions and was not easily moved from a position which he had taken. In this regard his autocratic disposition was matched by several faculty members, including some influential members of the Library Committee, who were of similar temperament.

In addition to the personal aspects of the situation, other circumstances limited the administration of the library and caused misunderstandings. The existence of many departmental collections, for which the librarian had some responsibility even though they were outside his official jurisdiction, led to inequities of library service. The limitations of the Doe Library building, which were becoming serious in the thirties, as well as the increased demands for service in spite of financial restrictions, were not adequately recognized by all faculty members. Furthermore, the California library reflected the growing administrative complexity evident in many academic libraries during that period. This fact was not sufficiently understood by many scholars who had been used to working with seminar collections or in libraries of much smaller institutions, and who resented imposition of the kinds of rules and administrative controls essential for a large library's operation.

The special committee's proposal to shift administrative authority from the librarian to an administrative board was contrary to the general direction in which the University's pattern of government and operation was developing in the twentieth century. Had it been accepted, the proposal could logically have raised the question of whether the University itself should have been administered directly by the regents, or by a special board made up of faculty members responsible directly to the regents, rather than by the president. No changes in the provisions for the library's government were made during the mid-thirties by the regents. The authority of the librarian in matters of administration, and of the Library Committee in allotting book funds and determining policies, remained as it had been.

The *By-laws and Standing Orders* were revised by the regents in 1938. The statement concerning the library was considerably shortened from the 1925 Orders, and changed so as to provide for the Los Angeles campus. These Orders, which remained in effect until after 1945, carried the library's governmental provisions even farther away from the closely prescribed regulations of an earlier era. Although the Orders defined the University's library resources, they did not describe the duties of the librarian or his relation to the University administration or the Library Committee. Neither did they directly delegate authority for the administration of the library to the librarian. Instead, the regents broadly gave overall administrative authority to the president, thereby allowing him, in turn, to delegate authority for individual departments of the University (as in the case of the library) to other officers of administration. In practice, however, the responsibilities of the librarian and the Library Committee continued the same as before the regents' Orders were revised.

Thus, over the course of half a century the governmental structure of the California library evolved from tightly regulated control by the regents to authority broadly delegated to the president, and from him to the librarian. Likewise, in matters of administration, responsibilities once carried by the Library Committee gradually came to be exercised by the librarian. These changes resulted in part from the need to meet the demands which both the University and the library's growth precipitated. More than this, however, they reflected the increasingly influential role of professional administrators at California, in the offices of both president and librarian.

Internal Organization of the Library

In 1900 no formal organization existed within the library. The staff included only four full-time members: the librarian, Joseph C. Rowell; the assistant librarian, J. D. Layman; the reference librarian, C. K. Jones; and a library assistant, Fannie Bonté. The organization of departments (later also divisions and services) developed gradually over the course of many years, and without advance planning. In general, the pattern was one in which organization followed function.

The earliest departmental designation was made in 1902, when H. Ralph

Mead was hired for the Catalog Department, and Arthur B. Smith for the Order Department. In 1904 Rowell reported that the work of the Accessions Department was the responsibility of Lillian Burt.[14] By 1910, the work of four departments was described by the librarian; these included the Order Department (A. B. Smith), Catalog Department (Pauline Gunthrop), Shelf Department (R. C. Woodmansee), and Binding Department (F. M. Bumstead).

After Harold L. Leupp became associate librarian in 1910, several changes were made in the library's organization. The Binding Department was discontinued about 1911, when binding operations were centralized within the University Printing Department. In 1912, when it was decided to reorganize the periodical records and to place entries in the public catalog, a Periodical Department was established. Also that year the name of the Order Department was changed to Accessions Department. Although the position of reference librarian had existed in 1900, it was not until 1913 that the Reference Department as such was mentioned in the librarian's report and described as "virtually a product of the new building."[15] About that time also the work of circulation was divided between the Loan and the Shelf Departments. When the handling of exchanges was transferred from the University Press to the library in 1914, the Exchange Division was created as part of the Accessions Department. After the decision was made in 1913 to reclassify and recatalog the collection, the Catalog Department was divided into Old and New Divisions. Thus, by 1915 the library was organized in six departments: Accessions (Sydney B. Mitchell); Catalog—Old Division (Pauline Gunthrop) and New Division (Edwin Wiley); Reference (Edith M. Coulter); Loan (Carleton B. Joeckel); Shelf (John A. Dean); and Periodical (Frank M. Bumstead).

Several changes were made between 1915 and 1928. After four years of operation, it was decided in 1916 to discontinue the Periodical Department and to divide responsibility for periodicals between the Accessions and Reference Departments. Likewise, the Loan and Shelf Departments were combined in 1918 under the superintendent of circulation, who was also given jurisdiction over the reserve book room. By 1921, the Old and New Divisions within the Catalog Department had outlived their usefulness and were discontinued. The changes effected during these years were

---

[14] "Librarian's Report," in *President's Report* (1904), pp. 98 and 102. Rowell did not explain how or exactly when these "departments" were created. Unless otherwise indicated, information on the library departments has been derived from the *Librarian's Reports* for the years cited.

[15] *Librarian's Report* (1913), p. 10.

made in order to consolidate library activities into more controllable units supervised by a small number of responsible staff members. By decreasing the number of departments from six to four, the librarian's span of control was also reduced, thereby allowing him to administer the library more efficiently.[16] The only unit not consolidated within the existing departments was the library's Photographic Service, which began operation in 1924, supervised directly by the librarian's secretary.

An important organizational change was made in 1928, when the Readers Department was established as a further move toward consolidating activities. According to Leupp, "the title 'readers department' was adopted to describe those library activities which exist primarily to bring the reader into direct personal contact with the resources of the library and to assist him in using them, as distinguished from those activities having to do primarily with the acquisition of books and their preparation for the shelves."[17] The main components of the newly created department were the Reference Division (including the Periodical Service, established in 1928) and the Loan and Shelf Division (including the reserve book room, opened in 1918, and the Rental Service, begun in 1929). In 1929 the Periodical Service was combined with the Exchange Division (formerly part of the Accessions Department) to form the Division of Serials and Exchanges; this new unit also became part of the Readers Department. Hence, by that time the number of departments had been reduced to three: Accessions, Catalog, and Readers. Separate from these departments were the Lange Library of Education and the Biology Library (after 1930), branches of the General Library, and the A. F. Morrison Memorial Library; the heads of these units were responsible directly to the librarian.

During the next ten years the library's organizational pattern remained essentially the same, although several new services and one new division were created. To meet the needs of students in the field of agriculture a separate reference room had been opened in 1921 and placed under the joint supervision of the Reference and Accessions Departments. In 1930 this became the Agriculture Reference Service and was located in the main reading room. Although financed jointly by the College of Agriculture and the General Library, it was considered a part of the Reference Division. As an adjunct to the Rental Service, the Library Extension Service was instituted by the Loan and Shelf Division in 1936 to meet the special needs

---

[16] Leupp described this organizational arrangement and his reasons for bringing it about in a letter to Stratton D. Brooks, President, University of Oklahoma, March 28, 1923, *Correspondence and Papers* (CU-12, Carton 8), University of California Archives, Berkeley.

[17] *Librarian's Report* (1929), p. 7.

of students enrolled in University Extension courses. Also about that time the Bindery Service was constituted under the Division of Serials and Exchanges to apportion funds and keep records of the library's binding orders.

The most important new unit established in the late thirties was the Documents Division. Proposed by Librarian Leupp in 1936, it was intended to centralize the acquisition and servicing of public documents and to coordinate the existing document collections located in departmental libraries as well as the General Library on the Berkeley campus. When Wilcox became the assistant librarian in 1937, he was placed in charge of carrying out plans for this new activity. His interest and background in working with public documents especially qualified him for this responsibility. The Documents Division was opened in February 1938.

In 1939 the last basic change in the library's organization during Leupp's tenure occurred. During previous years a number of facts had begun to indicate the need to divide the library's administration into two overall groups: public services and technical processes. The Readers Department had been successful in coordinating the reference and circulation activities. However, the exchange program had grown so large that it needed to be separated from the periodical service and aligned more closely with the work of acquisitions. Moreover, neither the two branch libraries nor the Morrison Library and the recently created Documents Division were administratively related to any of the existing departments. Concurrently there was also need to coordinate the activities of the Accessions and Catalog Departments. An acting head of the Accessions Department had been appointed during Bumstead's long illness, and subsequently assistant librarian Wilcox supervised this work. In addition, some fundamental changes were needed in the Catalog Department to accommodate the ideas of its newer members with the views of those who had served there for many years.[18]

When the appointment of Jens Nyholm as assistant librarian was announced in 1939, Leupp also described plans for regrouping library activities. Public services, including the Reference, Loan and Shelf, and Documents Divisions, plus the Morrison Memorial Library and the Biology and Education branch libraries, were placed under the jurisdiction of Jerome Wilcox (whose title was changed the following year from

---

[18] Leupp's views of this situation and the need for administrative reorganization were expressed in a letter to John Goodwin, Librarian, University of California at Los Angeles, Dec. 14, 1938, *Correspondence and Papers* (CU-12, Carton 27), University of California Archives, Berkeley. Further descriptive information has been derived from the *Library Staff Council Minutes* (1939–45), March 17, 1939.

assistant to associate librarian). Nyholm was responsible for the Accessions and Catalog Departments, the Division of Serials and Exchanges (which subsequently became the Division of Gifts and Exchanges), and the Bindery Service. Elinor Hand Hickox, formerly the librarian's secretary, was designated assistant to the librarian. In addition to continuing to supervise the Photographic Service, she was given authority over library personnel matters as well as equipment and supplies. The organization of the California library as it appeared after these changes is shown by the chart in figure 3.[19]

The administrative organization of the University of California library at Berkeley was compared by Herman H. Henkle in 1943 with that of Harvard and the Universities of Illinois and Texas.[20] At each of these institutions the librarian faced the problems of widely dispersed library resources. In order to deal with this situation Henkle found that "the administrative organization of all four libraries seems to have been undergoing gradual change in line with the fundamental principle that function should serve as the primary basis of administrative organization." He observed that steps had been taken in these libraries to establish clearly "the lines of control and responsibility," and that unity of management had been achieved. The main problem detected at California was the librarian's lack of authority over all collections on the campus, although he had responsibilities for purchasing and cataloging their books. A similar situation also existed at Harvard, whereas at Illinois and Texas the librarian had administrative control over all library resources on the campus. Finally, the trend was noted in each of the four institutions toward decreasing the span of control of the librarian as well as of other administrative officers. Thus, according to this study, the changes that had evolved in the structure of administration at California resulted in an organization comparable with three other major university libraries at that time.

STAFF

Aside from the contributions of individual people, several conditions existed at California that affected the overall staff situation during the years 1900 to 1945. The rapid growth in the size of the regular staff (from four persons in 1900 to eighty-four in 1945) was accompanied by the maintenance of high professional standards. Yet, despite the University's progres-

---

[19] Harold L. Leupp, "Library Service on the Berkeley Campus, University of California," *College and Research Libraries,* IV (1943), 212–7, 232; chart on p. 216. This article contains a description of the library's administrative organization as well as the chart shown in fig. 3.
[20] Herman H. Henkle, "Principles and Practice of Administrative Organization in the University Library," *College and Research Libraries,* IV (1943), 277–84.

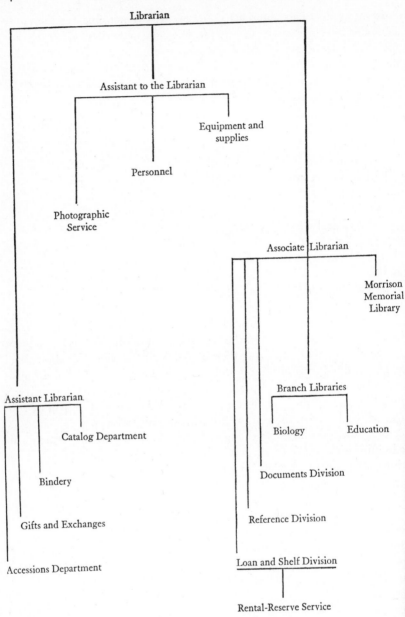

Librarian

Assistant to the Librarian

Equipment and
supplies

Personnel

Photographic
Service

Associate Librarian

Morrison
Memorial
Library

Branch Libraries

Assistant Librarian

Biology   Education

Catalog Department

Documents Division

Bindery

Reference Division

Gifts and Exchanges

Accessions Department

Loan and Shelf Division

Rental-Reserve Service

Fig. 3. Organization chart of the University of California library at Berkeley, 1940–1945.

sive record in matters of instruction and public service, the prevailing policy toward library personnel in terms of status, salaries, and benefits was conservative. Although this fact was quietly accepted by many library employees, the discontent of others caused periods of unrest and led to efforts to bring about changes.

In 1900/01 the total sum budgeted for library staff salaries was $7,260, of which Librarian Rowell received $2,400. As the size of the staff and total salaries began to increase, Rowell felt the need to adopt a "scale of compensation, with increase proportionate to terms of service."[21] However, no action was taken in this direction despite the fact that the total amount for staff salaries tripled in ten years ($22,600 in 1910/11). After Leupp became assistant librarian, a proposal was made to establish grades for staff members with stated salaries and annual increments, as follows:[22]

Grade	Salary	Annual Increases
Attendant	$30.00 to $50.00 per month	$60.00
Junior assistant	$50.00 to $75.00 per month	60.00
Senior assistant	$960.00 to $1,500 per year	60.00
Head of department	$1,500.00 per year up	100.00

Although this schedule was not formally adopted, it was accepted in practice for about ten years as the basis for determining salaries. As no substantial salary increases were made during that period, restlessness developed within the staff. By 1920 Leupp reported that valuable employees were leaving because of inadequate compensation, and he urged that a new salary schedule be adopted. Action was not immediately forthcoming, but by 1923 Leupp reported that a new schedule was in effect which established the following salary ranges:[23]

Librarian (equivalent to a full professor)	$4,000–$8,000
Associate librarian (equivalent to an associate professor)	$3,000–$4,000
Department head (equivalent to an assistant professor)	$2,700–$3,000
Senior assistants (equivalent to an instructor)	$1,800–$2,200
Junior assistants (equivalent to an assistant)	$1,200–$1,440
Clerical assistants (on full-time basis)	$1,080–$1,620

In 1927 a slight change was made when the maximum for senior assistants was increased to $2,300 (subsequently to $2,400) and the range for junior

---

[21] Joseph C. Rowell to Melvin G. Dodge, Associate Librarian, Stanford University, Jan. 27, 1902, in Rowell's *Letter Book* (1901–02), p. 216.

[22] "Librarian's Report," in *President's Report* (1912), p. 95.

[23] Harold L. Leupp to Stratton D. Brooks, President, University of Oklahoma, March 28, 1923; also Harold L. Leupp to John B. Kaiser, Librarian, Tacoma (Wash.) Public Library, Dec. 20, 1923, *Correspondence and Papers* (CU-12, Carton 8), University of California Archives, Berkeley.

assistants became $1,450–$1,700.[24] At that time also the librarian's salary was raised from $5,000 to $5,500.

In 1930, when Sproul took office as president, Leupp submitted another proposal for increasing salaries. This called for ranges of $1,500–$1,980 for junior assistants and $2,100–$2,900 for senior assistants; salaries for chiefs of divisions and branch librarians were to be raised from $2,500 to $2,700. The increases were accepted in principle by Sproul, but because of the effects of the depression at that time they were not adopted.[25] Although Leupp recognized the University's financial limitations, he also believed it was necessary for the library to retain its professional staff even if expenditures elsewhere had to be reduced. When the depression was most severe the University was forced to reduce on a percentage basis the salaries of all its employees.

As soon as the financial outlook began to improve, Leupp again urged that compensation for the library staff be increased. In 1936 he sent a proposal to the president calling for the following salary ranges, which represented an attempt to tie the salary scale for librarians to that of other groups in the University:[26]

Librarians, junior grade (in four steps, with $1,980 for a fifth
  step in special cases) .... $1,500–$1,860
Librarians, senior grade (in five steps) .... $1,980–$2,700
Chiefs of divisions and branch librarians .... $2,500–$2,900
Heads of departments .... $2,700–$3,300

The proposal was approved by Sproul and the regents, effective July 1937. At that time salary ranges of $3,300–$3,900 for the assistant, and $4,200–$4,800 for the associate librarian positions were also adopted. The librarian's salary, which had been increased to $6,000 in 1930, but subsequently reduced to $5,000 during the depression, was set at $5,500. This fact prompted Leupp to send the president a memorandum showing comparative statistics on college and university librarian salaries as follows: Columbia, $10,000; Michigan, $9,600; Chicago, $8,750; Yale, $8,000; Princeton, $7,000; Minnesota, $6,500; Illinois, $6,400; Dartmouth, $6,300; Syra-

---

[24] Harold L. Leupp to Charles H. Brown, Librarian, Iowa State College of Agriculture and Mechanic Arts, Ames, Iowa, Nov. 19, 1928, *Correspondence and Papers* (CU-12, Carton 11), University of California Archives, Berkeley.

[25] Harold L. Leupp to Robert Gordon Sproul, Nov. 16, 1931 (and with reference to letter of Nov. 10, 1930), *Correspondence and Papers* (CU-12, Carton 14), University of California Archives, Berkeley.

[26] *Library Staff Council Minutes* (1911–38), Sept. 4, 1936, also Harold L. Leupp to Charles W. Smith, Librarian, University of Washington, Aug. 4, 1938, *Correspondence and Papers* (CU-12, Carton 26), University of California Archives, Berkeley.

cuse, $6,100; Oberlin, $6,075; and Rochester, $6,000.[27] The Librarian's salary was raised to $5,700 in 1938, and to $6,000 the following year.

By 1942, in view of rising living costs, the library again faced the problem of inadequate compensation for its professional staff as well as clerical and student workers. Leupp appealed to the administration to rectify this situation. Although increases were granted in the student-employee wages, where the problem was most critical, and some cost-of-living bonuses were granted, salary and wage scales remained at their previous levels. Leupp's final proposal for salary increases was made in September 1944 when he recommended that the department heads, branch librarians, assistant and associate librarians receive higher compensation. In view of the impending appointment of a new librarian, no changes were made at that time. Before he retired in 1945, Leupp's salary had reached $6,500.

The size of the staff and the total amount expended for salaries at the University of California library may be compared with those of similar institutions. In a comparison of the ten university libraries whose book collections contained over one million volumes in 1943/44 (appendix A, table 6) statistics for staff size and salaries show that California ranked ninth in staff and sixth in salaries for 1920/21 as well as 1930/31, and eighth in staff and seventh in salaries for 1940/41.[28]

Aside from the matter of salaries, relatively little concern was expressed about the classification, status, and working conditions of librarians before the 1920's. Librarian Rowell had indicated in 1899 that the librarian was ranked as an associate professor, the assistant librarian as an assistant professor, and the reference librarian as an instructor.[29] The fact that he also requested library representation on the Academic Council at that time, however, indicated that the rank implied by these titles did not convey status equivalent to that of teaching faculty. No action was reported on Rowell's suggestion. Again in 1910 Rowell asked that membership in the Academic Senate be granted to "certain members of the library staff whose salaries ranged from $1,000 to $3,000."[30] Following Leupp's appointment

[27] Harold L. Leupp to Robert Gordon Sproul, March 18, 1938, *Correspondence and Papers* (CU-12, Carton 25), University of California Archives, Berkeley. Some figures were taken from "Library Statistics for Institutions of Higher Education," *American Library Association Bulletin*, XXXII (1938), 127; others, according to Leupp, were supplied from private sources.

[28] These years were selected because they represented periods when universities were relatively free from the abnormal effects of World Wars I and II and the depression, as well as the fact that statistics from a single, reliable source were readily available for each of them.

[29] Joseph C. Rowell, *Letter Book* (1899–1900), p. 117.

[30] Joseph C. Rowell to J. Henry Senger, Chairman, Committee on Membership of the Academic Senate, Sept. 6, 1910, *Correspondence and Papers* (CU-12, Carton 6), University of California Archives, Berkeley.

as associate librarian, both he and Rowell were admitted ex officio to Senate membership, although neither of them was explicitly given professorial title.

In several of his reports during this period the librarian acknowledged the staff's faithful service and cooperation despite the increasing pressure to keep abreast of the library's demands. Leupp announced in 1914 that staff members who wished would be granted time, subject to the approval of their department heads, to attend the annual conventions of the California Library Association. He also indicated that staff vacations were to be one month per year, part of which could be taken during the Christmas holidays if desired. However, vacation time was limited to 24 working days per year, and could not be accumulated beyond that. Vacations for clerical workers were to be two weeks per year.

Concern for staff status and benefits was expressed following World War I. Questions were raised by professional members about their designation as administrative employees of the University, since standards for their appointment required a college degree plus at least one year of library education, and especially since several of them were teaching librarianship courses. Requests were made in 1920 for professional staff members to be granted academic status and provided with insurance and pension benefits. Aside from incorporating into the regents' Standing Orders specific provision for the librarian's membership in the Academic Senate,[31] no action was taken on these matters. Permission was given in 1922, however, for senior assistants to take courses during working hours, provided they were given consent by their department heads.

In 1925 dissatisfaction with the University's policy toward librarians was expressed in a document drafted by several staff members and entitled "Statement Concerning the Status of the Library Staff of the University of California."[33] It began by stating, "The staff of the University Library has never been satisfied with the place accorded it in the University organization." After reviewing the qualifications of the staff and criticizing implications that librarians were clerical workers, the paper concluded:

The staff is convinced that it should have a definite status and be granted certain privileges merited by the character of its work. It believes that a distinctive classification carrying with it the title Librarian should be given to its members just as a distinctive classification has been given to certain groups of scientific workers. It is desired that the title Librarian be limited to those who have ful-

---

[31] *Regents' Minutes,* vol. XXII (1920–22), April 13, p. 11, and June 24, 1920, p. 91.

[33] "Statement concerning the status of the Library Staff of the University of California" (unpublished), 4 p., copy included in *Minutes,* University of California Library Staff Association (1933–46), University of California Archives, Berkeley, hereinafter cited as *Library Staff Association Minutes.*

filled the requirements for appointment to the staff, and that as a matter of record this group be given a place in "Officers and Students" following "Departments of Instruction with staff." It is further desired that the Librarians be granted the following privileges:

1. Vacation allowance of at least one month.
2. Provision for a retiring allowance.
3. The privilege of leave of absence for purpose of study.

The statement regarding vacation allowance was included because some members of the staff had inferred from a circular letter at that time specifying two weeks for "clerical workers" that vacations for librarians were about to be shortened. This was not the case, however.

After Sproul became president, several policy decisions affecting the library staff were made. In 1932 he authorized the titles "Librarian—senior, and junior grades" to replace those of "senior and junior assistants." It was also agreed that staff members in the public service departments would receive extra compensation for working on holidays when the other departments were closed. In addition, Leupp reported that annuity benefits similar to those of the faculty could be secured through the University by the library staff. In 1934 permission was granted for the publications of library staff members to be listed in the University's bibliography of faculty writings, which was issued in conjunction with the *President's Reports*.

Despite these provisions, the staff continued to feel during the thirties that its status in the University community was not adequately defined. In 1936 the Standards Committee of the Library Staff Association (organized in 1933) reported: "There has been a growing anxiety on the part of the staff over their increasingly lowered position the past few years with respect to rank, salary and professional opportunities."[33] The report suggested that all staff positions should be studied and a classification scheme established, based on duties performed; that library services be reorganized in order to group similar responsibilities more closely; that the work week, increased from 38 to 41 hours in 1932, be reduced to its former length; and that a clarified statement be issued regarding time granted for taking University courses. Although some librarians had previously been allowed three hours per week to take courses related to their work, it was felt that the subject content of such courses should not be so limited.

The Library Committee also expressed concern to the president on behalf of the staff and suggested that further consideration be given to the status of librarians in keeping with their educational backgrounds and experi-

---

[33] "Report of the Standards Committee of the University of California Library Staff Association" (unpublished; Dec. 10, 1935), 3 pp., in *Library Staff Association Minutes* (1933–46), copy appended to minutes for Jan. 14, 1936.

ence.[34] Accompanying its suggestions, the committee reported that all forty-four professional staff members had bachelor's degrees plus one year of library school training; in addition, nine persons had master's and three had doctoral degrees, and eighteen others had accumulated a total of 253 postgraduate course units in fields other than librarianship. The staff's proficiency in foreign languages included forty-four with knowledge of French, forty-one of German, twenty of Spanish, eight of Russian, seven of Italian, seven of Latin, four of Greek, three of Scandinavian languages, two of Chinese, and one each of Dutch, Polish, and Hebrew. The committee specifically recommended that the status of librarians should be clearly distinguished from that of clerical and technical workers, and should be more closely related to that of the faculty.

During the late thirties and early forties the library staff's status remained essentially unchanged. It was described by Leupp as "suspended between faculty and clerical."[35] Librarians were appointed on an annual-contract basis with no commitment regarding tenure. Vacation allowance of one month per year was granted, plus sick leave of one day per month, cumulative to a limit of 100 working days. Although short leaves of absence without salary deduction were allowed under particular circumstances and by special permission of the president, no provision was made for sabbatical leaves. Staff members were given time to attend library association and University meetings, and up to three hours per week for University courses. Retirement benefits were provided for librarians as well as other University employees when a pension-plan bill was passed by the state legislature in 1937.

California's policy regarding its library staff may be compared with that of other similar institutions at that time. A survey of thirty-seven large universities, reported by James A. McMillen in 1940, showed that eleven institutions had specific regulations regarding librarians' status, and of these, four classified professional staff as faculty.[36] Staff members were considered as speical professional groups at seven libraries, whereas twenty-six either considered them as administrative employees or gave them no specific designation. In 1946 Frank A. Lundy made an inquiry of thirty-

[34] "Summary of Statistics Relating to the Professional Staff of the Library" (including recommendations), sent by the Library Committee to Robert Gordon Sproul, President, University of California, Feb. 26, 1936, *Correspondence and Papers* (CU-12, Carton 46), University of California Archives, Berkeley.

[35] Harold L. Leupp to Richard Joel Russell, Library Committee Chairman, Louisiana State University, Baton Rouge, La., July 26, 1944, *Correspondence and Papers* (CU-12, Carton 41), University of California Archives, Berkeley.

[36] James A. McMillen, "Academic Status of Library Staff Members of Large Universities," *College and Research Libraries,* I (1940), 138–40.

five large colleges and universities regarding staff status.[37] He reported that librarians had been given academic rank equivalent to the faculty at eleven institutions, whereas eighteen other institutions were reported providing various degrees of academic recognition and privileges. He found that the University of California along with the remaining five universities (Cornell, Duke, Kansas, Missouri, and Wayne State) favored the development of a "unique status" for librarians. California's provisions, when compared with the findings of McMillen and Lundy, show that the University maintained a relatively conservative policy regarding librarian's status through the mid-1940's.

Three library staff organizations existed at California before 1945, each one serving particular needs of different groups. The Staff Council was established in 1911 at the initiative of Leupp, who had recently become associate librarian. The council was comprised of the department heads plus the librarian and associate librarian. One member of the council was elected to serve as secretary for one month, after which he automatically became chairman for a second month, and a new secretary was chosen. The council's purpose was to provide a structure for discussing library problems and administrative policies and procedures. Topics for consideration could be introduced by any member, thus representing the views or needs of all departments. Meetings were held weekly until 1917, when they became monthly. At that time, the terms of chairman and secretary were each extended to four months. In 1921 the librarian became the permanent chairman, and the position of secretary was filled successively for indefinite periods of time by other council members. The constituency was enlarged in 1928 to include on a rotating basis several of the subheads of departments. The assistant to the librarian became secretary of the council in 1939 and continued to hold that position until 1945.

The Staff Council was effective for some years in providing for an exchange of opinions and allowing members of the staff to participate in making administrative decisions. During the twenties and thirties, however, it began to lose its original democratic function; as Leupp became more autocratic the council increasingly became the means through which previously formulated administrative decisions were announced and procedures for their implementation discussed. The council continued to meet throughout Leupp's years as librarian.

The Staff Association was organized in 1933 and comprised "all members of the professional staff of the Library with a status equal or superior to

---

[37] Frank A. Lundy, *Faculty Rank for Professional Librarians* (M.A. thesis, University of California, 1948), 48 pp.

that of Librarian—Junior Grade."[38] The purpose of the association, as stated in its constitution, was "to enable us to act most effectively for the furtherance of our common interests, and also to foster among us the growth of professional spirit and to promote the general effectiveness of the Library service." Direction for the organization was provided by an Executive Committee, made up of representatives from the various departments, divisions, and branch libraries. This committee in turn elected a chairman, a secretary, and treasurer, who served for one-year terms. The functions of the association were broadly described. They included making recommendations to the administration regarding salaries and working conditions, considering matters related to professional standards and representation at meetings of professional organizations, and furthering professional and personal relationships among library staff members. In addition to regular monthly meetings for business and programs, occasional social gatherings were also held.

The early emphasis of the association was focused on matters affecting librarians' status and salaries. In time, however, it became more of a routine business and social organization. Through the efforts of its members a "Staff Manual" was issued in 1936, which proved useful in informing new employees about the organization of the library and regulations concerning librarians. The association's greatest value was to provide its members with a sense of professional consciousness and to afford a means for them to discuss common concerns pertaining to their work and the welfare of the library. With the rapid turnover in staff members during World War II, interest in the association waned. But in 1944 there was a renewal of interest which led to resumption of regular meetings and activities.

Finally, in 1940 the University of California Library Club was organized by the student assistants employed as clerical workers and pages. The club's stated purpose was "to encourage better fellowship among ourselves, to maintain congenial and cooperative relations with the library administration, and to better our service to the public."[39] The effects of World War II brought many changes among student assistants and caused the Library Club's gradual demise.

The three library organizations at California served useful purposes. They enabled staff members on various levels to exchange ideas among themselves and provided a means by which their opinions were expressed to the administration; they also focused the attention of staff members

---

[38] "Constitution of the Librarians' Association of the University of California" (unpublished; 1934), p. 1, copy in *Library Staff Association Minutes* (1933–46).

[39] "Library Assistants Organize," *Daily Californian,* April 24, 1940, supplement, p. 8.

and the administration upon the indispensable contribution of qualified and dedicated employees in providing library service of high quality.

California was fortunate in having had a very capable staff throughout the period 1900 to 1945. Unfortunately, however, tensions within the staff and conflicts between the staff and the administration developed periodically. Many of the younger librarians, especially during the thirties and forties, were frustrated and their enthusiasm was stifled because they felt that their capabilities were not sufficiently recognized. The formation of the Staff Association in 1933 was largely accomplished through the efforts of several "mavericks" who were unhappy with working conditions and hoped to improve them. This situation largely reflected the University's conservative policy of many years toward librarians and the autocratic attitude of Librarian Leupp in administering the library. On the other hand, the effects of the depression, followed by World War II, were also responsible for salaries remaining low and other benefits not being provided. Nevertheless, regulations concerning the staff were rigorously enforced by the administration, and often without adequate recognition that minor personal shortcomings were, in most cases, far outweighed by major professional accomplishments.

LIBRARY FINANCES

California's library appropriations from 1900 through 1945, in relation to the University's total operating costs on the Berkeley campus (appendix A, table 7), reveal several interesting facts. During the decade 1900–10, the library accounted for about 4 percent of the University's total cost of operation. After the completion of the Doe Library building and until the mid-1930's, between 8 and 9 percent of overall expenditures for education and research departments at Berkeley was for the library. From the late thirties to 1945, the library accounted for 6 percent of the total appropriation for the Berkeley campus. Thus, on an average during the total forty-five year period, library costs accounted for between 5 and 6 percent of overall University expenditures at Berkeley. This compared favorably with the median figure of 4.86 percent for eleven state universities (Texas, Michigan, Washington, Illinois, Iowa, North Carolina, Louisiana, Oklahoma, Kansas, Indiana, and Nebraska), reported by Coney, Henkle, and Purdy in 1940.[40] Among the ten university libraries with one million or more volumes in 1943/44 (appendix A, table 8), California ranked sixth

---

[40] Donald Coney and others, *Report of a Survey of the Indiana University Library . . . February–July 1940* (Chicago: American Library Association, 1940), pp. 34–5.

for 1920/21 and 1930/31, and seventh for 1940/41, in the total amount of salary and other library expenditures.

In 1902 a yearly library fee of five dollars per student was proposed in the Library Committee, but no action was taken. In 1909, however, the committee adopted a resolution recommending to the president and regents that all students pay a library fee of one dollar per academic term. This resolution was referred to the Academic Senate where it was voted upon and rejected in 1915.[41] As a result of the Library Committee's policy that duplicate copies of reserve books had to be purchased from other than library funds, by 1920 several departments had begun to collect book fees from students enrolled in their classes and to use this money to provide additional books for required reading. The inequities that resulted from this practice were soon apparent. Thus, the Committee proposed establishing a two-dollar-per-semester student book fee from which the entire reserve book collection would benefit. Upon recommendation of President Barrows, the regents voted in May 1921 to charge each student a library fee of five dollars per semester, beginning the following fall.[42] The library fee was eventually replaced by an incidental fee, from which an appropriation was made for reserve book purchases. This practice was discontinued in 1933, however, after the library's rental service had been established.

During the mid-twenties concern was expressed by the Library Committee that the overall cost of library operations was too high in relation to the amount spent for library materials. In the 1925/26 fiscal year, $58,749 was appropriated for books and binding; this amount was about 30 percent of the library's total budget. This proportion had decreased from about 38 percent in 1915/16, and 32 percent in 1920/21. The persistence of this concern led the library administration to undertake a cost survey intended to determine processing and cataloging as well as circulation costs. From January through June 1929 careful records were kept of the amount of staff time required for these activities. The results of the survey revealed the following per-volume costs: 65.5 cents for cataloging (72.6 cents including processing); 53.1 cents for recataloging; 7.9 cents for circulation; $1.74 for binding; and $1.59 for interlibrary loans.[43] According to the survey report, the processing and cataloging costs at California were lower than

[41] *Minutes,* University of California Academic Senate, vol. II (1915–20), Nov. 29, 1915, p. 30, hereinafter cited as *Academic Senate Minutes.*

[42] *Regents' Minutes,* vol. XXII (1920–22), May 12, 1921, p. 273; also, *Librarian's Report* (1921), pp. 4–5.

[43] Elinor Hand, "A Cost Survey in a University Library," *American Library Association Bulletin,* XXIV (1930), 411–12; also Harold L. Leupp, "The Cost Survey of the University of California Library," in *College and Reference Library Yearbook,* American Library Association, College and Reference Section, III (1931), 85–93.

the 77 cents reported five years earlier by the University of Illinois, but higher than the 67.7 cents given by Iowa State College of Agriculture and Mechanic Arts in 1929. The average of these costs at the three institutions was 72.4 cents, about equal to that at California. In 1930, after continued study, Leupp reported that the combined costs of ordering, plus gift and exchange activities, was 60.8 cents per volume.[44] Although the survey did not include the costs of periodic inventories, reference services, and general library administration, it did give members of the Library Committee as well as the University administration a greater understanding of the financial situation. It also showed that, as far as cataloging activities were concerned, California's costs then were comparable with those of two other research libraries. As Donald Coney, Leupp's successor, pointed out in 1952, university libraries lacked "a comprehensive, comparative cost study of their operations."[45] Unfortunately, this fact prevented further analysis or comparisons of California's library costs for the pre-1945 period.

The prevailing trend regarding library finances at California from 1900 to 1945 was one of steady increase. This trend was slow in developing before 1910 and showed fluctuations in subsequent years due to the effects of two World Wars and the depression of the thirties. Nevertheless, during this period the funds appropriated provided a strong research collection and a capable library staff to meet the growing needs of the University at Berkeley.

From a very simple basis in 1900 to a far more extensive and complex pattern in 1945, the necessary elements of library administration were developed and refined at California. Recognizing the need for a plan of government, the regents and presidents issued orders through which they delegated authority for the administration of the library; they also made reasonable financial appropriations for the library's support and appointed capable people to serve on its staff. Within the framework of the regents' Orders, the librarians developed a workable structure of internal organization as the means for directing and coordinating activities as well as reporting progress and needs to the University authorities. Despite some weaknesses in policies and practices that were apparent at various times, the library's administration responded positively to the steadily increasing demands of a rapidly expanding academic community.

[44] Harold L. Leupp to Charles H. Brown, Librarian, Iowa State College of Agriculture and Mechanic Arts, Ames, Iowa, June 12, 1930, *Correspondence and Papers* (CU-12, Carton 13), University of California Archives, Berkeley.

[45] Donald Coney, "Management in College and University Libraries," *Library Trends,* I (1952), 88.

CHAPTER VII

ORGANIZING BOOKS FOR READERS

PRIOR TO 1900, the California library was confronted with the problems of organizing and arranging materials in order to make them most useful to members of the academic community. After the turn of the century, however, the steady expansion of the University and the rapid growth of the collection considerably increased concerns for cataloging, classifying, and locating books on the Berkeley campus. Both the plans that were made and the activities carried out in these areas showed a unique combination of insight, imagination, and practical consideration by the library's leadership and members of the staff.

CATALOGING AND CLASSIFICATION

Cataloging and classification at California involved four significant developments: the use of the Rowell classification, the decision to reclassify into the Library of Congress system, the establishment of a depository catalog, and the division of the public catalog into author-title and subject parts. In addition, the accumulation of arrearages in cataloging as well as the acquisition at various times of large en bloc collections further complicated the processing of library materials.

THE ROWELL CLASSIFICATION AND RELATED CATALOGING DEVELOPMENTS

California's cataloging and classifying procedures developed very gradually before 1900 and were carried out almost exclusively by Librarian Rowell. The earliest catalog, which listed volumes in accession order following the pattern of the British Museum's *Numerical Catalog,* was a record of books received from the College of California. After his visit to eastern libraries in 1875, Rowell decided that books should have a flexible rather than a fixed location and that a card catalog instead of a book catalog should be constructed. By 1879 he had completed both a subject and an analytical author catalog of the library's holdings. Books were arranged according to broad subject groups which generally paralleled the University's organization of instructional departments and courses.

As the collection grew larger in the 1880's, Rowell realized that a more precise classification system was needed. Having studied the schemes of

Dewey and Cutter, he decided to devise one of his own. Rowell completed his plan in 1892, and by July 1894 he had classified the library's 60,000 volumes according to it. That year Rowell's scheme was published under the title, *Classification of Books in the Library.*[1] Devised primarily as an arrangement for books rather than a classification of knowledge, it used an arithmetical notation ranging from 1 to 999. Although Charles A. Cutter described Rowell's general arrangement of classes as "a cross between the Decimal and the Expansive Classification,"[2] its sequence of subjects showed closer similarity to the latter. This fact was especially evident in the location of language and literature, rather than history, near the end of the scheme. As the organization of departments and courses within the University had originally influenced Rowell's arrangement of books in the Bacon Library, his order of topics in the classification (especially within the sciences) largely reflected the same influence. To avoid using decimals to extend the division of classes, Rowell added lower case letters to the class numbers where necessary in order to provide for expansion. Serving as the sole basis of classifying books at California for almost twenty years, the Rowell scheme proved to be practical and adequate while the collection was under 200,000 volumes.

From 1900 until the collection was removed from the Bacon Library in 1911, several significant events occurred that affected cataloging and classification activities. The first step toward developing a regular cataloging staff was taken in 1902, when Edith Putnam Dart was appointed the library's first full-time cataloger. Her career at California was short-lived, however, for Rowell reported that "after a service of only one month, she was laid low by a fatal illness."[3] Later that year H. Ralph Mead was employed for cataloging, and by 1904 the librarian reported four people serving as catalogers.

In 1901 the library began to use printed catalog cards purchased from the American Library Association. The following year, when the Library of Congress initiated a card service, Rowell decided to subscribe to it. The dimensions of the new cards, different from those formerly used at California, led to a further decision to change the entire catalog to conform with the new standard size. For this project the typewriter was first introduced at the library, and by 1903 Rowell reported that half of the subject catalog was already completed. He also stated: "Our first year with the

---

[1] Joseph C. Rowell, *Classification of Books in the Library* [*of the University of California,*] University of California Library Bulletin, no. 12 (Berkeley: 1894), 49 pp.; (2d ed.; 1915), [109], 46 pp.

[2] Charles A. Cutter, "[Review of] Rowell Classification," *Library Journal,* XX (1895), 214.

[3] "Librarian's Report," in *President's Report* (1904), p. 98.

printed cards of the Library of Congress has been most satisfactory, and the work of our cataloguers has been considerably facilitated. A copy of our typewritten orders for new books is mailed also to the Library of Congress, and we secure at trifling cost the printed cards for practically all recent American books, for about one-fifth of English, and one-tenth of French and German books."[4] Rowell further indicated that from August 1902 to March 1903, 2,758 sets (including 8,773 printed cards) had been received at a cost of only $95.10. By 1908 the work of replacing old cards was completed.

In addition to these developments, the library's cataloging activities grew in size and complexity between 1900 and 1910. The use of printed cards necessitated closer adherence by the staff to the American Library Association's rules in cataloging works for which cards were not available, and often led to fuller treatment than had previously been given to many items. The collection's steady growth also required adjustments and expansion of the Rowell classification scheme at various times in order to accommodate many new works. During this period the library began to accumulate a "name list," consisting of slips with information concerning main-entry forms and dates, which eventually became the author-authority file. A shelf-list was also begun. Considering the changes that were made in cataloging procedures as well as the increase to almost 200,000 volumes, it was a genuine tribute to the staff's efforts and ability when Rowell reported in 1910 that "the current work of the catalogue department is well up to date."[5]

RECLASSIFYING INTO THE LIBRARY OF CONGRESS SYSTEM

After 1910 several conditions led to a reclassification of the California library. The closed-stack policy, adopted when the Doe building was occupied in 1911, necessitated greater reliance upon the catalog by library users. Cataloging errors and inconsistencies that had developed in former years were then considered more serious. In addition, the limitations of the Rowell classification had become increasingly apparent. Subject analysis was too inclusive in some fields yet almost completely lacking in others. Moreover, the scheme as originally devised for a collection of 60,000 volumes had never been expanded sufficiently to meet the library's needs. The development of the Library of Congress classification and list of subject headings, as well as the use of printed cards, had led Yale, Johns Hopkins, and the University of Chicago libraries to embark upon reclassification programs, and seemed to offer a solution to California's cataloging problems. Finally, Harold L. Leupp's appointment as associate librarian in 1910

---

[4] Ibid., p. 99.
[5] Ibid. (1910), p. 101.

provided the kind of new administrative direction required for the task of reclassifying.

In October 1911 Leupp discussed with the Library Committee a plan for reclassifying and recataloging the collection according to the Library of Congress system, and establishing a new dictionary catalog that would eventually replace the older author and subject catalogs. The committee reacted favorably and decided to recommend the proposal to the president. According to Leupp's estimates, if the current $7,000 annual appropriation for cataloging were raised to $18,000 for each of four years, the entire project could be completed.[6]

Rowell's reaction to Leupp's proposal was one of cautious interest. His personal modesty prevented him from taking affront at the replacement of his own classification scheme. Likewise, his open-mindedness and dedication to the library naturally inclined him to favor any change that promised improved service. Being frugal, however, he did express concern about the cost involved. In January 1912 he wrote to Ernest C. Richardson, librarian at Princeton: "Personally I have no objection to abandoning our present classification in favor of the L. C.; but in view of the very great expenditure involved (?$40,000), I am reluctant to approve such action until I feel assured, by the opinion of an unbiased and competent expert like yourself, that it is wise and advisable."[7] From this inquiry, as well as a similar one sent to Charles Martel at the Library of Congress, Rowell received replies which were favorable to the reclassification proposal. In the librarian's report that year, Rowell joined with Leupp in stating: "If the library continues to grow at its present rate of 30,000 volumes per year, delay in recataloguing will mean a rapid increase in the amount of work done twice."[8]

Additional funds were not appropriated in 1912, however, so the proposed project was held in abeyance. In February 1913 Leupp submitted a revised plan calling for recataloging and reclassifying books in history and the social sciences. These subjects comprised about 75,000 volumes, or slightly more than one-fourth of the total collection; it was estimated that they could be completed over a period of three years at an annual cost of $5,000. In offering this proposal Leupp stated: "A beginning in this field will not necessarily involve the expense of reclassifying and recataloging the entire collection, as work can be stopped at this point, if it seems best, without leaving the rest of the Library in any worse condition than it is at present;

---

[6] Harold L. Leupp, "[Report on] Recataloging Proposal," Feb. 9, 1912, *Correspondence and Papers* (CU-12, Carton 6), University of California Archives, Berkeley.
[7] Joseph C. Rowell to Ernest C. Richardson, Librarian, Princeton University, Jan. 23, 1912, *Correspondence and Papers* (C-B 419), Bancroft Library, Berkeley.
[8] "Librarian's Report," in *President's Report* (1912), p. 90.

but the experiment will show what can be done; what it will cost; and to what extent the Library service is improved." Within a few days President Wheeler replied, "I think you had better get into condition for beginning the recataloguing."[9] Consequently, Dr. Edwin Wiley, assistant classifier at the Library of Congress, was engaged to direct the new project. Nella J. Martin and Philena R. Sheldon, also from the Library of Congress, and Anne S. Pratt, from Yale, were appointed to assist Wiley in this activity.

The decision to adopt the Library of Congress system but to reclassify and recatalog the library's existing collections only in the fields of history and social studies left unresolved the matter of how to treat new books in other subject areas. In April 1913 Leupp sought the opinion of J. C. M. Hanson, formerly of the Library of Congress but then associate director of the University of Chicago library. Hanson reported Chicago's decision to classify new books according to the new system wherever schedules were available. Although he recognized the resulting disadvantage of having books in one subject arranged in two separate groups, Hanson suggested that such an arrangement would have the advantage of avoiding future double classification for thousands of volumes.[10] Leupp felt, however, that convenience to users in keeping all books on one subject together should be a prime consideration. The added fact that Library of Congress schedules had not yet been published for all subjects influenced the decision at California in favor of recataloging and reclassifying one group at a time. Meanwhile, new books were classified according to the old scheme until an entire class was ready to be changed. Leupp later defended this procedure, maintaining that, although allowing one subject to be divided into two groups seemed more economical, in terms of circulation and shelving costs as well as service to readers it would have been a false economy. Also, regarding the acceptance of classification designations and subject headings from Library of Congress printed cards with very few changes, he wrote, "We decided that variation from the L. C. program sooner or later would result in complications and difficulties; and that the advantage to be derived from following closely a carefully prepared scheme would out weigh occasional and probably temporary inconvenience."[11]

[9] Harold L. Leupp to Benjamin Ide Wheeler, President, University of California, Feb. 13 1913, and Benjamin Ide Wheeler to Harold L. Leupp, Feb. 17, 1913, *Correspondence an Papers* (C-B 419), Bancroft Library, Berkeley.

[10] Harold L. Leupp to J. C. M. Hanson, Associate Librarian, University of Chicago, Apr 14, 1913, and Hanson to Leupp, April 21, 1913, *Correspondence and Papers* (CU-12, Carto 46), University of California Archives, Berkeley.

[11] Harold L. Leupp to Donald B. Gilchrist, Librarian, University of Rochester, May 2 1932, *Correspondence and Papers* (CU-12, Carton 15), University of California Archive Berkeley. Leupp's views on continuing to classify into the old scheme were also expresse in this letter.

When reclassification and recataloging work was begun in 1913, the Catalog Department was divided into the Old and New Divisions. The value of maintaining two separate catalogs as opposed to combining them into one was also considered at that time. It was decided that author cards for new books in reclassified sections would be entered in the old author catalog, but that added entries for reclassified books would be withdrawn from the old classified subject catalog. At the same time a dictionary catalog was begun into which all new author, title, and subject cards were filed; this gradually replaced the older catalogs.

By 1914 the librarian was able to report substantial progress for the new cataloging and reclassifying activities. Classes J (political science), E and F (general and local American history) had been completed, and classes G (geography, anthropology, and ethnology) and H (social sciences) were in progress. Work was proceeding at the rate of about 1,000 volumes per month. It was estimated that approximately 52,500 cards, representing 11,300 volumes, were already contained in the new catalog. Printed cards from the Library of Congress had been available for about 90 percent of the titles thus far. Means were also being sought to have cards printed either locally or by the Library of Congress for the remaining 10 percent. Disappointment was expressed that the original $5,000 appropriation in the budget had been reduced, lowering the new cataloging staff from four persons to three and consequently slowing progress.

The reclassification and new catalog activities suffered a setback with the resignation of Miss Sheldon in December 1914 and of Wiley the following March. The effect of these staff losses, in light of the collection's 25,000-volume annual growth rate, led the librarian to report in 1915: "We are today, from the standpoint of the whole library, further from the goal than when we started."[12] Leupp urged that considerably increased funds be provided to enable the library to complete reclassification while the collection was still reasonably small. He stated: "The collection increases about twice as fast as the present recataloguing staff can work. If the staff were doubled it would just hold its own; if quadrupled the entire library would be covered in twelve years. . . . The question is between relatively light expenditure now and heavy expenditure later, with everything favoring the former alternative."[13]

Despite the appointment in July 1916 of Ellen A. Hedrick from Yale to succeed Wiley as head of the New Catalog Division, progress in reclassification was very slow for several years. Funds appropriated were increased,

---

[12] *Librarian's Report* (1915), p. 12.
[13] Ibid., p. 13.

allowing for some additional staff members to work in this area. However, the amounts budgeted were not substantial enough to provide the kind of comprehensive program for which Leupp had hoped. The librarian's report in 1916 indicated that almost 35,000 volumes (approximately one-tenth of the collection) were then in the Library of Congress classification. Later that year it was decided to discontinue the old author catalog and to consolidate its holdings in the dictionary catalog. Work on this project was begun early in 1917.

Progress in reclassification and new cataloging was reviewed regularly in the librarian's reports. By 1919, six years after the project had begun, about 108,000 volumes were completed, representing 27.5 percent of the total collection. Following the resignation of Miss Hedrick in 1921, and in view of the steadily increasing proportion of cataloging and classification using the Library of Congress system, the Old and New Divisions within the Catalog Department were discontinued. The addition of more staff members enabled the librarian to report by 1922 that about 230,000 volumes, almost one-half of the collection, were in the new classification scheme.

Even though progress was slow, Leupp remained convinced that the decision to reclassify the collection had been a wise one. By 1929 over 500,-000 volumes, about two-thirds of the collection, were classified according to the Library of Congress system. At that time work was begun on recataloging the departmental collections which were to become part of the new Biology Library (a branch of the General Library) in 1930. Other departmental collections were also subsequently recataloged.

In July 1933 financial limitations brought about by the depression forced a halt in recataloging and reclassifying activities. At that time, however, only the fields of law, languages, and literature remained in the old classification; together these books accounted for a little less than 20 percent of the library's holdings. In 1939, after the Burdach-Bremer collection was acquired, recataloging work in the field of German literature and linguistics was begun. It was envisioned then that the P classes could be completed in about six years. However, the turnover in the staff caused by World War II interrupted this work. By 1944 Leupp again expressed hope that reclassifying and recataloging the language and literature materials could be resumed shortly. He also recommended that the law collection be left in the Rowell classification indefinitely.

An overall view of the progress in reclassifying the California collection shows that on a percentage basis steady progress was made until the mid-thirties in converting from the Rowell to the Library of Congress classification. In terms, however, of over 220,000 volumes (18 percent of the library's holdings) remaining in Rowell as late as 1945, compared with approximately 260,000 volumes in the collection when the project was begun in 1913, the results subject the procedure to serious criticism. Despite Leupp's opinion that better service could be rendered during the process of reclassifying by not separating books within individual subject areas, his decision resulted in a divided library collection for many more years than was necessary.

The logical alternative would have been to begin classifying all new books into the Library of Congress system wherever schedules were available in 1913, and to provide temporary classification where schedules were forthcoming.[14] Concurrently, a reasonable number of books could have been recataloged from the older portion of the collection. Allowing for the possibility of changing approximately 16,400 volumes annually from Rowell, the entire project (except for law and some subclasses of language and literature) could have been completed in about sixteen years.[15] The only additional work would have been converting volumes from the temporary classification as the few remaining Library of Congress schedules were published.

Leupp acknowledged ten years after the reclassification project had begun that it was turning out to be an expensive undertaking. According to the cost-survey made in 1929, it was reported that the unit cost of recataloging was 53.1 cents per volume.[16] Leupp indicated that there had been mistakes in organization during the early stages, along with staff changes, that had caused progress to be slower than anticipated. Yet, in his opinion, the decision to change to the Library of Congress system was sound. Time proved him correct in this view. Delays and postponements in completing the work, however, proved him incorrect in his contention that continuing to use the Rowell system while reclassifying one subject at a time was the best method of procedure.

---

[14] According to Leo E. LaMontagne, *American Library Classification* (Hamden, Conn.: Shoe String Press, 1961), pp. 234–51, schedules published after 1913 were: C (history, auxiliary sciences), 1915; D (universal and old world history), 1916; BL-BX (religion), 1927; subclasses of P (language and literature), 1915–48. Schedule K (law) unpublished.

[15] In the period 1913 through 1930, for the fifteen years in which cataloging statistics were given in the *Librarian's Reports* (complete figures not given for 1913/14 and 1920/21), the total volumes cataloged in excess of those accessioned averaged 16,400 annually. On the basis of almost 260,000 volumes in the Rowell classification in 1913, and at the same rate of cataloging activity, these could have been recataloged and reclassified in about 16 years.

[16] Harold L. Leupp, "The Cost Survey of the University of California Library," in *College and Reference Library Yearbook*, American Library Association, College and Reference Section, III (1931), 91.

THE DEPOSITORY CATALOG

As early as 1902, Rowell suggested to Herbert Putnam, Congressional Librarian, that the University of California library "would be a good depository for a set of the new catalogue of the Library of Congress."[17] The advantages of a larger commercial and urban center were favored, however, and the catalog was subsequently established at the Mechanics' Institute Library in San Francisco. In 1906 the Institute Library was completely destroyed in the San Francisco fire. Although the library was reestablished, it was henceforth unable to fulfill the deposit conditions for servicing the catalog. As a result, upon completion of the Doe Library in 1911, the partially reconstituted depository catalog was transferred from the Institute to the University.

When the catalog was established at Berkeley, Ella Walker, formerly on the Library of Congress staff, was appointed its curator. By 1912 the librarian reported that the depository catalog included "all titles printed by the Library of Congress since the beginning of 1903; about 55,000 titles printed by the John Crerar Library; all titles so far printed by the Harvard University Library; and copies of all cards for German dissertations printed by the Royal Library in Berlin since August, 1909."[18] In addition, he indicated that cards from the University of Chicago library, as well as Library of Congress cards from 1898 to 1902, and 25,000 additional titles from John Crerar would be added the following year. Commenting further about the new catalog, Rowell wrote: "The use of this has not developed in any particular way just at present, but we already have found the collection exceedingly valuable for purposes of information, bibliographically and otherwise, and as a means also of knowing where a particularly rare book or edition may be found. The combined catalog, therefore, is particularly advantageous to libraries desiring books on interlibrary loans."[19] At that time depository catalogs had also been established at Columbia, Northwestern, Princeton, Chicago, Illinois, Michigan, and Yale universities.

Although it was planned that all cards for the depository catalog at California would be combined in one file, this was not achieved for several years. Because of the added work involved in filing and lack of sufficient staff time to check variations in forms of entry and to prepare necessary references, cards received from different libraries were kept in separate

---

[17] Joseph C. Rowell to Herbert Putnam, Librarian of Congress, Washington, D.C., Feb. 10, 1902, in Rowell's *Letter Book* (1901–02), p. 138.

[18] "Librarian's Report," in *President's Report* (1912), p. 90.

[19] Joseph C. Rowell, "Union Catalogs and Repertories: University of California," *Library Journal*, XXXVII (1912), 494.

files. In 1914 the work of checking, providing references, and interfiling was begun. Progress was very slow, however, for by 1915 the librarian reported the new unified file had been completed only from "A" through "Craig." Meanwhile, of course, many new cards were regularly being received, bringing the total number then on hand to almost 800,000. In addition to those from the libraries previously reported, entries were also being received from the Universities of Illinois and Michigan, and from the Newberry Library in Chicago. Interfiling progressed as the depository catalog continued to grow, and by 1919, when over one million cards were reported, all additions were being placed in a single file. By that time also, as part of a reciprocal arrangement, California had begun sending cataloging information for all its University publications as well as other requested titles to the Library of Congress, where cards were then printed.

The depository catalog continued to expand during the 1920's. The librarian reported in 1921 that the facilities provided for the catalog in the south corridor of the library's second floor had reached capacity, and that additional card cases were being installed in the hall along the building's west side. Four years later entries were also being received from the British Museum and Queen's University, Kingston, Ontario; by 1927 the size of the catalog reached 1,500,000 cards.

In 1936 Amy F. Wood (later Mrs. Jens Nyholm) and Evelyn Holcomb of the California staff reported the results of a study regarding methods used by eleven large libraries to administer their depository catalogs.[20] California faced a serious problem concerning space required for the ever-expanding catalog. Although most of the other libraries reported similar situations, some had already provided additional space and one (University of Chicago) was in process of combining its depository and official catalogs in order to conserve space. Regarding filing procedures, California reported that professional catalogers spent a total of about forty-five hours per week in this activity, but that all preliminary work was performed by clerical assistants. Filing procedures varied considerably among the other libraries, ranging from almost complete use of professional staff at some institutions to extensive use of clerical workers at others.

During the period 1930 through 1945, as the effects of the depression followed by World War II were being felt, the rate at which cards were received for the depository catalog declined. In 1940 Assistant Librarian

---

[20] Amy F. Wood and Evelyn Holcomb, "A Symposium Concerning Union Catalogs," *Library Journal*, LXI (1936), 90–5. In addition to California, other libraries included in this study were: Chicago (University), Columbia, Harvard, Illinois (University), Iowa State (University), John Crerar, Michigan (University), Minnesota (University, New York Public Library, and Princeton.

Nyholm reported that, in addition to those from the Library of Congress, California was currently receiving cards from the libraries of Chicago, Michigan, Stanford, and Wesleyan Universities, the John Crerar, William Andrews Clark, and Vatican libraries, and University Microfilms. He also indicated that the catalog at Berkeley contained entries accepted at various times from the American Library Association, the British Museum, Harvard, the National Library of Berlin, the Newberry Library, Queen's University (Kingston, Ontario), and the University of Illinois.[21] By June, 1945, California's depository catalog contained approximately 2,800,000 cards.[22]

DIVIDING THE PUBLIC CATALOG

By the mid-thirties the public catalogs in the University library had passed through several stages. The author and classified-subject catalogs established by Rowell in the late 1870's were used until 1913, when the dictionary catalog was begun. Entries continued to be added to the author catalog until 1917, when it was combined with the dictionary catalog. After 1913 entries for reclassified books were withdrawn from the classified-subject catalog. Although this catalog's size gradually declined, it continued to be used for that part of the collection which remained in the Rowell classification. In 1934 the library's *Handbook for New Students* described the public catalog (dictionary and classified-subject) as recording "all books belonging to the University Library, whether housed in the General Library or in other buildings on the campus."[23]

It was decided in the fall of 1937 to divide the dictionary catalog into author-title and subject parts. Several reasons underlay this decision. The increased number of users had caused crowding at the catalog. Moreover, some faculty members who mainly referred to the author and title entries had objected to cluttering the catalog with subject cards and even suggested their elimination. Finally, the catalog had outgrown its location in the northeast section of the loan hall. In conjunction with the need to provide space for additional card cases, the appropriate time for a major change had come.

Responsibility for planning and supervising this project was delegated to a member of the Catalog Department, Amy F. Wood. The work was divided into three stages. First, the cards within each catalog tray were

---

[21] Jens Nyholm to Arthur B. Berthold, Associate Director, Bibliographical Center and Union Library Catalog, Philadelphia, Dec. 14, 1940, *Correspondence and Papers* (CU-12, Carton 28), University of California Archives, Berkeley.

[22] This figure was derived from statistics reported in the *Biennial Report of the Catalog Department,* University of California Library (unpublished; 1944/45–1945/46), p. 13.

[23] *Handbook for New Students,* University of California Library (Berkeley: 1934), p. 6.

divided into separate author-title and subject groups. Two librarians, each devoting half-time to this activity, completed this division (involving 2,882 trays) between January 1 and May 13, 1938. Although subject cards were readily distinguished from other entries by their red headings, all cards had to be closely examined because of some inconsistencies and errors in cataloging. As part of stage two, it was decided that the new author-title catalog (the larger of the two halves) would remain in the location of the former dictionary catalog. Meanwhile, cases were provided at the west end of the loan hall for the new subject catalog. The amount of space needed for cards under the new arrangement was determined, and new labels for trays and cases were prepared. The third stage, which involved moving the cards and setting up the new catalog, was accomplished over the weekend of June 18–19 by four librarians from the Catalog Department and eight pages.

Hence, within six months the project was completed, and with virtually no interruption in the use of the catalog. The tasks of inserting necessary cross-references and some duplicate entry cards, as well as making corrections in filing, were carried out as follow-up activities. Aside from the cost of new card cases, the expenses involved included half the salaries of two librarians for four and one-half months, fifty-five dollars for marking and labelling, and seventy dollars in extra wages for weekend work. Leupp was well satisfied with the outcome of this endeavor, and wrote: "We have just finished dividing the catalogue, and the subject portion now occupies the west end of the Delivery Hall. The job was beautifully planned by Amy Wood, all preparations being made in advance and the actual transfer done last Saturday afternoon and Sunday. It was as nice a job of library engineering as I should want to see; the preparatory work has been going on for months according to a time schedule, and everything has clicked all the way through."[24]

In 1944 a study of library users' reactions to the divided catalog was made by Amy Wood Nyholm. Replies to 1,000 questionnaires submitted to students, faculty members, and library staff members showed that 74 percent of the respondents favored the divided catalog, claiming it was easier to use. The author-title catalog was used more than the subject catalog by 61 percent of those persons who replied. Although some serious complaints were expressed by those questioned, Mrs. Nyholm concluded that "the evidence supports a divided catalog for a large university population."[25]

---

[24] Harold L. Leupp to Peyton Hurt, Librarian, Williams College, June 22, 1938, *Correspondence and Papers* (CU-12, Carton 26), University of California Archives, Berkeley.

[25] Amy Wood Nyholm, "California Examines Its Divided Catalog," *College and Research Libraries,* IX (1948), p. 200.

PROBLEMS IN CATALOGING

Additional problems related to cataloging were faced by the library before 1945. An efficient and inexpensive method for reproducing catalog cards was sought, and some success was reported in 1903 when the typewriter was first used. After recataloging and reclassification work was begun in 1913, experiments were conducted with a multigraph machine; this device, however, proved unsatisfactory. About that time cards were also reproduced by the University Printing Department, but the cost soon made this plan prohibitive. Thereafter, until the 1930's, the library relied upon typing its own cards in addition to purchasing printed cards from the Library of Congress. Various mechanical devices were again considered in the thirties. A dexigraph machine was purchased in 1936 and used successfully thereafter to reproduce catalog cards by a photographic process.

Several times, particularly when large en bloc collections were acquired, the library developed arrears in cataloging. This situation was complicated by the recataloging and reclassification project, which also suffered many delays. Although in the past the Catalog Department had been able in due time to process these materials, staff disruptions during World War II caused this problem to become more serious. In 1942 Leupp reported that cataloging arrears numbered about 21,900 volumes, and a remedy for the situation was not in sight at that time.[26]

Before the division of the public catalog, the library adhered closely to the filing arrangement used by the Library of Congress. As the catalog became larger, students found it increasingly complicated and difficult to use. In 1933, therefore, Assistant Librarian Richards suggested a simplification in the filing rules. His proposal called for interfiling cards for all entries which began with geographical names, regardless of whether the place designation was an official part of the corporate entry or not. No action was taken, however, until after the catalog was divided. Then, in 1941, at the suggestion of Nyholm, several changes in the filing arrangement were put into effect. In addition to Richards' original proposal, these included simplifying the filing of complex personal names in the author-title catalog and disregarding all punctuation marks for headings filed in the subject catalog.

Two conclusions may be drawn from cataloging and classification developments at California from 1900 to 1945. Wherever possible in these activities the library functioned within the mainstream of commonly ac-

---

[26] *Librarian's Report* (1942), p. 8.

cepted library systems and practices during that period. In adopting the Library of Congress classification, using printed cards, following a dictionary arrangement for the public catalog, and sending cataloging information to the Library of Congress' depository catalog, California's performance was in keeping with that of many other large university and research libraries. At the same time, however, local initiative was shown in formulating policies and procedures to meet the library's particular problems. The method used in the reclassification project (although not completely satisfactory), the division of the catalog, simplification of filing arrangements, and experiments in reproducing catalog cards all attest to the thoughtful interest and imagination of the library staff and administration.

DEPARTMENTAL, BRANCH, AND SPECIAL LIBRARIES

In addition to the General Library, which contained the largest proportion of volumes, three other types of collections developed at Berkeley: departmental, branch, and special libraries. Each of these types served a distinctive function in providing library services. As early as 1915 Leupp reported that there were approximately 40 separate collections on the campus.[27] By 1945 this number had increased to over 90.[28]

DEPARTMENTAL LIBRARIES

Departmental libraries existed at the University before 1900. They were not planned but had evolved over a period of years in response to the particular needs of professors and students. As early as 1875 the president had reported that book collections for agriculture and mechanical arts had been set up in the lecture rooms used for those subjects. In his first report as librarian, Rowell indicated that in addition to the agriculture and circulating libraries there were collections in the "rooms" of five professors. When the Bacon Library was occupied in 1881, an attempt was made to consolidate all library materials in that building. However, within a few years books were being charged out to heads of departments for "departmental libraries." In time, these collections contained books purchased with department funds, as well as those borrowed from the General Library.

The regents' Orders in 1884 had not made provision for departmental libraries. By 1904, however, when a revised edition of the Board's *Manual*

[27] Harold L. Leupp to J. C. M. Hanson, Associate Librarian, University of Chicago, Jan. 26, 1915, *Correspondence and Papers* (CU-12, Carton 6), University of California Archives, Berkeley.

[28] *Volumes in the Libraries ... 1945;* libraries listed are the General Library, Biology, Lange (education), Boalt (law), Engineering, Giannini, Bancroft, Bureau of Public Administration, and 85 departmental libraries.

was issued, it stated that departmental libraries were considered "part of the working equipment of the departments to which they are attached, to be provided in the same manner as other equipment, *viz.,* by purchase with funds allowed the departments in the annual budget, or with special funds otherwise available for the use of the departments."[29] Funds assigned to the General Library were not to be used for departmental library book purchases. Although the University librarian was empowered to make both temporary and permanent deposits of materials to the departmental libraries, these collections were under the administrative control of the department heads.

Despite the regents' provision of a governmental basis and some broad policies for the departmental libraries, the functional relationship between these collections and the General Library was not clearly established. As student enrollment and book collections increased, supervision of departmental libraries became increasingly difficult. By 1910 when it was apparent that departmental library procedures needed to be formulated, Rowell sought the opinions of department heads and the Library Committee in order to draft a set of regulations. In February 1911 Rowell and Leupp issued a printed statement entitled *Regulations Governing Departmental Collections.*[30] It provided that: (1) departmental collections were to be available at all times to inspectors from the General Library; (2) department heads were to designate a custodian to supervise the collection and, in matters pertaining to it, to cooperate with the General Library; (3) the General Library was to catalog, arrange, and periodically inspect departmental libraries, and was to receive the cooperation of the department heads and library custodians in these activities; (4) books from the General Library were to be deposited in departmental libraries upon the request of department heads; (5) books so deposited were subject to recall or transfer at the request of the librarian; (6) departmental libraries were to be open at least three consecutive hours each day, Mondays through Fridays, while the University was in session; (7) departments were to report to the General Library all books received by gift or exchange for their collections. These regulations were subject to change by the librarian, if warranted, and were to become effective on July 1, 1911.

With President Wheeler's approval, this statement provided the basis of operation between the departmental libraries and the General Library.

---

[29] "Orders of the Board," Article 109, *Regents' Manual,* University of California (1904), p. 303.

[30] *Regulations Governing Departmental Collections,* University of California (Feb. 15, 1911), 2 pp., copy in box labelled, *CU Miscellany,* University of California Archives. Berkeley.

The regents likewise concurred and voted in 1913 to amend their Orders to state: "All books purchased for departmental libraries shall be cataloged by the librarian as part of the general library, and the Librarian shall furthermore make an annual inspection of the departmental libraries with a view to checking off the existing books against the catalogue, and shall, furthermore, make annual report to the President concerning the general condition of such libraries."[31]

In 1916 Leupp reported that the departmental collections varied greatly in size. Only seven, out of approximately thirty-two, contained over 1,000 volumes; as many as twelve collections had fewer than 100 books each. The total number of volumes in departmental libraries was about 42,500; in addition, some 6,000 volumes were on deposit from the General Library[32] Despite some improvements that had been achieved, the general arrangement for departmental libraries was unsatisfactory because of poor housing, inadequate space, absence of reference books, lack of staff, and irregular hours. Furthermore, annual inspections required by the regents had proved to be a burden for the General Library staff and had revealed in many collections considerable disorganization and poor management. Leupp felt that the departmental libraries should be limited to those books actually needed in connection with laboratory work or in department offices, and that it would be better for many of the smaller collections to be incorporated in the General Library.

The faculty's reaction to the departmental library situation was mixed. In 1917 the chemistry department requested the transfer of a large number of periodical files and journals to its collection from the General Library. When the matter was brought to the attention of the Library Committee, concern was expressed that such a request, if granted, would lead to similar appeals from other departments; furthermore, it would damage the General Library's collection as well as penalize other instructional departments that also sometimes needed the same materials. Thus, upon recommendation of the committee, the Academic Senate voted to approve "the general policy of maintaining a comprehensive central collection of books as against the distribution of these in departmental libraries, and of limiting the withdrawal of books and periodicals for deposit in departmental li-

[31] V. H. Henderson, Secretary of the Regents, to Joseph C. Rowell, May 19, 1913, *Library Committee Minutes,* Minute Book no. 2 (1910–21), copy included with minutes for May 19, 1913; also, "Standing Orders" [regarding the Departmental Libraries], in *President's Report* (1913), pp. 142–3.

[32] Harold L. Leupp, "Report of Departmental Libraries" (unpublished; 1916), 1 p., *Correspondence and Papers* (CU-12, Carton 6), University of California Archives, Berkeley.

braries to those which are exclusively used by the departments concerned and which are replaceable in case of loss."[33]

Following the Berkeley fire, which destroyed a large area of the city north of the campus in September 1923, concern was expressed for the safety of valuable materials in departmental libraries that were not housed in fireproof buildings. Aware of possible faculty opposition to the widespread withdrawal of deposited books from these collections, Leupp wrote to President Campbell: "I wish to present the case for your consideration, and to ask you either to authorize me to proceed with such withdrawal as may seem necessary to protect valuable material from fire risk, or, if you decide otherwise, to relieve me from responsibility for deposits allowed to remain in non-fireproof buildings against my judgment."[34] The matter was referred to the Library Committee where, in consultation with department heads, it was agreed that materials not vitally needed in departmental collections would be returned to the General Library.

The sincerity of Leupp's concern for the safety of library materials cannot be doubted, for the library had lost about 500 volumes that were in circulation during the fire. It was apparent, however, that he also saw this event as an opportunity to establish greater control over all library resources on the campus. Although the regents revised their "Orders Relating to the Library" in 1925, no substantial policy changes were made to improve the departmental library situation.

By 1932 there were seventy-one departmental collections at Berkeley, of which ten contained over 1,000 volumes each. At that time the General Library staff was no longer able to carry out the annual inventory of departmental libraries. Consequently, at Leupp's suggestion the president transferred this responsibility from the General Library to the departments beginning in 1934; each departmental library was also to be inventoried by the Comptroller's Office at least every four years. Among some eighty-five departmental collections on the Berkeley campus in 1945, the following each contained over 1,000 volumes: architecture (5,676); astronomy (2,418), chemistry (1,822), classics (1,713), engineering (10,272), geography (1,486), geology (2,829), philosophy (1,358), mining (4,692), music (1,066), paleontology (1,272), physical education—women (1,220), physics (3,946), vocational education (1,210), and plant pathology (1,390).[35]

[33] *Academic Senate Minutes,* vol. II (1915–20), April 22, 1918, p. 253.

[34] Harold L. Leupp to William Wallace Campbell, President, University of California, Oct. 4, 1923, *Library Committee Minutes,* Minute Book no. 3 (1921–45), copy attached to minutes of Oct. 9, 1923.

[35] George F. Farrier, *The University of California Library Postwar Building Program* (M.A. thesis, University of California, 1945), pp. 56–7. Farrier does not cite the source for these

The development of departmental libraries, according to Lawrence Thompson, was the common pattern in most American universities in the late nineteenth and early twentieth centuries. This was especially true at several prominent institutions, such as Harvard, Johns Hopkins, and the Universities of Chicago, Michigan, and Iowa. In the period between World Wars I and II, however, the trend away from departmental collections became apparent. According to Thompson, this was due to "the wholesale construction of new buildings in the 1920's, technical improvements in library service, and the increasing inter-dependence of all branches of knowledge."[36] Although the number of departmental libraries at Berkeley increased during that period, by the late thirties the need was also becoming quite evident for the consolidation of many of these collections into branch libraries that would be under the jurisdiction of the University librarian.

BRANCH LIBRARIES

During the 1920's three general conditions led to the development of branch libraries at California. First, administration and control of the departmental libraries was in most cases inadequate. Second, the Doe Library was crowded; although its ultimate book capacity had not been reached, the reading rooms were unable to accommodate the demands of the growing student body. Finally, the planning and construction of several new buildings afforded an opportunity to provide additional library facilities on the campus.

In 1922 President Barrows proposed to the regents that a fireproof structure be erected to house the combined libraries of the life sciences departments. Lack of funds prevented implementation of this suggestion. Leupp strongly favored the group library idea, and recommended in 1924 that it "be given a prominent place in the building programme of the University."[37] In addition to providing greater safety for valuable research materials, congestion in the General Library would be relieved, and better administrative control over library materials could be achieved. Regular hours similar to those of the General Library might be established and a more adequate staff provided. The threat posed to the campus by the Berkeley fire in 1923 also prompted consideration of moving departmental collections to fireproof buildings.

---

statistics; although figures were not available from the *Librarian's Reports* or office files for all departmental collections, the total number of volumes which Farrier stated was in general agreement with the total number reported in *Volumes in the Libraries . . . 1945.*

[36] Lawrence Thompson, "The Historical Background of Departmental and Collegiate Libraries," *Library Quarterly,* XII (1942), 49–50.

[37] *Librarian's Report* (1924), p. 6.

Meanwhile, in 1924, when Haviland Hall was completed and occupied by the School of Education, the first branch library was established. Book-storage facilities and a large reading room, a memorial to the late Alexis F. Lange, first dean of the School of Education, had been provided in this building. The departmental library and about 1,500 volumes in the field of education from the General Library were moved to this location. Added to these was Professor Lange's personal collection, given by his daughter. The University administration and the School of Education had already agreed that the new library was to be a branch of the General Library and under the jurisdiction of the University librarian. When opened in October 1924 the Lange Library of Education contained approximately 5,000 volumes, 10,000 pamphlets, and 92 current periodical titles. Administered by Faith E. Smith, a librarian with the rank of senior assistant, this branch was especially intended "as a research library for faculty and graduate students in the Department [*sic*] of Education."[38] In subsequent years Mabel E. Coulter, who succeeded Miss Smith in 1928, reported continued heavy use of the Lange Library. In 1934 an additional room in Haviland Hall was assigned to this library for supplementary book storage, and by 1944 plans were being made to enlarge its quarters.

Whereas the Lange Library of Education represented essentially the interests of only one instructional department, the Biology Library was a consolidation of about twelve former departmental collections. When the Life Sciences Building was being planned in the late twenties, President Barrows' earlier proposal for a group library was recalled. Space was allocated and preparations made to bring together the book collections of the departments that would occupy the new structure. The resulting library was to be administered as a branch of the General Library and was primarily intended to serve the research needs of faculty and graduate students. It was originally planned to combine in the new branch the books on biology from the General Library as well as the departmental collections. Since the stack area in the Life Sciences Building was only partially completed, however, the removal of books from the General Library was deferred until additional shelving could be provided later.

The Biology Library contained some 25,000 volumes and 450 current periodical files when it was opened in July 1930 and was supervised by M. Jessamine Abbott, a senior assistant on the library staff. The addition of a second tier of stacks allowed expansion of the collection to about 47,000 volumes by 1934. When the final two tiers were added in 1938, the Biology Library's capacity was increased to approximately 100,000 volumes. Mrs.

---

[38] *Ibid.* (1925), p. 4.

Abbott reported that heavy use of the collection by students and faculty members and the opportunity to provide more effective reference service were the great advantages of this branch library. After one year of operation, the success of the Biology Library led the Library Committee to report in 1931: "The University appears now to be committed to a future policy of decentralization, *not* by departments, but by groups of departments, the administration of these to remain under the central control."[39]

Plans for a third branch library were considered in 1931 when the Colleges of Mechanics and of Civil Engineering and the Department of Electrical Engineering were reorganized as the College of Engineering. Leupp proposed combining the departmental libraries and adding books on engineering from the general collection to form a new Engineering Library that would be administered as a branch of the General Library. The plan was approved in principle by the department heads and the University administration, but lack of funds prevented its implementation. Meanwhile, the former departmental collections in the fields of civil, mechanical, and electrical engineering were united as a new joint departmental library with financial support and supervision provided by the three departments. In 1942 Leupp renewed his proposal to establish a branch library for engineering as soon as possible. Action on this matter, however, was again deferred until after World War II. By 1945 the Engineering Library (still under the jurisdiction of the College of Engineering) contained over 10,000 volumes.[40]

In reviewing the development of branch libraries, Leupp recognized three conditions to justify establishing them. First, the departments involved were in a self-contained group having need for a common body of literature that was not generally essential to other departments. Moreover, use of library materials for such departments was in connection with laboratory or other similar research uses. Finally, these departments were located at a distance from the General Library. The success of the branch library plan at California (as well as at Illinois, Minnesota, Iowa State, and Brown)[41] encouraged other universities, especially after World War II, to adopt it as a reasonable solution to the problem of small and inefficient departmental libraries.

---

[39] *Library Committee Report* (1930/31), pp. 3–4.

[40] *Volumes in the Libraries . . . 1945.*

[41] Louis R. Wilson and others, *Report of a Survey of the University of Georgia Library . . . September–December, 1938* (Chicago: American Library Association, 1939), p. 69; also Dorothy H. Litchfield, "Departmental and Divisional Libraries," *College and Research Libraries,* II (1941), 238.

SPECIAL LIBRARIES

During the period 1900 through 1945 several special collections developed at California that were neither departmental nor branch libraries. Leupp described these collections as "not organically connected with any department but ... independently administered, with budgets of their own."[42] Included in this group were the Bancroft Library, the Bureau of Public Administration and Library of Economic Research, and the Giannini Foundation library.

After the Bancroft Library was moved to Berkeley in 1906, it was housed on the upper floor of California Hall, a recently completed classroom and administration building. Since the collection was not intended to be assimilated into the General Library, the regents established the Academy of Pacific Coast History to maintain this special library and encourage its use for historical research. According to its constitution, adopted by the regents in 1907, the Academy was organized with a president, vice-president, and secretary, and a council of twenty members plus the University president, ex officio. Frederick J. Teggart, formerly librarian of the Mechanics Institute Library in San Francisco and a noted scholar in the field of political institutions, was appointed and served as honorary custodian of the collection from 1906 until 1916.

It was anticipated that solicited subscriptions and gifts would provide sufficient funds to purchase additional materials for the Bancroft Library, and that the University would only underwrite the costs of housing, administration, cataloging, and binding. The Academy received donations averaging about $6,000 annually for the first few years; but by 1911, when the collection was transferred to the newly completed Doe Library, the president reported that Bancroft expenses had been taken over by the University. Thereafter, the Academy's main function was to guide the collection's development and encourage the use of its materials for writing and publishing.

Herbert E. Bolton, a professor in the history department, directed the Bancroft Library from 1916 until 1940, and again from 1943 to 1946. He frequently reported valuable additional materials acquired by purchase and gift, including collections of personal and family papers as well as the records of governmental agencies and commercial firms. From 1920 to 1930 approximately two-thirds of the master's theses and doctoral dissertations written in the field of history at Berkeley depended upon the use of

---

[42] Harold L. Leupp, "Library Service on the Berkeley Campus, University of California," *College and Research Libraries,* IV (1943), 213.

Bancroft materials, thus proving the collection an indispensable resource for teaching and scholarship. During these years the activities of the California Historical Survey Commission were also extensively supported by the Bancroft Library.

Although the director reported the collection's gradual growth, he also recognized and frequently expressed need for additional funds to provide more adequately for its development. Limitations of space that had developed by the twenties were partly relieved when the Bancroft Library was moved to the fourth floor of the Doe building in 1922, but accommodations there eventually proved inadequate for both staff and users. During the late thirties several plans were considered for housing the collection elsewhere on the campus. Improved facilities, however, were not provided until after World War II, when the library annex was erected with ample reading room, office, and storage space.

In terms of organization and administration, the Bancroft Library continued to remain separate from the General Library throughout the period from 1906 to 1945. Herbert I. Priestley, who had served as Bancroft librarian for many years, suceeded Bolton as director in 1940. At that time five additional people were regularly employed on the Bancroft staff, over $10,000 was being spent annually for books and binding, and approximately five hundred periodicals and newspapers were regularly being received. Following Priestley's death in 1943, Bolton again directed the library until George P. Hammond was appointed to the director's position in 1946. By then, in addition to its outstanding collection of newspapers, journals, and manuscripts, the Bancroft contained some 80,000 bound volumes.[43]

The Library of Economic Research was established in 1918, in association with the Department of Economics. Three years later the Bureau of Public Administration was organized in conjunction with the Department of Political Science. In 1926 the library resources of the Bureau of Public Administration and the Library of Economic Research were combined. The resulting library, located in the Doe Library building, was described in 1934 as "a pamphlet, document and periodical collection, serving chiefly as a research and reference library in the fields of public administration and economics."[44] By 1944 the Library of Economic Research contained about 150,000 items, mostly documents and reports issued by municipal and county governments, and was currently receiving some 1,500 serial publications. One librarian, four library assistants, four part-time clerical and

[43] *Volumes in the Libraries . . . 1945.*
[44] *Handbook for New Students,* op. cit., p. 22.

several student workers served on its staff, which was entirely separate from that of the General Library.

The Giannini Foundation was established at the University in 1928 to promote the study of agricultural economics, and in 1930 a research library was organized to serve the needs of the Foundation and the Department of Agricultural Economics. Located in Giannini Hall, this special library consisted primarily of pamphlets, bulletins, and reports. By 1945 it contained over 5,000 volumes and regularly received about 450 periodicals. The staff, which was responsible to the Foundation's director, consisted of one librarian and two clerical assistants.

Two other collections at California that had a semi-special status were the Law Library and the A. F. Morrison Memorial Library. The Law Library was under the jurisdiction of the School of Jurisprudence and thus actually qualified as a departmental library. It was distinguished from other departmental libraries, however, since special provisions were made by the regents for its financial support,[45] and it was housed in specially designed quarters in Boalt Hall. Moreover, the Law Library was considerably larger than any other departmental collection (over 80,000 volumes in 1945)[46] and had its own staff of librarians.

The Morrison Library, received as a gift and dedicated in 1928, was under the jurisdiction of the University librarian. Its unique status stemmed from the facts that it was an endowed library and that it served a special function as a recreation-reading collection. By 1944 the Morrison Library contained approximately 20,000 volumes.[47]

Service to the growing and changing needs of the University community was the motivating force in the evolution of departmental, branch, and special libraries, as in cataloging and classification developments at California. The problems of arranging the library's resources systematically and placing them in various useful locations on the campus were being met in a manner that was both practical and imaginative, and by a staff that was highly capable and dedicated in its work. Although centralized control over all these materials had not been achieved, the public catalog in the General Library served as the key to the collections that were under the jurisdiction of the University librarian, as well as to the departmental collections. Thus, by 1945 a combination of centralized organization in

---

[45] "Summary of Departmental Reports: Jurisprudence," in *President's Report* (1914), p. 35, and (1915), p. 41.

[46] *Volumes in the Libraries . . . 1945.*

[47] Clara Stow Douglas, "A University Browsing Library before the War and Now," *Library Journal*, LXIX (1944), 1084.

overall administration and technical processes, along with a pattern for more adaptable and increasingly decentralized public services, had been established for the major library resources on the Berkeley campus.[48]

[48] Approximately 1,175,000 of the 1,260,504 total volumes reported in 1945 were in collections whose holdings were shown in the General Library's public catalog. Calculations based on statistics reported in *Volumes in the Libraries . . . 1945.*

Chapter VIII

SERVING THE COMMUNITY OF SCHOLARS

Library materials were increasingly made available at California from 1900 to 1945 in response to the University's teaching and research needs. Although access to the stacks was limited after the Doe building was occupied in 1911, library hours and circulation services were extended. Moreover, the library's function in offering information and instruction came to be more fully recognized and developed. Underlying these accomplishments, policies were developed that brought materials and staff on the one hand, and users on the other, into a closer working relationship. The library thus adapted itself resourcefully during that period to the growing demands of a rapidly changing academic community.

Providing Library Materials

Several kinds of services and collections were developed for making California's library materials available to users. Depending upon their nature and purpose, they may be broadly grouped as: general circulation; reserve, rental, and other special-use collections; and interlibrary loans.

GENERAL CIRCULATION

Before 1900 various rules concerning the use of library books were in force. In general these rules were highly restrictive with regard to borrowing privileges. The earliest regulations, issued about 1870, allowed circulation of not more than three books per person to instructors, professors, and regents. Use of library materials by students was confined to the library premises. Borrowing privileges were granted to students in 1876, on condition that the student submit a written request on his behalf from a faculty member. The regents' Orders in 1884 made no provisions concerning circulating library materials except to specify penalties of fine or replacement cost for failure to return books.

A full set of rules, drawn up by Rowell and approved by the Library Committee and the president, was issued in 1887. Reference books were restricted to use in the library. Valuable works, volumes in sets, and files of periodicals could be borrowed only with the permission of the president. The remaining materials were allowed to circulate under the following conditions. Faculty members, regents, and University officers were allowed to borrow books for a period of ten days, with privileges of renewal. A limit of three books was allowed to students, who could borrow them overnight (4 P.M. to 9 A.M.) and weekends, or for longer periods with written approval of the president. People not associated with the University were allowed to consult books in the library with the consent of the librarian. In 1893 these rules were modified when the following statement was added: "The Librarian may use his discretion in issuing books ... to students requiring them for a longer period than one night."[1]

In 1900, when Rowell was on leave, Assistant Librarian J. D. Layman suggested that library rules be liberalized to allow students greater privileges. "Let one book at a time be loaned to freshmen," he wrote, "two to a sophomore, three to a junior, four to a senior, and five to a graduate student."[2] Although action on Layman's suggestion was not reported, the librarian did indicate increased circulation for a number of years after 1900. When the regents' Orders were revised in 1904, several provisions from Rowell's library rules of 1887 were officially adopted. Students were given borrowing privileges, but the loan period was not specified. No restriction was placed on length of circulation or number of books charged to faculty members, regents, or University officers, except that all books were to be returned each year on the Wednesday before Commencement. Use of reference books was still limited to the library building, and restrictions were placed on circulating volumes in sets, periodicals, and rare books. Statistics for books borrowed were not kept until 1909/10, but in that academic year 84,000 volumes had circulated for home use, and Rowell reported that "the present charging system for loans has been modified and improved during the last ten years."[3] Moreover, a loan desk, which had not been provided in the Bacon building, was being planned for the Doe Library.

In 1912, after the Doe Library had been occupied, library regulations permitted students to borrow books for a period of two weeks. Concern was then expressed, however, that faculty members who still enjoyed extended borrowing privileges were abusing them by retaining books longer than necessary. Consequently, in 1913 the Library Committee adopted a resolution that "Every member of the Academic Senate shall return books drawn by him, or shall renew charges for such books upon request of the

---

[1] *Library Rules of the University of California,* University of California Board of Regents (Sacramento: 1887), p. 2; the revisions adopted in 1893 were added in Rowell's hand.

[2] "Librarian's Report," in *President's Report,* University of California (1900), p. 86.

[3] Ibid. (1910), p. 100.

Librarian in accordance with regulations approved by the Senate."[4] The following year the committee voted to restrict borrowers from lending library materials to other individuals, and also stipulated that borrowers leaving the area for more than four days either return all library materials or make suitable arrangements with the librarian for their return, if needed. These regulations were subsequently approved by the Academic Senate.

Although two-week loans to students, as well as extended time for faculty members, remained in effect through 1945, several minor changes in the regulations were made. According to the *Library Handbook* issued in 1918, students were allowed to borrow four books at one time for home use. By permission of the associate librarian, exceptions were made in cases of special need and for graduate students. In 1925 the Library Committee lifted the restriction on the number of books that could be borrowed by honors students. This limitation was no longer specified at all in the 1934 and later editions of the library's *Handbook for New Students*. Beginning in July 1938 teaching assistants were permitted to borrow books from the library without a specified time limit.

While these changes were being made, the regents' policies regarding the library were also altered. According to the "Orders Relating to the Library" issued in 1925, the earlier regulations concerning circulation of books were replaced with a provision that the librarian "shall, with the advice and consent of the Library Committee, make general rules concerning the use of books and determine the classes of persons entitled to draw books, and penalties for violation of Library rules."[5] By 1938 the regents' *By-laws and Standing Orders* contained no statement pertaining to circulation of library books.

The library regulations of 1887 established a fine of five cents per day for each overdue book. This provision remained in effect until the Doe Library was occupied in 1911. At that time fines were abolished in favor of a system of recall notices and an appeal to the borrower's sense of responsibility in returning books. Unfortunately, the plan was not successful. In 1912 a fine system was reestablished; twenty-five cents was charged after the first day overdue, fifty cents on the fourth day, and one dollar on the seventh; higher amounts were charged for reserve books. By 1918 the system was slightly altered. A three-day "grace" period was allowed, following which fifty cents was charged until the sixth day, and one dollar until the tenth; thereafter, a student was subject to University disciplinary

[4] *Library Committee Minutes*, Minute Book no. 2 (1910–21), Nov. 17, 1913.

[5] "Orders Relating to the Library," in *Regents' Minutes*, vol. XXIV (1925–27), May 12, 1925, p. 81.

action for not returning books. In 1932, however, these provisions were ended in favor of those that had been in effect from 1912 to 1918.

Despite the fluctuations reported for reserve book and other special collections, both general circulation from the loan desk and total circulation showed a clear upward trend from 1910 through 1940 (appendix A, table 9). This fact was primarily accounted for by the rising student enrollment during those years. Yet, whereas enrollment increased 5.3 times from 1909/10 through 1939/40, library circulation multiplied almost seven times in the same period. During the two semesters of the 1939/40 academic year, on the basis of eighty-eight hours of service per week, an average of 468 library items was charged out each hour.[6] This circulation rate may be compared with about ninety books per hour in 1914/15, and approximately 310 in 1924/25. From 1914/15, three years after the Doe Library was occupied, to 1939/40, per-student library book borrowing had risen from forty-two to seventy-four books. This overall gain of 76 percent for the twenty-five year period amounted to an average per-student book circulation increase of 3 percent annually.

California's circulation may be compared with findings reported in 1938 by Carl M. White.[7] Using statistics gathered from twenty-three universities (California not included) for the years 1927/28 through 1936/37, White found that the average number of volumes borrowed per student increased from 40.08 to 48.41. This was a total gain of 20.78 percent for the decade, or an average of about 2 percent each year. Allowing for possible differences in reporting, California's 3 percent average annual increase exceeded that of the twenty-three institutions considered by White. Moreover, per-student book circulation at California during that period was considerably higher than the average reported in White's study.

Three problems were especially noted in connection with circulation activities from 1900 through 1945. Missing and lost books were a perennial concern. Samples drawn from the librarian's reports indicated that 300 volumes were missing for 1898–1900, 228 for 1911–13, 981 for 1929/30, and about 500 for 1938–40. In most cases losses from the departmental collections exceeded those from the General Library. Despite the closed-stack policy adopted when the Doe Library was occupied, frequent inventories of the departmental libraries, and attempts to improve the circulation system and establish greater control over the collections, a satisfactory solution to this problem was not found.

---

[6] *President's Report* (1940), p. 46.

[7] Carl M. White, "Trends in the Use of University Libraries," in A. F. Kuhlman, ed., *College and University Library Service* (Chicago: American Library Association, 1938), pp. 15–39.

The library encountered difficulties in circulating books to faculty members. In 1907 it became necessary for the Library Committee to vote that "officers and instructors shall sign charging slips when drawing books from the University Library."[8] The Library Committee called upon the president to intercede on behalf of the library in 1919 when it was found that materials charged to a particular professor had been sent by him to a faculty member at another university. The committee stated that such action was in violation of library regulations and reaffirmed its policy that "the rules of the Library should be strictly observed."[9] In its report for 1934/35, the Library Committee expressed concern that large numbers of books were charged out for long periods of time by some of the faculty, thus making these materials inaccessible to others.

Finally, congestion at the loan desk became a source of considerable irritation and complaint as student enrollments increased. Not only had the size of the loan desk and circulation area become inadequate, but the lack of a pneumatic tube and book-conveyor system limited the degree to which service could be improved. The situation was sufficiently critical by 1938 that Leupp authorized Enid F. Tanner, superintendent of circulation, to visit several eastern and midwestern university libraries in order to study their circulation facilities and methods. She reported that the basis for any significant improvement depended upon the installation of mechanical facilities between the loan desk area and the stacks. Despite Leupp's request for such equipment (he had made similar requests on several previous occasions), financial provision was not forthcoming. With the high turnover of student assistants during World War II, the service gradually became poorer rather than better.

RESERVE BOOK, RENTAL, AND OTHER SPECIAL-USE COLLECTIONS

The practice of reserving books for use in connection with particular courses had developed in the library before 1900. The regulations issued in 1887 indicated that books "reserved for class reference"[10] were not to be circulated outside the building. No description was given, however, of the procedures used for this activity.

After the move to the Doe Library in 1911, the reserve book collection was installed in the large reading room located on the north side of the main (second) floor. During the day books were to be used only within the building, but they could be taken out for overnight and holiday use;

---

[8] *Library Committee Minutes,* Minute Book no. 1 (1901–10), Sept. 23, 1907.

[9] Ibid., Minute Book no. 2 (1910–21), Dec. 22, 1919.

[10] *Library Rules of the University of California,* op cit., p. 4.

fines were charged for books returned late. Abuses of the system led to the removal of reserve books to the loan desk in 1916. Two years later the collection was moved to the ground-floor room (formerly the periodical room) west of the building's main entrance, where closer control was established over it. But within a few years, as demands for reserve books increased, this location was outgrown. In November 1922 the collection was again moved to the former Bancroft reading room on the first floor and, in response to changing demands, the service was broadened. Some books were restricted for two-hour use within the room, whereas others were allowed to circulate anywhere in the building during the day.

An experiment was tried in 1925/26, when the reserve books were again moved to the large reading room on the main floor. It was hoped that by providing seating for about 500 readers, keeping the books on open shelves, and establishing controls at the room's exits, the use of a charging system for daytime circulation could be eliminated. The plan was unsuccessful, as Leupp later wrote, because of "the impossibility of supplying books in the quantity needed to meet all demands of the larger classes, resulting in the stealing or hiding of books by students in times of pressure, and ... the large number of books and students handled in the room, making adequate supervision impossible."[11] Thereupon, the collection, which contained about 23,000 volumes, was returned to its former ground floor location which had been remodeled and enlarged.

Attention was again focused on the reserve book service when Professor Webster R. Robinson of the economics department was appointed chairman of a special committee to study the library's operation. The Robinson Committee had been created in 1927, at the request of the University's Budget Committee, in an effort to find ways to reduce the library's administrative costs. In its report, issued in 1928, the committee suggested the physical relocation of several library activities (some of which had already been planned). In addition, it recommended that the reserve book room again be enlarged and provision made for a "self-help" collection. Pending the librarian's study on the feasibility of operating a rental collection, action on the Robinson report was deferred.

In addition to heavy demands by students for service (daily circulation in 1935 ranged between 1,800 and 2,700 volumes),[12] the most recurrent

---

[11] Harold L. Leupp to Miss Gertrude Wulfekoetter, Assistant Librarian, University of Cincinnati, Aug. 30, 1930, *Correspondence and Papers* (CU-12, Carton 12), University of California Archives, Berkeley.

[12] Peyton Hurt, memorandum to Harold L. Leupp, April 22, 1935, *Correspondence and Papers* (CU-12, Carton 21), University of California Archives, Berkeley. Similar statistics were not reported in other years.

problem was that of rapport between the faculty and the library with regard to the reserve books. Requests to the faculty were made through the Library Committee that notice be given in sufficient time for materials to be assembled for reserve, and especially that books thus needed not be retained by instructors for their personal use. These efforts, however, proved to be only moderately successful. The decline in enrollment during World War II, along with the effects of changing emphasis in courses at that time, led to a decrease of about 75 percent in reserve book circulation from 1940 to 1944.[13]

Although the practice of reserving books was widely followed among university libraries in the twentieth century, California was one of the earliest institutions to develop it. In 1938 Theodore W. Koch wrote, on the basis of his investigations, that the reserve book system "had its beginning in the old Harvard College Library of 50 years ago."[14] According to the library rules in 1887, California was using reserve books at that time. Koch reported common problems at many institutions regarding reserve books, such as supplying sufficient numbers of duplicate copies, dealing with student abuses of the system, and securing faculty cooperation in providing information about items for reserve. Some universities had even worked out plans to limit the size of reserve collections. California's problems in dealing with reserve books were very similar to those encountered at other libraries before 1945.

In an attempt to reduce the administrative costs of reserve book service and to make books available to students for longer periods of time, the library opened a book rental service in August 1929. Only two copies of a title were kept in the reserve book room, and all additional ones were made available on a rental basis. At the rate of three cents per day, books could be retained until the end of each semester. Some criticism was voiced that the University, as a public-supported institution, was not justified in charging for the use of books. Objection was also expressed to the removal of all but two copies of a title from the reserve book room. Leupp defended the library's action, however, on the grounds that the rental plan allowed for the purchase of additional copies, and that students in large classes would face reduced competition in obtaining required reading materials. After one year of operation the librarian reported that over 22,000 volumes had been drawn, and $4,600 received from rental charges.[15]

---

[13] Helen E. Steedman, "The Effect of the War on the Loan and Shelf Division of the University of California Library," *College and Research Libraries,* V (1944), 206.

[14] Theodore W. Koch, "A Symposium on the Reserve Book System," in A. F. Kuhlman, ed., *College and University Library Service* (Chicago: American Library Association, 1938), p. 73.

[15] *Librarian's Report* (1930), pp. 5–6.

The rental service gained acceptance and its use increased in subsequent years. The rental desk was originally located on the ground floor in the corridor extending to the west of the main entrance-foyer area, with the collection housed in the small stack adjacent to the south side of the Morrison reading room. By 1935, however, these facilities were outgrown. The rental service was then moved into the reserve book room where its operation was coordinated with that of the reserve books. This combined unit was hence called the "Reserve Book-Rental Service." At that time Leupp wrote: "Our rental service for supplying in quantity, books required for collateral reading in connection with courses, has proved so successful that we are constantly receiving inquiries about it from other libraries."[16] He further indicated that the rental service was entirely self-supporting and that it had been able to provide added copies of books for every ten to fifteen students, according to the demands of individual courses. During the mid-thirties the rental service also began supplying books to people enrolled in the University Extension Division courses. Because of heavy administrative costs and other difficulties, this phase of the rental activity was discontinued by the library in 1943, when a similar service was instituted by the Associated Students of the University of California bookstore. In 1944 it was reported that of all library units, the rental collection had shown the smallest decline in circulation during World War II years. The prospects for rental collections relieving the pressure on reserve book resources in many universities led A. F. Kuhlman to comment in 1938 that "the operation of large rental libraries at the University of California and at the University of Chicago deserves further study and appraisal."[17]

Several other special-use collections, in addition to those for reserve and rental books, existed from 1900 through 1945 at California. The Case O collection, so designated because it was kept in the office of the librarian, (and not, as sometimes thought, because it was obscene) contained works of erotica. Use of these materials was limited to members of the Academic Senate and lecturers, and physicians at Cowell Hospital and the University Medical Center. Students were allowed access to them only upon presentation of a written request from a faculty member. The segregation as well as the restricted use of this literature was the object of student criticism on several occasions. An editorial in the *Daily Californian* in 1924 stated: "Regardless of subject matter, many of the works contained in

---

[16] Harold L. Leupp to Miss Bertine E. Weston, Editor, *Library Journal*, New York, July 3, 1935, *Correspondence and Papers* (CU-12, Carton 20), University of California Archives, Berkeley.

[17] A. F. Kuhlman, "How Reserve Book Collections Can Be Made Effective," in his *College and University Library Service*, op. cit., p. 105.

Case "O" are classics of literature. Why should students be denied the right to freely draw such books?"[18] Eight years later, responding to renewed questioning, Leupp defended the library's policy in this matter by saying: "Safeguarding student morals is not the task of the Library nor is it the motive behind restricting circulation of works of an erotic nature.... Protecting books from mutilation and theft is the primary object of restricting circulation."[19]

Case R, so designated because it contained rare books, was housed on the third floor of the Doe Library. Age, scarcity, contents, and physical makeup were the main factors that determined which books were included. Leupp described the library's policy regarding this collection when he wrote, "In general, in addition to rare and expensive books we now segregate examples of fine printing, unbound materials, very small books, some large volumes consisting mainly of plates, and books ... [that] would be subject to theft or mutilation in the stack."[20] Case R materials were available to faculty members and students but restricted to use within the library. When the library established its Treasure Room in the early thirties in connection with the Friends of the Library group, the Case R books became part of that collection. Christine Price was the curator of these rare materials during the thirties and early forties.

Two other segregated collections were Case B and Case M. Case B consisted of books that were considered too valuable to be shelved with the general collection but not rare enough to be assigned to Case R. These items, kept in a caged section of the stacks, were subject to limited circulation. Orchestral scores and other valuable works of music were set aside in Case M. Also subject to limited circulation, these materials were housed in a separate area on the second floor of the Doe Library.

Finally, the library had developed special collections for archival materials and maps. Rowell had begun collecting University reports and a wide range of historical materials even before he became University librarian. "While secretary to President Gilman in 1874–75," he wrote, "I was instructed to gather and bind all obtainable material of this nature. The resulting volumes ... may be properly considered the foundation and beginning of the Archives."[21] To these items he added the writings of faculty

[18] *Daily Californian,* Nov. 5, 1924, p. 4; another article on this subject appeared in the issue of Nov. 13, 1924, p. 7.

[19] Ibid., March 25, 1932, p. 2.

[20] Harold L. Leupp to Frank K. Walter, Librarian, University of Minnesota, April 26, 1928, *Correspondence and Papers* (CU-12, Carton 11), University of California Archives, Berkeley.

[21] Joseph C. Rowell, "A Brief Account of the University Archives" (unpublished; March 12, 1935), p. 3, in *Papers Read before the Staff Association of the University of California Library* (folder), University of California Archives, Berkeley.

members, master's theses, and doctoral dissertations. He also included the publications of California authors, although these were later transferred to Case R. The archives occupied a room on the third floor of the Doe Library and were under Rowell's care until his death in 1938. Thereafter they were serviced by the library staff until 1945, when May Dornin became the curator of the collection. Archival materials were available on a non-circulating basis for use by students, faculty, and other persons engaged in research work.

The library's map collection, also housed in a separate room on the building's third floor, contained approximately 22,000 items in 1944.[22] These materials were serviced by the staff of the Reference Division, and were available for use only on a noncirculating basis. Use restrictions were waived during World War II when some 3,000 maps were drawn for use by military agencies of the government.

INTERLIBRARY LOANS

During his early years as librarian, Rowell recognized both the limitations of California's collection and the need for libraries (especially in the West where book resources were meagre) to cooperate with each other. Therefore, in 1886 he requested authorization from the regents to participate in interlibrary loan activities. Interlibrary lending had been advocated ten years earlier by Samuel Swett Green of Worcester, Massachusetts, and had already gained acceptance by some eastern libraries.[23] The regents withheld permission until 1894, when they allowed Rowell to establish lending and borrowing arrangements with the California State Library in Sacramento. In 1897 this permission was extended to include the California Academy of Science library, and the following year Rowell was authorized to establish interlibrary loan arrangements with any other interested libraries.

In February 1898 Rowell wrote to 126 libraries throughout the United States, inviting them to cooperate with the University of California in an interlibrary loan arrangement. Replies were received from forty institutions willing to participate in this plan. Two years later Associate Librarian Layman reported, "The system of inter-library loans has been a decided advantage to us."[24] He regretted, however, the lack of printed catalogs

[22] Richard V. Teggart, "A University Library Reviews Its Map Collection," *Library Journal,* LXIX (1944), 1042.

[23] Samuel Swett Green, "The Lending of Books to One Another by Libraries," *Library Journal,* I (1876), 15–6; also [Melvil Dewey], "Inter-Library Loans," *Library Notes.* III (1892), 405–7.

[24] "Librarian's Report," in *President's Report* (1900), p. 85.

which made it difficult to decide where to send for particular items. For several years books were shipped at reduced rates via the Wells Fargo Express Company. When the discount privilege was discontinued in 1909, Rowell expressed hope that a library rate would be established by the parcel post service. Although requests were frequently sent to eastern and midwestern libraries, the bulk of California's interlibrary lending was with the State Library and Stanford University. In 1916 the librarian's report indicated that only one book had been lost thus far in all California's interlibrary loan transactions.

California's interlibrary loan statistics were not reported until 1909. During the years from 1909/10 through 1939/40, figures indicated that borrowing increased nine times (from 72 to 656 volumes), whereas lending multiplied eleven times (from 225 to 2,481 volumes).[25] In relation to its total interlibrary loan transactions, California borrowed an average of 24 percent as contrasted with lending an average of 76 percent for that period.

Despite the fact that borrowing libraries paid shipping costs, concern developed at California regarding time and labor expenses for lending about three times more volumes than it borrowed. Thus, an interlibrary loan code, based largely on those developed by the Library of Congress and Harvard, was adopted in 1920. The underlying philosophy of the code was that the library on the Berkeley campus was intended primarily as a research and reference collection for the use of the University's students and faculty, and was not to be considered a general lending library. Recognizing its obligations to the academic community at large, the library would lend "certain books to other libraries for the use of scholars engaged in teaching or writing or scientific investigation" but would not lend "books that should be in a local library or that can be borrowed from a library (such as a state or county library) having a particular duty to the community from which the application comes."[26] Loans were not made to libraries in the San Francisco Bay area since local residents could personally consult books in the University library.

As the Los Angeles campus and other branches of the University grew, they made increasingly heavy demands upon the library at Berkeley. Leupp indicated in 1930 that the library's policy was "more liberal in meeting requests of the branches of the University than of other institutions."[27] He

[25] Statistics derived from *Librarian's Reports* for years shown.

[26] *Inter-Library Loans,* University of California Library (January, 1920), 1 p., copy in *Library Committee Minutes,* Minute Book no. 2 (1910–21), following minutes for Dec. 22, 1919.

[27] Harold L. Leupp to Charles H. Brown, Librarian, Iowa State College of Agriculture and Mechanic Arts, Ames, Iowa, Feb. 6, 1930, *Correspondence and Papers* (CU-12, Carton 13), University of California Archives, Berkeley.

also acknowledged that California felt a heavy responsibility toward lending research materials to many other universities and small colleges in the West, as well as to public libraries that supplied the needs of local industries working in scientific fields. From the cost survey that was made in 1929, the expense for interlibrary loans (the costs of lending and borrowing were approximately the same) averaged $1.59 per volume.[28]

When financial limitations resulting from the depression were being felt in the thirties, California adopted a service-charge policy for lending to other institutions.[29] Effective in August, 1933, fifty cents plus postage was charged for a single volume, and 25 cents per title for additional items requested with the same order. At that time libraries were urged to consider requesting photostat copies of pertinent data rather than borrowing books. In 1934 a concession was made to branches of the University outside Berkeley, for which the charge was reduced to 25 cents per volume, with a maximum charge of one dollar per transaction. A limit of two dollars per transaction for other institutions was also set at that time. Although the *Library Journal* stated that, as far as then known, California was "the first library to adopt such a plan," it was later reported that Stanford had been charging for interlibrary loans since 1932.[30] The University of Nebraska also adopted a charge basis in 1933. California's policy remained in force until after 1945.

California's interlibrary loan activity may be compared with that of other large universities for the years 1927/28 through 1936/37 (appendix A, table 10). Considering the average annual number of volumes both borrowed and lent in this group, California ranked in third place after Chicago and Michigan, and ahead of Columbia, Illinois, Princeton, Minnesota, Pennsylvania, Cornell, and Stanford. Among these institutions California's average annual percentage was highest for volumes lent and lowest for those borrowed. Various factors, such as geographical location, library resources of local areas, and lending policies, undoubtedly influenced the interlibrary loan activities of these libraries. Yet California's overall standing may also be considered in part as indicative of the comparative strength of its collection at that time.

---

[28] *Librarian's Report* (1930), p. 8.

[29] Harold L. Leupp, "Service Charge for Interlibrary Loans," *Library Journal*, LVIII (1933), 791.

[30] "Editorials;" Nathan van Patten, "Inter-Library Loan Fees;" and Gilbert H. Doane, "Service Charge on Inter-Library Loans;" *Library Journal*, LVIII (1933), 780, 890, and 996 respectively.

PROVIDING INFORMATION AND INSTRUCTION

The University of California library served the academic community not only by supplying books and other research materials but also by furnishing information and instruction for its users. From 1900 through 1945, efforts were made to achieve these objectives by providing reference service, offering programs of library orientation and guidance in the use of bibliographical resources, issuing publications, and arranging exhibits related primarily to the book arts.

REFERENCE SERVICE

During the years before the Doe Library was occupied, reference service was provided on an informal basis at California. Rowell had not organized a reference department or reported specifically on "reference service." In paying tribute to Rowell, however, Leupp referred to "the kindly interest and the courteous personal service which those earlier readers received from the man who made the library."[31] Much can be inferred from Leupp's comment as well as his predecessor's prodigious activities in compiling bibliographies, guides, and a subject index to periodicals to indicate Rowell's great concern with providing information and reference assistance for library users.

The librarian's report for 1900 referred to C. K. Jones, second assistant on the staff, as the "Reference Librarian." Jones resigned during that year and the position was not mentioned again until 1910, when Rowell indicated that H. R. Mead was the "Reference Librarian." By 1913, and at various times thereafter, the librarian referred with increased frequency in his reports and correspondence to the activities of the Reference Department.

The Department's major responsibility was to provide information and assistance for library users. On several occasions from 1915 to 1920 the librarian reported the number of reference questions that had been answered. During the 1915/16 academic year, 15,665 inquiries were handled at the reference desk. In 1917/18 the staff replied to 105 requests for information by mail. An average of 239 questions per day was answered during the month of November, 1919. Unfortunately the librarian did not continue to report this kind of information in later years. Members of the reference staff also performed several other related tasks, such as compiling bibliographies, indexing publications, and servicing at various times the periodical, document, map, archive, and other special collections in the General Library.

---

[31] *Librarian's Report* (1919), p. 5.

An additional service was inaugurated in 1932 when Richard V. Teggart, who had been teaching in the economics department, was appointed to the reference staff. Teggart's initial responsibility was to advise and assist graduate students in the selection of thesis or dissertation subjects. His activities were gradually expanded to include working with advanced students in the broader areas of bibliography and research related to the social sciences.

In conjunction with reference services, plans were developed to provide assistance for users of the public catalogs. As early as 1915 a member of the staff was assigned the dual tasks of filing cards and aiding people in using the catalogs. The advisory service, however, was gradually absorbed by the reference staff and remained under its jurisdiction for many years. By the early thirties, the demands upon the Reference Department had grown to the extent that it was no longer able to provide continuous service at the catalogs. As a result, several members of the Catalog Department were assigned to assist with this work especially during the early weeks of each semester. Finally, in October 1939 a permanent Catalog Advisory Service was established. In addition to assisting users, the intent of this service was to relay information to the library's catalogers about difficulties encountered in using the catalogs.

During World War II, the Reference Department provided valuable help in locating needed information for many government agencies and defense industries. The University's document and map collections, and its holdings of many scientific journals and reference works, were especially useful in meeting these demands. The library and its reference collection had thus become a major center for war-related information on the West Coast.

How did reference service at California compare with that of other similar institutions? According to White's study in 1938, among eight universities the number of persons engaged in reference work doubled in the twenty-year period ending in 1938.[32] California's reference staff had increased that amount in about 15 years. Reference departments at these universities averaged between two and three persons each in 1918/19, and approximately six each in 1937/38; California's included four in the former year, and eight in the latter. In his study on this subject Samuel Rothstein noted that "the typical development of reference services in university libraries during the 1917–1940 period was one of only moderate progress. The chief positive accomplishment was the definite acceptance of refer-

---

[32] White, op. cit., pp. 29–30. In addition to California, these institutions were Chicago, Illinois, Iowa (University), Michigan, Minnesota, Northwestern, and Oregon (University).

ence work as a primary function of the university library, directed not only toward offering occasional guidance but frankly including the direct supply of information as well."[33] During that same period, California's reference staff was offering service considerably more advanced than that described by Rothstein.

LIBRARY ORIENTATION AND INSTRUCTION

Two kinds of library instruction were given, in addition to the general reference and catalog advisory services, during the period 1900–45. Drawing upon members of the staff, and with some outside librarians also as instructors, courses in library methods were offered for prospective librarians. Summer sessions for this purpose were held intermittently from 1902 through 1918, when full-credit courses were established during the regular academic year. Although library staff members were still primarily relied upon as teachers, instruction in librarianship was administratively separated from the General Library in 1922, when the Department of Library Science was created within the College of Letters and Science. Then, in 1926, largely through the efforts of Sydney B. Mitchell, and with the recommendation of Leupp, the School of Librarianship was established to offer courses at the graduate level. Thereafter, instruction was no longer given by members of the General Library staff.

During at least two periods, programs of instruction on the use of the library were offered for students by members of the library staff. In April 1904 Rowell received permission from the University's Academic Council for a series of eleven lectures to be given on successive Thursday evenings during the following fall semester. Offered by library staff members, these lectures were planned to provide general information concerning the arrangement and use of the collection, the catalog, important reference works, bibliography, the book trade, and book binding. Unfortunately, Rowell did not state the outcome of this endeavor. It was reported in the *Daily Californian* that about 50 persons had attended his introductory lecture.[34] According to the "Calendar" printed in the campus newspaper, only Mead's six lectures on reference work were scheduled thereafter. No other similar efforts by the library were reported until the early thirties.

In the fall of 1932 the Readers Department began conducting informative orientation tours for students. Leupp had suggested that a related program of instruction be developed, but reductions in the budget forced the in-

[33] Samuel Rothstein, *The Development of Reference Services*, A.C.R.L. Monograph, no. 14 (Chicago: Association of College and Reference Libraries, 1955), p. 83.
[34] *Daily Californian*, Sept. 12, 1904, p. 1.

definite postponement of this plan. The *Faculty Bulletin* in 1936 noted that library orientation tours were continuing to be offered each semester;[35] student participation, however, was on a voluntary rather than required basis. Tours were conducted by the head of the Loan and Shelf Division, and included visits to the loan desk, main reading room, reference desk, reserve book room, periodical room, Morrison Memorial Library, and the stacks.

At California several efforts were made apart from the library to offer help to undergraduates in using library resources. In 1921 G. D. Boyce, a teaching fellow in the Department of History, gave a course entitled "How to Use the Library." Also in the early twenties, members of the library saff were invited to give a series of lectures on library use as part of a first-year English course. Peyton Hurt reported in 1936 that "two undergraduate courses in library use and general bibliography . . . Librarianship 101 and Public Speaking 120," were being given.[36] The scarcity of information in official reports of the University and the *Daily Californian* about this kind of instruction indicate that special importance was not attached to library-use courses.

Hoping to determine the extent of library instruction being offered to undergraduate students at other institutions, Hurt made a survey of the graduate students at Stanford and California in 1932/33. He found that 62 percent of the combined group had received no instruction whatsoever on library use at the undergraduate or graduate levels. Special courses had been taken by 8 percent, and another 16 percent had received some library instruction in connection with other courses. Hurt concluded that "very little is done to instruct college students, graduate or undergraduate, in the use of the library."[37]

LIBRARY PUBLICATIONS

The printed page was used extensively at California during the period ending in 1945 to describe the collection and provide instruction on the use of the library. The earliest major effort in this direction came in 1880, when the "University of California Library Bulletin" series first appeared. Eighteen titles were published before the series became inactive in 1913; some were issued in second and third editions. An additional publication was released in 1942, as number 19 in the series (appendix F). Eleven titles

[35] *Faculty Bulletin,* University of California, V (Jan. 1936), 4.

[36] Peyton Hurt, *The University Library and Undergraduate Instruction* (Berkeley: University of California Press, 1936), p. 22.

[37] Peyton Hurt, *Use of the Library by Graduate Students* (unpublished; 1933), p. 20, University of California Archives, Berkeley; also his "The Need of College and University Instruction in the Use of the Library," *Library Quarterly,* IV (1934), 436–48.

were catalogs or bibliographical works that revealed many of the library's resources plus those of some other collections in the area. An additional six were items of literary or cultural value, and the remaining ones pertained to the Bacon and Doe Library buildings.

The series became inactive after 1913 for several reasons. Under Leupp's direction, greater emphasis was placed on the card catalog rather than bibliographies or indexes as the key to the collection. The development of the general reference service likewise reduced the necessity for providing printed catalogs and guides. Moreover, after the move to the Doe building attention within the library was focused more sharply upon specifically library functions; concern for the art collection and works of esthetic and cultural value, which had been the subjects of several series publications, shifted to other departments. Finally, during the twenties and thirties bibliographical publications, such as the *Union List of Serials,* reduced the library's need to issue similar works of its own. Some consideration was given in 1936 to reviving the "Library Bulletin" series. It was then proposed, however, that a new series, devoted more directly to library problems and with the title "Publications in Librarianship," should be issued instead. Action was deferred on this matter until after 1945.

Several publications in the form of guides or handbooks were also issued by the library. The earliest one appeared in 1888, with the title, *Library of the University of California: Subject Guide* (22 pages). It served as a finding device by indicating which alcoves of the Bacon Library contained books on particular subjects. Considering that the Rowell classification scheme had not yet been devised, and that books were then shelved according to broad subject groups, a location-guide had become very necessary. Library rules and other information pertaining to library use were not included in this booklet.

Shortly after the Doe Library was occupied, plans were made to issue a handbook. Lack of funds delayed publication until 1915, when a seven-page booklet entitled *University Library* was printed. Although this pamphlet provided a brief description of the building and its donor, plus a resume of current library statistics, it lacked information about the library's use, bibliographical facilities, and general regulations. Another publication, *Library Handbook, 1918–1919* (39 pages), was subsequently issued. In addition to providing historical and descriptive sketches, it furnished information regarding the classification system, circulation procedures, special collections, reference service, general rules and regulations, and library hours. This booklet was, in fact, the first real handbook published by the library, and was used throughout the 1920's.

Although the need for a revised and up-to-date edition of the handbook was expressed in the late twenties, it was not fulfilled until 1934 when the *Handbook for New Students* (25 pages) appeared. The contents of this booklet were similar to those of the previous ones, although its appearance and format were considerably more attractive. Later editions of the *Handbook*, with very minor changes, were issued in 1936, 1937, 1939, and 1941.

At the request of the Department of English, Frank M. Bumstead prepared a booklet, *The Use of the Library* (36 pages), that was published in 1921 for the University's "Syllabus Series." According to the author, the object of this work was "to enable the student to use the resources of the University Library intelligently, and to prevent the loss of time and energy caused by insufficient knowledge of library methods."[38] In addition to describing the useful features of many standard reference works and periodical indexes, it explained the meaning of the entries on catalog cards and suggested useful procedures to follow in compiling bibliographies. Intended primarily for undergraduate students, this publication suitably complemented the *Library Handbook*.

Under the library's auspices several other publications of a miscellaneous nature were issued. In 1900 Rowell wrote a three-page circular entitled *The University Library: A Little Talk about What Every Student Wants to Know*. It contained suggestions concerning the use of library materials and the development of good study habits. When the American Library Association met in Berkeley for its annual convention in 1915, and plans were made for those in attendance to visit the Panama-Pacific International Exposition in San Francisco, the library published a descriptive pamphlet, *The Library at the Exposition; a Survey*. With the financial assistance of Juan C. Cebrián, one of the library's notable benefactors, *Spain and Spanish America in the Libraries of the University of California, a Catalogue of Books* (two volumes), was published in 1928–30. During the years 1933 to 1939 the staff of the Morrison Memorial Library wrote short book reviews that were printed in a series of pamphlets called *Minute Reviews*.

Finally, the library was well represented through the years by articles that appeared in other publications. The campus newspaper, the *Daily Californian*, was used extensively to publicize library activities and changes in hours or regulations, as well as to describe notable new acquisitions. In January 1933 a series of five articles written by members of the library staff was published.[39] These brief accounts described the library's general opera-

[38] Frank M. Bumstead, *The Use of the Library* (Berkeley: University of California Press, 1921), p [5].
[39] *Daily Californian*, January 16–20, 1933, p. 4 (each issue). Titles of individual articles were: "A New World," "The Home of Books," "Book Room Magic," "For the Inquisitive," and "Morrison Memorial."

tion, circulation and reserve book procedures, use of the public catalogs, general reference service, and the Morrison Room. During the years before 1945 both the librarians and members of the staff also contributed numerous articles to many library and literary journals.

The type of library publication most noticeably lacking at California was a regularly issued list of new books. This matter was considered several times during the twenties and thirties, especially since acquisition lists were distributed by a number of other university libraries. The Lange Library of Education and the Agriculture Library reported newly received titles during part of that period, but estimated expenses prevented the General Library from offering this service.

EXHIBITS

Attractive and carefully planned exhibits were an important aspect of public service at the California library. In 1884, under Rowell's direction, the Loan Book Exhibition was sponsored to display examples of fine printing, book illustrating, and binding. Many valuable items from about seventy public and private libraries in the area, in addition to works from the University collection, were shown to some 1,780 visitors. In connection with this display the *Catalogue of the Loan Book Exhibition* was published as number five in the "Library Bulletin" series.

When the University celebrated its semi-centennial in 1918, the library provided an extensive exhibit of photographs, portraits, papers, and mementos to illustrate California's history and growth. Interest in exhibits was heightened by the display of gifts received and by the commemoration of special events. During the twenties and thirties much attention was given to showing works of fine printing, especially those presented by Albert M. Bender and other library friends. Interest in exhibits was also developed on several occasions by the display of unique items, such as coin, stamp, icon, and holographic signature collections. Special events of public interest and the accomplishments of notable persons were often used as the themes for exhibits. In 1934, to honor the 94th meeting of the American Association for the Advancement of Science, held in Berkeley, the library prepared an "Exhibition of First Editions of Epochal Achievements in the History of Science." In 1940, after Professor Ernest O. Lawrence of the California faculty was awarded the Nobel Prize for his contribution in physics, his medal and accompanying diploma were made the subject of a display. The library also used exhibits as the means to instruct students and other people about the use of library materials. A group of mutilated books was shown in 1937 along wih ten prepared posters on the theme "How Not to Use the Library."

Responsibility for preparing exhibits was shared by many staff members from most of the library's departments and divisions. During the thirties and early forties, Christine Price's contribution in connection with displays of rare and fine books was especially notable. Exhibits were usually shown for one month, although on special occasions they were held for longer periods. The library's exhibits drew many favorable comments from members of the University community, visitors, and descriptive articles that appeared in the *Daily Californian* and other Bay Area newspapers.

PROVISIONS FOR LIBRARY USE

The number of hours that the library was open for use gradually increased in the years before 1900. While the University was located in Oakland (1869–73), the library was open on weekdays only from 4 to 5 P.M. and closed altogether on Sunday. The hours were considerably extended after Rowell became librarian. Regulations printed in 1876 indicated that library hours were from 9 to 11:30 A.M., and 12:30 to 5 P.M., Monday through Friday. Except from 9 to 11:30 A.M. on Saturdays, the library remained closed weekends. According to the *Library Rules* issued in 1887, hours extended from 8:25 A.M. to 5:15 P.M. weekdays, except Saturday, when closing time was 1 P.M. In 1898, after the Bacon Library had been provided with electric lighting, three hours each evening, Monday through Friday, were added to the library schedule.

From 1911, when the Doe Library was occupied, until 1945, changes in library hours were relatively minor. The building was open weekdays from 8 A.M. until 10 P.M. Saturday closing time was changed from 10 P.M. to 6 P.M. in 1934. Sunday hours were from 9 A.M. to 5 P.M. until 1926; 9 A.M. to 10 P.M. from 1926 to 1934; and from 1 to 10 P.M. after 1934. On several occasions the library hours were extended to 11 P.M. during examination periods.

California's library hours during regular term time, on the basis of total hours per week in specified years, were as follows: 1869, six hours; 1876, thirty-seven and one-half hours; 1887, forty-seven and three quarter hours; 1898, sixty-two and three-quarter hours; 1911, ninety-two hours; 1926, ninety-seven hours; and 1934, eighty-nine hours. Kenneth J. Brough commented on library hours in his study *The Scholar's Workshop* and noted that "well past the middle of the nineteenth century, American colleges maintained hours of library service that now seem incredibly short."[40]

---

[40] Kenneth J. Brough, *The Scholar's Workshop* (Urbana: University of Illinois Press, 1953), p. 92.

According to Brough, in 1876 Columbia maintained twelve hours per week of service, Harvard maintained forty-eight, and Yale maintained thirty-six. By 1906 these hours had increased to eighty-seven at Columbia, eighty-two and one-half at Harvard, and seventy-five at Yale. In 1946 they were seventy-six at Columbia, seventy-five at Harvard, and eighty-four at Yale. From the mid-twenties through the early forties, according to Wilson and Tauber, the median number of hours that university libraries were open for service was about eighty-five per week.[41] Thus, by comparison with hours cited for other libraries, California's schedule was higher than the average.

While the collection was housed in the Bacon Library, access to the shelves was permitted for students as well as faculty members. The central-stack arrangement of the Doe Library, however, was planned for a limited-access policy in hope that the number of books missing from the collection each year could be reduced. Faculty members were granted nonrestrictive stack privileges. The signed request of an instructor plus the approval of the associate librarian allowed graduate students to obtain semester stack permits. In special cases, undergraduates were given access for short periods of time by applying at the reference desk.

Student complaints during the twenties caused the Library Committee to believe that restrictions on stack access were unduly limiting student use of the collection. Thereupon, in 1925 honor students were admitted to the stacks seven times each semester. Graduate students were accorded full stack privileges in 1926. These practices continued until the mid-thirties, when the librarian expressed concern for losses, extensive mutilation of materials, considerable displacement of books, and general disturbances that had developed from the more liberal policy. As a result, in 1937, a more restrictive policy was adopted. Aside from the faculty, only graduate students who had been admitted to either the qualifying examinations or candidacy for master's or doctoral degrees were granted stack privileges. Other graduate students were allowed limited access upon obtaining special permission from the Dean of the Graduate Division. Increased enrollments and crowded stacks during the late thirties, plus staff disruptions in the Loan and Shelf Division during World War II, caused these provisions to remain in force until after 1945.

Leupp was conscious of the failings inherent in limiting access to the stacks, especially as that practice affected the college students. In 1940 he stated that "establishment of an undergraduate or lower division library

---

[41] Louis R. Wilson and Maurice F. Tauber, *The University Library* (2d ed.; New York: Columbia University Press, 1956), p. 268.

physically separated from the present main building would be a comparatively inexpensive way to relieve over-crowding, would render possible for undergraduate students a quantity and type of library service which they need but do not and cannot receive under present conditions, and would fit readily into the comprehensive program for development of library service on the Berkeley campus."[42] During his remaining years as librarian, Leupp continued to express hope that the eventual establishment of an undergraduate library would provide students with freer access to books.

Until 1900 library privileges were limited to people who had some connection with the University. According to the *Library Rules* adopted in 1887, in addition to use by students, "regents, professors, instructors, and officers of the University (including affiliated colleges), and such benefactors of the University as may be designated by the Committee on Library and Museum,"[43] were allowed to draw books from the collection. When the rules were revised in 1893, these benefits were extended (upon payment of a five-dollar deposit) to University alumni also.

During the early decades of the twentieth century, policies regarding library use became less restrictive. In 1900 the Graduate Council proposed that Berkeley residents be allowed library privileges similar to those of students, provided they were recommended by two members of the Academic Senate and also paid a ten-dollar deposit. The regents adopted this provision in March 1901. Later that year, at the suggestion of the Library Committee, the president authorized library privileges for faculty members of the Pacific Theological Seminary (located in Berkeley) and the Berkeley Bible Seminary. Library use was further extended in 1904 when, according to the regents' Orders, it was granted, on the basis of endorsement by two members of the Academic Senate and payment of a ten-dollar annual fee, to any person who applied. According to the *Library Handbook, 1918–1919,* all University employees were permitted to use the library, and by 1920 faculty members from Mills College in Oakland also enjoyed this privilege.[44]

In 1925, by regents' action, the annual fee paid by California residents for library privileges was lowered from ten to six dollars. At the same time the five-dollar deposit basis for alumni and other former students was removed, and these people were expected to pay the six-dollar annual fee required of

[42] *Librarian's Report* (1940), p. 8.

[43] *Library Rules of the University of California,* op. cit., p. 4.

[44] Aurelia Henry Reinhardt, President, Mills College, Oakland, California, to David P. Barrows, President, University of California, Oct. 3, 1920, and Morse A. Cartwright, Executive Secretary, Office of the President, University of California, to Dr. Reinhardt, Oct. 15, 1920, photostat copies of original letters provided for author by the librarian of Mills College.

other citizens. This policy, which continued in force through the thirties and early forties, applied to persons enrolled in extension courses, students from other educational institutions in the area, faculty members from junior and state colleges, research workers in industrial firms, and all other citizens. By 1943 nonfee privileges had been extended to teachers in the University High School and other local schools related to the University's teaching program, visiting faculty members from out-of-state, government and war-related agencies, Extension Division instructors, and teaching assistants from Mills College. Subsequently, similar benefits were also given to faculty members from San Francisco State College. The practice of allowing any person free use of library books on the premises remained unchanged.

In his study of library practices at Harvard, Yale, Columbia and Chicago, Brough indicated that library use by persons not connected with the university was "a firmly established tradition at each of the four institutions."[45] Privileges were freely extended by all in the case of visiting scholars. In 1916 Columbia adopted a liberal policy of granting library benefits to students from many other institutions of higher education in the area and to the local public. By the late 1930's, however, Columbia found it necessary to establish more restrictive measures based upon a fee system. Marvin A. Miller found, in his study of circulation practices at seventy-one state universities and land-grant colleges in 1944, that "all libraries will and do make direct loans on occasion and by some arrangement, to individuals who have no official connection with the college or university."[46] He also stated, however, there was "little or no uniformity of practice among the groups of libraries as to lending to noncollege applicants."[47] In comparisons with Miller's findings as well as the observations of Brough, California's policy regarding library privileges was fairly typical of those at many other institutions before 1945.

The California library fulfilled its purpose as a service institution within the University during the period ending in 1945 in a manner that was generally progressive and forward-looking. Although its policies at times reflected a conservative outlook, there were clear evidences of a strong desire on the part of the library administration, supported by the Library Committee, the president, and the regents, to initiate changes wherever

---

[45] Brough, op. cit., p. 72.

[46] Marvin A. Miller, "Loan Clientele of State University and Land-Grant College Libraries," *College and Research Libraries,* VI (1944), 39–40.

[47] Ibid., p. 40.

these would increase the effectiveness of library service. With the passing of years, circulation and library-use practices became considerably more responsive to the needs of students. Moreover, the kinds and extent of reference services that were provided, the modifications in reserve book facilities and procedures that were made, and the book rental collection that was established all were directed toward bringing inquisitive minds and recorded knowledge together. Thus, among institutions of higher education, California deserved a well-respected place in terms of library service that was a vital resource for instruction in the community of scholars.

CONCLUSION

THE UNIVERSITY OF CALIFORNIA library at Berkeley was marked by several significant features in its development from 1900 to 1945. A large and distinguished collection was amassed to support the institution's teaching and research needs. The staff increased steadily not only in size but also in the degree of scholastic attainment, professional maturity, and dedication that it represented. Materials and services were well organized and administrative procedures effectively developed for the library to meet the University's expanding needs. The construction and subsequent enlargement of the Doe building, as well as the opening of branch libraries, provided almost continuously expanding facilities during that period to accommodate the rapidly rising numbers of books and readers.

What accounted for California's highly favorable library growth? The financial and cultural resources of the state were indispensable in creating a research library of quality. The emergence of the University as one of the nation's leading institutions of higher education and creative scholarship placed high priority on the library's development. Innovations in education and increased emphasis on graduate studies in the twentieth century focused attention upon academic libraries as information and use-oriented facilities rather than book repositories; at Berkeley response to this trend was clearly evident.

Of greater importance, however, to California's library development were the determined and influential men who decided its policies, appropriated its funds, appointed its staff, and directed its activities. During the course of forty-five years a strong combination of individuals with scholarly insight and concern for education on the one hand, and business experience and administrative skill on the other, was represented in the Board of Regents, the president's office, the Library Committee, and the position of librarian.

The regents, who were drawn largely from the state's political, business, and cultural leadership, included people of influence and purpose. By virtue of their public office, the governor, lieutenant governor, speaker of the assembly, president of the state Board of Agriculture, and state superintendent of public instruction served as regents. For a similar reason, the California Alumni Association president and the president of the Mechanics' Institute of San Francisco were board members. Among the prominent appointees (who also served on the regents' Library Committee) were Phoebe Apperson Hearst, a distinguished matron from one of the state's leading families and longtime University benefactress; James Kennedy Moffitt, a prominent Bay Area banker and industrialist who had contributed generously both to the University and the library; and Chester Harvey Rowell, a noted journalist, champion of political reform, and dedicated supporter of public education. Some of the library's best friends were regents who were instrumental in providing both publicly and privately for its financial, staff, and building needs.

The four men who successively served as University president between 1900 and 1945 determined to a major extent the library's development. Although varying considerably in their backgrounds, personalities, interests, and talents, they had in common an unusually high regard for the library. Using both personal influence and the power of their office, these men successfully presented the library's needs to the regents and to potential donors on numerous occasions. They were also effective in carrying out the regents' orders and dealing resourcefully in several instances with difficult library administrative problems. The interest and efforts of Presidents Wheeler and Sproul, the former confronted with a period of major change and rapid growth after the turn of the century, the latter with the adverse effects of the depression years followed by World War II, proved particularly beneficial to the library.

The loyalty and concern of the faculty were indispensable to the library's growth. Many of California's outstanding scholars served on the Library Committee and were faithful and dedicated in fulfilling their offices. Far from serving as rubber stamps for either the University administration or the librarian, these men contributed vision of what the library should become and determination to achieve the goal of excellence. A quality of academic independence combined with sound judgment enabled the committee for many years to counsel the librarian wisely in matters of collection building and administrative policies, and to press the president and regents effecively for adequate resources and facilities. Few libraries could obtain stronger support than California received from men such as A. C. Lawson, H. M. Stephens, G. P. Adams, C. A. Kofoid, R. J. Kerner, F. J. Teggart, and C. L. Camp. Many other faculty members took equally seriously their responsibilities in recommending titles and assisting where possible in their acquisition.

Although various other University officials helped to determine policies and to provide funds and facilities, the two men who served in turn as librarian were chiefly responsible for the library's direction. Each one was particularly well suited by personality, interests, and abilities to meet the demands of his respective period of service. Rowell's kindly and unpresumptuous manner, his skill in developing catalogs and bibliographical guides, and his creativity and diligence especially qualified him for the early period of the University's growth. During his years the nucleus of a strong collection was established, and innovations were adopted for its organization and use. Having seen the Bacon library outlive its usefulness, he helped to plan and urged construction of the Doe building. Through his personal commitment and dedicated service Rowell was a constant source of encouragement and support to the members of his staff.

Leupp possessed qualities that complemented those of Rowell, especially for the library's increased administrative needs. His training and previous library experience, combined with a strong sense of organization and great personal capacity for daily work enabled him to take over the library's direction at a critical time and to move it forward. Through his ability to evaluate and recruit people Leupp developed a capable staff. Moreover, he anticipated the library's future building needs and planned resourcefully to meet them. Leupp's determination to build a strong library was recognized by his colleagues and superiors, and proved to be a great asset to its successful growth.

Two thoughts appropriately concluded this account of the University of California library at Berkeley from 1900 to 1945. First, the library fulfilled its major purpose in serving the teaching and research needs of students, faculty members, and others who were drawn to its resources. Books, staff, and building facilities were all provided and organized in order to meet the intellectual needs of the academic community and its supporting society. Second, although larger collections existed in the East, the University of California represented the major library accomplishment in the nation's western half. Nearing mid-century, library growth at Berkeley helped to make that campus the leading center for research and higher education on the Pacific Coast.

APPENDIX A

TABLE 1

Library statistics of universities with enrollments of 5,000 students or more and libraries of over one million volumes in 1947, showing the number of volumes and rank among college and university libraries in 1900 and 1947, and the number of times for each library that its collection multiplied in size.

Institution	1900		1947		Number of times collection Multiplied
	Number of Volumes	Rank	Number of Volumes	Rank	
California (Berkeley) .	79,000	13[a]	1,422,494	7	18.0
Chicago..............	303,000	3	1,654,747	5	5.5
Columbia.............	300,000	4	1,836,590	4	6.1
Cornell..............	238,600	5	1,299,798	9	5.5
Harvard.............	548,500	1	4,968,316	1	9.0
Illinois..............	44,000	33[b]	2,076,312	3	47.2
Michigan............	140,000	8	1,309,720	8	9.4
Minnesota...........	60,000	20	1,474,580	6	24.6
Pennsylvania........	145,000	6	1,132,465	10	7.8
Yale................	309,500	2	3,642,730	2	11.8

Sources: *Report of the Commissioner of Education*, U. S. Bureau of Education (Washington, D. C. : 1899–1900), vol. II, pp. 1924–43. *Library Statistics of Colleges and Universities with Enrollments of 5,000 Students or More, 1946–47*, U. S. Office of Education, Circular no. 243 (Washington, D. C.: 1948), 2 pp. This source has been used because it is more reliable and complete than any source available for 1945.
[a] Shared 13th place with Georgetown University, Washington, D. C.
[b] Shared 33rd place with Tufts College, Medford, Mass.

TABLE 2

Funds provided by the University of California for the purchase of library books, shown at five-year intervals between fiscal years 1899/1900 and 1944/45, indicating amounts and percentages received both from gift and designated funds, and from general funds, and the total of all funds received.

Year	Income from Gift and Designated Funds		General Fund		Total Amount All Book Funds
	Amount	Percent of Total	Amount	Percent of Total	
1899/1900.	.....	....	......	....	$ 7,000[a]
1904/05...	$1,699	8%	$19,940	92%	21,639
1909/10...	3,975	13%	25,500	87%	29,475
1914/15...	3,100	12%	21,900	88%	25,000
1919/20...	8,872	29%	21,770	71%	30,642
1924/25...	7,478	20%	29,500	80%	36,978
1929/30...	9,142	13%	60,983	87%	70,125
1934/35...	5,717	10%	53,333	90%	59,050
1939/40...	5,846	8%	69,154	92%	75,000
1944/45...	5,705	9%	55,295	91%	61,000

SOURCES: Statistics for 1899/1900 cited from *Minutes*, University of California Board of Regents, vol. XII (1898–1900), May 9, 1899, p. 231. Statistics from 1904/05 through 1944/45 cited from *Financial Statements* (1902/03 1044/45), 43 reports in one volume. Percentages given have been calculated on the basis of statistics cited.
[a] No division appears for the amount of total funds received as income from gift and designated funds or from general funds.

TABLE 3

Statistics, shown at five-year intervals for the years 1919/20 through 1939/40, for current library expenditures (exclusive of salaries) for those universities with book collections containing over 1,000,000 volumes in 1943/44.

Institution	1919/20	1924/25	1929/30	1934/35	1939/40
California (Berkeley).	$26,612	$ 54,363	$118,127[a]	$ 74,610	$113,921
Chicago..............	51,359	78,372	191,859	120,725	108,169
Columbia............	73,900	103,600	175,506	129,414	198,298
Cornell..............	26,119	46,148	36,207[a]	52,772	57,470
Harvard.............	90,720	179,807[b]	326,939	251,348	266,516
Illinois.............	43,000	105,779	126,287	106,497	141,923
Michigan............	56,000	90,810	133,938	123,295	138,823
Minnesota...........	43,116	52,273	106,751	119,716	119,144
Princeton............	26,908	56,008	77,786	60,769	67,546
Yale................	29,240	86,507	165,967	154,374	183,461

SOURCE: *College and University Library Statistics*, 1919/20 to 1943/44, Princeton University Library (Princeton: 1947), 61 leaves.
[a] Expenditures exclude departmental library accounts.
[b] Statistics given are for 1925/26.

TABLE 4

University of California library appropriations, given at five-year intervals, 1911/12 through 1926/27, showing the amount of book funds, binding funds, and the percentage relationship of binding funds to book funds.

Years	Appropriation for Books	Appropriation for Binding	Percentage Relationship of Binding Funds to Book Funds
1911/12...............	$20,000	$ 5,000	25.0%
1916/17...............	25,000	5,000	20.0%
1921/22...............	35,500	10,000	28.2%
1926/27...............	46,000	10,000	21.7%

SOURCE: *Budgets*, University of California (1911/12–1926/27).

TABLE 5

University of California annual library appropriations for the years 1932/33 through 1941/42, showing the amount of book funds, binding funds, and the percentage relationship of binding funds to book funds.

Years	Appropriation for Books	Appropriation for Binding	Percentage Relationship of Binding Funds to Book Funds
1932/33...............	$77,000	$15,500	20.1%
1933/34...............	49,859	9,000	18.1%
1934/35...............	60,000	11,000	18.3%
1935/36...............	60,000	11,000	18.3%
1936/37...............	61,800	15,500	25.1%
1937/38...............	70,000	15,800	22.6%
1938/39...............	75,000	15,800	21.1%
1939/40...............	75,000	19,000	25.3%
1940/41...............	80,000	19,300	24.1%
1941/42...............	80,000	23,300	27.9%

SOURCE: Harold L. Leupp to Robert Gordon Sproul, President, University of California, Dec. 8, 1942, *Correspondence and papers* (CU-12, Carton 45), University of California Archives, Berkeley.

TABLE 6

University libraries with book collections over one million volumes in 1943/44, showing number of staff members and total amount expended for salaries in the years 1920/21, 1930/31, and 1940/41.

University	1920/21		1930/31		1940/41	
	Staff	Salaries	Staff	Salaries	Staff	Salaries
California (Berkeley).	28	$ 76,300	55	$152,068	86	$149,442
Chicago..............	94	124,118	116	236,407	100	164,508
Columbia...........	72	122,911	166	337,569	292[a]	457,767[a]
Cornell.............	20[b]	29,200[b]	21[c]	43,600[c]	47	86,520
Harvard............	..[d]	89,377	109	175,136	175	251,916
Illinois..............	42	57,984	69	135,770	138	212,903
Michigan...........	75	107,700	149	298,050	147	266,223
Minnesota..........	37	63,030	65	127,420	102	148,535
Princeton...........	51	71,440	64	111,615	74	114,459
Yale................	60	88,266	123	240,919	196	330,513

SOURCE: *College and University Library Statistics, 1919/20 to 1943/44*, Princeton University Library (Princeton: 1947), 61 leaves.
[a] Includes Bard College, Barnard College, College of Pharmacy, New York School of Social Work, Post-Graduate Medical College.
[b] Not including departmental libraries.
[c] Includes only General Library.
[d] Although figures were not given in this source, the Harvard Library was reported as having 116 staff members in 1912/13, according to "Statistics of University Libraries," *American Library Institute Papers and Proceedings* (1920), p. 3; and 65 full-time and 32 part-time employees in 1922, according to "Statistics of College and Reference Libraries," *American Library Association Proceedings*, XLIV (1922), 446-7.

TABLE 7

University of California financial statistics, at five-year intervals from 1899/
1900 through 1944/45, showing budgeted appropriations and amounts expended
for the library, and total operating appropriations or expenditures for the University at Berkeley.

Year	Library		Total University/Berkeley Operating Appropriations or Expenditures
	Budget	Expended	
1899/1900........	$ 12,940	$ 10,890	$ 387,000[a]
1904/05..........	33,930	39,674	723,000[a]
1909/10..........	......[b]	45,622	1,180,000[a]
1914/15..........	80,110	......[c]	913,006[d]
1919/20..........	100,482	......[c]	1,184,195[d]
1924/25..........	177,663	184,110	2,075,312[d]
1929/30..........	240,955	246,621	2,807,911[d]
1934/35..........	217,832	215,748	2,632,353[d]
1939/40..........	311,225	299,558	4,986,688[e]
1944/45..........	297,325	311,055	4,930,090[e]

SOURCE: Statistics cited have been derived from the following sources: *Report of the Secretary to the Board of Regents*, University of California (1899–1939); *Financial Reports* (1939/40–1944/45); *Budgets*, University of California (1914/15–1944/45); and *The Centennial Record of the University of California*, Verne A. Stadtman, ed. (Berkeley: University of California, 1967), pp. 295–6.
[a] Total University operating expenditures; separate figures not given for Berkeley.
[b] $16,870 budgeted for salaries; total appropriation not given.
[c] Separate figures for these items not given in years shown.
[d] Expenditures for education and research departments at Berkeley.
[e] Total appropriations for Berkeley.

TABLE 8

University libraries with over one million volumes in 1943/44, showing total
amount of salaries and other library expenditures (books, periodicals, and binding), in the years 1920/21, 1930/31, and 1940/41.

University	1920/21	1930/31	1940/41
California (Berkeley)...........	$115,800	$281,145	$262,380
Chicago.......................	190,264	420,509	288,498
Columbia......................	198,534	530,420	658,652[a]
Cornell.......................	69,152[b]	78,166[c]	143,484
Harvard.......................	196,430	540,527	524,359
Illinois.......................	110,984	270,659	359,577
Michigan......................	156,800	444,555	404,283
Minnesota.....................	111,318	241,309	256,931
Princeton......................	109,083	128,018	178,597
Yale..........................	150,987	424,090	510,348

SOURCE: Figures shown have been compiled on the basis of statistics cited in *College and University Library Statistics, 1919/20–1943/44*, Princeton University Library (Princeton: 1947), 61 leaves.
[a] Includes Bard College, Barnard College, College of Pharmacy, New York School of Social Work, and Post-Graduate Medical School.
[b] Not including departmental libraries.
[c] Includes only General Library.

Appendixes

TABLE 9

Circulation statistics for the University of California library, shown at five year intervals from 1909/10 through 1939/40, indicating number of items circulated from the loan desk, reserve book room, other service areas (specified by code), and total circulation, plus circulation of books per student.

Year	Loan Desk	Reserve Books	Other	Total	Per Student
1909/10.........	84,000[a]	....	106,000[b]	190,000	56
1914/15.........	81,114[c]	....	169,917[d]	251,031	42
1919/20.........	160,153[e]	459,740[f]	....	619,893	62
1924/25.........	249,425[e]	629,194[g]	....	878,619	83
1929/30.........	370,788[e]	222,733[h]	45,232[i]	638,753	56
1934/35.........	....	....	....	874,826[j]	66
1939/40.........	657,640[k]	568,388[h]	94,315[i]	1,320,343	74

Source: Statistics have been derived from the following sources: 1909/10 through 1929/30, and 1939/40, from *Librarian's Reports;* 1934/35, from *News Notes of California Libraries,* XXX (1935), 159. Per-student figures are based on total enrollment at Berkeley for years shown as reported in *The Centenial Record of the University of California,* ed. by Verne A. Stadtman (Berkeley: University of California, 1967), pp. 218–22.

a Home use.
b 100,000 estimated library use, plus 6,000 summer session.
c Home and overnight use.
d Day use.
e Day and home use.
f Day and overnight use.
g Includes 2-hour book room.
h Includes 2-hour book room and overnight use.
i Includes periodical room and rental books.
j Includes all books and periodicals.
k Includes General Library, plus Lange and Biology Branches.

TABLE 10

Average annual interlibrary loan statistics and percentages for ten university libraries based on informaton reported for the years 1927/28 through 1936/37.

Institutions	Number of Volumes Borrowed and Lent	Borrowed		Lent	
		Number of Volumes	Percent of Total	Number of Volumes	Percent of Total
California (Berkeley)....	2,260	425	19%	1,841	81%
Chicago................	4,220	971	23%	3,250	77%
Columbia...............	2,090	734	35%	1,356	65%
Cornell................	1,083	255	23%	828	77%
Illinois................	1,953	475	24%	1,478	76%
Michigan...............	2,440	650	26%	1,790	74%
Minnesota..............	1,353	717	53%	637	47%
Pennsylvania...........	1,146	350	31%	796	69%
Princeton..............	1,476	532	36%	943	63%
Stanford...............	988	338	34%	650	66%

Source: Calculations for California based on statistics derived from *Librarian's Reports* for 1928-31, 1934, and 1936, and from *News Notes of California Libraries* for the remaining years; calculations for the other nine institutions based on statistics reproted by Carl M. White, "Trends in the Use of University Libraries," in A. F. Kuhlman, ed., *College and University Library Service* (Chicago: American Library Association, 1938), pp. 32-3. Except for California, institutions shown are the nine (among a total of 14 included by White) with the highest total number of volumes borrowed and lent for the ten-year period considered.

APPENDIX B

"Leading American Library Collections,"[1] indicating (1) subject fields used to determine "the leading collections for advanced study and research" and showing those fields in which California (CU) was named, and (2) the rank among those libraries which were named in at least ten subject fields.

SUBJECT FIELDS

Literature and Languages

Classical	CU
English	CU
American	CU
German	CU
French	CU
Spanish	CU
Drama and Theater	—
Folklore	CU

History

United States	CU
Latin American	CU
Medieval	CU
English	CU
French	CU
German	CU
Italian history and literature	—
Spanish	CU
Near East	CU
Middle East (chiefly India)	CU
Far East (Chinese)	CU
Far East (Japanese)	CU
World War I (1914–18)	CU
Genealogy	—
American newspapers	CU

Fine Arts

Fine arts (general)	—
Archaeology (classical)	CU
Architecture	—
City planning and housing	—
Music	—

Philosophy and Religion

Philosophy	CU
Religion	CU
Jewish history and literature	—

Social Sciences

Sociology	—
Education	CU
Negro	—
Political science	CU
International law and relations	CU
Law	CU

Economics

Economics (general)	CU
Business administration	—
Labor and industrial relations	CU
Public finance and taxation	CU
Public utilities	CU
Transportation	CU

Science

Mathematics	CU
Astronomy	CU
Meteorology	—
Physics	CU
Chemistry	CU
Chemical technology	CU
Biochemistry	—
Geology	CU
Geography	CU
Maps	CU
Botany	CU
Cytology and genetics	CU
Mycology and plant pathology	CU
Taxonomy	CU
Zoology	CU
Entomology	CU
Genetics (zoology)	CU
Anthropology and ethnology	CU
Medicine	—
Bacteriology	CU
Pharmacology	—
Psychology	CU

Technology

Patents	—
Engineering	CU
Aeronautics	—
Agriculture (general)	—
Horticulture	CU
Forestry	CU
Soil Science	—
Animal Science	—
Veterinary science	CU

Printing History

Incunabula	—
Printing	—

[1] Robert B. Downs, "Leading American Library Collections," *Library Quarterly*, XII (1942), 457–73.

RANK OF LIBRARIES

1st, Harvard
2nd, Library of Congress
3rd, California (Berkeley)
4th, Columbia
5th, Michigan (Univ.)
6th, New York Public
7th, Pennsylvania (Univ.)
8th, Chicago (Univ.)
9th, Yale
10th, Cornell
11th, Minnesota (Univ.)
12th, Princeton
13th, Illinois (Univ.)
14th, Stanford
15th, Duke
16th, Texas

17th, Boston Public
18th, New York Univ.
19th, Newberry
20th, Wisconsin (Univ.)
21st, North Carolina (Univ.)
22nd, Johns Hopkins
23rd, Washington (Univ. at Seattle)
24th, American Antiquarian Society
25th, Brown
26th, U. S. Department of Agriculture
27th, Cleveland Public
28th, Huntington
29th, Iowa State
30th, Ohio State
31st, John Crerar
32nd, Massachusetts Institute of
Technology

APPENDIX C

Members of the Regents' Committee on Library and Museum, 1900–09.

Anderson, Alden (Speaker of the Assembly)* 1900–01
Earl, Guy Chaffee 1902–04
Ellinwood, Charles Norman 1907–08
Hearst, Phoebe Apperson. 1908
Hyatt, Edward (State Superitendent of Public Instruction)* 1907–09
Kirk, Thomas J. (State Superintendent of Public Instruction)* 1900–07
McEnerney, Garret W. 1904–09
Slack, Charles W. 1900–02
Taussig, Rudolph J. (President, Mechanics
    Institute of San Francisco)* 1901–03, 1908–09
Wheeler, Charles S. 1903–07

* Ex officio member of the Board of Regents by virtue of position.

APPENDIX D

Members of the Regents' Library Committee, 1919–20, and Committee on Library, Research and Publications, 1920–38.

Bowles, Philip E. 1919–22
Brown, Everett J. (President, California Alumni Association)*....... 1928–30
Cochran, George I. 1922–38
Cooper, William John (State Superintendent of Public Instruction)* .. 1927–29
Dexter, Walter F. (State Superintendent of Public Instruction)*...... 1937–38
Earl, Guy Chaffee 1920–21
Gallwey, John 1932–38
Gregory, Warren (President, California Alumni Association)*........ 1920–22
Haskins, Samuel M. (President, California Alumni Association)*.... 1930–32
Hotchkiss, Preston (President, California Alumni Association)*.... 1934–36
Kersey, Vierling (State Superintendent of Public Instruction)*...... 1929–36
Mauzy, Byron (President, Mechanics Institute of San Francisco)*.... 1919–29
Merrill, Charles W. (President, California Alumni Association)*...... 1924–26
Miller, Clinton E. (President, California Alumni Association)* 1922–24
Mills, James 1919–20
Moffitt, James K. 1919–38
Olney, Warren (President, California Alumni Association)*......... 1932–34
Rowell, Chester H. 1920–38
von Geldern, Otto (President, Mechanics Institute of San Francisco)*.. 1929–32
Wangenheim, Julius (President, California Alumni Association)*.... 1926–28
Wheeler, Charles S. 1919–20
Wood, William C. (State Superintendent of Public Instruction)*...... 1920–27

* Ex officio member of the Board of Regents by virtue of position.

APPENDIX E

Members of the Library Committee of the Graduate Council, 1901–11, and of the Academic Senate, 1911–45.*

Adams, G. P. 1912–20, 1925–34
Bacon, L. 1920–21
Bell, C. H. 1922–23
Bolton, H. E. 1919–20
Boodberg, P. A. 1944–45
Bowman, J. N. 1909–10
Brady, R. A. 1933–35
Bray, W. C. 1916–17
Brenner, C. D. 1943–45
Brightfield, M. F. 1942–44
Broek, J. O. M. 1944–45
Bronson, B. H. 1932–34
Bukofzer, M. 1944–45
Camp, C. L. 1936–45
Chambers, S. A. 1906–07
Chinard, C. G. 1917–19
Clapp, E. B. 1901–02, 1903–07, 1908–14
Cline, J. M. 1937–39
Costigan, G. P. 1926–27
Cottrell, F. G. 1909–10
Daniels, J. F. 1925–31
Davis, A. R. 1931–38
Davis, H. E. 1937–39
DeFilippis, M. 1938–41
Dennes, W. R. 1935–36
Emeneau, M. B. 1941–44
Essig, E. O. 1938–44
Etcheverry, B. A. 1918–20
Evans, G. C. 1934–35
Ferguson, W. S. 1907–08
Flügel, F. 1927–30
Foster, A. S. 1941–43
Foulet, L. 1909–12
Gay, F. P. 1911–16, 1919–20
Gordon, A. E. 1944–45
Hart, W. M. 1910–11, 1917–18

Haskell, M. W. 1908–09
Hoagland, D. R. 1921–22
Holbrook, R. T. 1919–20
Holmes, S. J. 1920–25
Jenkins, F. A. 1943–44
Kerner, R. J. 1929–32
Knight, M. M. 1935–38
Kofoid, C. A. 1931–35
Kurtz, B. P. 1923–25
Landauer, C. 1938–39, 1940–45
Lange, A. F. 1901–02
Latimer, W. M. 1925–28
Lawson, A. C. 1902–06, 1908–11, 1912–18, 1919–23
Leake, C. D. 1936–40
Lehman, B. H. 1921–22, 1927–32, 1933–35
Lehmer, D. N. 1920–21
Lenzen, V. F. 1930–34
Lessing, F. 1936–38
Leupp, H. L. (ex officio) 1910–17, 1919–45
Lewis, E. P. 1901–02
Linforth, I. M. 1930–31
Lipman, C. P. 1919–20
McCormac, E. I. 1918–19, 1923–24
McDonald, J. H. 1919–20, 1921–24
McMurray, O. K. 1916–20
Matthew, W. D. 1928–30
Merrill, E. D. 1927–30
Miller, A. C. 1902–11, 1912–13
Mitchell, S. B. (ex officio) . . 1917–19
Mitchell, W. C. 1911–12
Nitze, W. A. 1908–09

* Terms of appointment were for the academic year, beginning in the fall semester and extending through the spring semester; the committee remained inactive during the summer months.

Noyes, G. R. 1907–09
O'Brien, M. P. 1933–34
Patrick, G. Z. 1935–36
Paxson, F. L. 1939–45
Pepper, S. C. 1936–37
Petersson, T. 1920–23
Plehn, C. C. 1901–02,
    1918–23
Prescott, H. W. 1907–08
Price, L. M. 1930–31
Priestley, H. I. 1936–37
Radin, M. 1924–26
Reed, H. S. 1943–45
Reukema, L. E. 1931–33
Richardson, L. J. 1911–20
Rollefson, G. K. 1934–36
Rowell, J. C. (ex officio) 1901–19
Russell, F. M. 1931–33
Rynin, D. 1943–44
Sait, E. M. 1923–24
Schaeffer, P. B. 1932–33
Schevill, R. 1912–16
Schilling, H. K. 1902–06,
    1908–09
Setchell, W. A. 1918–19,
    1922–23

Stephens, H. M. 1902–07,
    1908–09,
    1910–19
Stewart, G. R. 1935–37,
    1939–42
Stewart, T. D. 1936–37
Stratton, G. M. 1903–04,
    1909–12
Stringham, I. 1904–09
Strong, G. W. 1937–40
Taliaferro, N. L. 1944–45
Taylor, A. 1940–43
Taylor, A. E. 1906–08
Teggart, F. J. 1924–29,
    1934–35
Thompson, I. M. 1935–36
Thompson, J. W. 1933–36
Tolman, E. C. 1920–22
Van Dyke, E. C. 1924–25
Van Nostrand, J. J. 1937–39
Vaughan, H. H. 1923–25
Wells, C. W. 1909–10,
    1918–21
Whipple, T. K. 1925–27
White, H. E. 1941–43
Williams, H. 1940–43
Woods, B. M. 1934–35,
    1939–41

APPENDIX F

Publications issued in the "University of California Library Bulletin" series, 1880–1942.

No. 1. *List of Periodical Literature.* Sacramento: 1880. 29 pp. *Co-Operative of Periodical Literature.* 2d ed. Berkeley: 1892. 54 pp. *Co-Operative List of Periodical Literature in the Libraries of Central California.* 3d, enlarged ed. Berkeley: 1902. 130 pp.

No. 2. *Notes on Library Progress and Description of the Bacon Art and Library Building.* [Compiled by Joseph C. Rowell.] n.p.: 1881. 8 pp.

No. 3. *Catalogue of the Library presented by Henry D. Bacon.* Sacramento: 1882. 22 pp.

No. 4. *Catalogue of the Bacon Art Gallery.* Sacramento: 1882. 14 pp. 2d ed. Sacramento: 1892. 15 pp. 3d ed. Berkeley: 1898. 16 pp.

No. 5. *Catalogue of the Loan Book Exhibition, held at the University of California, Berkeley, May 26th to 31st, 1894.* Sacramento: 1884. 96 pp.

No. 6. *Photographs of Sculpture presented by John S. Hittell.* Berkeley: 1885. 22 pp.

No. 7. *Catalogue of the Theological Library presented by Andrew S. Hallidie.* Berkeley: 1886. 50 pp.

No. 8. Stoddard, Francis H. *References for Students of Miracle Plays and Mysteries.* Berkeley: 1887. 67, [1] pp. chart.

No. 9. *List of Printed Maps of California.* Berkeley: 1887. 33 pp.

No. 10. Cook, Albert S. *Cardinal Guala and the Vercilli Book.* Sacramento: 1888. 8 pp.

No. 11. Gayley, Charles Mills, and Fred Newton Scott. *A Guide to the Literature of Aesthetics.* Berkeley: 1890. 116 pp.

No. 12. Rowell, Joseph C. *Classification of Books in the Library.* Berkeley: 1894. 49 pp. *Classification of Books in the Library of the University of California.* 2d, partially enlarged, ed. Berkeley: 1915. [109], 46 pp.

No. 13. Bailey, Thomas P. *Bibliographical References in Ethnology.* Berkeley: 1899. 25 pp.

No. 14. [Rowell, Joseph C.] *Tentative Plan Proposed for a New Library Building for the University of California.* Berkeley: 1901. [4] pp., 4 diagrams.

No. 15. Dixon, James Main. *A Survey of Scottish Literature in the Nineteenth Century (with some References to the Eighteenth).* Berkeley: 1906. 53 pp.

No. 16. Pinger, W. R. R., compiler. *A List of First Editions and Other Rare Books in the Weinhold Library.* Berkeley: 1907. 143, [1] pp.

No. 17. Mead, H. Ralph, compiler. *A Bibliography of George Berkeley, Bishop of Cloyne.* Berkeley: 1910. 46 pp.

No. 18. *List of Serials in the University of California Library.* Berkeley: 1913. 266 pp.

No. 19. Hale, Carolyn L., and Mary H. Lathe, compilers. *A Union List of Selected Directories in the San Francisco Bay Region.* Berkeley: 1942. 26 pp.

INTERVIEWS

(Name and position of interviewee, and place and date of interview.)

Camp, Charles L. (Professor emeritus, University of California; former member and chairman of the Library Committee): Berkeley, Oct. 18, 1967.

Coney, Donald. (University librarian, University of California, Berkeley): Berkeley, Oct. 13, 1967.

Dornin, May R. (Former library staff member and archivist, University of California; also former student in the School of Librarianship): Berkeley, Aug. 22, 1967.

Frugé, Grete. (Lecturer, University of California School of Librarianship; also former student in the School of Librarianship): Berkeley, Aug. 31, 1967.

Henkle, Herman H. (Executive director, John Crerar Library; former library staff member, University of California; also former student in the School of Librarianship): Chicago, Oct. 5, 1967.

Higgins, Doris F. (Former library staff member and head of the Catalog Department, University of California; also former student in the School of Librarianship): Berkeley, Sept. 20, 1967.

Jaffa, Aileen. (Former library staff member and head of the Agriculture Library, University of California; also former student in the School of Librarianship): El Cerrito, Calif., Oct. 17, 1967.

Keller, Dorothy B. (Head, Acquisition Department, University of California Library): Berkeley, Oct. 16, 1967.

Lenzen, Victor F. (Professor emeritus, University of California; former member of the Library Committee): Berkeley, Oct. 26, 1967.

Leupp, Beulah C. (Widow of the late Harold L. Leupp): San Mateo, Calif., Oct. 21, 1967.

Leupp, Graham M. (Son of the late Harold L. Leupp): San Mateo, Calif., Oct. 21, 1967.

Lundy, Frank A. (Director of Libraries, University of Nebraska; former library staff member and head of the Accessions Department, University of California; also former student in the School of Librarianship): Lincoln, Neb., Oct. 2–3, 1967.

Nyholm, Jens. (Director of Libraries, Northwestern University; former assistant librarian, University of California): Evanston, Ill., Oct. 4, 1967.

Richards, John S. (Former library staff member and assistant librarian, University of California): Carmel, Calif., Sept. 29, 1967.

Stewart, George R. (Professor emeritus, University of California; former member of the Library Committee): Berkeley, Oct. 31, 1967.

Uridge, Margaret. (Head, Reference Department, University of California Library; also former student in the School of Librarianship): Berkeley, Dec. 21, 1967.

Wilcox, Grace G. (Librarian, Ridgewood, New Jersey, Public Library; widow of the late Jerome K. Wilcox, former assistant and associate librarian, University of California): Ridgewood, N. J., Oct. 6, 1967.

BIBLIOGRAPHY

The following bibliography includes only those sources relating directly to the University of California and its library.

REPORTS, MINUTES, FINANCIAL STATEMENTS, AND ORDERS

California. University. *Budgets.* 1911/12–1944/45. 34 printed statements in 11 vols. (CU Archives, Berkeley.)

———. *Financial Reports.* 1939/40–1944/45. 6 printed reports in 3 vols. (Contents: Reports of the Secretary and Treasurer of the Regents, and Reports of the Controller. CU Archives, Berkeley.)

California. University. Academic Council. *Minutes.* 1894–1915. Unpublished. Vols. IV (1894–1905)–VI (1913–15). (CU Office of the Academic Senate, Berkeley.)

California. University. Academic Senate. *Minutes.* 1915–1946. Unpublished. Vols. II (1915–20)–VII (1931–33); Series II, vols. I (1933–34)–VI (1943–46). (CU Office of the Academic Senate, Berkeley.)

California. University. Academic Senate. Library Committee. *Financial Statements.* 1902/03–1944/45. 43 four-page printed statements bound in one volume. (CU Archives, Berkeley.)

———. *Minutes.* 1910–1945. Unpublished. 2 vols. (Minute Book no. 2, 1910–21, and Minute Book no. 3, 1921–45, are continuations of Minute Book no. 1, of the Library Committee of the Graduate Council, 1901–10. CU Archives, Berkeley.)

———. *Reports.* 1920/21–1923/24, 1925/26–1942/43. 22 mimeographed reports bound in one volume. (CU Archives, Berkeley.)

California. University. Graduate Council. Library Committee. *Minutes.* 1901–10. Unpublished, 276 leaves. (Minute Book no. 1, of the Library Committee of the Graduate Council, 1901–10, continued by Minute Books no. 2 and 3, of the Library Committee of the Academic Senate, 1910–45. CU Archives, Berkeley.)

California. University. Library. *Biennial Report of the Catalog Department.* Unpublished; 1944/45–1945/46. 26 leaves. (CU Office of the University Librarian, Berkeley.)

———. *Reports of the Librarian.* 1875/76–1944. (1875/76–1884/85 in mss.; 1885/86–1909/10 extracted from the *Reports* of the Regents' Secretary; 1910/11–1929/30 reprinted from the annual and biennial *Reports* of the President; 1931–44 in typescript form. CU Archives, Berkeley.)

California. University. Library. Staff Association. *Minutes.* 1933–46. Unpublished. 1 vol. (Includes miscellaneous papers of the Staff Association, 1925–47. CU Archives, Berkeley.)

California. University. Library. Staff Council. *Minutes.* 1911–45. Unpublished. 2 vols. (CU Archives, Berkeley.)

California. University. President. *Reports.* 1868/69–1942/44. 28 vols. (Biennial and annual, varies. 1868/69 in mss.; 1869/70–1880 included in *Reports* of the Regents; 1881/82–1942/44 printed separately. CU Archives, Berkeley.)

California. University. Regents. *By-laws and Standing Orders*. Berkeley: 1938. 73 pp. Later revised editions: 1940, 43 pp.; 1952, 66 pp. (CU Archives, Berkeley.)

———. *Minutes*. 1898–1946. Unpublished. Vols. XII (1898–1900)–XXXVI (1945–46). (CU Office of Regents' Secretary, Berkeley.)

———. *Regents' Manual*. Berkeley: 1884. 256 pp. Later revised editions: 1904, 356 pp.; 1907, 444 pp.; 1911, 444+62 pp. (CU Archives, Berkeley.)

———. *Reports of the Secretary to the Board of Regents*. 1875–1938/39. 17 vols. (Annual except 1901–04; becomes *Financial Reports, 1939/40–1944/45.* CU Archives, Berkeley.)

California. University. Regents. Committee on Library and Museum. *Minutes*. 1881–1906. Unpublished. 2 vols. (Book no. 1, 1881–1905; Book no. 2, 1905–06. CU Office of Regents' Secretary, Berkeley.)

California. University. Regents. Committee on Library, Research and Publications. *Minutes*. 1920–22. Unpublished. 1 vol. (In addition to Minutes of Committee on Library, Research and Publications, also includes minutes of several other Regents' committees. CU Office of Regents' Secretary, Berkeley.)

Sproul, Robert Gordon. *Report of President Robert Gordon Sproul to the Regents of the University of California, September 18, 1942.* Mimeographed. 2 pp. (CU Archives, Berkeley.)

COMPILATIONS AND COLLECTIONS

California. University. *Descriptive Pamphlets*. 4 vols. (Contents: compilations of printed pamphlets, magazine articles, letters, addresses, and clippings on miscellaneous topics related to the University from 1869 through 1952. CU Archives, Berkeley.)

———. *Gifts Received*. 1892–97, 1923–47. 3 vols. (Contents: clippings from printed reports and lists of gifts received by the University. CU Archives, Berkeley.)

———. *Historical Pamphlets*. 6 vols. plus 1 box. (Contents: compilations and separate copies of clippings, pamphlets, and miscellaneous items related to the University both before and after 1900. CU Archives, Berkeley.)

———. *In Memoriam*. 1931–48. 3 vols. (Compilations of booklets printed annually or biennially, and containing brief biographical statements for faculty members deceased within the previous year or biennium. CU Archives, Berkeley.)

California. University. Controller. *Record of Donations Received by the University of California*. 1868–1950. 6 vols. ([Part I], 1868–1940, compiled 1941, 3 vols.; [Part II], 1940–50, compiled 1952, 3 vols. CU Office of Gifts and Endowments, Berkeley.)

California. University. Library. *Bancroft Library Miscellany, 1898–1949.* 1 vol. (Contents: compilation of reports, correspondence and papers related to the Bancroft Library. CU Archives, Berkeley.)

———. *Borrowing Privileges*. 1 file folder. (Contents: miscellaneous papers, reports, copies of regulations. CU Office of the University Librarian, Berkeley.)

———. *CU Anthology. A Collection of Evaluations which have been made of the Library Collections on the Berkeley Campus of the University of Cali-*

fornia. Compiled by Marion A. Milczewski for the Library Council. Unpublished; 1954. 24 leaves. (Contents: reports of evaluations made during the period 1935 through 1953. CU Archives, Berkeley.)

———. *CU Miscellany*. 2 boxes. (Contents: miscellaneous papers, reports, and correspondence related to the University library. CU Archives, Berkeley.)

———. *Catalog Department*. 1 box. (Contents: copies of classification schedules with notes, letters, reports, and miscellaneous papers pertaining to cataloging and classification activities. CU Archives, Berkeley.)

———. *Cebrián Gifts*. 1 box. (Contents: mss. and typescript lists of books given by Juan C. Cebrián to the library, 1912–26. CU Archives, Berkeley.)

———. *Correspondence and Papers*. 1878–1945. 46 cartons. (Contents: Rowell periodical index; correspondence relating to the planning and move into the Doe Library; bookplates; general correspondence, 1911–45; Leupp files, 1919–45. CU Archives, file series no. 12, Berkeley.)

———. [*Library*] *Handbooks, Orientation, etc.* 1 box. (Contents: library handbooks, guides, orientation booklets and leaflets, copies of library rules and regulations. CU Archives, Berkeley.)

———. *Library Miscellany*. 1915–56. 1 vol. (Contents: compilation of printed programs and copies of journal articles related to the library. CU Archives, Berkeley.)

———. *Library Scrap Books*. 1911–50. Unpublished. 2 vols. (Contents: clippings of newspaper articles related to the library; compiled and with notes by J. C. Rowell for the period through summer, 1936, and by May R. Dornin after 1936. CU Archives, Berkeley.)

———. *Morrison Library*. 1 box. (Contents: miscellaneous papers and pamphlets containing book reviews, descriptions of exhibits, and book lists. CU Archives, Berkeley.)

———. *Serials Department*. 1 box. (Contents: mimeographed lists of serials received at various times during the period 1936–60, and copies of departmental regulations. CU Archives, Berkeley.)

———. *University Library, Bacon + Doe Library, Historical Materials*. 1 box. (Contents: miscellaneous uncataloged programs, papers, clippings, booklets, etc. related to the University libraries. CU Archives, Berkeley.)

———. *University Library Exhibits*. 1 box. (Contents: notes, printed programs, and miscellaneous information related to library exhibits for the pre-1900 through 1945 period. CU Archives, Berkeley.)

California. University President. *Correspondence and Papers*. 1900–45. 610 cartons. (Indexes for these materials make possible access to papers pertaining to the library. CU Archives, file series no. 5, Berkeley.)

Lawson, Andrew C. *Correspondence and Papers*. 22 boxes, 14 cartons. (Bibliographical "key" to these materials makes possible access to papers pertaining to the library. Bancroft Library, file series no. 602, Berkeley.)

Leupp, Harold L. *Collected Writings*. 1923–43. 1 vol. (Contents: compilation of copies of six published articles written by Leupp. CU Archives, Berkeley.)

Mood, Fulmer. *Survey of the Libraries of the University of California, 1945–48*. 4 cartons. (Contents: notes of interviews and collection inventories, correspondence, ms. copies of drafts for final report. CU Archives, file series no. 5.55, Berkeley.)

Rowell, Joseph C. *Correspondence and Papers.* 1887–1935. 3 boxes. (Contents: scrapbooks, letters, clippings and pictures, record of visit to libraries in the East, 1875, with notes, and papers pertaining to the acquisition of the Bancroft Library. Bancroft Library, file series no. 419, Berkeley.)

———. *Letter Books.* 1878–1907. 15 vols. (Contents: original, carbon, and mimeographed copies of librarian's correspondence and papers. CU Archives, Berkeley.)

———. *Writings.* 1880–1920. Unpublished. 3 vols. (Contents: compilations of Rowell mss. and copies of published articles. CU Archives, Berkeley.)

MISCELLANEOUS PAPERS, DOCUMENTS, AND STUDIES

Appel, Leslie H., and J. A. Arnott. *Study of the Illumination of the Main Reading Room of the Doe Library.* Unpublished B.M.E. thesis. University of California, 1912. 16 leaves. (CU Archives, Berkeley.)

California. University. *Green Pastures of the Mind.* University Explorer series, no. 843. Mimeographed; 1944. 5 leaves. (Copy of script used for radio broadcast on Sunday, Apr. 23, 1944, describing the Morrison Memorial Library and its service to men in uniform during World War II; Clara Stow Douglas, informant. CU Archives, Berkeley.)

———. *Library on a Spool.* University Explorer series, no. 914. Mimeographed; 1945. 5 leaves. (Copy of script used for radio broadcast on Sunday, Sept. 16, 1945, describing the photographic service at the University library; Elinor Hand Hickox, informant. CU Archives, Berkeley.)

———. *Sidelights on a Saint.* University Explorer series, no. 89. Mimeographed; 1935. 7 leaves. (Copy of script used for radio broadcast on Tuesday, Aug. 20, 1935, describing Irish mss. and illuminations in the University library; Professor Douglas Chrétien, informant. CU Archives, Berkeley.)

———. *Volumes for Victory.* University Explorer series, no. 835. Mimeographed; 1944. 5 leaves. (Copy of script used for radio broadcast on Sunday, Feb. 27, 1944, describing reference service provided by the University library for war needs; Bess Lowry and Jerome K. Wilcox, informants. CU Archives, Berkeley.)

California. University. Library. *Current Periodical Subscriptions, 1912–1913.* Unpublished; [1914]. 102 leaves (Contents: lists of periodicals currently received, and name of agent and subscription price for each title. CU Archives, Berkeley.)

———. *Division of the Catalog.* Unpublished. 2 pp. (Provides description of method used to divide the public catalog in 1938. Originally undated and unsigned; date of April 21, 1947, and signature of Doris Higgins added with memo at top of p. 1. CU Office of the Catalog Department of the Library, Berkeley.)

———. *How Not to Use the Library; An Exhibit of Mutilated Books.* 1937. 1 case. (Contents: 10 mounted photographs with texts prepared by Peyton Hurt, Enid Tanner, and Amy Wood, for exhibit March 1–15, 1937. CU Archives, Berkeley.)

———. *The Kiang Chinese Library as Described by S. C. Kiang Kang-Hu.* Unpublished; [1919]. 3 leaves. (CU Archives, Berkeley.)

———. *Library Historical and Descriptive Documents.* Unpublished; [1875–

1935]. 25 leaves. (Contents: mss. and typescript copies of four papers and one letter related to the early history of the library. CU Archives, Berkeley.)
———. *Volumes in the Libraries of the University of California, 1 July 1945.* Mimeographed; February 1946. 1 p. (CU Archives, Berkeley.)
California. University. Library. Staff Association. *Constitution of the Staff Association of the University of California [Library].* Unpublished; [1933]. 4 leaves. (By-laws appended to copy of Constitution, [1936]. 2 leaves. CU Archives, Berkeley.)
———. *Papers Read before the Staff Association of the University of California Library.* Unpublished; [1934–44]. 1 folder. (Contents: typescript copies of papers read by staff members. CU Archives, Berkeley.)
———. *Staff Association Celebration of Library Silver Jubilee, 1910–1935.* Unpublished; 1935. 23 leaves. (Contents: transcripts of reminiscences by Joseph C. Rowell, Harold L. Leupp, and May R. Dornin. Bancroft Library, file series no. 419, Berkeley.)
———. *Staff Manual.* Unpublished; 1936. 121 leaves. (CU Archives, Berkeley.)
California. University. Regents. *Library Rules of the University of California.* Sacramento: 1887. 6 pp. Revised edition: 1893. 3 pp. (CU Archives, Berkeley.)
California University. Registrar. *Student Enrollment, Degrees Conferred, 1869 to 1945/46.* Statistical Addenda, Part II, October, 1946. Berkeley: 1946. 33 pp. (CU Archives, Berkeley.)
Coney, Donald. *Rowell of California.* Unpublished; [1954]. 24 leaves. (CU Archives, Berkeley.)
Farrier, George F. *The University of California Library Postwar Building Program.* Unpublished M.A. in Librarianship thesis. University of California, 1945. 84 leaves.
Halvorson, Homer. *A Study of the Library Needs of the English Department of the University of California.* Unpublished M.A. in Librarianship thesis. University of California, 1934. 51 leaves.
Hurt, Peyton. *Use of the Library by Graduate Students; A Study of Their Ability, Instruction, Frequency of Use, and Desire for Instruction.* Unpublished; [1933]. 96 leaves + 15 pp. (CU Archives, Berkeley.)
Merritt, Ralph P. *After Me Cometh a Builder: the Recollections of Ralph Palmer Merritt.* Unpublished; 1962. 140 leaves. (Typescript of tape-recorded interviews conducted by Corinne S. Gilb in 1956 for the Regional Cultural History Project, University of California, and used by permission. Bancroft Library, Berkeley.)
Mood, Fulmer. *A Survey of the Library Resources of the University of California: Berkeley, La Jolla, Los Angeles, Mt. Hamilton, Riverside, San Francisco and Santa Barbara.* Berkeley: Library Photographic Service, 1950. 2 vols., photocopy of typescript. (CU Library, Berkeley.)
Multhauf, Robert P. *History of Science Collections in the Library of the University of California, Berkeley, with Comparative Evaluations of Other Libraries in the San Francisco Bay Area.* [Berkeley], University of California General Library, 1953. 77 leaves. (CU Archives, Berkeley.)
Rowell, Joseph C. *The Beginnings of a Great Library: Reminiscences by Joseph C. Rowell.* Unpublished; 1938, 23 leaves. (CU Archives, Berkeley.)

Smith, Dora. *History of the University of California Library to 1900.* Unpublished M.A. in Librarianship thesis. University of California, 1930. 168 + 40 leaves.

Stephens, Henry Morse. *The Bancroft Library: Remarks by Professor H. Morse Stephens before the California Library Association, Feb. 27, 1906.* Unpublished; 1906. 4 leaves. (Typescript copy of address included in the Henry Morse Stephens papers. Bancroft Library, file series no. 926, Berkeley.)

Stevens, Frank C. *Forty Years in the Office of the President, University of California, 1905–1945.* Unpublished; 1959. 187 leaves. (Typescript of tape-recorded interviews conducted by Amelia Roberts Fry for the Regional Cultural History Project, University of California, and used by permission. Bancroft Library, Berkeley.)

Whitney, C. Mason. *Architectural Development of the University of California.* Unpublished; 1934. 2 vols. (Includes descriptive information on the Doe Library. CU Archives, Berkeley.)

BOOKS

California. University. *Brief History of the University of California.* [Berkeley: 1966]. 61 pp. (Prepared by the Office of University Relations.)

———. *The Centennial Record of the University of California.* Edited by Verne A. Stadtman. Berkeley: University of California, 1967. 586 pp.

California. University. Library. *Book Plates of the University of California.* [Berkeley]: 1936. 101 pp.

———. *Catalogue of the Loan Book Exhibition Held at the University of California, Berkeley, May 26th to 31st, 1894.* University of California Library Bulletin, no. 5. Sacramento: 1884. 96 pp.

———. *Cooperative List of Periodical Literature.* University of California Library Bulletin, no. 1. 2d ed. Berkeley: 1892. 54 pp.

———. *Cooperative List of Periodical Literature in Libraries of Central California.* University of California Library Bulletin, no. 1. 3d, enlarged ed. Berkeley: 1902. 130 pp.

———. *List of Periodical Literature.* University of California Library Bulletin, no. 1. Sacramento: 1880. 29 pp.

———. *Spain and Spanish America in the Libraries of the University of California, A Catalogue of Books.* Berkeley: 1928–30. 2 vols. (Contents: vol. 1, the General and Departmental Libraries, compiled by Alice I. Lyser; vol. 2, the Bancroft Library, compiled by Eleanor Ashby; initiative and financial assistance for publications provided by Juan C. Cebrián.)

Ferrier, William Warren. *Origin and Development of the University of California.* Berkeley: Sather Gate Book Shop, [1930]. 710 pp.

Fitzgibbon, Russell H. *Libraries of the University of California.* Berkeley: [University of California], 1965. 92 pp. (Provides brief historical and descriptive sketches of libraries on all campuses of the University.)

Jones, William Carey. *Illustrated History of the University of California . . . 1868–95.* San Francisco: F. H. Dukesmith, 1895. 413 pp.

Kurtz, Benjamin P. *Joseph Cummings Rowell, 1853–1938.* [Berkeley: University of California Press, 1939.] 60 pp.

Mitchell, Sydney B. *Mitchell of California; the Memoirs of Sydney B. Mitchell,*

Librarian, Teacher, Gardener. [Edited and] with a preface by Lawrence Clark Powell. Berkeley: California Library Association, 1960. 263 pp.

Pettitt, George A. *Twenty-eight Years in the Life of a University President*. Berkeley: University of California, 1966. 254 pp. (An account of the Presidency of Robert Gordon Sproul, including excerpts from his addresses and writings.)

Rowell, Joseph C. *Classification of Books in the Library*. University of California Library Bulletin, no. 12. Berkeley: 1894. 49 pp.

———. *Classification of Books in the Library of the University of California*. University of California Library Bulletin, no. 12. 2d, partially enlarged, ed. Berkeley: 1915. [109], 46 pp.

Sibley, Robert, ed. *The Romance of the University of California*. San Francisco: H. S. Crocker Co., for the University of California Alumni Association, 1928. 59 pp.

Towle, Katherine A. *The University: An Introduction to the Berkeley Campus*. [Berkeley]: 1936. 62 pp. (Printed as *University of California Bulletin*, XXX: 4, [1936] entire issue; provides a brief summary history of the University to 1936, and a description of rules, regulations, courses, student life, and activities.)

Wheeler, Benjamin Ide. *The Abundant Life*. Edited by Monroe E. Deutsch. Berkeley: University of California, 1926. 385 pp. (Contains excerpts from Wheeler's addresses and writings during his years as University President.)

PAMPHLETS

Bumstead, Frank M. *The Use of the Library*. Berkeley: University of California Press, [1921]. 36 pp.

California. University. Library. *Dedication of the Library*. [Berkeley: 1912]. 29 pp. (Provides descriptive information about the Doe Library and addresses delivered at the dedication; reprinted from *University of California Chronicle,* XIV (1912), 332–58. CU Archives, Berkeley.)

———. *The Dedication of the Library of French Thought ... at the University of California, on September 6 (Lafayette Day), 1917; to which is added a Brief Description of the Collection*. Berkeley: 1918. 36 pp.

———. *Exhibition of First Editions of Epochal Achievement in the History of Science . . . on Display at the University Library*. Berkeley: University of California Press, 1934. 48 pp.

———. *Handbook for New Students*. Berkeley: 1934. 26 pp. (Contents: general descriptive information, rules and regulations, library hours, etc.) [revised]. Berkeley: 1936. 24 pp. [revised]. Berkeley: 1937. 24 pp. [revised]. Berkeley: 1939. 24 pp. [revised]. Berkeley: 1941. 25 pp. (CU Archives, Berkeley.)

———. *Laying the Corner-stone of the Doe Memorial Library*. [Berkeley: 1909]. [6] pp. (Contains addresses delivered at the corner stone laying ceremony; reprinted from the *University of California Chronicle,* XI (1909), 45–50. CU Archives, Berkeley.)

———. *Library Handbook, 1918–1919*. Berkeley: [1919]. 39 pp. (Contents: general descriptive information, rules and regulations, library hours, etc. CU Archives, Berkeley.)

———. *Library of the University of California: Subject Guide.* Berkeley: 1888. 22 pp. (CU Archives, Berkeley.)

———. *Notes on Library Progress and Description of the Bacon Art and Library Building.* [Compiled by Joseph C. Rowell.] University of California Library Bulletin, no. 2. n.p.: 1881. 8 pp.

———. *Presentation of the Commendatore M. J. Fontana Library to the University of California, Thursday, May 29, 1924.* Berkeley: [1924]. [4] pp.

———. *University Library.* Berkeley: 1915. 7 pp. (Contents: biographical sketch of Charles Franklin Doe, description of the Doe Library, and general statistics of the library. CU Archives, Berkeley.)

Hurt, Peyton. *The University Library and Undergraduate Instruction.* Berkeley: University of California Press, 1936. 42 pp.

[Rowell, Joseph C.] *Tentative Plan Proposed for a New Library Building for the University of California.* University of California Library Bulletin, no. 14. Berkeley: 1901. [4] pp. (Includes 4 diagrams by Rowell of floor plans for the proposed new library.)

Sproul, Robert Gordon. *Inaugural Address of Robert Gordon Sproul as President of the University [of California], October 22, 1930.* Berkeley: [University of California], 1930. 29 pp.

ARTICLES

Anderson, Otillia C. "A University Library Reviews Its Map Collection; the Cataloger's Point of View," *Library Journal,* LXX (1945), 103–6.

Backus, Jean. "World War II Research; the Library's Wartime Collection is Surveyed," *California Monthly,* XLIX (1942), 22–3, 38–40.

Bolton, Herbert E. "The Bancroft Collection at Berkeley, California," *Library Journal,* XLIV (1919), 227.

Branch, Nelle U. "The Agricultural Libraries of the University of California," *American Library Association Bulletin,* XXIV (1930), 377–9.

Brown, Charles H. "Harold L. Leupp, Administrator," *College and Research Libraries,* VI (1945), 353–4.

Coney, Donald, and Julian G. Michel. "The Berkeley Library of the University of California: Some Notes on Its Formation," *Library Trends,* XV (1966), 286–302.

Coney, Donald. "The University Library," *California Monthly,* LXIII (1953), 26, 41–6.

Coulter, Edith M., and Christine Price. "Classification of University Library Personnel," *Library Journal,* LII (1927), 661–2.

Cutter, Charles A. "[Review of] Rowell Classification," *Library Journal,* XX (1895), 214–5.

Dornin, May R. "The A. F. Morrison Memorial Library at the University of California," *American Library Association Bulletin,* XXIV (1930), 413.

Douglas, Clara Stow. "A University Browsing Library before the War and Now," *Library Journal,* LXIX (1944), 1083–5.

Hand, Elinor. See [Hickox], Elinor Hand.

"Harold L. Leupp and the University of California Library," *California Library Association Bulletin,* VII (1945–46), 28.

Haverland, Della B. "Joseph Cummings Rowell," *Pacific Bindery Talk,* VII (1935), 151–4.

[Hickox], Elinor Hand. "A Cost Survey in a University Library," *American Library Association Bulletin,* XXIV (1930), 411–2.

Hickox, Elinor Hand. "University's Photographic Service in Peace and War," *Library Journal,* LXX (1945), 730–3.

Higgins, Doris F. "Catalog Adviser Service at California," *College and Research Libraries,* VII (1946), 64–6.

Hurt, Peyton. "The Need of College and University Instruction in the Use of the Library," *Library Quarterly,* IV (1934), 436–48. (A condensation of his study, *Use of the Library by Graduate Students.*)

Leupp, Harold L. "The Cost Survey of the University of California Library," *College and Reference Library Yearbook,* III (1931), 85–93.

———. "Joseph Cummings Rowell," *Library Journal,* LXIV (1939), 286.

———. "Library Service on the Berkeley Campus, University of California," *College and Research Libraries,* IV (1943), 212–7, 232.

———. "The Library the Heart of the University," *Library Journal,* XLIX (1924), 619–22.

———. "Moving the University of California Library," *Library Journal,* XXXVI (1911), 458–60.

———. "Service Charge for Interlibrary Loans," *Library Journal,* LVIII (1933), 791.

Lowry, Bess. "Reference Work and the War," *College and Research Libraries,* V (1944), 331–4.

MacIver, Ivander. "The Exchange of Publications as a Medium for the Development of the Book Collection," *Library Quarterly,* VIII (1938), 491–502.

———. "Gift and Exchange Division in Wartime," *College and Research Libraries,* VI (1944), 35–7.

———. "The Round Table: Year's Study of Exchange," *Library Journal,* LIX (1934), 168–9.

Morrow, Irving F. "Recent Work at the University of California," *Architect and Engineer,* L (1917), 39–49.

[Nyholm], Amy F. Wood. "California Divides Its Catalog," *Library Journal,* LXIII (1938), 723–6.

Nyholm, Amy [F.] Wood. "California Examines Its Divided Catalog," *College and Research Libraries,* IX (1948), 195–201.

[Nyholm], Amy F. Wood. "Four and Twenty Years After; A.L.A. Returns to the University of California," *Library Journal,* LXIV (1939), 486–9.

Pettitt, George A. "Library Honors," *California Monthly,* XLIX (1942), 21, 44.

Priestley, Herbert I. "History on File," *Saturday Review,* XXVI (Oct. 30, 1943), 18–9. (Description of the Bancroft Library, Berkeley.)

———. "Manuscript Collections in the Bancroft Library," in American Library Association Committee on Archives and Libraries, *Archives and Libraries.* Chicago: American Library Association, 1939. pp. 64–70.

Richards, John S. "The Rental Service in the University of California Library," *Library Journal,* LVI (1931), 795–6.

Rowell, Joseph C. "Departmental Libraries of the University of California." *Library Journal,* XLI (1916), 710.

———. "Union Catalogs and Repertories: University of California," *Library Journal,* XXXVII (1912), 494.

———. "The University of California Library," *Public Libraries,* IV (1899), 212–3.

Schilling, Hugo Karl. "The Weinhold Library," *University of California Chronicle,* VIII (1905), 144–50.

Sproul, Robert Gordon. "The Place of the Library in Higher Education," *American Library Association Bulletin,* XXIV (1930), 332–8.

Steedman, Helen E. "The Effect of the War on the Loan and Shelf Division of the University of California Library," *College and Research Libraries,* V (1944), 203–6.

Tanner, Enid F. "Rental Service," *Library Journal,* LX (1935), 674–5.

Teggart, Richard V. "A University Library Reviews Its Map Collection," *Library Journal,* LXIX (1944), 1040–2.

Thompson, Lawrence S. "Necrology: Harold L. Leupp," *College and Research Libraries,* XIII (1952), 271.

"U. C. School of Librarianship," *Pacific Bindery Talk,* IX (1937), 125.

"University of California Library of French Thought," *Library Journal,* XLIII (1918), 408.

Wilcox, Jerome K. "Documents Division in World War II," *College and Research Libraries,* VI (1945), 108–11.

Williams, Edwin E. "The Library Looks Across the Pacific," *California Monthly,* XXXV (1935), 18. (Description of the Kiang Chinese collection in the University library.)

———. "News—One Hundred Years Old," *California Monthly,* XXXVI (1936), 22–4, 41–2. (Description of the Clerbois newspaper collection in the University library.)

Wood, Amy F. See [Nyholm], Amy F. Wood.

NEWSPAPERS AND JOURNALS

Daily Californian (University of California student newspaper). Sept. 12, 1904; Aug. 24, 1915; Feb. 12, 1919; Oct. 17, 1919; Nov. 5, 1924; Nov. 13, 1924; Sept. 13, 1929; Sept. 23, 1929; Jan. 16–20, 1933; Apr. 24, 1940 (supplement); Aug. 30, 1943.

Faculty Bulletin (University of California). Vol. V (1936).

News Notes of California Libraries. Vol. I (1906); Vol. XXV (1930) ;Vol. XXX (1935); Vol. XLI (1946).

University of California Chronicle. Vols. I (1898); III (1900); V (1903); VI (1904); VIII (1906); IX (1907); X (1908); XI (1909); XII (1910); XIII (1911); XIV (1912); XV (1913); XVI (1914); XVII (1915); XIX (1917).

INDEX

Abbott, M. Jessamine, 64, 144, 145
Academy of Pacific Coast History, 146
Accessions Department, 20–21, 110, 112
Acquisitions: sources of volumes added (1910–1940), 6; faculty purchases, 22–23; en bloc collections, 23–33 *passim*
Adams, George P., 78, 105, 175
Administration: participation of Regents in, 68–69; library government, 103–109 *passim;* library rules, 103–104; librarian's authority, 103–104, 105–106; faculty proposal for library reorganization, 105–107; internal organization, 109–113; comparison with other libraries, 113; organization chart, 114
Administrative Committee on University Library, 99. *See also* Library Committee
Agriculture Library, 6, 148, 168
Agriculture Reference Service, 111
American Library Association, 167
Archives, 158
Ashby, Eleanor, 81

Bacon, Henry Douglas, 79, 84
Bacon Library: description of, 84; cost, 84; lighting, 85; alternations and addition, 85; evaluation of, 86; demolition of, 86
Bancroft Library, 15, 146–147; volumes (1945), 6; acquisition of, 24–25; Rowell's efforts to acquire 44–45; original location in Doe building, 91; re-location to fourth floor, 95, 147
Barrows, David Prescott, 71–72, 124, 143
Bender, Albert M., 32, 57, 81, 168; and Friends, collection, 81
Berkeley Bible Seminary, 171
Binding, 33–34; Department, 110; Service, 112, 113; appropriations for, 179
Biology Library, 6, 111, 144–145
Boalt Hall, library. *See* Law Library
Boehtlingk, A. A., collection, 33
Bolton, Herbert E., 23, 146, 147
Bonté, Fannie, 42, 109
Book collection, 5, 6, 38–39, 177, 183–184
Book funds: amounts and rate of growth, 6–7; allocation of, 9–10; General Interest Fund, 11; Librarian's Fund, 11; during Wheeler's administration, 70; during Barrows' administration, 72; during Campbell's administration, 72; during Sproul's administration, 74; statistics, 178, 179
Book selection: by faculty, 8–11 *passim;* by

librarian, 11; by staff, 11–12; policies, 12, 16, 18–19; report of Survey Committee, 16–18; appointment of bibliographer, 21–22
Borrowing privileges. *See* Circulation
Boston Evening Transcript, 31
Boyce, G. D., 165
Branch libraries, 143–145
Brayton Hall, 83
Bronson, B. H., 23
Brough, Kenneth J., 169–170, 172
Brown, Arthur, 99
Brown, Charles H., 39–40
Bumstead, Frank M., 20, 53, 63, 110, 167
Burdach-Bremer collection, 31–32, 132
Bureau of Public Administration library, 6, 147
Burt, Lillian, 110

Cajori, Florian, collection, 30
California Academy of Science library, 159
California State Library, 159, 160
Californiana collecting, 15
Camp, Charles L., 78, 175
Campbell, William Wallace, 72–73
Carpentier, Horace W., 7
Case B collection, 158
Case M collection, 158
Case O collection, 157–158
Case R collection, 158
Catalog Advisory Service, 163
Catalog Department, 110, 112, 163
Cataloging: use of Rowell classification, 126–128; use of printed cards, 127–128; reclassification to Library of Congress system, 128–133; dictionary catalog begun, 131; public catalogs described, 136; division of catalog, 136–137; card reproduction methods, 138; arrearages, 138; filing arrangements, 138
Cébrian, Juan C., 80–81, 167
Chambers, Samuel A., 22
Circulation: regulations before 1900, 150–151; regulations followed in Doe Library, 151–152; regulations for faculty, 151–152, 154; fines, 152–153; statistics, 153, 182; comparison with other institutions, 153; book losses, 153; borrowing privileges, 171–172
Clapp, Edward B., 77
Clark, George, 23, 45, 59
Clerbois, Léon, newspaper collection, 31

MANAGEMENT
BY
MULTIPLE
OBJECTIVES

MANAGEMENT BY MULTIPLE OBJECTIVES

Sang M. Lee

PBI

a petrocelli book

new york / princeton

1 2 3 4 5 6 7 8 9 10

Typesetting by Backes Graphics
Designed by Diane L. Backes

Library of Congress Cataloging in Publication Data

Lee, Sang M., 1939–
    Management by multiple objectives.

    Includes bibliographical references and index.
    1. Management by objectives. I. Title.
HD30.65.L43   658.4'012   81-10516
ISBN 0-89433-083-7   AACR2

7066490

To my parents with love

CONTENTS

Preface

This book is about a modern management approach. Management by multiple objectives is a new way to integrate management systems and modern management technologies in order to achieve multiple and often conflicting organizational objectives. This book attempts to provide a basic understanding of underlying concepts, techniques, and resources required to design and implement an effective MBMO system in organizations. It presents ideas and approaches based on management theories, management science modeling methodology, computer science applications, and most recent research findings on managerial economics.

Management functions have increased in both complexity and magnitude over the past thirty years. This change has been due, in large part, to a drastic change in the nature of management and the environment within which it operates. While organizations have become much larger and more complex, management functions have become more specialized. Natural resources and key materials required for operations have become increasingly scarce, forcing managers to evaluate action alternatives more carefully while considering environmental constraints. Ecology and pollution control have become household words, the Middle East crisis and Persian Gulf oil supply have been more than merely international news, and government regulations and consumer groups have began to exert greater impact on organizations.

As managers have increasingly been held accountable for the achievement of key organizational objectives, not only to stockholders but also to other outside interest groups, they have looked for more sophisticated approaches to the analysis of complex management systems. Consequently, we have seen a wide popularity of the traditional MBO concept. Many organizations have tried MBO with varying degrees of success. One of the important reasons for the less than expected success of the fine concept of MBO is the lack of analytical approaches to consider multiple and conflicting objectives. MBMO utilizes the most current management science and computer-based approaches to management by multiple objectives.

There are numerous books on MBO. Most of these books can be classified into two broad categories: popular practitioner-orientated books that are interesting to read but offer nothing really new to competent managers, and comprehensive theoretical texts that deal primarily with behavioral implications of MBO. I have attempted to write a book which is interesting yet presents new concepts and approaches for multiple-objective decision making.

This book is directed to those who aspire to become effective managers and staff specialists. It can be used as a text or a reference book by students of business, public administration, social sciences, and engineering. It can also be used as a reference or training handbook by practicing managers and staff personnel.

This book has three parts and nine chapters. Part I presents the conceptual framework of MBMO. It consists of two chapters: chapter 1 is on introduction to MBMO and modern management, and chapter 2 is devoted to the MBMO process. Part II examines various elements of MBMO. Chapter 3 discusses the formulation process of long-range goals and strategic plans. Chapter 4 presents formulation of multiple organizational objectives. Chapter 5 is devoted to formulating operational objectives, while chapter 6 provides formulation of action plans. Chapter 7 is concerned with the problems associated with implementation of the MBMO system, and, finally, chapter 8 presents the review, evaluation, and control to close the MBMO loop. Part III examines the future of MBMO. Chapter 9 discusses advantages, limitations, pitfalls, and the future of MBMO.

This book is based on my previous 13 books and some 130 research articles on management decision making. In writing the book, I have relied heavily on suggestions and criticism of my colleagues and students. I have benefited a great deal from suggestions made by my colleagues Lester Digman and Fred Luthans of the University of Nebraska-Lincoln and a good friend Edison Diest of Wadsworth Publishers who read the manuscript many times. I also express my sincere thanks to my office staff, Joyce Anderson, Jane Chrastil, Cindy Knuth, Cindy Gnirk, and Angela Sullivan, for their expert typing.

Finally, I express my love to my family, especially my daughters Tosca and Amy, for their many lost evenings. Perhaps now I can say yes when the girls ask me "can you play a game with us now?"

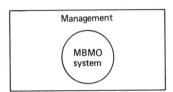

Part I: Introduction to Management by Multiple Objectives (MBMO)

Part I will provide the conceptual framework of management by multiple objectives. It presents the general background concerning the definition, functions, approaches of management, and how they fit into the process of management by multiple objectives.

Part I consists of two chapters. Chapter 1 is an introduction to MBMO and modern management. Chapter 2 presents the MBMO as a management system.

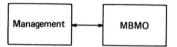

1

Introduction to MBMO and Management

This book is about management. It is about a management concept, philosophy, and style that has been quite widely accepted by scholars, practicing managers, administrators, and consultants during the past twenty years. Management by objectives (MBO) has been accepted by many as a pragmatic and effective management approach. Many organizations, both public and private, have applied or integrated some features of MBO to their management functions with varying degrees of success. We have seen some flowery accolades as well as harsh criticisms of the approach.

Like any other management concept, MBO comes in various names, emphases, formulations, and processes. Scholars and consultants have developed comprehensive packages (books, brochures, training aids, films, etc.) and sold the generic approach under many different variations. Some of the popular variations, in addition to "management by objectives," have been "administration by objectives," "individual goal-setting," "management by objectives and results," "planning-programming-budgeting system (PPBS)," "zero-base budgeting," and "management by objectives and priorities." In most cases, the MBO approach is applied for a better overall management performance, a better performance appraisal of employees, more effective planning and decision making, a better organized training and development program, a more effective motivational and incentive system, or a means to increase the level of employee participation in the management process.

Management by objectives is generally accepted as a sound normative approach to management by academicians, practicing managers, and consultants. The basic theory of MBO is that the *best way to manage things is to involve people in setting objectives and then direct needed resources toward them in an organized manner*. It is a simple but powerful management approach. The basic problem with MBO is not in its concept but in its weakness as a functional system. It has been more of a philosophy than a system. In other words, thus far MBO as a management approach has not been self-contained as an operational system that could be implemented. There have been numerous books that describe the basic philosophy and concept of MBO in general terms. There have also been numerous "how to" kits and packages about the MBO process. However, most of these publications are simply a detailed outline of the MBO concept. For example, some popular books on MBO go even so far as to define the formulation process of an objective as "to (an action plan here for a single key criterion) by (a target date for accomplishment here) with (a specified maximum resource requirement here)" without even suggesting any analysis of the relationships among inputs (resource requirements), outputs (objective attainment), time dimensions, uncertainties, ramifications of such an MBO program for other components of the organization, etc.

A major weakness of the MBO process resides in the methodological area—pulling all the relevant parts together in a systematic way to achieve the basic goal of MBO. Thus, frequently the MBO implementation process becomes an exercise of listing wishful thinking, generating self-protective paper work, and creating an unmanageable mishmash. Undoubtedly, we can say that the MBO implementation process provides an opportunity for everyone in the organization to gain a broader insight about the functions and interrelations among various departments and personnel. However, such a secondary benefit without the achievement of the primary purpose may not warrant the efforts, resources, and organizational turmoil usually required of an MBO implementation process.

The author believes the essence of management is decision making to achieve desired results. With or without systematic analysis, the decision maker utilizes a process which transforms relevant data into useful information for action. As we try to make the MBO process comprehensive and effective, it inevitably involves the systems approach. A system is a whole composed of a set of components with certain relationships among the components and their attributes that serve to perform a function. The MBO process can likewise be viewed as a system that has various components, and relationships among these components, along with a set of objective criteria in

order to improve organizational effectiveness.
process as a system presents us not only with
importantly, with a methodology for practical i
book is intended to develop the management b
(MBMO) process as a functional system.

Another important weakness of the traditional MBO approach is
its total neglect of multiple and often conflicting objectives involved in real-world situations. Treatment of multiple objectives that
compete for organizational resources is not as simple as the MBO
approach contends. For example, it is almost a futile and useless
exercise to develop an objective such as "to increase profit by 5
percent this fiscal year" without analyzing other objectives that conflict with the profit objective in terms of trade-offs, resource requirements, and priorities. A functional MBO system must be capable of performing a systematic analysis of multiple objectives.
Recent research in the field of management science provides us
with that capability.

MBMO is a modern management system that employs systematic
approaches to set multiple organizational objectives and develop
activity plans to direct needed resources toward them in an organized manner. The features that distinguish MBMO from the traditional MBO approach are (1) it employs a system-orientated methodological approach; (2) it explicitly analyzes multiple conflicting
organizational objectives; (3) it utilizes the most current technical
(information systems, management science, and computer-based
modeling techniques) and technological (interactive and simulation-
based decision making with the aid of computers) approaches.

There is no one right way to develop and implement MBMO, as
there is no one best way to manage all organizations. The appropriate MBMO approach depends upon the particular curcumstances
and conditions under which the organization functions. Thus, the
objective of this book is to provide the basic knowledge and understanding required to implement MBMO in any organization—
private business firms, government agencies, or nonprofit organizations. This book is intended to develop the MBMO process as a
self-contained management system that could be implemented in
real-world situations.

Part I provides an overview of the conceptual framework of the
MBMO system in the management context. Chapter 1 introduces

e reader to MBMO and its roles in modern management concepts. Chapter 2 outlines the system of MBMO with all of its major components and their relationships.

Part II deals with each major component of the MBMO system in greater detail and depth, with emphasis on the practical implementation of the system. Chapter 3 presents the importance of long-range goals and strategic plans to organizations. Chapter 4 discusses the formulation and analysis of multiple objectives. Chapter 5 provides an insight into the formulation of operational objectives. Chapter 6 is devoted to the formulation of action plans. Chapter 7 presents the implementation phase of the MBMO system. Chapter 8 discusses the final phase of the MBMO process—review, evaluation, and control.

Part III examines some practical problems to be anticipated in the MBMO system implementation and discusses future research needs. Chapter 9 presents benefits, limitations, systematic approaches, and the future of MBMO. It also discusses organizational problems faced with the MBMO implementation and possible approaches to resolve them.

MANAGEMENT SCIENCE AND MBMO

The specific origin of the concept of MBO is not known, just as the origin of management is not known. Although many academicians trace the MBO concept to the days of the Old Testament, Koran, and ancient Greek philosophers, there is no practical value in seeking a detailed historical analysis (for a good history of MBO, see the book by Odiorne in the References). The idea of defining objectives and implementing relatively systematic resource allocation schemes for results can be readily found in the management styles of many early entrepreneurs as well as in some early management texts.

The basic theoretical foundation of MBO, if there ever was such a thing, can be found in operations research and management science. Operations research activities originated in the United Kingdom early in World War II. An urgent need for the most effective military tactics and strategies necessitated a scientific approach to analyze various logistics problems. The British, and later the American military authorities, formed groups of scientists to do research on military operations (with the goal of achieving mission objectives in the most efficient way). It has been said that their studies were instrumental in the victorious air battles over Britian, the island campaign in the Pacific, the battle of the North Atlantic, and other phases of the war.

After the war, operations research moved into business, government, and other institutions in the United States. The name "management science" became a popular substitute for operations research as the concept and areas of application were broadened to more than "operational" problems. Management science deals with the application of scientific tools, models, and computer-based analysis to provide more concrete information relevant to managerial problems.

Decision making is the most fundamental function of management. As a matter of fact, Herbert A. Simon, an eminent scholar of management and the Nobel laureate in 1978, states that decision making is synonymous with management. Increased emphasis on rational decision making is the result of the aggregate effects of advances in management technology, the ever increasing complexity of environment, and the improved capability of modern managers. In order to improve the rationality in decision making, greater emphasis has been placed on techniques that would provide more concrete information about the decision environment and the outcomes of available alternatives. Hence, the trend of decision making has developed toward the management science and computer-oriented approaches. Management science has thus become an integral part of modern management.

The management science approach emphasizes the following aspects of the decision problem:

1. Analysis of the nature of the management problem

2. Analysis of the decision environment and its interaction with the organization

3. Definition of organizational objectives

4. Definition of system constraints and priorities of the decision maker

5. Determination of available resources

6. Analysis of technological activities of the system

7. Determination of decision and activity levels to achieve objectives

Management science permits a scientific approach to MBO. Management science as well as systematic approaches to management decision making may well have contributed more toward the acceptance of MBO than is usually appreciated by managers and scholars. When the organization involves complex technologies (chemicals, electronics, mechanical processes, etc), when there exists an increasing materials shortage (energy, petroleum, certain vital metals, etc.), and when managerial problems involve complex processes (production, inventory control, construction, assembly line balancing, location-allocation, working capital management, capital budgeting, customer information processing, and the like), the role of management science is especially important in implementing MBO.

Although management science has contributed a great deal to systematize and operationalize the MBO process, it has often neglected the human aspect of management. Management systems, regardless of how well conceived, modeled, analyzed, and solved, cannot exist in a vacuum. The system functions and dysfunctions because of people. The human aspect of management—motivation, development, leadership, psychological needs, etc.—constitutes the essence of any MBO system.

Unfortunately, traditional management theorists have concentrated only on the human side of MBO, seeking an improved management effectiveness through objective-orientated performance appraisals, incentive systems, training and development programs, participative management processes, and the like. Too often the interrelationships among system components, environmental factors, system constraints, priorities of the decision maker, etc., have been neglected. Thus, many behavioral-orientated MBO processes have resulted in less than anticipated results. In order to develop an operational MBO, one must consider both systematic as well as human aspects of management.

In today's complex organizational environment, management attempts to achieve a set of objectives to the fullest possible extent in an environment of conflicting interests, incomplete information, and limited resources. Management's effectiveness can be measured by the quality and degree of achievement of organizational objectives. Therefore, recognition and definition of organizational objectives provide the foundation for management.

Management functions are also constrained by environmental factors such as government regulations, economic and political situations, people's concern for certain special issues (i.e., pollution, energy, nuclear power generating plants, consumer protection, etc.) and international politics and economic situations. In order to chart the best course of action in these puzzling times, therefore, a comprehensive analysis of multiple and often conflicting organizational objectives and environmental factors must be undertaken.

Important developments in the field of management indicate that management by multiple objectives is perhaps the most difficult and important issue. Martin K. Starr, editor of *Management Science* and a past president of The Institute of Management Science (TIMS), in his address to the 1975 TIMS conference stated that in his opinion, the most important research topic in the area of management today would be the area of multiple-objective decision making. Warren Bennis, eminent scholar in the field of organizational development, in his address at the 1975 American Institute for Decision Science Conference stated that organizations, as well as society in general, have become so fragmented into various interest and value groups that there no longer existed one predominant objective for any organization. Consequently, one of the most important and difficult management decision problems is to achieve an equilibrium among the multiple and conflicting interests and objectives of the various components of the organization.

Several recent studies concerning the future of the industrialized society (e.g., *The Limits to Growth*) have echoed this same theme that when a society is based on enormous technological development and change, stability of the system must be ensured by achieving a delicate balance among such multiple objectives as food production, industrial output, pollution control, population growth, use of natural resources, international cooperation for economic stability, civil rights, and equal opportunity provisions. Management by multiple objectives is a very important aspect of management today, and it certainly will be the central issue in the 1980s.

There have been numerous studies published in the management science field during the past 15 years concerning multiple-objective decision making. Several techniques and their applications to real-world management problems are providing new dimensions for

MBMO as an operational system. One of the most promising techniques is goal programming. Goal programming is a powerful tool which draws upon the highly developed and tested technique of linear programming, but provides a simultaneous solution to a complex system of multiple objectives. The most important characteristic of goal programming is its realistic and pragmatic approach to management decision making. It has the following special features:

1. An explicit consideration of the existing decision environment —system constraints, organizational climate and management philosophy, and the judgment of the decision maker

2. A flexible approach to the definition of management objectives

3. Incorporation of the decision maker's priorities as an integral part of the model

4. Capability to perform interactive analysis feedback and control of the system (trade-offs among objectives; effects of changing technological coefficients, levels of objectives, and priorities; addition or deletion of constraints or variables)

5. Capability to perform computer-based solutions and model simulations

6. Recognition of the human side of management in the MBO process

In order to operationalize the MBO process, we shall develop the MBMO process based on the framework of the goal programming approach (not necessarily its modeling and computer-based solution procedures). The goal programming methodology provides the means to pull together all the essential parts to make the process work. (See Appendix A for the concept of goal programming for MBMO.)

MANAGEMENT IN HUMAN ORGANIZATIONS

Organization is one of the most important creations of mankind. As a matter of fact, the primary distinguishing characteristic of mankind has been the capacity to learn about the environment and transmit such knowledge into an organized effort to accomplish desired goals. This is also the basic issue of economics. Most human organizations, whether they are business enterprises, government agencies, or social institutions, have evolved in such a way as to narrow the gap between desires (objectives) and resources (human and non-human inputs).

A very important characteristic of human organization is its ability to direct and coordinate combined efforts of people for common goals, regardless of individual differences. Organizations can continue to exist and grow even though top managers and key employees come and go. The combined efforts of a handful of people, even millions of people, can be coordinated and directed toward common goals—to conquer foreign lands, to create sophisticated electronic thinking machines, to obtain live pictures of Saturn through a satellite, to monitor the pulse of the world economy.

Thus, our lives are based on and controlled by organizations. We work for organizations, develop certain loyalties to organizations, and receive pensions and social security benefits from organizations when we retire. Finally, we may join a senior citizens organization for companionship and other activities. Organizations exist because they serve certain purposes in the society. In order to serve the purpose well, the organization sets specific objectives to achieve within the environmental constraints of time, resources, governmental regulations, union contracts, management philosophy, etc.

The lifeblood of an organization is management. In spite of all else, if management falters, an organization cannot long survive. The roles and importance of management for organizations have increased dramatically during the past fifty years. Although there are numerous reasons for this trend, we can single out the following factors: the increasing complexity of the environment, the increasing role of technology for the survival and prosperity of the organization, the greater financial and capital resources required for continuous operation, and the changing psychological needs of people within organizations.

Management may well be one of the most widely used terms today. We use it when discussing problems of ecology, energy, health care delivery systems, law enforcement, correctional programs, higher education, emergency rescue efforts, mental health, etc., in addition to more traditional business-related functional areas. It has been said that the earliest known use of the term "management" in its modern connotation traces back to the year 1714 and the publication of a 48-page booklet in London by Jonathan Swift entitled, "The Management of the Four Last Years (of the reign of Queen Anne) Vindicated."* This author has also seen "Management of the Parish Proceeding" in early eighteenth century church records of Scotland. Regardless of the orgin of its use, management has become increasingly important as the decision problems and environment we face have become more complex.

Management has different meanings for different people. Everyone knows pretty much what a private does in the Army, a secretary in an office, an assembly line worker at a General Motors plant, a salesperson in a sporting goods store, and a nurse at a county hospital. However, we have no standard view of the manager's job. What they are and what they do depends entirely upon the organization, geographical locations, the departments, the expertise of the managers, number of people working under them, and many other relevant factors.

WHAT IS MANAGEMENT?

Over a half-century ago Mary Parker Follet defined management as "getting things done through people." This broad and vague definition is still a very good description of management; getting things done implies achieving objectives. Management operates as a dynamic living system by integrating human, financial, and physical resources in such an effective way that the output becomes greater than the simple sum of its inputs.

In a more detailed manner, we can define management as:

A process of achieving a set of objectives in the most efficient way within the given constraints.

This definition is more accurate since it emphasizes that (1) management must have definite directions for the organization—a coordinated set of multiple objectives; (2) management must seek the most efficient way to achieve the objectives—in terms of operational

---

Academy of Management Newsletter, vol. 8, no. 2, 1978.

plans, work assignments, selecting and motivating qualified employees, and evaluation of results; and (3) management must work within the environmental constraints, both external and internal to the organization.

Traditionally, management has been regarded as the art of "getting things done." Thus, it emphasized the "art" of performing the job, for example, the individual manager's natural leadership qualities, with a strong connotation of a military commander's abilities. On the other hand, many recent studies have emphasized the "science" of management meaning "systematic problem solving and decision making." In reality, management is a combination of art and science where certain attributes and systematic analysis are both required. In science, we can predict the phenomenon with a definite probability of occurrence when ingredients of a process are accurately determined. For example, we know the result of a chemical process with a 99.99 percent accuracy when chemicals are added together in a given environment. However, the accuracy of scientific experimentation or prediction is impossible to obtain in a management process because the ingredients (people and resources) are unpredictable and the environment is dynamic.

Modern management recognizes the dynamic nature of the process, and, as such, a basic function of modern management has become management of disturbance or problem solving. Management of change and disturbance in people (their value system, attitudes, behaviors, etc.), materials and other resources (especially technical and technological aspects of resources), and the environmental setting constitute the very core of the modern management process.

THE PROCESS AND BASIC FUNCTIONS OF MANAGEMENT

Based on our definition of management, we can depict the simplified process of management as in Figure 1.1. The entire process depends upon the unique environmental constraints including the physical location of the organization, external forces (governmental regulations, economic and market conditions, and other socioeconomic factors), available organizational resources and their unique characteristics (people, materials, capital, technology, etc.), and the like.

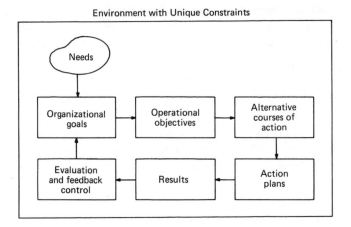

FIGURE 1.1   A simplified management process

The organization exists as it serves to meet some needs in its environment. Thus, needs are the basis for formulating the long-term organizational goals. Organizational goals often are stated in an abstract, elusive, or unclear manner. For example, a police department may define its basic organizational goal as "providing safety, peace, and order in the community." Although we know what the goal statement says, it is unclear as to how such a goal could be measured and achieved. Thus, a set of operational objectives, toward which resources and organizational efforts can be directed, must be formulated.

In order to identify the most effective way to achieve the set of objectives, it may be necessary to evaluate many alternative courses of action. This process involves a host of complex activities, for example, an analysis of priorities of objectives, evaluation of existing alternatives, exploration of additional alternatives, a systematic analysis of alternatives in terms of their cost-benefit measures, and the like. Once alternatives are evaluated, the action plans must be formulated. This phase is also complex and involves planning, organizing, controlling, staffing, and coordinating before action plans can be implemented.

Once results are obtained from action plans, evaluation and feed-back control need to be undertaken. This process enables management to modify organizational goals and objectives, re-establish priorities of objectives, determine new sources of information in order to make the decision process more effective.

Management functions are those generic activities or tasks necessary to make the management process operate. A common way of describing management functions, presented by numerous texts and findings from a countless number of research publications, can be listed as planning, organizing, controlling, directing, and staffing. Some researchers with a strong scientific or systems background argue that management functions involve decision making, problem solving, and systems analysis.

The principles of good management present the normative approach—what managers *should* do for the organization. Many recent studies concerning what real-world managers actually do on the job clearly show a gap between the ideal and the real (see Mintzberg; Sayles; and Stewart). It is not that practicing managers do not realize that ideal principles are good or that they do not want to do a good job. The basic problem is how to adapt ideal principles to the real functions they are supposed to be doing for the organization. In other words, insisting on the normative approach may lead us into a dream world.

Many empirical studies about what managers actually do provide us with a descriptive picture that reveals that managers' actual tasks appear to vary from the principles of management. Although our understanding of reality should be the foundation for any action, the principles of management functions should not be based solely on actual observations of what practicing managers do on the job. The primary reason for this is that such an approach would lead to a self-perpetuating process without improvement.

Now, let us take a look at the contradictions between the principles versus the reality of management functions in Table 1.1 (with seemingly great but in reality only slight exaggerations). It should be apparent that what managers actually do appears to be vague, sporadic, impromptu, and reactive chain of uncoordinated activities. For example, let us listen to the comments of a former project engineer for construction of a nuclear power plant who has recently

TABLE 1.1
Contradictions between principles and reality

Principles of Good Management	*What Managers Really Do*
Rational decision making and problem solving	Most decisions are made by subordinates, postponed, ignored, or negotiated.
Systematic planning, organizing, controlling, directing and staffing	Most of these activities are delegated to staff subordinates, calls short meetings to go over summaries with the staff, and signs the documents.
Clearly thought out objectives and goals	A number of objectives worked out with subordinates and other managers tend to be in conflict and competitive with that of other departments; priorities are not consistent with organizational objectives; tend to list objectives that are easily achieved.
Well-organized action plans and daily routines	A daily work schedule of unplanned meetings, a series of telephone calls, and impromptu decisions for numerous items.
Providing clear leadership and direction to subordinates	Management by exception, guidelines are discussed only when subordinates raise questions or challenge the manager's leadership, most of the time is spent with lateral managers or outsiders.
Job authority and responsibilities	The gap between the work authority and responsibilities increases as one moves up the organizational ladder.
Analysis of results and feedback evaluation of action plans	Such activities take place by subordinates only when they are demanded by higher managers. Tasks usually continue without clear-cut beginning and end.
Motivating subordinates by analyzing individual's personal goals and organizational goals	A negotiated process with superiors and peer groups. Says "nice work" once in a while to subordinates.

been promoted to manager of the materials management division at a public utility:

> I am supposed to be responsible for the materials management functions of this utility, a job of $160 million annually. When I tried to perform my duties, making the final purchasing and inventory control decisions, the whole organization went berserk. The Engineering Division Manager told me that he is the one who decides what to buy and the Production and Distribution Division Managers told me they are the line mangers who would tell me when to buy, how many, and when to deliver them.
>
> When I was a project engineer for the nuclear plant construction, I didn't have organizational clout because we had a matrix organization for the project. Then, when I became the materials manager I thought I would have the kind of power you read about in management books—a tough-minded decision maker with impeccable devotion to the organization. Now I know that the gap between the job authority and job responsibilities increases rather than decreases as you move up the organizational ladder. I certainly had more influence as a project engineer.
>
> Do you know how I spend most of my working hours? I spend most of my time trying to find ways to increase my job authority and power—I study books, talk with outside consultants, and then write memos to other division managers about what proper materials management is about. Right now all important decisions on materials, purchasing, and inventory control are made by people in other divisions. We just take care of the paper work— purchase orders, stock status computer printouts, vendor records, advertising for bids, etc. We can save millions of dollars if they would let me centralize all materials functions under my control. I am afraid that I may be either fired or leave the organization before I am given the managerial authority that I need to function properly.

We must recognize that management is a human process, and as such there exists an enormous gap between aspirations (good management principles that managers are all for) and actuality (disorganized chain of random events). Management is not an optimization process where the optimal decisions are sought for the organization at all times. Rather, it is a "satisfying" process. The manager attempts to achieve satisfactory ends for the organization's objectives given limited managerial abilities, scarce resources (especially time), limited information, vague organizational purpose, and an unstable set of priorities for objectives.

Furthermore, the management job involves the systems concept: coordination of various interrelated dynamic and changing forces, interests, values, and system components in such a way as to achieve an equilibrium. Management is really a process of managing distractions, disturbances, and dynamic forces toward vaguely defined organizational objectives. As such, management functions are not really planning, organizing, controlling, etc. per se, but the process by which the manager sees to it that these functions are adequately carried out by people. If we accept this description of the management process, the seemingly wide gap between the principles of management and reality becomes relatively small.

In reality, then, good and effective management functions involve the following activities:

1. Secure competent subordinates who can carry out operational, staff, or managerial responsibilities effectively.

2. Strive to demonstrate to superiors and peers in the organization how valuable his or her contributions are for the organization.

3. Seek personal goal attainment and greater power in the organization's politics.

4. Believe in people and motivate subordinates by helping them achieve their personal goals that are congruent with organizational goals.

5. Have a broad perspective, positive attitudes, and be self-confident in accepting managerial responsibilities.

6. Become a center of information for others in the organization (get answers for them) and be decisive when an action is required.

7. Maintain organized routines and contingency plans for emergencies, and manage time effectively.

8. Reject the status quo and seek improvement for the organization.

MANAGEMENT APPROACHES

Management functions require three basic types of skills: technical, conceptual, and human. The technical skills are those directly related to the performance of work that contribute to production and distribution of goods or services. The conceptual skills represent the cognitive ability to synthesize, grasp the situation, plan for future actions, and make effective decisions. The human skills or leadership abilities enable one to influence the attitudes and behaviors of others toward a common goal by encouraging, helping, and educating. The relationship between the organizational hierarchy and managerial skills is shown in Figure 1.2.

A unique aspect of managerial functions is that they require more conceptual and human skills and less technical skills as one moves up the organizational ladder. Yet, in many organizations technical skills represent the primary evaluations criteria for advancement. We are all too familiar with the following examples:

- A very diligent and hard working assembly line worker is promoted to a foreman's position and immediately runs into all sorts of problems in managing the workers.

- A very good traffic control officer is promoted to a sergeant and put behind a desk. The police department lost the best street cop and acquired a very ineffective manager.

- A well-known psychiatrist is appointed as the director of the State Mental Health Agency, and the entire program became chaotic.

- A nationally known history professor is selected as the new president of a university and soon the university is in mass confusion.

Another striking aspect of managerial skills is that one's conceptual and human skills can be easily transferred from one top management position to another but not his or her technical skills. An effective university president becomes president of a large corpora-

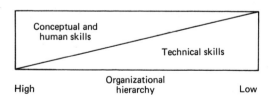

FIGURE 1.2 **Organizational hierarchy and management skills**

tion and turns out to be an effective chief executive officer. A president of a large manufacturing firm becomes the dean of a business school and gradually transforms it into the best in the country. Undeniably, the development and possession of conceptual and human skills are an important prerequisite to becoming an effective manager.

In the management literature various approaches to management have been suggested. Some of these are bureaucratic organization approach, behavioral approach, management science approach, human relations approach, contingency approach, systems approach, and the like. Here we shall discuss several approaches that are oriented more toward managerial skills.

EXPERIENCE, INTUITION, AND JUDGMENT

The intuitive approach based on the manager's experience and judgment has been widely practiced in the past and still is today. Experience is a wonderful source of knowledge. As a matter of fact, the education process is primarily a way of learning things in a relatively short period of time through others' experience without doing it ourselves. Story telling (also known as case studies in the management field) has long been an effective way to transmit knowledge in the human history. Confucius, as early as 500 B.C., recognized the value of experience when he said, "I hear and I forget, I see and I remember, I do and I understand."

Good work experience (not repetitive but new and broad experience) is a prerequisite to becoming an effective manager; however, the value of experience is decreasing in today's technological society. Scientists tell us that as much as 90 percent of the knowledge we have today has been created during the past ten years. In view of the long history of mankind, this statement clearly demonstrates the enormous rate of change we experience in today's environment. The problems of today and of the future are radically different from those faced by our forefathers. The energy problem is a good example of this; its complexity, magnitude, and newness is such that it is not feasible to resort to our problem-solving methodology of the past. Thus, in addition to experience we need conceptual skills to mobilize quickly all available information and knowledge in order to survive in our troubled environment.

SPECIALIZATION

Specialization has been an effective way to perform various management functions. Many managers are specialists in a sense. The production manger could be a specialist who has worked for a number of years in the production area as a design engineer, production staff member, quality control manager, and assistant production manager. A personnel manager is a specialist in human resources management. Likewise, a marketing manager could be a specialist who came up through the marketing research area.

A specialist by definition is one who knows almost everything there is to know about a narrow field, in other words, a person with well-developed technical skills. The demand for specialists in organizations has increased drastically during the past thirty years. Accordingly, the importance and influence of specialists have also gained a great deal. The financial analyst, information systems expert, organizational development specialist, computer and operations analysis expert, the environmental impact analysis specialist, the marketing researcher, the affirmative action officer have become important people in organizations.

GENERALIZATION

When society is based on such a rapid rate of change, generalists are also needed. A generalist is one who knows something about almost everything. When a problem arises the generalist should have enough knowledge about the expertise that would be needed to face it. Some managers are generalists who are familiar with almost every facet of the organization's functions. The generalist lacks a depth of technical skills but is supposed to make up for it with broad conceptual skills.

A GENERALIST WITH A UNIVERSAL MIND

In today's complex organization, a manager *must* have an in-depth knowledge of at least one function area, be it production, marketing, finance, materials management, or personnel. Without such expertise his or her contribution would be severely limited. At the same time, the manager must possess a broad perspective and insight about the organization's roles, the nature of the existing environment, and the interactions that are necessary between the organization and environment. In other words, the manager must have conceptual as well as technical and human skills. Thus, Kenneth Boulding states that today's organizations need people who are specialists with universal minds.

A very interesting story that exemplifies this viewpoint is told by H.Z. Halbrecht as follows:

> A recent Ph.D. in operations research was hired by a metropolitan city government. His job was to find a good location for a sewage disposal plant somewhere in one of the boroughs. A few weeks later he came to his supervisor. He had the model; he had spent an awful lot of money on computer time; and he announced "I've got the optimum location for it." When his supervisor heard "optimum" he started to duck, but thought he would listen to him anyway. Then the fellow showed how he came up with the location. Now, everybody who is high up in any city administration (who has also got a little bit of brains and who has lasted more than six months) has an address book in his pocket, because it's great to know all the theories about public administration and city management, but before you do anything drastic, it's nice to know who lives in the area that you are going to pick for the sewage disposal plant. And, by an odd coincidence, the optimum location picked was two blocks from the Chairman of the City Finance Committee's home. The supervisor suggested that that was not the "optimum" location, and this fellow got furious. "Are you looking for a political solution or for a truthful solution?" The man who replaced the first fellow was put on that assignment and was told to find the best "workable" solution.*

There is a definite need to improve communication between specialists (often staff managers) and generalists (often line managers). Specialists must understand the broad environmental, organizational, and political aspects that must be considered in the management process. Managers, on the other hand, must recognize the value of professional expertise of specialists that could be effectively utilized for managerial decision making. As pointed out by British philosopher C.P. Snow, "What we need to do is humanize the scientist and simonize the humanist."

---

*H.Z. Halbrecht, "If Your Students Aren't Marketable, What's Your Future?" *Decision Sciences*, 4(1973): quoted with permission of Decision Sciences

SUMMARY

MBO has been widely accepted as a general and normative management approach. Its basic idea is quite simple: the best way to get things done is to determine the objectives and get required resources to achieve them. Although the idea of MBO is simple, it requires a systematic approach to make the process functional. There have been enough advances in the field of management science so that the MBO process can be both systematic and also humanistic enough to make it work. The new process of MBO is suggested here as MBMO. It shows great promise of being an effective approach to manage any system, organization, or system problems in the 1980s.

REFERENCES

Boulding, Kenneth. "The Specialist with a Universal Mind." *Management Science* 14(1968): 647-53.

Churchman, C.W. *The Systems Approach*. New York: Delacorte Press, 1968.

Drucker, Peter. *The Practice of Management*. New York: Harper & Row, 1954.

Halbrecht, H.Z. "If Your Students Aren't Marketable, What's Your Future?" *Decision Sciences* 4(1973): xiii-xix.

Koontz, H., and O'Donnell, C. *Principles of Management: An Analysis of Managerial Functions*. New York: McGraw-Hill, 1972.

Lee, S.M. *Goal Programming for Decision Analysis*. Philadelphia: Auerbach, 1972.

——. "Goal Programming for Decision Analysis of Multiple Objectives." *Sloan Management Review* 14(1973): 11-24.

Lee, S.M., and Moore, L.J. *Introduction to Decision Science*. New York: Petrocelli-Charter, 1975.

Meadows, D.G., et al. *The Limits to Growth*. Washington, D.C.: The New American Library, 1972.

Mintzberg, Henry. *The Nature of Managerial Work*. New York: Harper & Row, 1973.

Morrisey, G.L. *Management by Objectives and Results in the Public Sector*. Reading, Mass.: Addison-Wesley, 1976.

Odiorne, G.S. *MBO II: A System of Managerial Leadership for the 80's*. Belmont, Calif.: Fearon Pitman, 1979.

Raia, A.P. *Managing by Objectives*. Glenview, Ill.: Scott, Foresman, 1974.

Sayles, L. *Leadership: What Effective Managers Really Do . . . and How They Do It*. New York: McGraw-Hill, 1979.

Stewart, R. *Contrasts in Management*. London: McGraw-Hill, 1976.

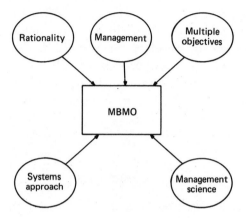

2

The MBMO System

A well-known scientist decided that he had been a bachelor long enough, or at least that he should seriously consider whether to get married or not, and if so to whom. Being a rational man, he sat down and enumerated the advantages and disadvantages of the marital state and the kind of qualities that he should look for in choosing a wife. As for the advantages—and I quote from his notes, "Children (if it please God), constant companionship (and friend in old age), charms of music and female chit-chat." Among the disadvantages—"Terrible loss of time, if many children forced to gain one's bread; fighting about no society." But he continued, "What is the use of working without sympathy from near and dear friends? Who are near and dear friends to the old, except relatives?" And his conclusion was: "My God, it is intolerable to think of spending one's whole life like a neuter bee, working, working, and nothing after all. No, no won't do. Imagine living all one's day solitarily in smokey, dirty London house—only picture to yourself a nice soft wife on a sofa, with good fire and books and music perhaps—compare this vision with the dingy reality of Gt. Marlboro Street." His conclusion: "Marry, marry, marry." Having decided that he ought to get married and having listed the desirable qualities of a future spouse, he then proceeded to look for a suitable candidate. He had several female cousins, so that there was no need to search outside the family circle. He dispassionately compared their attributes with his list of objectives and constraints, made his choice and proposed to her. Needless to say, he lived happily ever after. The scientist in question—Charles Darwin; the year, 1837. (Eilon, p. 3)*

For our purposes the above story points out several important aspects of the management process and environment. The first aspect is that rational decision making, upon which the concept of

---

*Quoted with permission from *Operational Research Quarterly*.

MBO is based, has been with us for a long time. As a matter of fact, man's desire to achieve his objectives has led to continuous efforts to comprehend the norms and conditions under which the environment functions. The increase in man's body of knowledge has produced new scientific and technological discoveries and inventions. Man has thus acquired a greater margin of control over nature, providing new opportunities for growth and further development. However, man's control over nature is also the genesis of the problem of decision making, since different decisions may result in different consequences. Man attempts to select the best course of action from a set of alternatives in order to achieve his objectives as completely as possible.

The second item that needs to be pointed out in the Darwin story is that MBO is constrained by environmental factors. Charles Darwin was a superb scientist and therefore was able to be rational in selecting his course of action. The five wives of Henry VIII certainly must have wished that he was more rational in deciding his marital problems. For some reason, Darwin limited his search for a bride within the family circle. Although he thought he made the optimum decision, it might have been a suboptimum solution at best. This special constraint he imposed might have been due to his family training, personality, or the accepted life-style during that period of time in England. In other words, the way we define the decision environment presents a host of constraints to the decision-making process.

The third aspect which deserves our attention in the Darwin story is that complex real-world problems involve multiple, sometimes conflicting, objectives. It is precisely this element of complexity which has led to a host of difficulties in the management process. As we discussed in chapter 1, management by multiple objectives is a fact of life in the manager's job—no treatment or discussion of the management process is complete without it. Now, let us review several important aspects of MBMO in greater detail.

THE CONCEPT OF RATIONALITY IN MANAGEMENT

One of the primary incentives for man to pursue knowledge is the basic human and environmental problem of trying to satisfy unlimited human desires with limited resources. This has always been the most troublesome human problem. There are two possible approaches to solve this human problem. One is to increase available resources. For an individual, this approach may take the form of the Protestant work ethic. Or it may take a form of scientific endeavors that will enable him or her to utilize existing limited resources in a more efficient manner. Finally, it may mean a scientific break-through that creates new uses for relatively abundant resources, such as water, air, sunshine, and so on.

The second basic approach is for an individual to limit his or her desires so that the existing resources become sufficient enough to satisfy them. For example, one may choose to have a small cottage in the mountains and meditate ten hours, have only two meals, and work four hours a day. The two approaches are quite different, but both have found wide practice in the history of human society.

The first approach, the Protestant work ethic, is clearly a general philosophy of Western culture. One who accumulates wealth through hard work or innovative ideas becomes a successful person. The economic rewards of hard work also usually result in social and psychological rewards. In short, "money talks" for the fulfillment of human desires. In the United States millionaires are often more respected than statesmen, artists, scholars, or religious leaders. Since we live in an age of scarce resources (and they are becoming scarcer every day), it may be inevitable and appropriate for those who ac-quire greater control over resources to receive social respect.

The second approach, limiting one's desires, has been a long-accepted practice in Eastern cultures, although it is gradually dimin-ishing. By exercising strong self-discipline, self-control, and some-times even self-denial, one reduces his or her desires to the very min-imum, even to the subsistence level. This philosophy can be broadly defined as asceticism. Ascetics usually introduce some philosophic or religious accent into their daily life in order to enrich their "inner" happiness. Physically, asceticism is far from a comfortable way of life; however, many have found it a meaningful life-style as they re-ceive social respect for their philosophy, knowledge, and courage to endure physical hardships. If not completely ascetic, an austere way of life has long been advocated in many Asian countries as the gen-tlemanly life-style. For example, even today many Japanese million-aires spend their leisure by enjoying "small pleasures" at home, such as practicing calligraphy, playing "go" (complicated Oriental chess-type game), composing poems, or watching the birds. It is interest-ing to note that traditionally the elite group in such societies was comprised of royalty, politicians, and scholars, all of whom were primarily engaged in the perpetuation of past norms and/or in literary or artistic endeavors. It now seems ironic that the socially elite who advocated an ascetic way of life not only ruled those who were directly involved in the actual production of goods and services but also received their respect.

The point of this discussion, aside from the pros and cons of Eastern and Western culture, is that in a society where limitation upon human desires is advocated, MBMO is unlikely to play an important role. In other words, MBMO becomes important in a cultural setting where the way of life is geared toward greater control over and efficient use of resources to fulfill desires. Therefore, MBMO is not equally applicable in different environments. Realistic analysis of one's environment is an important prerequisite for an effective application of MBMO.

The traditional economic theory postulates an "economic man," who is "economic" and also "rational." The economic man is an "optimizer" in the Western cultural sense. He is assumed to be one who allocates his resources in the most rational manner to optimize his welfare and has knowledge of the relevant aspects of his environment. He is also assumed to possess a stable system of preferences and the skill to analyze the alternative courses of action in order to achieve his desires. In the classic economic theory, we often assume that the concept of economic man provides the basic foundation for the theory of the firm. In other words, we often think that the management process of an organization is or should be like one employed by the economic man.

Recent developments in the theory of the firm have cast considerable doubt on whether the concept of economic man can be applied to management of today's complex organizations. According to broad empirical investigation, there is no evidence that any one individual is capable of performing a completely rational analysis for complex decision problems. Also, there is considerable doubt that the individual's value system is exactly identical to that of the organization, which is a group of individuals. There may be lack of agreement in determining what is best for the organization as a whole. Furthermore, the manager is actually often incapable of identifying the optimum choice, either because of his or her lack of analytical ability or because of the complexity of the organizational environment.

The concept of economic man does not sufficiently provide either a descriptive or a normative model for the decision maker in an organization. Because of the organismic limitations of the decision maker, his or her decision making will at best be a crude approximation of global rationality.

There is an abundance of evidence that suggests that the practice of management is affected by the epistemological assumptions of the manager. Indeed, the practice of scientific methodology and rational choice is not always directly applicable to management. The manager is constantly concerned with his or her environment and always relates possible decision outcomes and their consequences to the environment with its unique conditions. Stated differently, the manager is extremely conscious of the implications of the decision to his or her surroundings rather than simply considering isolated economic payoffs. This concern with the environmental context of the decision prompts a variety of modifications that further moves the manager from the traditional concept of "rational" behavior to one of "bounded rationality."

The manager is then, in reality, one who attempts to employ an "approximate" rationality in order to maximize the attainment of organizational goals within the given set of constraints. The manager may fall far short of being a completely rational person, but his or her behavior may at least be "intentionally" rational. If we define MBMO as a rational choice process within the context of the manager's environmental concern and his or her limited knowledge, ability, and information, the paradox between the economic man and manager in reality becomes increasingly vague. Discrepancies still remain between the theory of rationality and the realities of human life. These discrepancies, however, may provide valuable information for the analysis of human behavior in the organizational environment.

MULTIPLE OBJECTIVES IN ORGANIZATIONS

We are now comfortable with the notion that the management process must consider environmental factors, multiple objectives, and bounded rationality. The organization interacts with the existing environment and generates two sets of goals: system constraints and organizational objectives. System constraints represent the absolute restrictions imposed by the environment. For example, there are only seven days in a week (time constraints), the production capacity in a short run is limited to certain available hours (manpower constraints), the tax payment must be made based on the tax laws (regulatory constraints), the distribution should be limited to demand and storage capacity (physical constraints). System constraints must be satisfied before any organizational objectives can be considered. Organizational objectives represent desired levels of certain outcomes. For example, desired level of pollution control, desired level of profit, desired diversification of investments among various available alternatives, desired market share for each product, and the like are good illustrations of objectives. Figure 2.1 is a schematic presentation of the relationships between system constraints and organizational objectives in the MBMO framework.

Although most scholars and practicing managers agree that organizations indeed have multiple objectives, there exists much varied opinion about organizational goals for business firms. Herbert Simon indicated that business organizations must consider profit, social responsibility, power, prestige, and job security collectively. White has identified goals with respect to their internal and external environments. External goals are comprised of market goals, company image, relative power and position with respect to other corporations within the same industry. Internal goals are such things as financial and production goals.

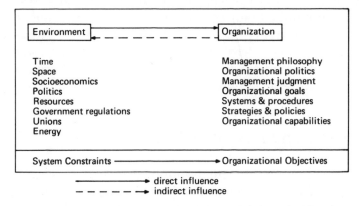

FIGURE 2.1 Environment and organizational objectives
in the MBMO framework

Shubik investigated the goal structures of 25 corporations as described by the top management. The study revealed a wide range of political, social, economic, and ethical aspects. The items most frequently stated as the primary goal of corporations were as follows:

Primary Goal	Frequency
Personnel	21
Duties and responsibilities to society	19
Consumer's needs	19
Stockholder's interest	16
Profit	13
Quality of product	11
Technological process	9
Supplier relations	9
Corporate growth	8
Managerial efficiency	7
Duties to government	4
Distributor relations	4
Prestige	2
Religion as a guide in business	1

Morris stated that managers are primarily concerned with such goals as sales volume, the organization's rate of growth, market share and industry position, favorable corporate image, satisfactory labor relations, job satisfaction, and public service. The results of a survey conducted by England indicated the following:

Goals	% rating goal as highly important	% indicating goal significant for success
Organizational efficiency	81	71
High productivity	80	70
Profit maximization	72	70
Organizational growth	60	72
Industrial leadership	58	64
Organizational stability	58	54
Employee welfare	65	20
Social welfare	16	8

Perrow conducted yet another survey and found that important business goals are societal impact, consumerism, profitability, product quality, political aims, and community services. Cyert and March described a set of prescriptive and constraining goals for corporations. Prescriptive goals were defined as raising profits, increasing market share, making the company a much better place to work, and becoming a better citizen. On the other hand, constraining goals entailed the following: actions that violate no laws, liqiuidity that is neither too high nor too low, and earnings that do not fall below a specified amount per share.

Some theorists may still claim that a variety of noneconomic goals are simply means to a long-run profit maximization. But a series of five- to ten-year short-run goals could form a long-run noneconomic goal for a period of 50 to 100 years. Then, should we define the concept of long-run as a time period running well over the span of a human life? On the other hand, we can interpret profit only as an intermittent/intermediate goal which serves as a means to fulfill other more important goals such as long-run prosperity of the organization, welfare of the employees and stockholders, and contribution to the society. Philip Selznik, a well-known social scientist, observed that when an organization is in operation with many contributing forces to keep it alive, management tends to forget the task of defining its objectives. Perhaps some may argue that the multiplicity of vague organizational goals represents an attempt to escape from the task of clearly defining goals of the organization— its continued existence may be the overriding goal.

The idea of multiple objectives is much more readily accepted for governmental or public orgainzations. For example, suppose a city government is to formulate a long-range economic plan. The plan can easily include such objectives as construction of new water tanks, extension of the existing public transit system, paving of streets, beautifying the downtown area, improving garbage and sewage services, overhauling the welfare programs, instituting new job-training programs, expanding the metropolitan airport facilities, and the like.

Organizations have multiple objectives, regardless of their form, purpose, or people who work in them. A systematic management process capable of handling multiple and conflicting goals based on their priorities and resource requirements should be the central concern of management. The MBMO system is such a process. Appendix A presents a management science approach (goal programming) to the implementation of MBMO.

MBMO AS A SYSTEM

As we discussed in chapter 1, application of the MBO concept in organizations has gone through three distinct stages: performance appraisal, management planning, and an integrated management process. In the early stage of MBO development, its concept was adopted as a better way to appraise managers' performance. The scope of this application was generally limited to subordinates and their immediate supervisor. As McGregor pointed out, the manager was put in a very uneasy position in evaluating individual subordinates' personal worth to the organization. In the second broad stage of MBO development in the 1960s, the concept of MBO was used for management planning for the entire organization. No doubt the influence of the Federal Planning Programming and Budgeting System (PPBS), widely touted during the early 1960s, was a strong impetus to business organizations for the application of MBO. MBO was evolved as a scheme to tie plans, budgets, and programs to objectives. During the past several years MBO reached the third stage where it has become an integrated management process that includes formulation of organizational objectives, long-range strategic plans, decision making, action plans, and feedback and control. At this stage, MBO is based on an interaction between the organization's goals and top management and managers at all levels, rather than either a top-down or bottom-up process.

Management by multiple objectives is not merely a style, philosophy, technique or procedure. It is an integrated management system—a way to pull management functions together in a systematic and logical manner to formulate and achieve a set of objectives. The major elements of the system and key steps of the MBO are presented in Figure 2.2. They key steps of the system can be identified as follows:

1. Set Organizational Goals	Evaluate environmental conditions, organization's unique factors, and then formulate broad long-range organizational goals.
2. Formulate Multiple Objectives	Formulate explicit organizational objectives and analyze them in terms of their priorities for the organization.
3. Formulate Operational Objectives	Formulate specific, detailed, short-term work objectives at the divisional, departmental, or individual manager's levels.
4. Formulate Action Plans	Develop a set of action plans to achieve operational objectives. Action plans will include determining manpower needs, training and development needs, career development and manpower planning, performance appraisal plans, and employee motivation plans to implement action plans. Also, it is essential to establish plans to secure, control, and systematically allocate capital and materials to implement the action plans.
5. Implement the System	Determine the system implementation strategies in terms of personnel, resource requirements, planning and expected problems and strategies to resolve them.
6. Review, Evaluation, and Control	Evaluate the results of the action plans and make necessary modifications based on periodic reviews for the entire system.

   Now we shall discuss the major elements of the MBMO system in greater detail.

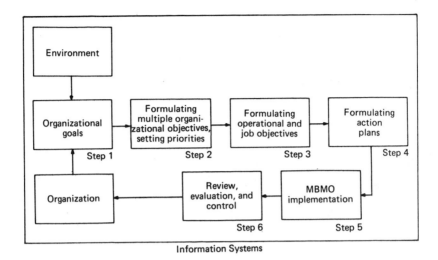

FIGURE 2.2 Major elements of steps of MBMO

MANAGEMENT INFORMATION SYSTEMS

As a system, the MBMO process is composed of certain elements and their relationships to achieve a set of objectives. In order to make the system function effectively, important and timely information must be retrieved, processed, stored, and utilized. Since MBMO is also a human process, it requires a good communication system that can serve as the catalyst in pulling all human efforts together.

The primary functions of management information systems for MBMO involve the following:

- Identify and obtain information, from both external and internal sources, that would be required in setting long-range organizational goals.

- Analyze relationship among organizational objectives, priorities of objectives, and alternative courses of action, and work activities. Process this information for use in various elements of the MBMO system.

- Identify data input requirements, data collection methods, and information-flow patterns for systematic analysis and decision making.

- Design a system of information and communication flows for feedback control and updating of the MBMO support elements.

SETTING ORGANIZATIONAL GOALS

This step involves the following questions: "What is the basic purpose or mission of the organization in the society?" "Why and how does the organization exist?" "What type of organization does it want to become?" Any human organization must serve a purpose and satisfy certain needs in the society. It exists in a given environment with its unique set of factors. Also, it has certain organizational characteristics, such as the size, location, management philosophy, stage of its growth, physical and human capabilities, and the like. Based on all such information, management must formulate broad long-range organizational goals.

FORMULATING MULTIPLE OBJECTIVES

Broad organizational goals present the general direction in which an organization should move. However, such a direction alone cannot provide explicit targets toward which the organization should direct its resources. Formulating organizational objectives in explicit and measurable criteria is the most important element of the MBMO process. For example, an overall service goal to the customer can be more clearly defined by such things as (1) improvement of the product quality, (2) maintenance service for the customer, (3) product information brochures, (4) reasonable price for the product, and the like. Once organizational objectives are formulated, they can be further refined and broken down into departmental objectives and personal work objectives. In this way, work activities will be coordinated toward achieving the overall organizational objectives.

SETTING PRIORITIES

It is human nature to desire more than one can possibly achieve. Organizational objectives are no exception to this rule. Since multiple objectives are competing for organizational resources, there is a need to set priorities so that important organizational objectives are achieved before less important ones are considered. This is one aspect of the MBMO process which has been generally neglected by managers. A sound priority structure is as essential as formulating realistic objectives.

ANALYZING ALTERNATIVE COURSES OF ACTION

It has been said that any decision problem which does not have alternatives will result in a bad decision. Once multiple objectives are formulated and their priorities determined, strategies or possible ways to achieve these objectives should be explored. The set of available alternatives may not be exhaustive. It is sometimes necessary to develop new alternatives through a thorough systems analysis. However, it is extremely difficult to determine how exhaustive the alternative search should be, since the process may cost a great deal of money, time, and effort. Once all feasible alternatives have been determined, they should be carefully analyzed in terms of their cost-effectiveness in achieving organizational objectives. This process is further complicated when we introduce the time dimension to the effectiveness—short term versus long term. This is where management science models are very useful in determining the relative merits of available alternatives.

CHOOSING SPECIFIC ALTERNATIVES

Decision making takes place throughout the management process, from the analysis of environment to reviewing results of action plans. Systematic decision making is especially needed for choosing alternative courses of action. When all relevant information is obtained about feasible courses of action, the decision has to be made in choosing specific action. The decision-making process should be as rational and systematic as possible. However, quantitative data or model results do not automatically become decisions. We must recognize the fact that the decision-making process is based on the personal style of the manager. The manager may use his or her intuition and judgment about many other factors that are not quantitative and could not be examined explicitly, e.g., organizational politics, personal insights about future outcomes, environmental factors, etc. The manager uses all available data and information to enrich and sharpen his or her judgement so that the final decision will be at least "'intentionally rational" in the environment of uncertainties, intangibles, and incomplete information.

DEVELOPING ACTION PLANS

When alternatives are selected through the decision-making process, action plans must be developed. This step involves scheduling activities, resource allocations, manpower needs, and proper control of event sequences. A host of network and planning models can be applied so that the objectives would be achieved effectively.

HUMAN RESOURCES MANAGEMENT

MBMO is a human process. Without effective human resource management, we cannot expect an effective MBMO system. Thus, it is essential to develop a well-planned and coordinated human resources management process encompassing performance appraisal, behavior reinforcement, employee motivation with appropriate compensation plans, training and development, career paths, and long-range organizational manpower planning.

CAPITAL AND MATERIALS MANAGEMENT

We live in an environment where important raw materials are becoming increasingly scarce. The growing shortage of key materials has a profound impact on management. For some manufacturing firms, materials cost has surpassed 50 percent of the total cost of the product for the first time. Effective and systematic management of needed capital and materials (securing the source, capital budgeting, purchasing systems, inventory control, materials resource planning, warehousing, project scheduling, etc.) is an integral part of management and MBMO.

FEEDBACK CONTROL SYSTEM

Organizational goals and objectives are to be achieved by a set of action plans in the MBMO process; however, it would be rare indeed if action plans result in the exactly expected attainment of objectives. Thus, corrective action is essential, since there is a need to evaluate the results of the action plans and make necessary modifications so that the desired results could be obtained. Since the environment changes, it is quite possible that previously established goals, plans, objectives, criteria for cost-effectiveness, etc., are no longer appropriate. Thus a systematic feedback and control of the MBMO process is essential to maintain the system current and effective.

MANAGEMENT APPROACHES WITH THE MBMO SYSTEM

As a result of the MBMO system and its acceptance by organizations, several changes are likely to occur in traditional management approaches.

PURPOSE-ORIENTED MANAGEMENT

The MBMO system requires an organization to be purpose oriented, from top management to the low-echelon employee. The work activities will be planned and carried out according to organizational objectives rather than just "by the book" of company procedures. The question "What does this activity contribute toward important organizational objectives?" will continually be asked before resources are committed. There will be more emphasis on such things as zero-base budgets, cost-effectiveness, and priorities for objectives.

INFORMATION- AND ANALYSIS-BASED MANAGEMENT

An effective MBMO system also requires an efficient management information system (MIS) and systematic decision making. With the ever increasing complexity of the environment and its vital impact on the organization's survival, information management becomes extremely important. Accurate and timely information must be processed in order to predict the future state of affairs with an acceptable degree of accuracy.

There will be more widespread application of management science models to generate additional information. The use of computers for everyday management will be more prevalent. With the availability of inexpensive but powerful microcomputers and minicomputers, even small organizations can be more systematic in handling materials, inventory control, marketing research, payroll, and scheduling.

Decentralization of decision making will be more common in large organizations with economical installation of departmental computing facilities. Managers, especially at the lower and middle levels, will be required to be competent users of computers and management science. Large independent and centralized departments of computing or management science at the corporate level will be rare. Such staff personnel will be part of the line departments. They will be involved in actual use of decision support systems rather than simply advising the line personnel.

MANAGEMENT OF MULTIPLE OBJECTIVES

Management will be vitally concerned with the analysis of multiple objectives, not only with their formulation but with priorities and trade-offs. There exists an ever increasing pressure in the simultaneous satisfaction of government regulations, economic optimization, and other organizational goals. Materials shortage (e.g., energy) and increasing costs are forcing managers to be more concerned with the economic optimization (minimizing operational costs). Yet, government regulations to cope with the same basic problem have forced organizations to be further removed from economic optimization. We will see more direct conflict between the organization's economic survival and other objectives that are related to social responsibilities of the organization.

Managers will be held increasingly more accountable with regard to the legitimacy of their objectives, priorities, and conflict resolution among objectives. Thus, we will see greater application of systematic approaches in dealing with multiple goals and their trade-offs. Computer-based interactive approaches will be more widely used in objective formulation and priority setting.

INCREASED CONCERN FOR PRODUCTIVITY

The essence of MBMO is to increase the efficiency of the organization. Productivity of human, physical, and financial resources will continue to be management's central concern. In order to improve the cost-effectiveness of the management process, three important areas should be evaluated: (1) productivity of human resource, (2) more effective management of capital and materials, and (3) more efficient management process. In order to implement an effective MBMO system, management must commit itself to the training, development, self-improvement, and motivation of the human resource. The human resource and its effective utilization will continue to hold the key to the survival and prosperity of the organization under the MBMO system.

INCREASED ATTENTION TO GROUP BEHAVIOR

As we focus attention on the human resource, group behavior will become increasingly more important than the individual worker's behavior. It has been pointed out by many scholars that one of the important reasons for the poor showing of American workers in the world productivity race is management's failure to recognize the importance of workers' group behavior. Harvard sociologist Ezra F. Vogel contends in his book *Japan as Number One: Lessons for America*, that perhaps the most important reason for the phenomenal productivity increase of Japanese workers is their group-conscious behavior patterns. It is terribly important for Japanese to belong to groups; group loyalty and confidence in group values are driving forces for Japanese workers. The study of group behavior, especially the importance of the sense of shared purpose to motivation and productivity, will receive greater attention from management under the MBMO system.

MANAGEMENT OF CAPITAL, ENERGY, AND MATERIALS

With the increasing scarcity and cost of acquiring capital, energy, and materials, an effective management of these resources will become almost as important as the management of human resources. As Harvard economist Martin Feldstein points out, the American economy suffers from a lack of capital formation due to low savings. He singles out inflation and government taxes that penalize savings as the main causes of declining savings. Efficient management of capital, energy, and materials will further require systematic approaches based on computer-based information systems and management science. Cost-savings from these resources represent a 100 percent contribution to profits, while cost savings in other areas (e.g., marketing channels) may represent only a very small net contribution to profits.

MORE SYSTEMATIC CONTINGENCY MANAGEMENT

We will probably see more drastic future changes in the environment than we have in the past. We will see a shortage of energy, materials, water, clean air, and many other resources. We will also see some important technological breakthroughs—cheaper and more powerful microcomputers, new inventions concerning energy, new transportation methods, etc. We can expect many political and economic crises in the international arena. These changes will have varying degrees of impact on the organization.

An organization cannot be totally reactive to a situation, functioning without plans. Nor can it be totally proactive with every possible contingency planned for changing situations. Under the MBMO system, however, the basic targets are clearly defined and people can use their imagination to get there. With the availability of information systems, management science models, and computational facilities, contingency management will be more systematic and orderly.

CLOSER INTERACTION WITH EXTERNAL FACTORS

The MBMO system is an open system. It breathes in external factors in the form of environmental constraints, needs, and information. The feedback control system monitors such information so that the entire MBMO system remains current and effective. Thus, we can expect the organization to have closer interactions with external forces: government agencies, international situations, socioeconomic factors of the environment, consumer concerns, and the changing market situation.

KEY TERMS OF MBMO

At this point it is appropriate to define a number of terms which are widely used in MBMO. For example, the reader may have difficulty differentiating the terms "mission," "goals," "objectives," and "targets."

Mission: This is a very broad and general statement about the basic purpose of the organization (e.g., a public utility's mission would be to provide electric and gas services to the customer).

Goal: This is a more precise statement of a purpose than the mission but may not be a quantifiable description of a hoped-for accomplishment. It tends to be relatively long range in its time frame, five years or longer (e.g., to increase the market share in the East Coast area during the next five years).

Objective: An objective is an explicit, clear, and specific statement about a desired accomplishment in quantifiable terms. Objectives are based on goals, and they are to lead toward accomplishing goals. An objective can be long term (up to five years). Usually, however, they are short term, six months to three years. It is necessary to define objectives in quantitative criteria with specific time constraints (e.g., to decrease the traffic fatality rate by 10 percent during the next year).

Target: A target is a finer breakdown of an objective. It is a very specific desired state that contributes toward achieving an objective. Targets are expressed in a very short-term time frame (e.g., to introduce a new curriculum for the college by November 15 for the Academic Committee review).

Priority structure for objectives: This represents an ordering of objectives in terms of their importance to the organization. Priorities may be based on either numerical or hierarchical weights. The numerical weights in terms of utilities or coefficients of regret are also called cardinal weights. The hierarchical weights are ordinal or preemptive priority weights. Thus, the most important objective should be pursued until it is attained or reached the point beyond which no further improvement is possible before the second most important objective is considered.

SUMMARY

This chapter has presented background material as well as the essential elements of the MBMO system. MBMO is not merely a management style but a methodological system that gets things done in a systematic way. We must recognize the many relevant factors that influence the MBMO system such as the changing concept of rationality, multiple and often conflicting objectives, and the systems approach that utilizes scientific analysis of inputs, process, and outputs. As a management system, MBMO provides many positive features that would be most useful in facing the ever changing environment in which we live and many difficult managerial problems it will bring us in the future.

REFERENCES

Cyert, R.M., and March, J.G. *A Behavioral Theory of the Firm*. Englewood Cliffs, N.J.: Prentice-Hall, 1963.

Eilon, S. "Goals and Constraints in Decision-Making." *Operational Research Quarterly* 23(1973): 3-15.

England, G.W. "Organizational Goals and Expected Behavior in American Managers." *Academy of Management Journal* 10(1967): 108.

Feldstein, Martin, "Commentary." *Newsweek*, June 4, 1979.

Lee, S.M. *Goal Programming for Decision Analysis*. Philadelphia: Auerbach, 1972.

Lee, S.M., and Moore, L.J. *Introduction to Decision Science*. New York: Petrocelli-Charter, 1975.

McGregor, D.M. "An Uneasy Look at Performance Appraisal." *Harvard Business Review* 35(May-June 1957): 89-94.

Morris, W.T. *Management Science in Action*. Homewood, Ill: Irwin, 1963.

Perrow, C. "A Framework for the Comparative Analysis of Organizations." *American Sociological Review* 32(1967): 194-208.

Selznik, P. *Leadership in Administration*. Evanston, Ill: Row, Peterson, 1957.

Shubik, M. "Approaches to the Study of Decision-Making Relevant to the Firm." *The Journal of Business* 34(1961): 101-18.

Simon, H.A. "A Behavioral Model of Rational Choice." *Quarterly Journal of Economics* 69(1955): 99-118.

Vogel, E.F. *Japan as Number One: Lessons for America*. Cambridge, Mass.: Harvard University Press, 1979.

White, C.M. "Multiple Goals in the Theory of the Firm." In K.E. Boulding and W.A. Spivey, eds. *Linear Programming and the Theory of the Firm*. New York: Macmillan, 1960.

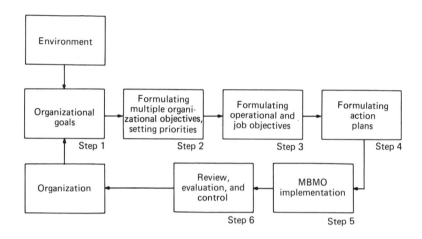

Part II: The MBMO Process

MBMO is not only a management style or philosophy but also an integrated system. As such, it requires certain basic elements and steps. This part presents these elements of MBMO and how they should be put together to make the system function.

Part II consists of the following chapters:

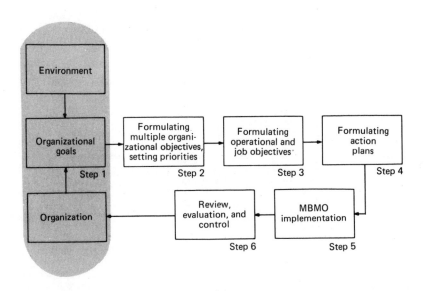

3

Long-range Goals and Strategic Plans

Elton Mayo, a truly outstanding pioneer of modern management, recognized the need for a systematic management process in order to achieve organizational objectives. He listed the following as the three persistent problems of management in modern, large-scale industry:

1. The application of science and technical skills
2. The systematic ordering of operations, and
3. The organization of teamwork—that is, of sustained cooperation.

Although Mayo did not specifically mention MBO or MBMO, what he had in mind was essentially the process of MBMO. The MBMO process is an integrated system that utilizes coordinated human efforts and scientific approaches in order to achieve organizational objectives in the most efficient manner.

In this chapter we shall discuss the initial element of MBMO, formulating long-range goals and strategic plans. More specifically, we shall focus on analyzing the environment, evaluating organizational capabilities, developing organizational purpose and missions, formulating goals and strategic plans, and the role of management in the organizational goal development process.

Figure 3.1 presents a simple illustration of the organizational goal development process. The environment with its unique economic, political, social, technological, physical, and international factors will determine the needs of the organization's clientele. The organization's survival and continuing success is determined by its ability to meet the client's or constituent's needs effectively.

The organization's capabilities to provide goods and/or services to satisfy the external needs are determined by internal factors such as human, financial, physical, technological, and managerial re-

49

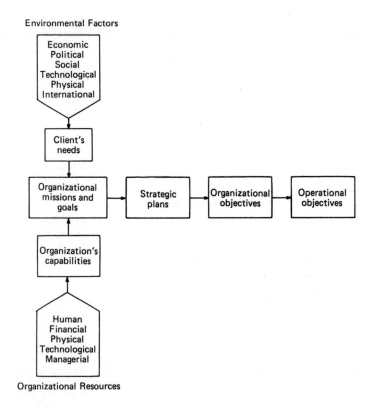

FIGURE 3.1 Development process of organizational goals.

sources. Management analyzes the required external needs in view of the organizational capabilities. From this analysis, management develops organizational missions, goals, and strategic plans. Detailed and specifically defined organizational objectives, in turn, will be developed from organizational strategic plans and become the basis for more detailed operational objectives.

ANALYZING THE ENVIRONMENT

Organizations function in a given external environment. An organization is an open system that constantly interacts with the environmental factors and their change. Thus, the survival and growth of an organization could be determined by capabilities and adaptability of the organization to external factors. External environment is subject to constant fluctuations and long-term changes. However, the organization has very little or no control over such things as government regulations, socioeconomic conditions, actions of foreign governments and international relations (e.g., OPEC's price increases, Japan's stringent import quotas for American goods, Iran's Islamic government, tension in the Middle East, etc.), actions of competitors, special issues or concerns of people at a given time (e.g., nuclear power plants, inflation, etc.), technical and technological developments, and the existing political climate.

In order to ensure survival and growth, the organization must continually monitor and analyze such external factors and their possible future changes in terms of their impact on the organization. An organization must provide goods and/or services needed in the present and future environment. Thus, analysis of the existing needs of people, a thorough market research, is a prerequisite for survival. Such analysis should provide information for the following important management problems:

1. *The market*: What types of products or services are demanded by people? Are we providing some of these products or services? Who are the primary customers? Are there opportunities to increase our market share? What will the future market be like?

2. *Products or services*: What are the existing demand and supply conditions, prices, qualities, and life cycles of the products or services? What is the existing competition? What opportunities or future changes in the market can we expect? Are there opportunities to introduce new products or services successfully?

3. *Financial aspects*: What level of financial resources would be required? What kind of return on investment can we expect? What does the future look like in terms of financial opportunities?

4. *Potential risks*: Are there some obvious risk areas in the environment? Are there opportunities to reduce the degree of risk in these areas? What are the possible courses of action in order to reduce the risk?

A systematic and critical analysis of the external factors and their change is a vital requirement for developing organizational missions, goals, and strategic plans. This analysis process should provide important information concerning the existing needs, opportunities, risks, and the magnitude of organizational resources required to survive and succeed in the given environment.

EVALUATING ORGANIZATIONAL CAPABILITIES

External environmental factors constitute the absolute system constraints—the decision space must be restricted to the area that satisfies all restrictions. The decision space must be further modified based on the organizational capabilities. An evaluation of organizational capabilities involves not only assessing available internal resources for management actions but also the general philosophy and characteristics of the organization. Two organizations with exactly the same internal resources will not function in the same way because differences exist in management philosophies, human value systems, and the stage of organizational growth.

Analyzing the organization's capabilities should provide information about its strengths as well as its weaknesses. Management can use such information as a basis for determining what the organization can actually do—exploring future opportunities, setting organizational goals, developing strategic plans, and committing necessary resources. The following are key elements which should be considered in the analysis of an organization's capabilities:

1. *Organizational characteristics*: What is the basic philosophy of management in running the organization? Where is the organization in terms of its growth state—a new firm, a mature organization, highly diversified and decentralized, an international firm, a financially troubled organization, or what? What are the product or service lines? Where are products in their life cycle? What are the existing and expected future states concerning competition, market, external relations (government, customers, unions, etc.)?

2. *Human resources*: What is the capability of management personnel? How does employee productivity compare with other organizations? Do employees have the appropriate technical skills to compete and succeed in the market? Are employees motivated and happy in the organization? What are future

needs involving human resources—manpower requirement, training and development, personnel system needs, etc.?
3. *Technological resources*: What is the current state of technologies in the organization? What changes or improvements should be made in currently available technologies in order to survive and prosper in existing environment? What are the trends in technological development that should be explored in the future?
4. *Financial resources*: What is the current financial situation? Can the organization meet future challenges successfully with the existing financial resources, or should new arrangements be explored? What are the current and expected rates of return on investments? What is the organization's ability to secure short-term and long-term external capital?
5. *Physical resources*: What is the existing condition of physical plant, equipment, and supply of materials? What is the current and expected future production capacity? How effective are policies and procedures dealing with physical resources? Do operating costs compare favorably with competitors? What are some of the areas where potential cost savings can be made? Are materials management systems efficient in utilizing the existing physical resources? What are the future physical resource requirements to support the organization's sustained growth?

The evaluation of an organization's capabilities in terms of its resources and special characteristics is essential for developing organizational goals and long-term strategic plans. This evaluation process should be systematic and continuous so that any major changes can be readily monitored and adjustments incorporated.

DEVELOPING LONG-RANGE GOALS

ORGANIZATIONAL PURPOSE OR MISSION

A clearly defined purpose or mission statement is important for an organization in developing its long-range plans and broad organizational policies. A statement of the purpose encompassing the nature and roles of the organization provides not only a sense of direction and a common purpose, but also a justification for its very existence. The statement of organizational purpose should also identify key performance or result areas that serve as the criteria for determining the importance of long-term actions.

Unfortunately, in implementing the MBO system, organizations tend to bog down in developing the mission statement. Quite frequently, this process becomes such a political issue with each department or division competing to glorify its roles for the organization. It is not unusual to see an organization spending countless hours of meeting time (by the goals and mission committee) generating enormous amount of paper work with very questionable future impact.

The purpose or mission statement should be broad yet succinct. The detailed statements of organizational goals and specific objectives will be developed subsequently with considerable deliberation, and thus it is not necessary to spend "5,000 man-hours" to develop an elaborate and detailed purpose or mission. Such lengthy preparation not only consumes an inordinate amount of organizational resources but also tends to discourage people and causes them to lose their enthusiasm for MBO. Thus, in the MBMO system, the process of developing the purpose statement for the organization is integrated into the organizational goal development element.

The organizational purpose or mission statement should encompass the following key elements:

- *Nature of the organization.* What is the primary purpose and function of the organization? Why does it exist? What needs in the society does the organization satisfy? How are these needs expected to change in the future?

- *Clientele.* Who are the customers or constituents? How well does the organization serve its customers? What improvements can be made in meeting the customer's needs? What kind of potential is there in attracting new customers?

- *Organizational characteristics.* What is management's basic philosophy in pursuing the organization's purpose? Do organizational structure, management style, decision making, and organizational climate reflect management philosophy?

What are some unique characteristics of the organization when compared with competitors? What are the possible changes and improvements that can be made in the organization to make it more effective?

- *Financial requirement.* What is the required financial return on investment in order to grow at a satisfactory rate? How is the organization doing when compared to the desired growth rate? In what areas can the organization make improvements in the future?

- A clear and concise statement of the organizational purpose serves as the basis upon which an effective MBMO system can be built. An inordinate amount of effort should not be expended for developing the organizational purpose. But it must be developed on a correct and firm basis, otherwise all other blocks of the MBMO cannot be built upon it.

LONG-RANGE ORGANIZATIONAL GOALS

Formulating the organization's long-range goals and subsequent strategic plans represents the first major step of MBMO. Figure 3.2 presents this process in a schematic point of view. Long-range goals are more detailed versions of the organizational purpose or mission. For example, a metropolitan police department may state its basic purpose or mission as "to maintain peace, order and law observance in the community." However, its long-range goals may be defined as "to prevent crime and reduce the incidence of suppressible crimes per capita in the city."

Long-range organizational goals must contribute to achieving various elements of the organizational purpose or mission. Thus, the system constraints imposed by the environmental factors and internal constraints imposed by the organizational characteristics and capabilities must be carefully considered in formulating organizational goals. The bounds defined by the constraints provide the decision space within which goals are to be formulated. Thus, the constraints are qualifiers for the long-range goals.

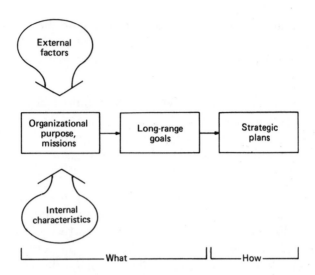

FIGURE 3.2 Formulating long-range goals and strategic plans.

Every goal defined must somehow contribute to the achievements of the organizational purpose. Thus, development of long-range goals must be within the realms of organizational purpose or missions already identified, rather than identifying new directions for the organization. The directions have been identified already. The exact paths to follow would be determined by the long-range goals.

It is of course possible to develop long-range goals that are not already indicated in the organizational purpose or mission statement. Such an exceptional case could occur when exact paths to follow were not known when the purpose statement was prepared. For example, if an organization decides to formulate a goal such as "install an integrated management information system based on the new generation computer just announced by IBM during the next three years," it may be a new goal which was not explicitly described in the purpose statement.

In summary, long-range goals are developed based on the guidelines indicated in the organizational purpose or mission statement. Most likely, exceptions may be found in the area of innovative goals representing desired conditions that do not currently exist but will contribute to the organizational purpose.

A goal is a simple and concise statement which expresses a desired result or a state to be achieved. Long-range goals can be classified into three basic categories: maintenance, performance, and innovative, as shown in Figure 3.3.

MAINTENANCE GOALS

Maintenance goals are intended to stabilize desirable existing conditions. Many organizations tend to ignore or neglect some of the good things they have already achieved. For example, suppose that an organization has a very favorable public image; it may take the condition for granted and neglect to maintain the favorable situation while pursuing new goals. Maintenance goals represent the backbone of an organization.

PERFORMANCE GOALS

Performance goals represent the improvement of effectiveness in key result areas. Performance goals are formulated because existing conditions are not acceptable or desirable. For example, suppose that a firm has only 3 percent of the market share. This may not be a desirable share of the market. Thus, it may present a performance goal such as "to increase our market share by 50 percent (to 4.5 percent of the industry) during the next five years with less than proportionate increase in the marketing costs."

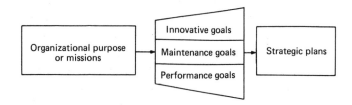

FIGURE 3.3 Formulation process of the long-range goals.

Innovative Goals

Innovative goals represent new desired conditions that the organization does not presently have. For example, an electronics firm may want to introduce new product lines in the microcomputer market, or an organization may want to develop a new management information system (MIS) based on the most advanced computer system. An innovative goal may not be tied directly to the organizational purpose or mission statement, however it should specify any preparation effort required to improve the organization's capabilities. For example, an integrated MIS based on a new computer system would require two years of planning time, 12 man-years of human resources, and $5 million.

The three types of goals are not necessarily complementary or mutually exclusive. They may coexist but with different priorities; also, they may be competitive for organizational resources. Thus, there are several important elements that deserve more detailed consideration before formulating long-range goals:

- The time horizon of the goals

- Approximate resource requirements of each of the goals

- Relationships between the goals and the organizational purpose

- Measurement criteria for the goals

- Organizational structure and goals

The time horizon

Long-range goals are not likely to be achieved at exactly the same point in time. As a matter of fact, some long-range goals, especially maintenance goals, may never be terminated—they are continuing. Development of an integrated MIS goal will be terminated when the system is installed and operating. On the other hand, maintaining a favorable public image of the firm may be interminable.

Approximate resource requirements

It is imperative to know at least the approximate resource requirements of the goals. Of course, the resource requirement at this point is approximate by necessity, a ball park figure must be available. Otherwise, many long-range goals may be a list of wishful thinking that can never be pursued because of the limited organizational resources.

Relationships between the goals and the organizational purpose

Since the purpose is expressed in a general abstract statement and goals are not precisely measurable at this point in time, precise relationships between the goals and the purpose cannot be measured. Nonetheless, the general relationships must be determined. Thus, high priorities will later be assigned to objectives derived from those goals which are important contributors to the primary purpose of the organization.

Measurement criteria

In order to monitor progress toward the goal and ascertain the final acheivement, certain measurement criteria should be developed for the goals. It is especially important to develop a set of clearly understood measuring criteria for interminable maintenance goals, as exemplified below:

Goal	*Measuring Criterion*
To improve the product quality through effective quality control programs	The number of customer complaints and returned products during the time period for the goal as compared to statistically projected figures

Organizational structure and goals

Another important element which deserves close attention is an analysis of the organizational structure in view of the long-range goals. Is the structure well streamlined so that an effective coordination among various divisions and departments can be ensured for the achievement of the goals? Are there major or minor changes necessary for the long-range goals that have been formulated? An efficient organizational structure is an important requirement for successful achievement of long-range goals.

An actual list of long-range organizational goals may contain any number of innovative, maintenance, and performance goals. The magnitude, time range, and the nature of goals will be determined by the organizational purpose and internal capabilities. The organization should have relatively accurate past data for its maintenance goals. A higher degree of uncertainty and risk exist for performance goals, and extremely high levels may exist for innovative goals. Therefore, in order to reduce the risk of overextending the internal capabilities, it is imperative to forcast the resource requirements of performance and innovative goals as accurately as possible. Furthermore, the organization must be realistic in developing innovative goals, as they involve a very high degree of uncertainty and an extended time range.

During the process of developing the organizational purpose, abstract issues and management philosophies are of prime importance. However, as long-range goals are being analyzed more concrete data need to be collected. The required data are not only for the external and internal constraints, but historical as well as projected data concerning organizational performance, innovative projects, and future conditions.

DEVELOPING STRATEGIC PLANS

Once long-range organizational goals are formally developed, strategic plans need to be formulated. Strategic plans represent the means to achieve long-range goals; thus, they generally need to be long term. A set of sound strategic plans should include the following key elements: a set of long-range goals; a list of major steps and key activities for the goals; a systematic ordering and sequencing of steps and activities; a network or planning timetable of steps and activities; an accepted means and criteria to measure progress; a set of priorities for the goals; and a list of required resources including financial, physical, material, and manpower resources.

Strategic plans are relatively long term by necessity, but they need not be uniform in terms of magnitude, time range, and required resources. The primary reason, of course, is the difference in the nature of goals in regard to whether they are maintenance, performance, or innovative goals as well as the priority assigned to the goals. For example, research and development for new product lines would be a major long-term innovative goal, while overhauling of the wage and salary system could be a relatively minor and short-term goal.

A simplified strategic planning process is illustrated in Figure 3.4. Essentially, it involves determining what an organization wants to do during the planning horizon in order to achieve long-term goals. The three basic notions that must be analyzed are what the organization "ought to do," "can do," and "wants to do." The "ought to do" indicates an ideal situation based on rationality. The "can do" represents the organization's capabilities within the given set of external and internal constraints. The "wants to do" represents a commitment based on a compromised or bounded rationality, as we discussed in chapter 2, which is derived through analysis and judgment of all available data based on management's values, goals, and philosophies. The decision-making process based on available data and human judgment to determine the commitment plans is the core of the strategic planning step.

The strategic planning process begins with an analysis of the opportunities, threats, strengths and weaknesses of the organization in view of available information accumulated in the data base. Several key elements of the data base that need to be analyzed are summarized as follows:

1. **Needs and desires of clients or constituents**
   Customers
   Community
   Government
   Unions
   Stockholders
   Suppliers
   Creditors, etc.
2. **Past conditions of the organization**
   Past performance in providing goods or services
   Return on investment
   Sales
   Profits
   Managerial abilities
   Public image and public relations

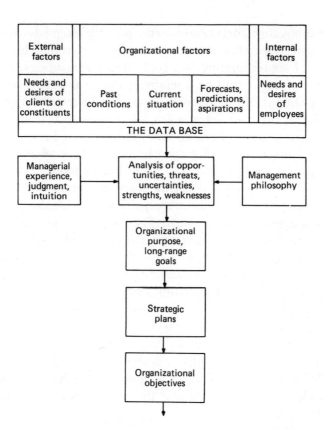

FIGURE 3.4 The strategic planning process (Adapted from
***Management Policy and Strategy* by A.G. Steiner and**
J.B. Miner, Reprinted)

Marketing capabilities
Research and development
Labor relations, etc.
3. **Current situation in the organization**
Financial
    profit
    sales
    debt
    return on investment
    liquidity, etc.

Efficient use of resources
  productivity
  human resource cost vs. total revenue
  sales or profit per employee
  training and development
  wage and salary administration
  capital and physical facilities utilization, etc.
Managerial capabilities
Staff capabilities
Employee motivation
  job satisfaction
  turnover
  absenteeism, etc.
Product service markets
  market share
  market potential
  market maturity
  product/service life-cycle
  strengths and weaknesses, etc.
Technological capabilities
  technology availability
  research and development
  computational capabilities
  management information systems
  potential changes
  strengths and weaknesses, etc.
Competition
  price
  product—service
  quality
  market share
  technology
  research and development, etc.
Social responsibilities
  public service
  public image
  consumer protection
  environmental concerns
  social contributions, etc.

Organizational considerations
    organizational structure
    information processing and communication
    organizational flexibility and change
    strengths and weaknesses, etc.

4. **Forecasts and predictions for future conditions**
Economic conditions
    general condition—GNP, inflation, employment, etc.
    projected sales
    market potential
    energy costs
Competition
    new products or services
    technology
    price
    quality, etc.
Technology
    new developments
Social conditions
    special issuses and concerns (Proposition 13,
      nuclear power plants)
    values and attitudes
    crime
    population
Political conditions
    international tension
    actions of power groups (OPEC, superpowers)
    government regulations, etc.

5. **Needs and desires of employees**
Rank and file employees
Staff and professional
Managerial personnel
Board of directors

THE ORGANIZATIONAL PROCESS OF GOAL DEVELOPMENT

MBMO is not intended to be an addition to existing management
tasks; rather, it is an integrated and systematic way to manage an

organization. It should be clear, therefore, that every function, unit, and employee in the organization will be affected by the MBMO system. Thus, the importance of actual commitment and participation of top management in MBMO can be easily understood. It should be understood clearly throughout the organization that organizational planning (including the purpose, long-term goals, policies, etc.) is the responsibility of top management. The top manager (chief executive officer, president, or chairman of the board in nonprofit organizations, or head of governmental agencies) is architect of the organization's future, and thus he or she is the chief planner.

As the chief planner, top management has several responsibilities. George Steiner lists the following: (1) making sure that the climate in the organization is congenial to doing effective planning; (2) making sure the system is organized in a fashion appropriate to the organization; (3) if a planner is employed, seeing to it that he or she is the right person for the job and have the person report as close to the top of the organization as possible; (4) getting involved in doing the actual planning; and (5) having face-to-face meetings with those who draw up plans for the top manager's review and approval.

It is important for the top management team to provide the guidance and thrust for the MBMO system. We are not suggesting a strict top-down management style. However, some essential information needed for developing strategic plans are available only from top management. Top management must be actively involved in actual formulation of organizational purpose, long-range goals, and strategic plans. Such participation provides essential inputs for the MBMO system concerning top management perceptions in regard to external and internal factors as well as management philosophies. Furthermore, top management participation demonstrates its commitment to the MBMO system, and helps to motivate all members of the organization to participate in the MBMO process.

Since the MBMO system is a total way to manage an organization by and with objectives, all members of the organization should be involved. The organizational purpose and mission generally flow down from top management, while unit objectives, work activities, and methods flow up from the bottom of the organization, as shown in Figure 3.5. All members of the organization help shape the purpose and long-range goals of the organization, but they must be accepted and approved by top management. Organizational units present their objectives, activities, and work methods to the higher level management; then, the organization's operational objectives and measuring criteria are determined jointly. Actual action plans, unit objectives, individual objectives, and work methods will be refined and modified following the final determination of organizational objectives.

There exists a cascade approach and a subsequent upstream flow of information in the goal-setting process of MBMO. The cascade approach is basically the top-down flow of information and guidelines. The upstream approach represents a bottom-up flow of employees' objectives, concerns, work methods, and units' objectives. The two-way flow of information and communication ensures a great deal of commitment, enthusiasm, and participation in the MBMO process. Figure 3.6 presents the organizational participation in MBMO.

EXAMPLE—A LARGE PETROLEUM CORPORATION

The exact process to be used for developing organizational purpose, missions, and long-range goals depends upon the unique characteristics of the organization (type of organization, type of industry, size

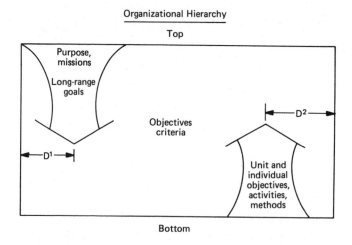

FIGURE 3.5 Organizational process of MBMO

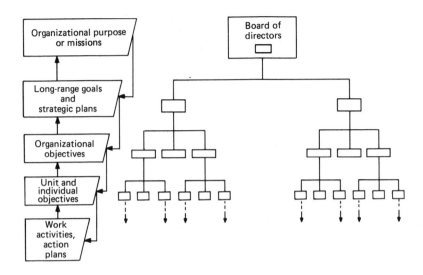

FIGURE 3.6 Organizational participation in MBMO

of the organization, growth stage of the organization, competition, market, technology, management philosophy, etc.). However, there are certain basic elements, issues, and steps that need to be evaluated as we have discussed in the chapter. Below is a simplified illustration of the organizational purpose, long-range goals, and strategic plans developed for a large petroleum organization.

1. The Basic Organizational Purpose
   Search, explore, find, refine, produce, and market energy resources, primarily oil and gas for American customers.
2. Long-range Goals
   a To manage the company operation so that a satisfactory and stable rate of growth can be achieved through reinvestment of a major portion of the company's profit.
   b To recognize the essential value of energy resources for the customer and the nation and strive to satisfy customer needs at the most reasonable cost.
   c To take systematic risks to identify, explore, and develop new sources of energy for organizational growth.
   d To provide a stable and challenging work environment for all employees.

e   To conduct the company's activities in a lawful, ethical, and moral way.

f   To provide a stable and satisfactory rate of return on investment to the stockholders.

g   To recognize the social responsibilities of the firm and contribute to social good as a citizen in the community.

3. Strategic Plans

a   Increase the company's market share by 5 percent during the next 5 years.

b   Explore at least 3 new potential sites during the next 6 years.

c   Continue to participate in social support and clarity programs.

d   Continue the current dividend payment policy during the next 5 years.

e   Implement new management training and employee development programs during the next 3 years.

f   Continue the research and developmental programs for shale oil and solar energy.

SUMMARY

This chapter has presented the first basic element of the MBMO system—formulating long-range and strategic plans. The organizational purpose and visions are developed based on an analysis of the external environment and the internal organizational capabilities. The cascade effect of the MBMO process begins with a clear and concise statement of the organizational purpose. Long-range goals are developed to achieve the organizational purpose. Three broad areas encompassing maintenance, performance, and innovative goals must be developed. Then, a set of strategic plans are developed to attain long-range goals. It is absolutely essential that top management participate directly in the goal-formulation process and make a strong commitment to MBMO for its successful implementation.

REFERENCES

Lee, S.M., and Moore, L.J. *Introduction to Decision Science.* New York: Petrocelli—Charter, 1975.

Mayo, Elton. *The Social Problem of an Industrial Civilization.* Boston: Harvard University, Division of Research, Graduate School of Business Administration, 1945.

Morrisey, G.L. *Management by Objectives and Results for Business and Industry.* 2d ed. Reading, Mass.: Addison-Wesley, 1977.

Odiorne, G.S. *MBO II: A System of Managerial Leadership for the 80's.* Belmont, Calif.: Fearon Pitman, 1979.

Raia, A.P. *Managing by Objectives.* Glenview, Ill.: Scott, Foresman, 1974.

Simon, H.A. "Rational Decision Making in Business Organizations." *American Economic Review* 69(1979): 493-513.

Steiner, A.G., and Miner, J.B. *Management Policy and Strategy.* New York: Macmillan, 1977.

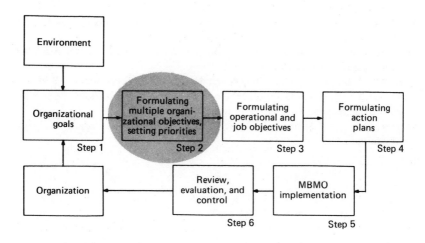

4

Formulating Multiple
Organizational Objectives

Developing the organizational purpose or mission, long-range goals, and strategic plans represents the first basic element of the MBMO process, which involves the formulation of directions and guidelines by upper management. In order to direct resources, human efforts, and work activities toward organizational goals, clearly and explicitly defined objectives are essential. Such organizational objectives must be formulated within the guidelines of long-range goals and strategic plans as well as lower division capabilities. In other words, the objective formulation process—the heart of MBMO—is at the crossroads of the top-down and bottom-up approaches involved in the MBMO process. Figure 4.1 presents a simple representation of the objective formulated element in the MBMO process.

The folklorists of the Orient say that once a Chinese king (there were a number of small kingdoms in China around 500 B.C.) asked Confucius how he should achieve his lifelong goal of bringing peace to the world (at that time, the entire territory of China). Confucius asked for a piece of paper and a brush to write down his reply. Legend tells us that Confucius wrote nine characters and walked out after throwing away the brush. The nine characters the sage wrote present the characteristically profound philosophy of Confucius— "Cultivate yourself, control your family, govern the nation, and then peace shall come to the world." Perhaps what Confucius was trying to tell the king was that a broad goal cannot be achieved until more clearly defined objectives and subobjectives are achieved. The wisdom of Confucius has earned him a special place in the MBMO hall of fame.

As the story of Confucius indicates, a cascade effect should be recognized in the MBMO process. The organizational purpose, long-range goals, and strategic plans present a set of important factors

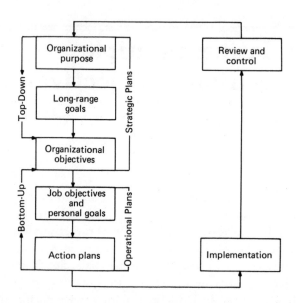

FIGURE 4.1 The objective formulation element
in the MBMO process

that are critical for formulating objectives. Thus, a careful analysis
of previous steps should help to formulate various objectives. In this
chapter we shall discuss the following topics: (1) identifying multiple objectives, (2) determining the objective levels, and (3) setting
priorities for objectives.

IDENTIFYING MULTIPLE OBJECTIVES

WHAT IS AN OBJECTIVE?

An objective is an explicit, clear, and specific statement in quantifiable terms about a desired state. An objective can represent a relatively long-term accomplishment, i.e., six months to three years.
An objective usually contains four basic elements: an accomplish-

ment plan, an objective criterion, a quantitative measurement, and a time constraint within which the desired state is to be achieved. For example, viable objectives can be formulated as follows:

To increase the *market share* by *10 percent* during *this fiscal year.*

To reduce the *number of burglaries* by *5 percent* during the *next 6 months.*

To achieve the *donated blood* level of *1,000 pints* during the *coming campaign.*

We should notice here that the objective statement does not include the rationale or justification for its existence. The rationale or justification, the "why," was already defined in the organizational purpose and goals. The action plans and methods, the "how," will be determined after the objective is formulated. The formulation of objectives involves basically "what" (criteria), "how much" (quantitative levels of the objectives), and "when" (the time deadline). The objective criterion is the only firm element in the objective formulation process. The objective levels (how much), the time deadline (when), and the resource requirements (at what cost) are variable parameters. These parameters are determined only after a careful analysis of conflicts among objectives, technological coefficients (resource requirements associated with work activities that will lead toward the achievement of a given objective), available resources and capabilities, and the priorities for the objectives.

Not all objectives can be precisely expressed in quantitative criteria. Thus, we need to recognize the two forms of objectives: quantitative and qualitative. As illustrated earlier, a quantitative objective indicates the direction of a desired change, the criterion, the degree or amount of change and the time constraint. It is of course desirable to have as many quantitative objectives as possible.

Qualitative objectives not only do exist but they are often of high priorities. Qualitative objectives, such as "improving the public image of the organization," also indicate the direction of change and/or the criterion, but they do not indicate the exact degree or amount of change. Whenever possible, qualitative objectives are replaced by surrogate quantitative objectives.

HOW IS THE FORMAT OF OBJECTIVES DETERMINED?

Any objective can be classified into two basic types: maintenance and improvement. A maintenance objective is to preserve a favorable existing condition. An improvement objective (either performance or innovative) is to make a change in the existing condition. The desired change could be to reduce or increase an existing objective level (the performance objective) or to introduce an entirely new condition (the innovative objective) which is perceived to be superior to the existing condition. Since the format of a maintenance or an innovative objective is simple or self-explanatory, we shall discuss here only the performance objective.

FORMAT OF A QUANTITATIVE PERFORMANCE OBJECTIVE

Many organizational objectives seek to improve existing conditions. They are either internally oriented (e.g., improving productivity of workers) or externally oriented (e.g., improving the public image of the firm). The basic attempt of an objective would be to change the existing conditions in a particular direction which is perceived desirable to achieve organizational goals.

All performance objectives must contain the direction of change, the condition (criterion) to be changed, the amount or degree of change desired, and the time constraint for the change. For example, let us consider the following objective: To increase the market share by 5 percent during the next 3 years.

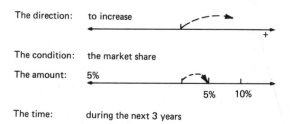

The direction:	to increase
The condition:	the market share
The amount:	5%
The time:	during the next 3 years

The basic performance objective can be further modified later for divisional or individual objectives. For example, the above market share objective can be modified as follows: to increase the market share of the patient bathing system in the Great Plains sales district by 5 percent during the next 3 years. For now, let us simply say that the basic format of a performance objective should be stated in quantitative terms for the desired change, the degree of change, and the time constraint. The primary reasons for quantifying objectives are (1) quantitative terms allow a more accurate analysis of the relationship between the contributing work activities and the objective level; (2) quantitative terms allow the formulation of models that could be used to manipulate model inputs, parameters, and objective levels; and (3) quantitative terms allow objective evaluation of the performance.

FORMAT OF A QUALITATIVE OBJECT

Qualitative objectives are formulated when the desired change in the existing condition cannot be expressed in a quantitative measurement or when the determination of precise quantitative measurements would require excessive time, cost, or effort. Consider the following qualitative performance objective: To improve the public image of the organization during the next year. Conceivably, a qualitative objective is such that it does not allow any quantification. However, in most cases, qualitative objectives can be replaced by a set of surrogate quantitative objectives that are proven to be related to the desired conditions of the objectives. For example, let us reexamine the above stated qualitative performance objective as follows:

Original objective

    The direction: to improve

    The condition: the public image

    The amount: ?

    The time: during the next year

Surrogate objectives

    The direction and condition:

      1. Decrease the number of customer complaints

      2. Increase the organization's community service activities

      3. Increase the number of the organization's information brochures distributed to the community

      4. Increase the quality control efforts for the organization's products

The amount:
1. 10% -
2. 5% +
3. 20% +
4. 10% +
The time: during the next year

Although we may not have precise correlation coefficients between the original qualitative objective and each of the surrogate quantitative objectives, we can readily accept that those surrogate objectives are generally related to the original objective. A good idea is to substitute qualitative objectives by related indirect surrogate quantitative objectives whenever and as much as possible.

MULTIPLE OBJECTIVE CRITERIA

In chapter 3 we discussed that an organization must have three basic types of objectives in order to survive and grow: maintenance, performance, and innovative. Maintenance objectives are necessary to ensure the organization's existence. In this sense, these are perhaps the prerequisite objectives for survival; however, the status quo or "control" which prevents change should never be the ultimate objective for any organization. Improving its contribution through improved effectiveness and new activities—managing change—is important for organizational growth.

We should note here that an objective criterion (e.g., profit, market share, customer relations, social responsibility, etc.) may encompass all three types of objectives. For example, for the market share objective criterion we may have the following separate objectives:

maintenance objective: to maintain the current market share (5 percent of the industry total) during the coming year.

performance objective: to improve the market share in the Great Plains region by 10 percent during the coming year.

innovative performance: to negotiate and open a sales office in Japan and achieve $1 million export during the coming year.

The same type of differentiations can be made for other objectives such as profit, employee relations, etc. It should be evident that organizations not only have multiple objective criteria, but the multiplicity further increases because the objectives can take any of the three different types of formats.

Organizational objectives must encompass specific activities, quantitative criteria whenever and as much as possible, the desired results to be accomplished by the organization, and a specific time constraint. These objectives should include both the economic and noneconomic areas of the organization, as discussed in chapter 2. Formulation of specific organizational objectives in a given organization requires the identification of key objective criteria or key result areas that would contribute toward the achievement of organizational goals. Identification of multiple key criteria in a governmental agency or nonprofit organization may be simpler than in the private sector because their mission—the purpose of their existence—is often more explicitly stated than it is for the private company.

Here we shall consider only the multiple objective criteria of business organizations. As shown in chapters 1 and 2, there has been extensive research into the analysis of organizational objectives in the management literature. Although numerous studies of this subject have not shown unanimity, a number of multiple objectives have been generally accepted as essential for any business organization.

MARKET OBJECTIVE

The market objective is concerned with securing a satisfactory volume of sales for the organization's products. The market objective may take several different forms. For example, it may be described as "to attain 25 percent of the industry market share during the next year," or it could be "to achieve $5 million total sales for the coming year," or it may be expressed in terms of sales volume, such as "to achieve the total sales of 50,000 units of the product next year." In addition, the market objective can also be expressed in terms of a maintenance, performance, or innovative objective.

PROFIT OBJECTIVE

The profit objective, a necessary concern of any business organization, can be expressed in many different ways, such as the rate of return on investment, earnings per share, profits to total revenue ratios, etc. Profit maximization, the objective so vehemently advocated in traditional management theory, is usually not the predominant objective associated with profit. The profit objective may take the following forms: "to achieve the rate of return on investment of 12 percent during the next three years," or "to increase profits by five percent during the next year," or "to achieve the satisfactory profit level of $5 million during the next two years."

PRODUCT OBJECTIVE

The product objective involves the production and distribution of the organization's primary products (or services). This objective usually involves certain desired results concerning specific products. Again, it may take the form of a maintenance, performance, or innovative objective. Some illustrative examples of this objective would be "to introduce a new simplified camera in the $400-$500 range for nonprofessional customers during the next two years," or "to phase out the large-size V-8 automobiles by 1983," or "to increase the sales of the new patient bathing tubs to 1,000 in the Midwest sales region during the next two years."

FINANCIAL OBJECTIVES

An organization may have a number of financial objectives, such as the desired debt ceiling, capital structure, capital budgeting, portfolio management, working capital, cash flows, common stock or preferred stock issues, dividend payments, etc. Some financial objectives might be "to increase the monthly cash inflow by 10 percent during the next year," or 'to maintain a minimum working capital of $2 million within the next two years," or "to continue the dividend payment policy of 30 percent of the profit."

HUMAN RESOURCES OBJECTIVES

Human resources objectives deal primarily with helping and developing employees to achieve their personal objectives while working toward the organization's objectives. Many objectives in this area may not be quantified easily, such as motivation, training and development, job satisfaction, and the like. However, some of these objectives could be expressed in quantitative terms. For example, there may be objectives such as "to reduce the turnover rate to 15 percent during the next year," or 'to reduce the absenteeism to less than two percent by the end of next year," or "to send all senior managers to at least one week of top management training programs at universities by the end of 1982," or "to conduct a two-day supervisory management training program for all first-line managers by the end of next year."

PHYSICAL FACILITIES OBJECTIVES

Physical facilities objectives are concerned with the organization's physical capabilities to support its productive activities. These objectives can also take a variety of forms, such as productive capacity (in units), assembly lines, square feet of the plant facilities, fixed charge or costs, etc. Some objectives could be "to increase the full reserve capacity to the 30-day demand (20 million barrels) by the end of next year," "to increase the manufacturing plant facility space to one million square feet by 1983," or "to increase production capacity to 20 aircraft per month during the next three years."

RESEARCH AND DEVELOPMENT OBJECTIVES

Research and development objectives involve not only technical aspects but also innovative ideas to improve organizational effectiveness. These objectives could be expressed in terms of new technology, dollars, or other criteria. For example, a research and innovative objective may read as "to develop an electric car in the $5,000 range, with a capacity of 150 miles before recharge, by 1985."

Productivity Objectives

Productivity objectives may be related to technology, employee motivation, or training and development. Productivity objectives could be formulated in quantitative terms such as "to decrease the unit cost of the product by 5 percent during the next year," or "to decrease the labor cost to 35 percent of total cost during the next two years."

Organizational Development Objectives

Organizational development objectives are concerned with improving organizational effectiveness through changes in the organizational climate, processes, structure and functional relationships. Examples would be "to develop a decentralized organizational structure for various divisions by 1982," or "to set up the Far East sales office in Tokyo within three years."

Social Contribution Objectives

Social contribution objectives represent the organization's activities or financial contributions to various civic or social causes. Some examples would be "to sponsor an annual special Junior Olympics for handicapped children in the community," or "to hire and train at least 20 minority hard-core unemployable persons every year."

DETERMINING THE OBJECTIVE LEVELS

Determination of the appropriate objective levels is perhaps as important, if not more so, as identifying the objective criteria. Yet, most MBO books or papers do not even mention this important aspect of the objective formulation. For example, an objective could be formulated as "to reduce the production cost by 10 percent during the next fiscal year." The basic question we can raise would be, why 10 percent but not 5 percent or 15 percent? The objective level stated should not be determined arbitrarily but be based on legitimate reasons.

There are many reasons for determining the most appropriate level of a given objective.

SATISFYING OF OBJECTIVES

Managers usually attempt to achieve a set of multiple objectives based on the perceived importance of these objectives for the organization and thus assign certain priorities to objectives. In most cases, priorities are assigned to achieving a given objective rather than to the objective criterion. For example, a manager may assign the highest priority to an objective, such as "to increase the market share by 5 percent in the Great Plains district," rather than assigning the priority to "market share" per se. In other words, the central driving force of the management process is 5 percent of the market share.

We have already recognized the multiplicity of organizational objectives and their possible conflict. If the market share objective is in conflict with other objectives assigned lower priorities, achievement of 5 percent increase in market share would be possible only at the expense of achieving those conflicting objectives. If the objective level for market share is set at a higher level than actually justified, a substantial inefficiency would result. Therefore, it is essential to analyze conflicts among these objectives through trade-offs. Without such analysis, it is impossible to achieve the satisfying solution which provides economic and operational efficiency to the system.

CHALLENGE AND MOTIVATION

If an objective level is so low that it can be obtained easily without any effort, people will receive little satisfaction due to the lack of challenge. Paradoxically, if an objective level is so high that it is beyond reach of even the best efforts of the workers, people will be frustrated with the situation. In order to provide work challenge and satisfaction (that will lead to a high level of motivation), the objective level should be at an appropriate level. It should provide a challenge to incorporate imagination and "stretch" efforts on the part of the work team to achieve the objective level. Simultaneously, the probability of attaining the objective level should be high when required efforts are provided.

Many managers tend to play it safe by arguing for lower objective levels or limiting their objectives to maintenance types only. Thus, they may boast a 100 percent attainment record for their objectives. Effective managers, however, are not afraid to face challenging objectives. Their good efforts, whether or not the objective level is completely attained, should be rewarded. Furthermore, if good efforts on the part of the manager and his or her subordinates could not achieve the objective level, then their experience should be used as a guide in setting a similar objective level in the future.

Although we recognize the importance of setting an appropriate objective level, when it comes to actually doing it, it is easier said than done. One must gather relevant information and data about activities that contribute to the achievement of the objectives, degree of conflict with other objectives, trade-offs among the objectives, and environmental factors that affect the objective. It is not easy to determine what data are necessary, how much data would be sufficient, and how to analyze them.

Some possible sources of data or analyses that would be useful for setting the objective level are below:

1. *Historical data*—past records within the organization as well as externally available data such as government statistics, industry reports, published research papers, etc.
2. *Future analysis*—published studies in the area of future analysis concerning social, economic, and political conditions
3. *Trend analysis*—simple explanation of past trends or complex curve-fitting analysis
4. *Regression and other multivariate analyses*—predictive models for a certain objective criterion based on a set of independent variables

5. *Custom-made models*—designing analytical or computer-based simulation models to analyze the relationship between the objective criterion under consideration and other objectives and to provide the degree of conflict and trade-off information

SETTING PRIORITIES FOR OBJECTIVES

As we discussed in earlier chapters, it is human nature to desire more than is available. The same principle applies to organizational objectives. Regardless of how organizational objectives are determined, there would be more organizational objectives than can possibly be achieved with the available resources. Consequently, all objectives cannot be achieved, and there is a need to establish a priority structure that would ensure that at least the important objectives would be achieved with the available resources.

The priority-setting process is one of the most important managerial decisions. The priority structure represents a choice activity of management about what objectives should be achieved at the expense of other objectives. Setting priority involves an exercise of individual judgment, whether it is done by one person or by a group of individuals. Although an increasing number of systematic approaches have been developed to make the process more effective, no technique has been suggested to replace human judgment that synthesizes a variety of factors involved in managment objectives such as internal and external elements, emergency situations, short-term versus long-term benefits, and the like.

There are two important inputs to the priority-setting process: the cost-benefit ratio, and distinction between system and goal constraints. The cost-benefit ratio provides an economic efficiency measurement—the value of the output in relation to the input cost for a given action plan. The system constraints represent those that must be satisfied before any organizational objectives are to be considered. Once such constraints, representing the external and internal realities, are satisfied, then goal constraints that represent desired objective levels should be analyzed.

There are many intuitive, subjective, or systematic approaches that have been suggested for the setting of priorities. We shall review here several of the most promising.

TREND ANALYSIS

We can perform a simple trend analysis for all major organizational objectives. For example, for a given objective we can determine where we are now, where we will be if the past trend continues, and where we should be. The analysis can be shown in a simple graph as in Figure 4.2. Point A represents the current level of the objective criterion (e.g., profit, market share, etc.). Point B is the projected point where the objective level would be at the end of the planning horizon t_1. Point C represents the desired level of the objective at the end of the planning horizon t_1. Then, the absolute difference $|C - B|$ represents the deviation between where it would be and where it should be. If the deviation is favorable (i.e., the projected outcome is better than the desired outcome), this objective should be assigned a very low priority. On the other hand, if the deviation is unfavorable (i.e., the projected outcome is lower than the desired outcome), the objective under analysis should receive a greater amount of attention.

It should be noted here that the unfavorable deviation measurements (either absolute or percentage value) for the objectives would not be a sufficient basis for assigning priorities. However, if some of the objectives have generally the same degree of importance, the deviation measures could be used as differentiating factors. For example, suppose that the following objectives are accepted as prime importance for the organization: market share, profit, and employee productivity. Let us further assume that the trend analysis yielded the following information:

Objective	Deviation between Should Be and Would Be
Market share	+5%
Profit	-12%
Employee productivity	-27%

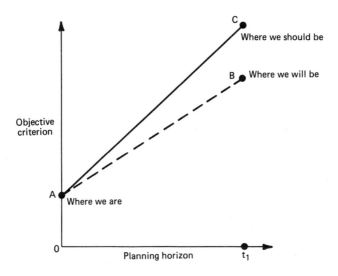

FIGURE 4.2 Trend analysis for objective levels.

Given the above information, the managers would be most concerned with the productivity objective, followed by the profit objective, and finally the market share objective. Thus, we can assign priorities based on the deviations between the desired level and the projected level of various objectives.

PRIORITY HIERARCHY CLASSIFICATIONS

Another simple approach that can be easily used for setting priorities for objectives is the priority hierarchy classification. For example, we can develop four hierarchic groups: must, highly desirable, desirable, and nice to achieve. Figure 4.3 presents the priority heirarchy classifications and measures within each classification.

"Must" are those objectives perceived essential by management for the survival and long-term prosperity of the organization. "Highly desirable" represents those objectives which play important roles in improving the overall performance of the organization. These objectives may not be directly related to the survival of the organization but they may be considered important by management. "De-

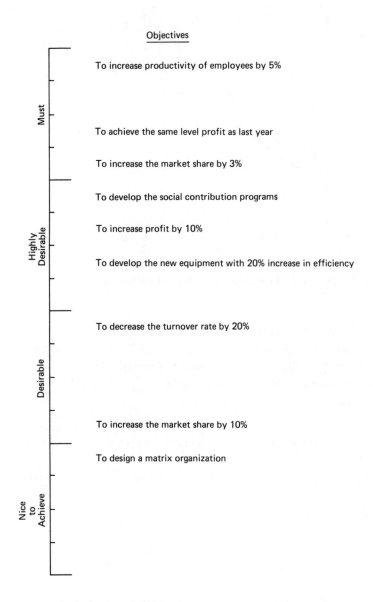

**FIGURE 4.3 Priority hierarchy classifications
and illustrative objectives**

sirable" objectives are those considered important for the long-term success of the organization but are not at all urgent. "Nice to achieve" are frill objectives that represent some pet projects that are desirable for improving organizational performance in certain areas. These "nice to achieve" objectives could be scrapped or reduced in scale if they are in conflict with higher priority objectives or a lack of resources.

It should be emphasized here once again that objectives can be decomposed by levels as well as by the orientation (maintenance, performance, and/or innovative). Thus, an objective can appear in each of the four classifications with different objective levels or orientation.

THE PAIRED COMPARISON METHOD

We accept the notion that management by multiple objectives based on priorities is an effective management process. The process of priority setting is extremely important and complex when there are a large number of objectives under consideration. One possible method of obtaining a priority structure for multiple objectives is to present a list of objectives to the decision maker (or a decision-making group) to rank them in the order of importance or preference.

Actually this process is not a novelty to practicing managers. Managers usually work with a set of policies or procedures that have already assigned some implicit priorities to objectives. Also, managers motivate or evaluate the performance of their subordinates based on the objective criteria and their priorities set in advance. As a matter of fact, quite often effective managers make work agreements annually with subordinates concerning their roles, responsibilities, and work activities that would contribute toward the achievement of important organizational objectives.

The paired comparison method is a simple process that can provide some check on the consistency in the value judgment of the decision maker. In this method the decision maker is simply asked to compare the objectives two at a time and indicate which is more important in the pair. This procedure is carried on until all possible pairs of objectives are analyzed for comparative value judgment. From this analysis a complete priority ranking can be obtained for the objectives in terms of their importance to the organization.

Suppose there are five objectives: O_1 (market share), O_2 (profit), O_3 (customer satisfaction), O_4 (employee relations), and O_5 (research and development). If there are n number of objectives, the total number of pairs to be evaluated will be $n(n-1)/2$. For example, for five objectives the total number of pairs would be $5(5-1)/2 = (5 \times 4)/2 = 10$.

Now we can list the objective pairs and ask the decision maker to check which one is more important for each of the pairs by $>$ (the objective on left is more important than on right in the pair) or $<$ (the objective on right is more important than the one on left). For example, let us assume that the decision maker's judgment for the paired comparison is as follows:

$O_1 > O_2$	$O_2 > O_4$
$O_1 > O_3$	$O_2 < O_5$
$O_1 > O_4$	$O_3 > O_4$
$O_1 > O_5$	$O_3 < O_5$
$O_2 < O_3$	$O_4 < O_5$

In order to derive the complete priority structure for the objectives, we rearrange the preference judgment so that all the "more important than" signs will point in the same direction, as follows:

$O_1 > O_2$	$O_2 > O_4$
$O_1 > O_3$	$O_5 > O_2$
$O_1 > O_4$	$O_3 > O_4$
$O_1 > O_5$	$O_5 > O_3$
$O_3 > O_2$	$O_5 > O_4$

The most important objective must be more important than four other objectives. In other words, the most important objective should appear on the "more important than" side of the list four times. Objective O_1 indeed appears four times on that side. Similarly, the second objective in importance should appear three times on the "more important than" side. Objective O_5 qualifies as the second priority objective. In general, if there are n objectives, the objective with the rth priority ranking should appear $n-r$ times on the "more important than" side of the preference judgment list. In this example case, the priority ranking of the five objectives considered would be as follows:

Priority Ranking	Objective	$n - r$
1	O_1 (market share)	$5 - 1 = 4$
2	O_5 (research and development)	$5 - 2 = 3$
3	O_3 (customer satisfaction)	$5 - 3 = 2$
4	O_2 (profit)	$5 - 4 = 1$
5	O_4 (employee relations)	$5 - 5 = 0$

Although the paired comparison method described above looks complex, it can be done rather quickly by using a matrix form. For example, let us suppose that there are n number of objectives that need to be evaluated in order to establish the priority structure. We can construct a matrix which shows a vertical and horizontal listing of objectives as in Figure 4.4. This type of matrix is often used to analyze correlations among variables. Since we do not need to compare an objective to itself, the diagonal line is darkened to cross out the space.

The paired comparison matrix can be used by following the four simple steps shown on the following pages.

Objectives	1	2	3	4	5	6	—	—	—	N	Number of pluses	Priority rank
1	◪											
2		◪										
3			◪									
4				◪								
5					◪							
6						◪						
—							◪					
—								◪				
—									◪			
N										◪		

FIGURE 4.4 The paired comparison matrix

Step 1

Starting with Objective 1, evaluate its importance against that of other objectives horizontally. If it is more important than the other objective, put a + sign in the space. If Objective 1 is less important than the objective being compared with, put a - sign in the space.

	1	2	3	4	5	6	7	8	9	10
Objective 1	◺	+	−	−	−	−	−	−	+	−

Objective 1 is perceived as more important than objectives 2 and 9, but as less important than all other objectives.

Step 2

Now the evaluation result obtained in Step 1 should be transposed, that is, list the + or - evaluations vertically in the Objective 1 column. Since the horizontal evaluation performed in Step 1 is for Objective 1 versus each of the other objectives, when we list the same information vertically + becomes - and - becomes +. For example, in Step 1, Objective 1 is rated as more important than Objective 2. When we come down in the Objective 1 column, we will be evaluating Objective 2 versus Objective 1. Since Objective 1 has already been rated as more important than Objective 2, the space should have a - sign.

	1	2
Objective 1	◺	
2	−	◺
3	+	
4	+	
5	+	
6	+	
7	+	
8	+	
9	−	
10	+	

The horizontal evaluation is transposed and all - are made + and all + are made -.

Step 3

Continue the procedures outlined in steps 1 and 2 for all of the objectives under consideration. The evaluation is always initiated horizontally on the right of the diagonal line and then transposed vertically.

	1	2	3	4	5	6	7	8	9	10
Objective 1	⧄									
2		⧄	+	+	−	−	+	−	+	−

	1	2
Objective 1	⧄	
2		⧄
3		−
4		−
5		+
6		+
7		−
8		+
9		−
10		+

Step 4

Sum the number of + signs horizontally for each of the objectives. The next column represents the priority ranking for each of the objectives. In order to obtain the priority rank we simply find $(n - s)$, where n = total number of objectives being evaluated and s = sum of + signs.

As an example, let us consider 10 objectives as shown in Figure 4.5. Their priority structure is shown on the following page.

Objectives	*Priority*
Product development	1
Profit	2
Research and development	3
Pollution control	4
New wage plans	5
Productivity	6
Market development	7
Social contribution	8
Market share	9
Organizational change	10

Objectives	1	2	3	4	5	6	7	8	9	10	Number of pluses	Priority rank
1. Market share		+	−	−	−	−	−	−	−	−	1	9
2. Organizational change	−		−	−	−	−	−	−	−	−	0	10
3. Social contributions	+	+		−	−	−	−	−	−	−	2	8
4. Profit	+	+	+		+	+	−	+	+	+	8	2
5. Pollution control	+	+	+	−		−	−	+	+	+	6	4
6. Research and development	+	+	+	−	+		−	+	+	+	7	3
7. Product development	+	+	+	+	+	+		+	+	+	9	1
8. Productivity	+	+	+	−	−	−	−		−	+	4	6
9. New wage plans	+	+	+	−	−	−	−	+		+	5	5
10. Market development	+	+	+	−	−	−	−	−	−		3	7

FIGURE 4.5 Example of the paired comparison matrix

Although the paired comparison method works well in most cases, it can cause some problems when the number of objectives under consideration is large and the decision maker's judgment is not consistent. For example, suppose the decision maker rated objectives as follows:

$$O_2 > O_5 \,; O_5 > O_3 \,; O_3 > O_2$$

Obviously, there exists logical inconsistency in the decision maker's judgment. It is hoped that a review of the situation by the decision maker would clear up the problem. The paired comparison method can be used effectively not only to establish the priority structure of the multiple conflicting objectives but also as a checking device for the consistency of the decision maker's judgment.

It may appear that the paired comparison method is an impossible technique for decision problems that involve numerous conflicting objectives. Fortunately, however, many situations involve only a limited number of conflicting objectives, usually less than 10. Hence, the paired comparison would be a simple enough task.

COST-EFFECTIVENESS ANALYSIS

Another approach that can be used for setting priorities for objectives is cost-effectiveness analysis. Since the MBMO process attempts to satisfy multiple and conflicting objectives rather than optimize one objective, the cost versus effectiveness measurement is an important criterion for setting priorities. The cost-effectiveness measurement does not provide automatic priority weights. It simply provides information that sharpens the manager's judgment in determining the priorities.

The cost-effectiveness measure is usually a nonlinear function—increasing at an increasing rate in the early stage and increasing at a decreasing rate in the later stage. Thus, it can also be an important criterion in determining the objective levels. For example, the marginal effectiveness value provides much information as to where the cut-off point should be in terms of the objective levels.

Since we are not dealing with a problem which has objectives with a commensurable criterion (i.e., values that can be measured on some unit basis such as dollars, number of people, etc.), the cost-effectiveness measures must be evaluated based on subjective judgment. For example, suppose the activities (or objectives) we are considering have the following information:

Activities	Cost (million $)	Expected Result
Research and development	2.5	New product design
Wage and salary study	0.5	More effective compensation plans— higher level of motivation
Handicapped children's olympic	0.1	Better community relations
Pollution control	5.0	Meet government regulations
Marketing research	1.5	More effective market penetration

From the above information we can easily see that cost-effectiveness measures are all in different criteria—there is no commonality. Managers must use their subjective judgment in weighing not only the objective criteria but also the cost associated with them.

COMPUTER-ASSISTED INTERACTIVE APPROACH

The priority setting process cannot be considered independently without analyzing the associated objective levels. In other words, there is no uniform way to determine priorities for various objective criteria. The actual priorities must be based on the unique characteristics of the situation the organization is in as well as the nature (e.g., maintenance, performance, innovative) and exact levels of the objectives. For example, an organization may state that one of its important objectives is to achieve a satisfactory level of profit. It would be extremely difficult to assign a priority to this objective because we do not have any idea what a satisfactory level of profit means. On the other hand, suppose that the same organization lists three separate (decomposed) objectives about the profit goal as follows: (1) achieve the same level of profit as last year; (2) increase the profit level by 10 percent; (3) maximize the profit. We should have no difficulty in evaluating these three objectives in relation to other objectives.

The computer-assisted interactive approach is a very effective way to determine priorities under varying conditions of the decision environment. The primary advantage of the interactive approach is that it can help the decision maker to sort out important information about the environment, complex interrelationships between objective levels and priorities, and trade-offs among conflicting objectives. More specifically, the approach has the following advantages:

1. It can evaluate and provide information on how many more objectives are formulated than can realistically be achieved.
2. It can identify unrealistically high objective levels (i.e., over-optimism or wishful thinking on the part of the managers), more than can be achieved.
3. It can analyze the complex interrelationships between varying objective levels and priorities that would be almost impossible to analyze mentally on the part of the manager.
4. It can provide trade-off information among those objectives that are in conflict. This information can be used to adjust both the objective levels and priorities.
5. It uses already available technology in most organizations.

On the other hand, the computer-assisted interactive approach has certain requirements. The two most important requirements are:

1. It requires modeling of the MBMO process. The multiple objectives being evaluated must be put together as a quantitative model so that the input-output relationships and interactions among the objectives can be evaluated.
2. It requires trained personnel who can design models, interact with the system, and interpret the results of the output.

Although there are many different ways to develop an interactive approach, we shall discuss just one possible method here. The interactive system is installed on an IBM 370-158 computer and consists of a control program (CP) and the conversational monitor system (CMS). The system allows the user to create and edit files (programs, problems, etc.) and to execute programs conversationally. The interactive system can be used to analyze the impact of the following four most prevalent changes in the MBMO system: (1) changes in objective levels; (2) changes in input or output coefficients (these are sometimes referred to as technological coefficients); (3) addition or deletion of objectives; and (4) changes in priorities assigned to various objectives (see Appendix A).

Perhaps the most dramatic advantage of the computer-assisted interactive approach is its capability to generate information concerning trade-offs among conflicting objectives. This information can be used to adjust the objective levels as well as priorities assigned to the objectives in such a way as to attain a satisfying solution which achieves objectives as closely as possible based on their priorities.

SUMMARY

The broad organizational purpose, missions, and long-range goals determine the basic directions of top management. In order to operationalize the broad goals and direct required resources to achieve the goals, explicitly stated objectives must be formulated. The objectives require precise quantitative criteria, desired levels, time constraints, and appropriate priorities. If the goal is so abstract that explicit objectives cannot be determined, surrogate or pseudo-quantitative objectives should be formulated.

Many MBO books and related papers provide only superficial treatment of the priority-setting process; however, this is of fundamental importance for an effective MBMO system. In this chapter we devoted a great deal of attention to various approaches that could be used in setting priorities. The objective formulation process can be best described by Figure 4.6. Once the organizational objectives are completely formulated, we move down to the lower level of management where job objectives will be identified.

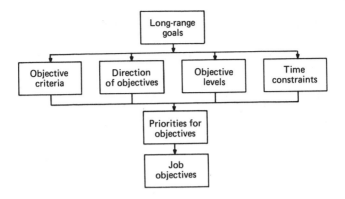

FIGURE 4.6 The process of organizational objectives formulation

REFERENCES

Drucker, Peter. *The Practice of Management*. New York: Harper & Row, 1954.

Lee, S.M. *Goal Programming for Decision Analysis*. Philadelphia: Auerbach, 1972.

Lubans, V.A., and Edgar, J.M. *Policing by Objectives*. Hartford, Conn.: Social Development Corp., 1979.

Morrisey, G.L. *Management by Objectives and Results in the Public Sector*. Reading, Mass.: Addison-Wesley, 1976.

Odiorne, G.S. *MBO II: A System of Managerial Leadership for the 80's*. Belmont, Calif.: Fearon Pitman, 1979.

Raia, A.P. *Managing by Objectives*. Glenview, Ill.: Scott, Foresman, 1974.

Simon, H.A. "Rational Decision Making in Business Organizations." *American Economic Review* 69(1979): 493–513.

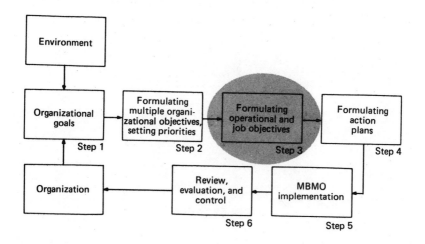

5

Formulating Operational Objectives

The MBMO system in reality is not a totally scientific process; nor is it a totally behavioral and psychological process of human interactions. It is a system based on a combined process of human interactions and systematic analysis. Thus, neither the traditional behavioral MBO approach nor the purely scientific approach alone would suffice for the MBMO system—both are needed.

Organizational objectives are relatively long range and broad in their scope. Thus, there is a need to convert organizational or strategic objectives to operational objectives. Operational objectives are more specific, detailed, short-term work objectives at the divisional, departmental, subunit, or individual managers' levels. In the MBO literature, it has been advocated quite frequently that the cascade process of developing the organizational purpose—long-range organizational goals → strategic plans → objectives— should be repeated for divisions, departments, and other subunits in the organization. In other words, the MBO process should look something like the one shown in Figure 5.1.

The cascade process shown in the figure is like a waterwheel process. Although such a repetitive process at every level of the organization would be an interesting learning experience for many people, the cost-effectiveness would never justify such a process. As a matter of fact, the most negative aspects of MBO have been the enormous paper work and time consumption required by the process. Thus, divisions, departments, subunits, or individuals should not repeat the cascade process, but instead they should be concerned only with formulating operational objectives. The MBMO process, then, should look like the one described in Figure 5.2.

As we discussed earlier, the heart of an effective MBMO system is the formulation of quantifiable organizational objectives and their

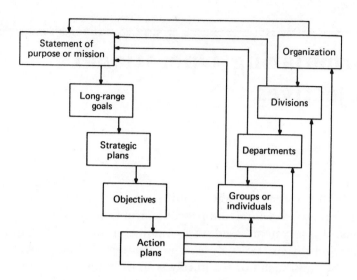

FIGURE 5.1 Cascade process of MBO

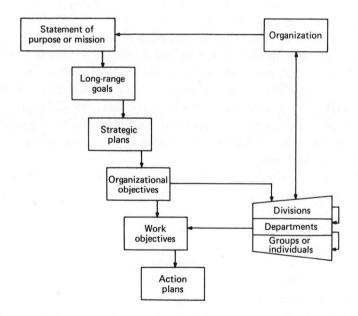

FIGURE 5.2 Work objectives formulation process in MBMO

priorities. Perhaps the second most crucial aspect of MBMO is determining operational objectives. This is where the "gear" is applied to get the machine rolling. At this level organizational objectives are operationalized through accountability and personal commitments.

The exact process of formulating operational objectives at the divisional, departmental, or subunit levels depends upon the unique characteristics of the organization. Thus, the process must be tailored for the organization. The type of industry the organization is in, the size (in terms of sales, employees, profit, assets, etc.), the stage of organizational growth, the organizational structure, the management philosophy and style, and similar conditions of the organization all play important roles in determining the objective formulation process at the middle or lower organizational hierarchy.

In this chapter we shall examine the following aspects of the operational objective formulation process:

- Basic steps of the operational objective formulation process
- Formulating divisional and departmental objectives
- Formulating individual job objectives
- General guidelines for formulation of operational objectives

BASIC STEPS OF THE
OPERATIONAL OBJECTIVE FORMULATION

Although each organization requires a unique process for formulating operational objectives, the following represent the general steps that could be applied in any organization:

1. Objective formulation group
2. Dividing each key result area of the organizational objective into subareas
3. Assigning operational objectives to subunits
4. Developing specific measures for key areas
5. Projecting the resource requirements
6. Setting the target date

THE OBJECTIVE FORMULATION GROUP

The formulation of operational objectives requires vertical and horizontal coordination in the organization. Although ideally all members of the organization should be involved, realistically, a manageable group of busy individuals must be involved in the formulation process. It is important that managers or key individuals of all major operational units are included in the objective formulation process. For example, in formulating the organizational objective, the board of directors, the chief executive officer, and all senior vice-presidents (or equivalent) should be involved. Thus, the "linking pin" principle can be preserved. Figure 5.3 shows the typical linking pin arrangement in formulating objectives at various organizational levels.

In real-world situations, the objective formulation process requires a great deal of information and work expertise. Thus, the

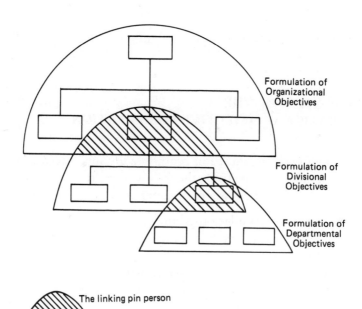

FIGURE 5.3 Linking pin concept

objective formulation group is usually well represented by such staff personnel as data processing specialist, economist or statistician, management scientist, marketing researcher, materials management analyst, etc. These staff people supplement the working knowledge and experience of line managers in providing specialized expertise in formulating operational objectives.

The group must perform a thorough analysis of the following factors that affect the operational objectives:

- Review of external factors affecting the organization
- Review of internal factors affecting the operational objectives:

    organizational objectives

    historical trends

    current resource allocations within the organization

    current performance of various organizational subunits

    organizational limitations

    relations and interactions among organizational units

- Review of subunits' operational capabilities

DIVIDING EACH KEY RESULT AREA OF THE ORGANIZATIONAL OBJECTIVE INTO SUBAREAS

The organizational objective has already identified an explicit result to be accomplished. Now in order to operationalize this objective, we must subdivide the busy result area. For example, let us suppose that the busy result area identified in the organizational objective is market share. This key result area could be subdivided into industrial products, consumer products, and export products. Then, the subareas can be further fragmented into other subareas based on such things as product line, type of product, distribution patterns, demand patterns, price, etc. This process would provide the opportunity to identify the "critical few" key result subareas that yield a relatively greater proportion of the results. Furthermore, through this process we can assess the relative importance or priority of each subarea for the organizational objective.

ASSIGNING OPERATIONAL OBJECTIVES TO SUBUNITS

Once the key result area identified in an organizational objective has been subdivided into several major subareas, operational objectives must be formulated to accomplish the key result subareas. These operational objectives should be analyzed by the objective formulation group at an appropriate level and assigned to divisions, departments, or other lower subunits in the organization. For example, the subdivided market share objective could be formulated as operational objectives for various regional sales offices, product sales departments, or even to the individual sales person.

DEVELOPING SPECIFIC MEASURES FOR KEY AREAS

The next step is to develop specific measuring criteria for each of the key subareas. These criteria are to be used in evaluating the performance of progress. Undoubtedly, the past performance data could serve as the basis in developing certain measures. However, the relevance of the past data depends upon the nature of the objective—maintenance, performance, or innovative. For example, for certain maintenance objectives, the past performance data could serve as the target. However, for performance objectives, the past performance data should be increased significantly. On the other hand, for certain innovative objectives, it would be extremely difficult to establish the appropriate measure. Some illustrative examples of measures are:

- Increase in total sales measured in dollars for the year, with a standard (satisfactory level) of $10 million

- Customer relations measured by the reduction of returned products, with a standard of 2 percent per year

- Market share increase measured by the percentage of our sales of the industry sales, with a standard of 3 percent per year

PROJECTING THE RESOURCE REQUIREMENTS

Operational objectives cannot be accomplished without resources at any level, divisional or departmental. As a matter of fact, the objective criteria standards must be developed based on available or projected resources within the organizational subunit. There should be no strict precedence requirement of resources before objective levels can be determined. Undoubtedly, the available resources are important constraints only after they become known or determined by management. However, quite frequently the amount of resources available or allocated to certain subunits is a direct function of desired objective levels and their priorities. In other words, the ends are not always determined by the means, but frequently the means are determined by the desired ends.

SETTING THE TARGET DATE

The desired standards or objective levels (or subareas of the lay result criteria) should be accomplished by a certain target date. The time requirement is surely a function of available resources and the desired objective levels. The process of setting the target date should be conducted the same way as setting the objective levels. The target date should be such that accomplishing the desired results within the time constraint is challenging and also attainable with good efforts.

As we have discussed in earlier chapters, all of the organizational and operational objectives may not be quantified in explicit measures. In some instances, quasi or surrogate quantitative objectives could be formulated to represent qualitative or subjective objectives. If such substitution is impossible, the qualitative objectives should be used as they are defined. Although they do not render themselves to explicit analysis, clearly defined qualitative objectives would be much better than none at all. At least we should be able to monitor the organization's progress toward the qualitative objectives.

FORMULATING DIVISIONAL AND DEPARTMENTAL OBJECTIVES

In order to formulate divisional and departmental objectives, the general steps outlined above should be implemented. The broad organizational objectives must be decomposed or subdivided among the divisions in such a way that they can be operationalized. When we say "operationalize," we are implying that the key result areas are identified so explicitly that resources can be directed toward them with the appropriate accountability, responsibility, and controls.

If a division contains several middle management levels (departments, subunits, etc.), several objective formulation groups should be formed. Thus, although the basic process of formulating operational objectives remains the same, several cascading steps may be necessary to coordinate objectives at the various organizational levels. The linking pin concept will be effective in coordinating the work of the objective formulation groups at different levels.

A common procedure for developing the divisional objective employs the bottom-up process. The lowest subunit objective formulation group, which is composed of the line manager, lowest level managers, and appropriate staff personnel, formulate their objectives first and send them up to the next higher objective formulation group for their review and modification. This higher group then will aggregate the operational objectives of the lower subunit groups and pass them along to the next higher level, and so on. Although the bottom-up process appears to be a sensible approach, in reality it is not the most effective way. In order to make the bottom-up approach productive and effective, there should be a constant two-way communication. The top-down communication must convey the organizational objectives (key result areas, objective levels, target dates, priorities, etc.) and available resources in the orgnization as well as in divisions. The bottom-up communication carries various possible objective achievements with different resource levels, priorities, target dates, etc. The dual approach, then, is the most effective way to formulate divisional and departmental objectives.

Figure 5.4 represents the general two-way approach to formulate divisional and departmental objectives. The organizational objectives categorized in maintenance, performance, and innovative areas are prioritized before they are decomposed at the divisional level. The divisional objective formulation group analyzes the constraints or bounds imposed by the organizational objectives and sends down the information. The divisions or departments report their possible contribution toward organizational objectives in terms of a detailed list of operational objectives that could be accomplished within the constraints. The two-way communication remains active until all significant differences are ironed out by the objective formulation group.

The divisional level objective formulation group is also required to aggregate the expected results of the departmental (or subunits')

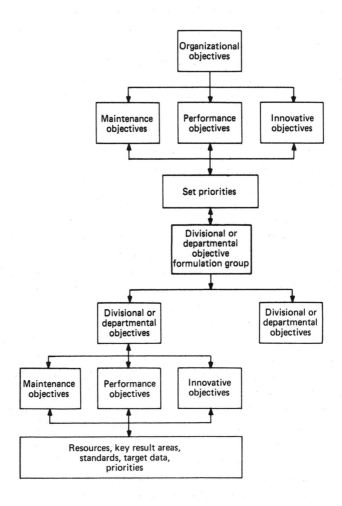

FIGURE 5.4 Two-way approach to formulate divisional objectives

objectives. In an organization with a traditional structure, the aggregation procedure is usually a straightforward mathematical operation. For example, in order to achieve the organizational objective of market share, suppose that each of the three divisions set their objectives as follows:

Last Year's Sales

Division 1	$12 million
Division 2	$10 million
Division 3	$20 million
Total	$42 million

Divisional Objectives

Division 1	Increase sales by 15%
Division 2	Increase sales by 10%
Division 3	Increase sales by 8%

With the above proposed increase in sales by each division, the objective formulation group can easily determine the aggregate sales increase for all the divisions as follows:

Division 1: 15% x $12 million = $1.8 million: 4.29% of total sales

Division 2: 10% x $10 million = $1.0 million: 2.38% of total sales

Division 3:   8% x $20 million = $1.6 million: 3.81% of total sales

Aggregate $4.4 million: 10.48% of total sales

Although the above is obviously an oversimplified illustration, more complicated situations can still be analyzed. For instance, some products of the divisions may be complementary (e.g., automobile sales and auto parts) or competitive (e.g., hardbound and paperback editions of the same book). The interrelationships between and among divisional activities must be analyzed in order to predict the aggregate effect of all the dimensions' operational objectives.

From our discussion thus far, we can easily recognize the danger of pursuing suboptimization by each of the divisions. In other words, each division may pursue the best or optimal combiniation of operational objectives for only that division. For instance, the marketing department may try to increase the market share by 20 percent during the next year through aggressive promotional efforts and price cutting. Although this effect may achieve the primary objective for the marketing department, it may be detrimental to the organization as a whole because of the loss of profit. The same reasoning can be applied to the objective of an engineering department which attempts to develop a product that is the most advanced technologically in the market with very little attention given to the cost. In order to achieve the organizational objective—the global optimum —divisions may need to formulate operational objectives that are less than optimal for a specific division.

The coordination of divisional (or departmental) objectives in order to accomplish organizational objectives has been an important area of research in management science. The approach has been generally described as the decomposition method. This approach was initially developed as a computational device to solve a large-scale mathematical programming model for a decentralized system. However, with ever increasing computer capabilities, the approach has become a methodology to coordinate divisional (subordinate) units' activities by the central (superordinate) unit in such a way that the organizational objectives could be as closely accomplished as possible.

In the decomposition approach, the central unit sends down information to divisions concerning the organizational objectives, their priorities, and the available resources at the headquarters level. Based on this information, the divisions formulate their own objectives and activity plans and submit them to the central unit. The central unit then analyzes the cost-effectiveness of the divisional plans in terms of their resource requirements and contribution toward organizational objectives. The top-down and bottom-up communication continues until the divisional plans and cost-effectiveness measures reach the equilibrium stage.

The decomposition approach is perhaps the most promising method for formulating operational objectives at the divisional (or departmental) level. The approach is not only systematic but it is also based on the two-way communication principle. Furthermore, the approach provides important managerial implications associated with divisional coordination which can be used to develop the management information system as well as the organization.

FORMULATING INDIVIDUAL JOB OBJECTIVES

Formulation of organizational and divisional (departmental or other subunits) objectives define the parameters, resources, and priorities with which individuals must work within the organization. In order to make the organization function properly in pursuit of its objectives, individual manager's job objectives must be formulated. This phase is also one of the most critical aspects of the MBMO system because this is where accountability and personal commitment to certain work activities are made. Formulating individual job objectives requires the combined technical, conceptual, and human skills of managers.

Formulating individual job objectives involves identification of common group goals and the coordination of individual efforts for acheiving them. Unquestionably, the basic emphasis is on the desired states in the future—where the organization should be going and how it should get there. However, it is also equally important to ascertain individual manager's roles in the organizational pursuit and how the welfare of the individual will be affected. The key element in the individual job objective formulation process is the determination of the individual's personal goals and how they can best be achieved by working toward the organizational objectives.

Figure 5.5 presents the individual job objective formulation process in the MBMO system. The individual manager's objective setting provides not only the opportunity to have his or her commitment to the organization in writing, but it also lets the individual see how his or her managerial roles would contribute toward organizational objectives. Thus, the individual job objective formulation process can become an important motivator through active involvement, participation, and interaction with other members of the organization in determining the future of the organization.

Managerial functions are complex, especially in large organizations. It would be extremely difficult, if not impossible, to formulate job objectives encompassing every responsibility area of an individual manager. Once again, we have to utilize the "critical few" principle. The emphasis must be placed on those objectives or activities that are critical in achieving the key result areas with high priorities. Although the "critical few" principle sounds great at this stage, its direct application involves complications. If the organiza-

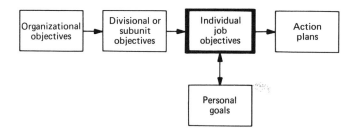

FIGURE 5.5 Formulation of individual job objective process
in the MBMO system

tional objectives and the general personal goals are compatible, the best way to achieve personal goals would be to work toward the organizational objectives. However, if there exists some conflict between organizational and personal goals, identification of the critical few for the organizational goals may not receive the appropriate priorities. Thus, the individual objective formulation process is an important managerial phase where motivation, accountability, job responsibility, performance standards, future activity planning, and personal development goals are developed.

MANAGERIAL JOB OBJECTIVES

There are basically three managerial job objectives that need to be formulated: normal job objectives, special job objectives, and personal improvement objectives. The normal job objectives include the three general key result areas that are already defined by organizational and divisional objectives—maintenance, performance, and innovative. These objectives should be subdivided in key result areas when they reach the individual manager. The manager's job objectives would be to delineate his or her key functions that contribute toward achieving organizational objectives. The manager's own priority structure of key functions must conform to that of the organizational and divisional priority structures for objectives.

The special job objectives include the functions required to fulfill special assignments, projects, or emergency responsibilities. These functions are usually carried out simultaneously with the normal job objectives. The assignment of appropriate priorities must be determined through consultation with superiors. Some examples of the special objectives would be:

> "To immediately change the mortgage approval policy for the minimum cash requirement from 5 percent to 20 percent due to the high prime rate."
>
> "To reduce personnel cost by 5 percent and operating cost by 10 percent below the budgeted amounts."
>
> "To implement Saturday morning banking hours by the end of the next month."

The personal improvement objectives are concerned with the individual manager's job-related skills and potential. The personal improvement objectives can be formulated in such a way to integrate the individual's personal goals with organizational objectives. Although the most direct purpose of formulating personal improvement objectives is to improve the individual's work performance, it has more long-term and implicit benefits. For example, personal improvement objectives could serve as a challenge for personal growth, a chance for advancement, and added job responsibilities. They can become a very strong motivational force.

There are numerous opportunities to improve one's technical, conceptual, and human skills. Opportunities such as taking training and developmental courses offered by universities, professional organizations, and the organization; on-the-job coaching; conducting research and publishing professional papers based on the research; and various continuing education programs. Another very important area of personal improvements is in the area of health (mental as well as physical). One cannot live up to his or her potential and make contributions to the organization if the individual is not healthy or cannot cope with stress, both personal and job induced.

The nature and variety of an individual's improvement objectives depend upon the stage of the person's career as well as the unique conditions of the organization at a given point in time. Nevertheless, the personal improvement objectives allow the individual to recharge for future contribution. As such, these objectives are as important as other individual job objectives.

THE FORMULATION OF JOB OBJECTIVES

When we are at the stage of formulating individual job objectives, it is assumed that the following aspects of the MBMO process have already taken place: a set of explicitly defined organizational objectives has been determined; the key result areas of organizational objectives have been further subdivided, and clearly defined divisional (or departmental and subunits) objectives have been formulated; and also through the objective formulation group and other communication channels, all of the key elements involved in the individual job objective formulation have been thoroughly analyzed.

The individual job objective formulation process is basically the same as formulating organizational or divisional objectives. Perhaps the only real difference would be that the process at the individual job level is not as complex as at higher organizational levels. Let us list several essential steps here.

IDENTIFY KEY JOB FUNCTIONS

A manager's position carries a certain set of job responsibilities that are important for achieving the organization's goals. Therefore, the initial step required to formulate an individual manager's job objectives is to identify the key job functions required to achieve high-priority organizational (and thus divisional) objectives. The types of information needed for this step would be:

Which of my functions are directly and indirectly related to divisional and organizational objectives?

Which of my functions and activities contribute most to the clearly identified key result areas that have been assigned high priorities?

What are the current, possible, and desired levels of my performance in the key result areas?

What are the most cost-effective ways to carry out my most critical functions?

How would my functions interrelate with those of others—needing support of others, giving support to others, or complementing the work of other units of the organization?

ESTABLISHING JOB OBJECTIVES WITH
EXPLICIT TARGETS AND DATES

This is where the individual manager makes a firm personal commitment concerning job objectives in terms of targets and the time constraint. The procedure we discussed for the organizational and departmental objectives applies equally here. Thus, the targets and their deadlines should be *challenging, attainable, measurable* (quantitatively if at all possible), and directly related to important organizational objectives. At this point, the assignment of priorities is not really critical, as the key result areas and their priorities have been determined already at higher organizational levels.

ESTABLISHING APPROPRIATE
PERFORMANCE STANDARDS

The basic standard of performance for any work involves the analysis of input and output. For example, the quantity and quality of output in relation to the cost and time requirements as inputs could be used as the performance standard. Such standards must be established for all key functional areas of the individual manager. Since performance standards are of fundamental importance for employee motivation, career advancement, and compensation programs, they must be developed in close consultation with superiors and subordinates. Furthermore, these standards should be documented in writing so that no future misunderstanding will occur. The standards are by no means permanent; they must be evaluated continually, updated, or modified so that they can be realistic, measurable, attainable, and also relevant. The key motivating force in the MBMO system lies in the individual commitment to certain personal job objectives based on measurable criteria, appropriate standards of performance, and an effective performance appraisal and reward system.

COMMUNICATING AND REVIEWING THE OBJECTIVES

When the individual's job objectives are formulated in a written document, they should be communicated with other members of the organization with whom the manager interacts closely. Such communication involves not only superiors, subordinates, and peers, but it should also include various objective formulation groups. Such communication reveals clearly the key result areas, the aspiration levels, priorities, and target dates. The information is very helpful to others in formulating their job objectives. For example, a subordinate has a clear understanding as to what are important key result areas and guidelines in formulating his or her own job objectives. Also, the manager is "on record" with his or her commitment.

The communication process also provides an opportunity to receive inputs from other members of the organization in terms of suggestions, reviews, analysis, and additional information. Based on such inputs, the manager may need to modify or revise his or her job objective statements. The entire process of job objective formulation is usually an interactive one where relevant parties interact with the individual's tentative list of objectives. Although this process may sound never ending, once the basic procedure is set up and everyone becomes accustomed to working within the framework, it should be easy to follow. Furthermore, in most organizations individual job objectives are formulated once a year. Thus, this process need not be an additional burden to most people. Figure 5.6 presents a typical format that could be used in documenting the individual manager's job objectives and evaluating the progress.

SOME GUIDELINES FOR DEVELOPING OPERATIONAL OBJECTIVES

A well-known French philosopher once said, "Do not sacrifice today for an uncertain tomorrow." We strongly disagree with his reasoning. Since all tomorrows are uncertain, we should sacrifice some of today in order to be better prepared for tomorrow—tomorrow is inevitable. The very purpose of the MBMO system is based on this belief that planning for tomorrows is a good way to manage the state of affairs, be it that of an organization or an individual.

Most managers already accept the basic MBMO concept. As a matter of fact, they can talk eloquently about the importance of objectives and planning. However, when it comes to actually formulating objectives in writing and communicating with others con-

Name _Fred Shen_ Position _Plant Mgr._ Date _7/1_ Dept. _Production_

Reviewer _J. M. Green_ Position _VP-Production_ Date _7/5_ Dept. _Mgt._

Individual Job Objectives	Related Organizational Objectives	Related Divisional Objectives	Priority	Expected Cost	Results		Dates	
					Target	Actual	Target	Actual
1. To reduce the inventory level by 2%	Increase operational efficiency of the firm by 5% during the next year	Reduce the operating cost to 5% below the budget	P_1	10 man months and 20 hours of computer time	Reduce to $1.47 million		6/30	
2.								
3.								

FIGURE 5.6 Individual job objectives format

cerning objectives, managers tend to be timid or often "too busy" to handle such paper work. This sytematic approach is a necessary prerequisite for any effective management system—MBMO or other. A well-prepared set of objectives represents the individual's commitment to work toward certain targets that are beneficial to the organization. Although there is no "one right approach" to formulating operational objectives, experiences and empirical studies have identified several important guidelines concerning the operational objective formulation process:

1. *It should identify a specific action to be performed.* Any objective can be achieved only when required actions are taken. The commitment to take those actions is the key contribution of the objective-setting process.
2. *It should identify one single key result area to be accomplished.* Identification of a specific key target result is essential in order to evaluate objectively the actual performance against the target.
3. *It should specify the target date (deadline) for the completion of a given objective.* Any objective could be accomplished in an infinite period of time. A specific commitment to achieve an objective must include the target date. It is also an important criterion in evaluating the actual performance.
4. *It should specify the maximum expected cost for accomplishing the objective.* Accomplishing an objective at all costs is not the basic approach of MBMO. In other words, the objective achievement must be worthwhile only in realation to the associated cost of achieving it—cost-effectiveness is the foundation of the MBMO process.
5. *It should be a challenging target for members of the organization involved.* Formulating and working toward an objective should and could serve as an effective motivational vehicle; it should provide a challenge for everyone involved in achieving the objective.
6. *It should be measurable, tangible, and attainable.* Operational objectives should be formulated in quantitative terms if at all possible. Furthermore, such objectives should be realistic in terms of its attainability.

7. *It should be consistent with the organizational purpose, goals, and objectives.* Operational objectives must be relevant and contribute directly to higher level organizational goals. Furthermore, their priorities must be consistent with priorities of the related organizational objectives.

8. *It should be well communicated to those who will be contributing to or evaluating its actual results.* It is essential that objectives are formulated jointly with superiors, subordinates, and peers so that others know what to expect from the individual subunit or manager. This process is especially important as a motivational factor for subordinates who will be contributing toward its attainment.

9. *It should be recorded and communicated in writing.* Once operational objectives are formulated, they should be recorded and communicated in writing so that any future misunderstanding can be minimized. Such written records can be valuable information sources for future references.

SUMMARY

Formulating operational objectives is the point at which organizational goals and objectives are transformed into operationalized key targets. Relevant and clearly defined operational objectives provide the focus toward which commitment and accountability can be directed. This is also the stage where the individual manager can evaluate the relationship between organizational objectives and personal goals. Thus, this process should not be regarded as a paper work-generating stage of the MBMO process. If an individual manager cannot use this process effectively, he or she may fail to achieve organizational objectives, individual goals, and also personal goals of subordinates.

REFERENCES

Lubans, V.A., and Edgar, J.M. *Policing by Objectives*. Hartford, Conn.: Social Development Corp., 1979.

Morrisey, G.L. *Management by Objectives and Results in the Public Sector*. Reading, Mass.: Addison-Wesley, 1976.

Odiorne, G.S. *MBO II: A System of Managerial Leadership for the 80's*. Belmont, Calif.: Fearon Pitman, 1979.

Raia, A.P. *Managing by Objectives*. Glenview, Ill.: Scott, Foresman, 1974.

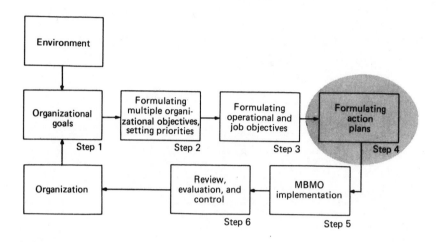

6

Formulating Action Plans

Formulating organizational purpose, long-range goals, strategic plans, clear organizational objectives, and concise departmental and industrial work objectives describe the nature and state of the desired ends. Although these MBMO phases specify the "why" and "what" of the desired states, they do not present the *means* of achieving the ends. The action plans are concerned with the "how"—or methods—to achieve the desired set of multiple objectives.

Many approaches that have been suggested for managerial planning and control—such as the planning-programming-budgeting system (PPBS) and zero-base budgeting (ZBB)—tend to concentrate on planning and formulating of objectives but often neglect the methodological aspect of management. In order to be operational, a system must be capable of identifying the means or a set of action plans to achieve the desired ends.

An action plan must specify what, how, when, and by whom a certain activity or a set of activities should be undertaken in order to achieve objectives. Action plans are typically developed only for performance and innovative objectives; they are not usually developed for maintenance objectives. The primary reason is that for maintenance objectives, a set of well-established routine activities is usually outlined based on the past experience.

Figure 6.1 presents the basic inputs to and functions of action plans in the MBMO process. Action plans hold the key in connecting planning, decision making, and actual resource-allocating activities. In addition to providing the means to the ends, action plans also facilitate a control over the entire MBMO process through measurement of work performance and progress. The control property of action plans is especially valuable for qualitative objectives that are difficult to quantify. Action plans developed for qualitative objectives are approximate means that are presumed to lead to the achievement of objectives. Thus, the progress of action plan implementation is the best estimate of the degree of qualitative objective achievement.

The process of formulating action plans provides many managerial benefits, some of which are:

1. Provides the opportunity to analyze resource requirements (time, money, manpower, physical facilities, technology, etc.) to achieve a set of multiple objectives.
2. Tests the feasibility of objectives—whether they are achievable, whether they are realistic, and the soundness of priorities assigned to objectives.
3. Identifies conflicts and trade-offs among objectives under consideration.
4. Identifies the required activities—what, when, how, how much, by whom, and in what sequence.
5. Helps to identify the most efficient ways to achieve the objectives among many available alternatives through a systematic evaluation of alternatives.
6. Necessitates the identification of required work relationships and interactions among various available resources—people, different functions in the organization, resources, technology, etc.
7. Provides a more realistic anticipation about the expected outcome of the planning process and future activities designed to achieve desired objectives.
8. Delineates the work responsibility and accountability as to who will see to the accomplishment of action steps toward objectives.
9. Provides a rational basis for resource allocation to various components in the organization through budgeting.
10. Helps to develop a systematic sequence of activities with appropriate time requirements through scheduling.

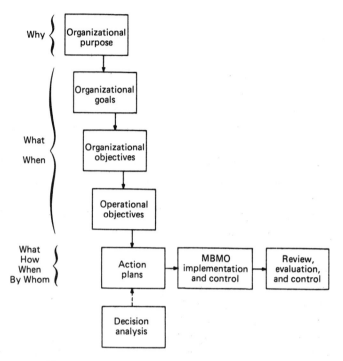

FIGURE 6.1 Formulating action plans

The action planning process consists of the following five basic steps:

1. *Programming action plans*—determining what actions are required to achieve a set of objectives

2. *Scheduling activities*—developing a time-phased plan for the actions determined in step 1

3. *Budgeting*—determining resource requirements and allocating resouces accordingly

4. *Managing responsibility*—assigning responsibility for major activities that are required to achieve a set of objectives

5. *Reviewing and controlling*—analyzing all steps of action planning and revising plans as necessary before their actual implementation

PROGRAMMING ACTION PLANS

"QUICK AND DIRTY"
ALTERNATIVE EVALUATION SYSTEM

Programming action plans basically involves laying out the best possible approach to follow in order to achieve set objectives. This step includes evaluation of alternative courses of action currently available, exploring additional alternatives, analyzing all economically feasible alternatives, and determining the most satisfactory alternative.

Let us suppose that a firm has set as its objective to "increase the total sales of products by 5 percent during the coming year." The marketing department has identified the following existing alternatives:

1. Increase advertising and marketing efforts
2. Increase bonus to the sales force
3. Increase sales force
4. Train field sales force

In addition to the existing alternatives, the marketing department has developed the following additional (new) alternatives:

1. Develop a new advertising and promotion campaign
2. Develop new compensation plans for the sales force
3. Reorganize regional sales organizations for local emphasis
4. Develop a new sales budgeting system for regional offices and provide greater autonomy
5. Develop a new sales training program
6. Introduce a new warranty and service system
7. Introduce a cash rebate campaign for new customers

Once all feasible alternatives have been identified, they can be evaluated in a rather simplistic and crude manner as shown in Table 6.1. This evaluation method presents only a "quick and dirty" way to analyze alternatives. For a more complex real-world problem, a computer-based management science approach can be used.

TABLE 6.1 A "quick and dirty" alternative evaluation

Objective: Increase total sales of products by 5% during the coming year

Existing alternatives	Resource requirement*	Degree of contribution to objective†	Feasibility under system constraints‡	Total score
1. Increase advertising and marketing efforts	3	4	1	8
2. Increase bonus to sales force	4	3	2	9
3. Increase sales force	5	2	3	10
4. Train field sales force	2	5	2	9
New alternatives				
5. Develop new advertising and promotion campaign	6	1	5	12
6. Reorganize regional sales organization—local emphasis	3	2	6	11
7. Develop a new sales budgeting system—regional autonomy	3	4	3	10
8. Develop a new sales training program	3	3	2	8
9. Introduce new warranty and service system	5	3	4	12
10. Introduce cash rebate campaign	6	1	5	12

* Very high resource requirement = 6; very low resource requirement = 1

† Very low degree of contribution = 6; very high degree of contribution = 1

‡ Very low feasibility = 6; very high feasibility = 1

The "quick and dirty" alternative evaluation system is based on three basic criteria—resource requirement, degree of contribution to the objective, and the feasibility under the currently existing environmental and organizational constraints. The scoring system is based on a 6-point scale as shown below:

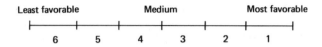

Regardless of the criterion under consideration, 1 is the most favorable score and 6 the least favorable. Thus, an alternative with the least total score would be regarded as the most desirable one.

The resource requirement item represents an approximate total monetary cost in terms of the present value. Required resources may be in dollar costs, managerial manpower, new personnel, space requirements, etc. These resources should be roughly converted to an actual dollar value common denominator. If an alternative requires a great deal of resources it would be less desirable; thus a score of 6 should be assigned. On the other hand, if an alternative could be easily implemented with a relatively insignificant cost, it would receive a score of 1. For example, training field sales force (alternative 4) can be implemented at a reasonable cost; thus, a score of 2 is given. However, developing an entirely new advertising and promotion campaign (alternative 5) requires a considerable amount of resources, and a score of 6 is assigned to this alternative.

The degree of contribution to the objective under consideration is also scored on a 6-point scale. An alternative with most direct and significant contribution to the objective is assigned a score of 1, and an alternative with a minimum or questionable contribution would be given 6.

Feasibility under system constraints indicates whether or not an alternative could be implemented without changing organizational policies, external regulations, or established work procedures. If it can, a score of 1 is assigned. For example, increasing the efforts and budget of the existing advertising and marketing programs (alternative 1) would require no forseeable disturbance; thus a score of 1 is assigned. On the other hand, reorganization of regional sales organizations in order to provide a more local autonomy (alternative

6) would require considerable planning, reassignment of personnel, relocation of people, possible unrest among the employees, and a considerable amount of cost. Thus, this alternative receives a score of 6.

The total score is a simple sum of scores on the three criteria we considered. If a different weighting scheme is appropriate for the criteria (i.e., each of the criteria is not considered equal in importance), a differential weighting method can be applied.

The "quick and dirty" alternative evaluation scheme can be used to eliminate some inferior alternatives before a more comprehensive analysis is performed. For example, we might say that for the short-term sales objective we have in mind all alternatives with scores higher than 10 points total should be eliminated from further consideration; thus, alternatives 5, 6, 9, and 10 could be dropped from further analysis. Among the remaining alternatives, we may want to select one, two, or other combinations based on the same three criteria that we considered. The "quick and dirty" approach is especially useful for brainstorming by a group of planners, a task force committee, or an executive group. This technique is an elementary way to screen existing and newly generated alternatives. It should not be used as a permanent and final evaluation system of alternatives.

MANAGEMENT SCIENCE METHODS FOR PROGRAMMING ACTION PLANS

There exists a variety of ways to design a custom-built management science model to evaluate various alternatives. However, before a quantitative model is designed for analysis, the following important factors need to be considered:

1. *Mutual exclusiveness*. Certain alternatives cannot be implemented simultaneuosly. For example, if a cash rebate program is introduced for new customers, then an increased maintenance and warranty program may not be possible.

2. *Complementarity*. If a certain alternative is selected for implementation, then it automatically requires one or more of other alternatives. For example, a new branch office is to be opened in Japan and it must be accompanied by a training program of some local Japanese employees for the operation.

3. *Organizational and enviromental politics.* Certain activities may involve politically sensitive issues either internal or external to the organization. Such sensitive issues must be analyzed carefully.

4. *System constraints.* There are certain constraints that must be satisfied before objectives can be pursued. Governmental regulations (e.g., equal opportunity and affirmative action laws), clearly established organizational policies and procedures, and contracts with various parties must be considered as system constraints.

5. *Special manpower requirements.* Certain activities require specialized skills, managerial manpower, and particular capability of individuals.

6. *Special equipment requirements.* In addition to special manpower needs, certain activities may require additional facilities and/or specialized equipment such as large cranes, computers, electronic gear, etc.

7. *Special time requirements.* Certain activities must conform to established time schedules such as fiscal year, union contract periods, sequencing of tasks, legislative sessions, and the like.

Once the above factors have been analyzed thoroughly, the next step is to implement a management science approach when it is appropriate. The management science modeling approach requires quantification of the problem as a mathematical model. Some objectives would not render themselves to such a systematic analysis. Determining whether or not management science could be applied to a given situation involves judgment and is an art in itself.

The basic steps of the management science modeling approach are as follows:

1. *Analyze the environment and the objective.* This step involves a general understanding of the situation, problem, or the objective under consideration. It would require finding various functional relationships among the involved departments and individuals, key decision makers, responsibilities, and the final authority for action plan implementation.

2. *Obtain support through involvement.* The key to any successful implementation of action plans is gaining the support through involvement of key personnel—superiors, top management, sub-

ordinates, user departments, support units, and other affected parties. Without the active participation and blessing of these people, action plans cannot be implemented effectively.

3. *Determine the appropriate method.* There are many different ways to model a problem situation. In addition to selecting a technical modeling approach (e.g., simulation model, curve-fitting, linear programming, goal programming, inventory model, queuing model, break-even analysis, etc.), it is also very important to decide how comprehensive or simple the modeling approach should be. A simplified model is easy to formulate, solve, and manipulate to generate information. However, the generated information may not be accurate enough to suit the situation. On the other hand, a comprehensive model may not be cost effective or timely even though it provides more accurate information.

4. *Develop the model and obtain results.* Once the basic nature of the model is determined as outlined above, a management science model can be formulated. Model formulation is not a simple step. It involves a continuous checking and reviewing process so that the final model will be functional. Once the model is developed, it should be run (most likely on a computer) to generate required information. It must be emphasized here that the purpose of a model is not simply to obtain a solution. It should be run many different ways while changing assumptions, parameters, objective levels, priorities, etc. Thus, the model should provide enough relevant information to answer "what if" type questions.

5. *Develop action plans.* Based on the information obtained from the model, a set of action plans should be developed. These plans could be used for the pilot run to check whether or not they are functional, or have the user departments test the action plans. At this step, plans could be modified or revised after testing and review.

6. *Implementation of action plans.* At this step, plans become activities. Implementation requires coordination and directing of various resources toward the desired objective.

7. *Review and control.* After the implementation phase, progress toward the desired objective must be evaluated carefully. This step is an essential part of the entire process, as it is here that the validity of the model can be assessed. Modification of assumptions, parameters, objective levels, priorities, and sequence and

timing of activities can be made and the loop continues. The information obtained from the actual result of activities becomes the basis of control.

A comprehensive example of the management science approach is presented in the Appendix. Appendix A presents the concept of goal programming for MBMO, and Appendix B provides an application example of goal programming.

DEVELOPING PLAN ACTIVITIES

Whether we apply a "quick and dirty" or a management science approach to program action plans, eventually we must develop a list of plan activities. The analysis of plan activities allows us to establish proper target dates, resource requirements, and primary responsibility for particular activities. For example, let us assume that the plan activities for the objective "increase sales by 5 percent during the next year" are to be developed. Table 6.2 presents a simplified version of the plan activities chart.

TABLE 6.2 Plan activities chart

Plan activities	Time	Resources	By whom
1. Analyze environment and objective (increase sales by 5% during next year while inflation is about 15%)			
a. Economic forecast	NOW + 2 wks.	20 computer-hrs. 40 man-hrs.	Systems Analysis Econ. Forecasting
b. Sales trend analysis	NOW + 2 wks.	20 man-hrs.	Mkt.

TABLE 6.2 Plan activities chart (continued)

Plan activities	Time	Resources	By whom
c. Marketing efforts analysis	NOW + 2 wks.	5 man-hrs.	Mkt.
d. Regional sales trends	NOW + 2 wks.	5 man-hrs.	Mkt.
e. Sales productivity analysis	NOW + 2 wks.	10 man-hrs.	Mkt./Systems Analysis
2. Obtain support through involvement.	NOW + 5 wks.		
a. Sales division mgr.	NOW + 3 wks.	4 man-hrs.	Mkt.
b. Regional sales managers.	NOW + 3 wks.	$2,000; 48 man-hrs.	Mkt.
c. Marketing dept.	NOW + 4 wks.	2 man-hrs.	Mkt.
d. Sales people	NOW + 5 wks.	$500; 6 man-hrs.	Mkt.
3. Determine appropriate method	NOW + 10 wks.		
a. Sales forecasting model	NOW + 8 wks.	30 man-hrs.	Mkt./Systems Analysis
b. Promotional effectiveness model	NOW + 8 wks.	10 man-hrs.	Mkt./Systems Analysis
c. Sales effort allocation model	NOW + 10 wks.	10 man-hrs.	Mkt./Systems Analysis
d. Training effectiveness evaluation	NOW + 7 wks.	5 man-hrs.	Personnel/ Systems Analysis
e. Bonus system evaluation	NOW + 7 wks.	6 man-hrs.	Mkt./Fin.

TABLE 6.2 Plan activities chart (continued)

Plan activities	Time	Resources	By whom
4. Results of the analysis	NOW + 14 wks.	15 computer-hrs.	
a. Simulation study	NOW + 13 wks.	40 man-hrs.	Mkt./Comp.
b. Sensitivity analysis	NOW + 13 wks.	20 man-hrs.	Mkt./Comp.
c. Testing assumptions	NOW + 14 wks.	3 man-hrs	Mkt./Comp.
5. Develop action plans	NOW + 20 wks.		
a. Increase advertising budget by 10%	NOW + 20 wks.	$100,000	Pres.
b. Develop new sales training program	NOW + 18 wks.	$20,000; 40 man-hrs.	Mkt./Personnel
c. New bonus system	NOW + 17 wks.	$40,000; 30 man-hrs.	Fin.
d. Increase sales force by 2%	NOW + 20 wks.	$125,000	Mkt.
6. Implementation of action plans	NOW + 30 wks.	300 man-hrs.	Mkt.
7. Review and control	NOW + 45 wks.		
a. Advertising effectiveness	NOW + 45 wks.	30 man-hrs.	Mkt.
b. Sales force effectiveness	NOW + 45 wks.	20 man-hrs.	Mkt.
c. Bonus system	NOW + 35 wks.	10 man-hrs.	Mkt./Fin.
d. New sales force productivity	NOW + 40 wks.	10 man-hrs.	Mkt.

The real value of the plan activities chart is that it provides a brief summary of what needs to be done, by when, at what cost, and who is accountable for the completion of each of the activities. Furthermore, this chart provides valuable information for other steps that would be required for controlling action plans such as scheduling, budgeting, and reviewing.

SCHEDULING ACTIVITIES

Scheduling is a systematic way to plan activities so that the objective will be achieved in the most effective way. Scheduling *is not* simply determining time requirements for activities, and it *is not* simply finding a proper sequence or precedence requirement among activities. It is a combination of all timing, sequencing, and arranging of activities in a logical manner.

The key to good scheduling involves being realistic and expecting unusual situations. There are many useful techniques now available widely for systematic scheduling, such as PERT (program evaluation and review technique), CPM (critical path method), GERT (graphical evaluation and review technique), and other network analysis techniques. Most organizations have systems analysts, management scientists, or a few recent M.B.A.s who would be happy to work with these scheduling techniques.

Below are some tips that may be very useful in developing a good schedule.

1. *Determine the absolute deadline.* It is always nice to know when the end result must be obtained.
2. *Determine the earliest starting point.* There is much preliminary work that needs to be done before action plans can be developed, such as clearance by the top management, approval of the budget, approval of the departmental objectives, etc.
3. *Break each activity into subactivities or tasks.* Frequently, an activity consists of a series of tasks, and scheduling of these tasks may be necessary before the overall schedule can be developed.
4. *Estimate the time requirement for each task and then each activity.*

5. *Determine the required sequencing, simultaneous (parallel) running, complementarity, or mutual exclusiveness among activities and tasks.* As stated earlier, certain tasks or activities must be contiguous, while others can be done in parallel. Such relationships must be analyzed carefully in advance.

6. *Determine the critical path—the sequence of tasks or activities that represents the longest cumulative time requirement.* Identification of the critical path provides highlights of which tasks and activities should be controlled very closely in order to keep on schedule.

7. *In order to schedule realistically, first start from the end and work back, and then start from the beginning and work forward.* This approach enables one to be more realistic as to how much time can be allocated to each task or activity by indicating its scheduling leeway, or "slack."

8. *Develop a GANTT Chart.* In addition to or in preparation for developing a PERT or CPM network, a GANTT Chart should be prepared. A GANTT Chart provides important information that is necessary to develop a final network-type schedule for analysis. Various relationships among activities can be presented concisely in a GANTT Chart, such as contiguous, complementary, parallel, or mutually exclusive realtionships. Figure 6.2 presents a typical GANTT Chart.

9. *Prepare for contingencies.* Emergencies may occur in any situation. Natural disasters, bad weather, international or national emergencies, labor strike, death of key executives, etc., can possibly prolong the critical path. Although "crashing" at a high cost may keep the schedule intact, it is not always possible (especially when a series of emergencies occurs) or desirable, except as a last resort. Thus, a contingency plan should be developed for the unexpected.

TIME MANAGEMENT

Time is the most precious resource for everyone. No one has more time than others. As such, one who manages his or her time well will succeed in life. The same logic applies to organizations. If organizations and their key personnel use time effectively, they will

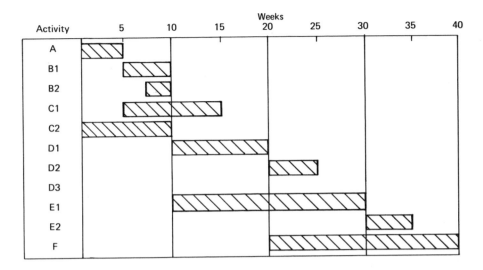

FIGURE 6.2 A GANTT Chart schedule

succeed together. Although there have been a number of popular books published on time management and some people do extensive consulting on the topic, it is nothing unusual or different from the basic MBMO approach.

The basic approach of time management can be summarized concisely as follows:

1. Determine long-term goals.
2. Formulate short-term objectives that contribute to long-term goals.
3. Assign priorities to these objectives.
4. Plan activities or actions that would lead to important objectives.
5. Analyze multiple goals, their conflicts, and trade-offs as accurately as possible.
6. Schedule activities in an appropriate sequence and order.
7. Delegate authority and responsibilities.
8. Identify time wasters and try to avoid them:
   lack of planning
   unrealistic goals and objectives
   wrong or lack of priorities
   overcommitment

lack of proper schedules
routine and trivial paper work
visitors
telephone calls
meetings
failure to delegate
9. Review and control the time management process.
10. Determine the best use of time *now* based on priorities, action
plans, and schedules.

BUDGETING

Budgeting is one of the most widely used and debated terms in
management. The term "budgeting" suggests an air of bureaucracy
where a higher authority doles out a few bucks to do impossible
tasks. Or, many taxpayers think of budget as something that always
takes a few more dollars from their pockets every year. In reality,
budgeting is simply a bridge which connects the desired ends and
action plans.

Budgeting is not a one-step operation where we allocate resources
to various organizational components to get the job done. It is a
continuous operation which encompasses the following three basic
steps:

1. Determine the total required resources to achieve a set of desired objectives of the organization.
2. For a given amount of resources, determine their best allocation so that the desired objectives will be achieved to the greatest possible extent.
3. Continue the process of adjusting objective levels and priorities, requesting additional funds with good justifications, and
reallocating resources within the budgeted amount based on
changing environmental factors.

In most situations, budgeting is based on the historical trend,
that is, the new budget is simply a sum of the last year's budget plus
some additional percentage based on new required projects and the

inflation factor. Thus, the only activity involved in budgeting would be politicking and step 2 where allocation of funds is determined. However, since Proposition 13 in California we are more keenly aware of the need for systematic ways to devolop the budget. Newer management systems such as PPBS (planning-programming-budgeting system) and ZBB (zero-base budgeting) have become quite popular and are helpful in reallocating resources.

Perhaps the most important aspect of budgeting is step 1 where a clearly developed set of objectives, action plans, or programs is presented as the basis for budget request. If the requested budget is not fully funded, it is a clear evidence that the stated objectives are not expected to be achieved fully during the budget year. Steps 2 and 3 are more of an internal control process, i.e., allocating budgeted funds in such a way as to operate in the most efficient way to achieve important objectives.

IMPORTANT FACTORS IN BUDGETING

Budgeting is the most important and powerful management control tool. Budget allocation is perhaps the clearest indication of management's perceived importance of a given department and its activities. A good example would be the greatly increased budget of the Department of Defense in 1980 after the Iranian and Afghanistan crises.

In budgeting, money is the common denominator. However, many tasks and projects are planned in terms of time, number of people, person-hours, and required materials and equipment. Thus, there is a need to translate other resources into dollar terms. Other resources commonly involved in the budgeting process are as follows:

1. *Human resources:* The greatest proportion of most budgets is payroll for human resources—FTEs (full-time equivalents), man-years, work hours, workdays, etc.
2. *Materials, supplies, and services:* In order to support human activities, a variety of materials, supplies, and other services are required.

3. *Facilities, equipments, and technology:* Action plans may also
   require buildings, warehouse, office space, stadium, durable
   equipments, specialized technology-based tools such as computers and word processing systems, etc.
4. *Time:* A frequently ignored resource is time. We hear words
   like "time is money." We receive interest when we deposit
   money in savings for a given period of time. When a project is
   not completed within a contracted time period, the contractor
   pays a penalty.

Most managers can readily relate to the above resources when
they are considering action plans. Therefore it is necessary first to
estimate resource requirements for activities and then translate the
resources into dollars for budget preparation.

BUDGETING PROCESS

Since budgeting is an important management control mechanism,
it should be approached analytically and realistically. In order to
achieve a set of objectives in a cost-effective manner, action plans
must be analyzed carefully in terms of their resource requirements
and possible benefits (contributions to objectives). Actually, this
work has already been completed in the programming part. The
translating of required resources into dollars is often called the costing process. This process must be executed based on past records,
trends, probabilistic forecasting of the future outcomes, and managerial judgment.

Quite frequently, managers would like to have a slightly padded
budget for self-protection in case of estimating errors or contingencies. Although such practice may be comforting to the manager,
it could quickly become a general and accepted practice throughout the organization. Then the system no longer serves the purpose.
In this day of inflation, international tension, energy shortage and
Proposition 13, we must believe in budget integrity. Budget integrity
implies that a budget is prepared systematically and realistically so
that it represents the least cost estimate for undertaking the tasks
to be accomplished, and then living within the given allocation.

Since President Carter's implementation of it in the federal government, zero-base budgeting (ZBB) has become popular. The basic philosophy of ZBB is establishing budget integrity. Today we see many variations of ZBB, such as 90 percent or 110 percent base budgeting. ZBB rejects the historical budgeting process and requires an evaluation and justification of all programs anew for the new fiscal period. 90 percent budgeting is concerned with indicating what could be accomplished with a 10 percent decrease in total allocation. On the other hand, 110 percent base budgeting is an approach utilized to develop a list of action plans with a budget increased by 10 percent.

MANAGING RESPONSIBILITY

A very important step in action planning is to determine who will see to the successful completion of major tasks and activities in order to achieve a set of objectives. This responsibility involves not only managing the tasks of a unit but also coordinating or interfacing with other work units. The programming and budgeting steps have already determined the manpower and other resource requirements, schedule of tasks, who would be involved, and how much money would be required to complete certain tasks. At this step, several key questions need to be asked: Who should be held responsible for various tasks of action plans? What is the nature of the responsibility? What type of coordination is required with other units? Who is responsible for the coordination?

Managing responsibility for action planning in MBMO requires a systematic approach. Many conventional management tools are not very effective in managing responsibility. For example, a simple organizational chart simply gives a list of who reports to whom or a "pecking order." On the other hand, a job description simply presents a broad and general description of what one is expected to do on the job. Thus, they do not reveal clearly the nature of responsibility to get the necessary activities completed to achieve a set of multiple objectives. One critical aspect of a managerial position which is completely void in job descriptions or organizational charts is the necessity to manage complex interfaces and interrelationships on the job.

One innovative idea that could be used for managing responsibility in action planning is the Responsibility Analysis Chart (see Melcher, p. 35 and Raia, pp. 76-78), sometimes called a Linear Responsibility Chart. Figure 6.3 presents a typical Responsibility Analysis Chart for action planning. Plan activities required to achieve a given objective are listed on the left. The list of management personnel who would be involved in the planned activities is presented in the middle of the chart. The nature of responsibility codes are entered in appropriate cells for a given activity and a given management personnel. The nature of responsibility can be defined as follows:

G = General responsibility: The manager has the overall accountability to oversee the successful completion of the activity.

O = Operating responsibility: The person has the direct operational responsibility for the activity.

S = Specific responsibility: The manager has responsibility for specific aspects of the activity.

C = Consultative responsibility: The individual should be consulted for ideas, information, advice, and approval before final decisions are made for the activity.

N = Notification responsibility: The manager should be notified about the decision as to action to be taken.

A = Approval responsibility: The individual must approve the decision before action is taken.

The Responsibility Analysis Chart would be very useful to the vice-president of sales in analyzing working relationships with other managers and departments in achieving the sales increase objective. Although the method to complete this chart is contingent upon the objective, its magnitude, time horizon, and many other factors, it is best to involve many individual members of the task force. The group analysis approach reveals a great deal of hidden information about interactions among various individual managers and departments that are needed to complete a task. Furthermore, the group approach usually paves a smooth road of progress toward the actual implementation of activities.

Objective: Increase sales by 5% during the coming year
Date: 3/5

Plan Activities	President	VP-Sales	VP-Marketing	VP-Production	VP-Finance	VP-Personnel	VP-Research & Design	Mgr-Management Science	Mgr-Reg. Sales	Mgr-Computer Operations	Responsibility Code
1. Increase advertising budget by 10%		G	O S	D	D			N	N		
2. Develop a new sales training program		O S	G	N		S		C			G = General O = Operating S = Specific C = Consultative N = Notification A = Approval
3. Develop a new bonus system for sales personnel	A	O	G	C	S	N	N	C N	C N	C N	
4. Increase sales force by 2%		G	N			S		O			

FIGURE 6.3 Responsibility analysis chart

REVIEWING AND CONTROLLING

Action planning is not a one-shot operation. A process of reviewing and controlling continues throughout the planning process—during the programming, scheduling, budgeting, and implementation phases of action planning. However, there are two distinct phases of reviewing and controlling: ante- and postimplementation. The anteimplementation review and control process is concerned with making sure that the planned activities are realistic and the most appropriate ones for the desired objective. In this sense this phase is primarily proactive in nature. On the other hand, the post-implementation review and control process is primarily concerned with how to use the information of actual results of activities in such a way as to improve the effectiveness of future decisions. Thus, this phase is more reactive in nature.

Human information processing capability is quite limited. Because of this cognitive limitation, we must simplify the complex real-world problem. We attempt to utilize systematic and/or analytical approaches in order to identify key variables that explain a major proportion of a given phenomenon. In the process we leave out important system constraints, variables, or interrelationships among system components. It is also possible that the dynamic environmental conditions have changed so significantly that the assumptions used for the analysis are no longer valid. Thus, we must continuously review the situation to uncover valuable new information and then use it in such a way to control the action planning process to be productive.

There are many reviewing and controlling approaches. However, the following represent the most widely used methods:

1. *Individual analysis.* This approach is considered by an individual manager or a member of the task force. Basically, it is rechecking the action planning process one more time as objectively as possible.
2. *Group analysis.* This approach can be used by the task force, insiders and outsiders within the organization, and the task force members and outside consultants. It can generate some fresh looks, or outsiders' viewpoints, that could be extremely valuable to those who have been too close to the project.
3. *Outside expert analysis.* It is usually quite beneficial to invite a well-known expert in the area concerned and make certain that all important factors have been thoroughly analyzed. The outside expert's assistance is especially useful when a planned activity has far-reaching consequences to the environment, customers, government agencies, management-employee relations, and suppliers.
4. *Subordinate-superior analysis.* Another popular approach is a continuous analysis by key members involved in the activity and their superior.
5. *Peer group analysis.* This is basically a free-for-all type peer "rap session" where they can attack and defend each other's ideas. The potential benefit of this analysis is generation of new information stemming from an uninhibited discussion of various aspects of action planning.

Although the idea of reviewing and controlling is quite sound, the degree to which one indulges in this process is a key importance. If 70 percent of the action planning efforts are used for review and control, the process tends to get bogged down and people can become disillusioned quickly with the MBMO approach. On the other hand, if only 1 percent of efforts is expended for review and control, the action planning would look like a hit-and-run activity. A careful analysis of the importance, complexity, and magnitude of the objective and activities is necessary to determine an appropriate level of reviewing and controlling efforts.

SUMMARY

Developing and implementing action plans represent the positive steps to direct resources to action in order to achieve a set of multiple objectives. Action planning involves five basic steps: programming, scheduling, budgeting, managing responsibility, and reviewing and controlling. Perhaps the most important step would be programming, since this is where broad objectives are broken down into subobjectives or activities. Also, this step generates various alternatives and evaluates them in terms of their cost-effectiveness. This process is a prerequisite for the remaining four steps.

Once a set of activities is determined, a systematic way to schedule them is necessary. Another key step is to allocate resources wisely and effectively so that the maximum result could be obtained with a given amount of budget. The action planning is a complex process. It can easily become an arena for organizational power struggle and bureaucratic paper work. This makes a clear delineation of managerial responsibility for various facets of the process extremely important. Finally, a sound management practice always requires a process of continuous review and control. MBMO is no exception to this rule.

REFERENCES

Lee, S.M. *Goal Programming for Decision Analysis*. Philadelphia: Auerbach, 1972.
——. *Goal Programming Methods for Multiple Objective Integer Programs*. OR Monograph 2. Atlanta: American Institute of Industrial Engineers, 1979.
Melcher, R.D. "Roles and Relationships: Clarifying the Manager's Job." *Personnel* 44(May-June 1967): 33–41.
Morrisey, G.L. *Management by Objectives and Results in the Public Sector*. Reading, Mass.: Addison-Wesley, 1976.
Raia, A.P. *Managing by Objectives*. Glenview, Ill.: Scott Foresman, 1974.

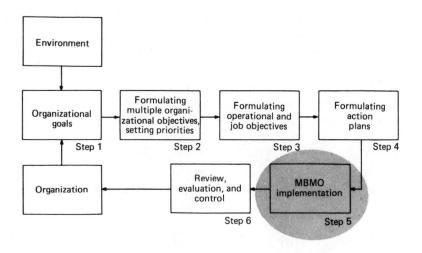

7

Implementation of the MBMO System

The preceding chapters have discussed the important components and steps of the MBMO system. This chapter is devoted to the most important phase of MBMO—putting the system to work, or implementation. The degree of success in applying MBMO is quite often determined by how the organization implements the system. If an organization approaches the implementation phase with proper systematic plans, efforts, time, and resources, it will most likely enjoy the maximum benefits of the system (see McConkey, p. 99).

In implementing the MBMO system, there are several key issues that need to be answered, some of which are (1) Who should be responsible for the implementation? (2) Who should be involved in the process? (3) What are the most likely problems we should expect to encounter? (4) What strategies should be used to resolve these problems? (5) What are the required resources for implementation? and (6) How can we plan ahead for system implementation? We shall discuss these questions from both empirical and theoretical viewpoints and provide important guidelines for MBMO implementation.

FACTORS IMPORTANT FOR SUCCESSFUL MBMO IMPLEMENTATION

Several factors have been pointed out by many empirical studies as being important for successful MBMO implementation. They are (1) top management involvement and support; (2) consistent management philosophy; (3) effective communication; (4) a clearly developed organizational structure; (5) effective management information systems; (6) adequate managerial and technical skills; (7) proper integration with other functions of management; (8) proper allowance for contingencies; (9) effective change strategies; and (10) commitment to reduce bureaucracy.

145

TOP MANAGEMENT INVOLVEMENT AND SUPPORT

It has been clearly established by many studies that the involvement and visible support of top managers are crucial for managing by multiple objectives. The very foundation of the MBMO system rests upon the organizational purpose, long-range goals, and strategic plans to be established by top management. Thus, without top management's full commitment, the whole process becomes an exercise in futility. Furthermore, since MBMO generally requires large-scale changes in job responsibilities, authority, organizational structure, organizational policy and work procedures, top management involvement becomes imperative.

CONSISTENT MANAGEMENT PHILOSOPHY

The MBMO system is based on certain values, approaches, and philosophy. It is based on the belief that greater efficiency and harmony can be obtained in a workplace when individuals are encouraged to exercise self-motivation, self-control, creativity, and systematic approaches. If management's philosophy is visibly contrary to the underlying MBMO principles, the MBMO system implementation cannot be successful. For example, if top management views and uses MBMO as a means to suppress and control members of the organization, the MBMO system can quickly turn into another tricky game.

EFFECTIVE COMMUNICATION

MBMO is a human process. In order to bring out the best imagination and efforts from members of the organization, clear communication is essential. Effective communication results in commitment rather than compliance. Commitment results in voluntary behavior based on positive attitude, whereas compliance results in involuntary behavior based on neutral or negative attitudes. Thus, effective communication encourages innovation and creativity on the job. It also encourages harmony, mutual understanding, and group cohesiveness for teamwork. Furthermore, it promotes systematic and rational approaches to problem solving, decision making, and action planning. Effective communication is indeed the MBMO catalyst.

CLEARLY DEVELOPED ORGANIZATIONAL STRUCTURE

As stated already, delegation, self-motivation, and coordination are important elements of MBMO. In order to delineate the responsibilities of various work units and personnel, a clearly developed organizational structure is needed to provide fundamental information about personal and work unit responsibilities. Such information helps to define work content, coordination needs, and administrative responsibilities that are necessary to implement the MBMO system.

EFFECTIVE MANAGEMENT INFORMATION SYSTEMS

A management information system is concerned with collecting, storing, processing, and transmitting information necessary for effective managment decision making. MBMO is basically a human information system. Information is needed to develop organizational objectives, action plans, trend forecasting, review and control, and all other facets of MBMO. The success of MBMO implementation is thus based on the effectiveness of management information systems.

ADEQUATE MANAGERIAL AND TECHNICAL SKILLS

MBMO implementation requires various managerial and technical skills. Managers must possess conceptual skills in formulating organizational objectives, quantifying many abstract objective criteria, developing models to represent complex problems, and making decisions with action planning. Perhaps the most crucial skills needed on the part of the manager are human skills—abilities to communicate, coach, counsel, involve, and motivate others for a set of common objectives. Managers also need certain technical and analytical skills concerning the basic functions of the organization. For example, a manager should know what the important factors are that influence sales and how to analyze them. In order to secure adequate managerial and technical skills required of managers, training and development programs must be developed prior to the MBMO implementation.

PROPER INTEGRATION WITH OTHER FUNCTIONS OF MANAGEMENT

MBMO cannot exist in a vacuum. It must be properly integrated with many other functions of management. For example, objective formulation must be integrated with marketing research, new product development, capital budgeting, management science modeling, training and development programs, and data processing. Furthermore, it is imperative that a proper reward and punishment system be operational for MBMO implementation. Such integration is especially important in view of the required individual innovation, self-control, and self-motivation in the MBMO system.

PROPER ALLOWANCE FOR CONTINGENCIES

MBMO is a human process. Thus, the inexact nature of human judgment and relationships must be taken into account. Since quantitative objectives are convenient and exact, many people tend to overemphasize them, and generally neglect qualitative objectives. Such a mistake can be minimized by allowing some contingencies for qualitative objectives. Also, the uncertainties of the external and organizational environment would most likely result in unexpected changes.

EFFECTIVE CHANGE STRATEGIES

Since MBMO implementation can be a drastic change in some organizations, careful change strategies prior to system implementation must be prepared. They not only help to answer such critical questions as how the system should be developed, how it should be implemented, who should be involved in the system, etc., but they also lessen the anxiety and unrest among members of the organization.

COMMITMENT TO REDUCE BUREAUCRACY

MBMO is a complex management system. Implementation of MBMO generally requires a great deal of coordination, communication, and cooperation among personnel and work units. Thus, the system frequently requires additional paper work and bureaucracy in its initial implementation. As a matter of fact, many organizations abandon the management by objectives process after the objective preparation stage because the whole process gets bogged down with excessive paper work and bureaucracy. It is important for the organization, especially top management, to make a commitment to reduce bureaucracy and paper work as much as possible by eliminating duplicate systems.

PREPARING FOR CHANGE

The preceding section discussed a number of factors important for a successful MBMO implementation. Checking to see if most of the necessary factors exist in the organization can be used as an assessment process prior to MBMO implementation. In addition to this assessment, the organization must take necessary steps to prepare for change—the MBMO system implementation.

Introduction of MBMO as the basic management process may require significant changes not only in management practice but also in personnel work procedures and expectations. Organization members must work, behave, and think differently. For an effective implementation of MBMO we must minimize negative consequences of such change and find ways to motivate the personnel to be effective with the new system. Organizational change is a complex topic in itself and certainly the discussion here cannot be comprehensive. We shall simply discuss some important issues involved in preparing for organizational change.

MANAGERIAL ASSESSMENT

The first major step when considering MBMO implementation is managerial assessment of all of the above-described necessary factors. This assessment process should be conducted by a planning or task force group appointed by top management. The assessment should answer not only whether or not the organization is substantially ready to embark on MBMO, but also find an answer to the fundamental question, "Do the expected benefits outweigh the costs (including organizational disturbance and unrest) associated with MBMO implementation?" It is not advisable to adopt MBMO or any other system because of either its conceptual attractiveness or "other firms have it" syndrome without fully realizing the required organizational change and disturbance. The results of this assessment must be evaluated thoroughly by top management before any actual planning work for MBMO is initiated.

PLANNING FOR ORGANIZATIONAL CHANGE

Planning is essential for any significant organizational change. The planning process should produce and communicate the following information:

- What needs to be changed
- Why change is necessary
- How change will be carried out
- Who will be involved in the change process

- When change will take place
- Expected organizational benefits from change

The planning period for MBMO is perhaps the most sensitive phase for organization members. The way the planning process is carried out has enormous impact upon the implementation phase and eventual effectiveness of the system. Once a go-ahead decision has been made, the chief executive officer must take charge and outline the following important aspects through the top-level managers: immediate changes that are necessary, appointment of a task force or planning group, and assessment for change in policies, work procedures, information requirements and flows, training and development programs, job descriptions, functional relationships among various work units, and communication systems.

Perhaps the best way to initiate the planning work is by a task force group composed of all key individuals (linking pin idea) and some outside experts if possible. It is important to find experts who have professional expertise about MBMO yet do not have any vested interest in specifics of organizational politics. Thus, outside consultants or resource persons should be involved in the planning phase. Without such professional expertise, the planning work could become an arena for misdirection and internal politics, a source of undesirable rumors, and an exercise in wishful thinking. In order to provide prestige, credibility, as well as appropriate responsibility to the task force group, top managers must be actively involved in planning meetings.

MANAGING RESISTANCE TO CHANGE

According to a theory of social change proposed by Kurt Lewin, any situation where change is proposed has dynamic forces working in opposing directions. The *driving forces* attempt to move the situation toward the direction of desired change. The opposing forces, called *restraining forces*, attempt to resist the driving forces and keep the situation from moving toward the desired change. A dynamic equilibrium is achieved between the two set of opposing forces. Lewin contends that any increase in the driving force will most likely be accompanied by an increase in the restraining forces. Thus, achieving a desired change in a smooth and permanent way would be through three basic steps: (1) identifying and blunting the courses of the restraining forces; (2) increasing the driving forces toward the desired change; and (3) achieving a new level of equilibrium between the opposing forces closer to the desired change by reinforcing positive behaviors.

Identifying and removing or blunting the causes of resistance to change should start during the planning phase. Most widely recognized causes of resistance to change are:

1. *Uncertainty.* People fear the unknown. When one's security and stability are threatened, it tends to create resistance.
2. *Threat to vested interests.* People build comfortable routines, work procedures, norms, personal status, and involvements in various internal and external groups at a work situation. A proposed change is a threat to such vested interests.
3. *Not being involved.* When people feel that they are not part of the driving forces, they tend to resist a change because of a lack of ownership interests in the concept.
4. *Ineffective communication.* Perhaps the most prevalent cause of resistance is due to ineffective communication. The justification and reasons for change might not have been communicated clearly to all members of the organization. Or, people may interpret the proposed change in many different ways due to an ineffective communication system.
5. *Feeling of inadequacy and fear of failure.* Frequently people recognize the need for a change but resist because they may feel inadequate or have fear of failure in the new environment. Such fear has been widely observed whenever an organization introduces a computer-based information system.
6. *Excessive work.* Often people fear that a proposed change will simply add work to their current job responsibilities. Also, people fear the generation of a great deal of paper work, especially when they are not convinced about the necessity of a proposed change.
7. *Ignoring the existing values and norms.* People tend to resist change when it is perceived as a threat to existing values, standards, and norms currently existing in the organization.

In order to reduce the restraining forces to change, several strategies can be employed, perhaps the most widely accepted of which are:

1. Involve members of the organization in planning as well as actual implementation of the MBMO system.
2. Open channels of communication, vertically and horizontally, in order to provide downward information as well as feedback on desired changes and people's reactions toward them.
3. Create and maintain the credibility of top management's interest and commitment in the desired changes.
4. Attempt to keep the MBMO planning process completely open. When people feel assured that the process is not done in secret, behind the scene, or in private, a trust can be built for the system.
5. Recognize and honor established work procedures or group norms as much as possible. If changes are required, involve the people who will be affected.
6. Recognize an MBMO catalyst, a new member of top management or a consultant to the chief executive officer with whom some key personnel could work together to reassess current organizational problems and generate new approaches.
7. Management must provide reinforcement to positive behaviors toward the desired change. A successful experience with MBMO and continued management support will gradually transform the new system into a way of life, thus achieving a new equilibrium and stability within the organization.

PERSONNEL TRAINING AND DEVELOPMENT

As discussed earlier, there are certain technical and managerial skills required in the MBMO system. The organization must develop a comprehensive training and development program to provide such skills. The MBMO system does not allow personnel simply to maintain status quo or "muddle along" in the organization. They must know how to develop individual work goals, departmental objectives and action plans, and to work toward the achievement of organizational objectives.

The training and development program must deal with such basic issues as what MBMO is, how people will be involved, what changes will be necessary, and what skills will be needed to perform effectively in the system. Such a program is an excellent vehicle not only for training but also for communicating and winning over people for the proposed change.

The nature of the training and development programs, either developed internally or brought in by outside experts, will vary greatly based on the needs of the organization as determined by an assessment process. However, it is important that the programs provide levels of minimum skills and knowledge that are required in MBMO. For example, abilities to plan, identify problem areas, make decisions in a rational and organized manner, lead people in a participatory way, manage change, and manage time are all very important skills that need to be developed.

IMPLEMENTING MBMO

When all preparations are completed, the actual MBMO implementation approach must be determined. Once again, there are many different ways or combinations of implementation approaches that could be used, depending upon unique aspects of the organizational environment. Let us look at several well known approaches.

TOP-DOWN IMPLEMENTATION

This is a widely practiced managerial approach. Top managers prepare the basic purpose of the organization, long-range goals, organizational objectives, strategic plans, and major departmental objectives. The general direction, target, and guidelines are clearly presented for subordinate divisions and departments. Based on the directives and guidelines from top managers, subordinate managers will participate in preparing their own departmental objectives, action plans, and work procedures.

The top-down approach has several important advantages: (1) it coordinates activities of the entire organization toward the achievement of organizational objectives (i.e., satisfying global objectives) rather than working toward divisional objectives; (2) it provides a clear understanding of management philosophy, policies, and guidelines and thus alleviates any misinformation; (3) it provides immediate credibility to the MBMO system; and (4) it minimizes the effort required for the most time-consuming, tedious, and political phases of the system.

This approach also has some grave shortcomings: (1) it tends to demand compliance rather than generating commitment on the part of most organization members; (2) it tends to create bureaucratic policies and procedures, thus inhibiting creativity and innovative ideas by subordinate personnel; (3) it encourages employees to work based on the "books" rather than taking voluntary responsibilities for the achievement of objectives.

BOTTOM-UP IMPLEMENTATION

This approach is opposite to top-down implementation. The MBMO process may start from the lowest level managers, although the initial planning process can begin at any level below the top managers. The lower level managers develop their departmental (or sectional) objectives, individual work objectives, action plans, and work procedures. As their proposals are moved up to higher level managers, they will be modified and consolidated in order to formulate the objectives of superordinate units.

The bottom-up approach has the following advantages: (1) it promotes greater participation and commitment on the part of lower level employees; (2) it reflects more precise relationships and interactions among various operational units of the organization; and (3) it encourages creativity and new ideas by lower level employees.

It also has a number of disadvantages: (1) it tends to make the MBMO planning and implementation process drift because of lack of top-level directions and petty politics at the lower level; (2) it has the danger of creating a suboptimal management approach where departmental objectives take priority over all the overall organizational objectives; and (3) it may create an undesirable tendency that organizational objectives are formulated by subordinate managers rather than by the top managers.

LINKING PIN IMPLEMENTATION

In this approach the manager of each work unit prepares unit objectives, action plans, and work procedures with key personnel. However, this process takes place as part of a total program where managers of superordinate divisions also participate by providing the top management guidelines, direction, and organizational objectives. Thus, this approach is a combination of top-down and bottom-up approaches.

Major advantages of the linking pin implementation are (1) it promotes team effort and commitment to group norms; (2) it allows the formulation of realistic unit objectives within the constraints provided by top management; and (3) it provides better communication both vertically and horizontally. Perhaps the single most important weakness of this approach is that some unit managers may be reluctant to reveal to rival peers or subordinates certain unique work activities or problem areas.

IMPLEMENTATION BY OPEN PARTICIPATION

The open participation approach is intended to encourage a wide interest and involvement from all members of the organization. Usually several different levels of groups need to be organized for initial orientation, training, planning, and then implementation. Although the concept is quite appealing, the practical logistics for an open participation program require a great deal of organization. The major advantage of this approach is that it tends to encourage self-motivation, commitment, and low level of resistance to change on the part of organization members.

This approach has several severe drawbacks: (1) participants are not at the same general level of understanding about management and MBMO, thus an effective training is extremely difficult; (2) since the program is based on voluntary participation, quite often many members participate in only part of the program; (3) some participants merely attend the meetings to show their faces, while a few others may attend to disturb or obstruct the implementation.

As stated earlier, there is no one right approach of MBMO implementation for all organizations. However, most successful implementations of organizational changes indicate that there should be a clearly planned program which uses some top-down and some bottom-up approaches while taking advantage of the linking pin and the open participation concepts.

IMPLEMENTATION STRATEGIES AND STEPS

There are basically three MBMO implementation strategies: (1) an internal coordination person or committee takes charge of implementation; (2) an outside consultant or organization takes the responsibility; and (3) a combined group of key individuals from the organization and outside experts forms a task force for implementation.

The internal coordination committee approach is perhaps the most economically feasible avenue for many organizations. Also, the key individual may have intimate knowledge about what needs to be done and how to coordinate the efforts of many different work units. However, this approach also has a danger of "the blind leading the blind;" all the work may become an expensive learning exercise but nothing more.

The outside consultant or consulting organization approach is often a very expensive but simple way to bring about change. Furthermore, consultants often bring with them rich experience of actual implementation of a similar system at many other organizations. Thus, they know how to avoid common pitfalls during system implementation. However, the organization must take over the system sooner or later. This approach tends to encourage organization members to rely too much on the expertise of outside consultants in implementing and operating the system.

The third approach represents a combination of outside experts who provide general guidelines and technical knowledge, while internal personnel provide the detailed functional relationships and work procedures in the organization. In most situations this combined task force approach works best.

The actual implementation steps can take any of the three basic forms: organizationwide total implementation, vertical unitwide step implementation, or horizontal levelwide step implementation. Let us discuss these approaches in greater detail.

ORGANIZATIONWIDE TOTAL IMPLEMENTATION

This approach is a clean-sweep complete implementation for the entire organization. It is most appropriate for small organizations where span of control is relatively short, the number of operational functions is limited, and the coordination relatively simple to attain. Complete, all at once implementation requires a great deal of advance planning, training, and time commitment by top management.

Since this approach will result in a very hectic or even chaotic situation at the initial stage of implementation, there must be flexible plans to respond and make necessary changes quickly. Such corrective plans based on review and control must be formulated in advance.

The total implementation approach has several important advantages: (1) it has a sweeping and complete impact of the system on the organization; (2) it will involve all functional units simultaneously and thus they can learn the system together; (3) since it involves the entire organization, any petty jealousy or pockets of resistance could be avoided; and (4) as this approach has a short implementation period, the total start-up efforts and cost could be the least among the available options.

This approach also has several disadvantages: (1) it requires such a hectic and chaotic pace of implementation that many small mistakes may be unnoticed and become bad organizational habits; (2) because of its large-scale change, extensive external assistance may be required and organizational members may resent the system as a consultant's project; and (3) because of its large scale and hectic pace, the entire organization may concentrate on system implementation and neglect the basic objectives the system is intended to help achieve.

VERTICAL UNITWIDE STEP IMPLEMENTATION

This approach represents a cautious way to the MBMO system. It tests the MBMO system feasibility by implementing it in one vertical unit such as the production, research and development, or sales department. This approach is most appropriate for large decentralized organizations with diverse operational functions. The vertical, one-unit-at-a-time implementation approach allows the organization to concentrate on a test run and make the final decision as to whether or not the system should be implemented in the entire organization.

Major advantages of this approach are (1) it does not disrupt the entire organization and thus requires only a limited amount of managerial commitment of time and efforts; (2) the test or experiment can be used as a training device for other units' personnel; (3) because of its limited scale any mistakes or problem areas can be identified easily and corrective actions taken; (4) the one-unit implementation may require only minimal, if any, external assistance and thus provide the opportunity to bring forth the employee commitment to the change; and (5) a "showcase" implementation results.

This approach has several disadvantages. Although these disadvantages are real, they can be controlled relatively easily by imaginative managers. Some of these are (1) because of its small-scale implementation, frequently insignificant problems can be magnified and color a wrong picture for the MBMO system; (2) perhaps the most serious disadvantage is the weight assigned to the test run (as the test run is critical for the system's complete implementation, selection of a wrong unit will be fatal to the system); and (3) because of its limited scope of one-unit implementation, the possibility of people opposed to the MBMO system wrecking the system is relatively high.

HORIZONTAL LEVELWIDE STEP IMPLEMENTATION

This also is a one-step-at-a-time approach. However, it involves one horizontal level of the organization at a time rather than one vertical unit at a time. The implementation process moves from one level to the next as the system progresses. In most organizations the process is top down, starting at the top level and expanding to the next lower level. This approach is most appropriate for meduim-size organizations with some diversified operational functions but with limited decentralization. This approach would not be as hectic as the organizationwide total implementation but not as simple or conservative as the one unit at a time approach. In fact, this approach is very attractive for most state agencies, universities, hospitals, etc.

Major advantages of this approach are (1) it is an orderly process requiring relatively limited time and effort; (2) because of its one-level-at-a-time approach, personnel at each level can provide training and experience to employees at the next lower level; and (3) because of its levelwide top-down approach, the broad guidelines and constraints of the overall organization can be carried on to the lower levels.

One principle disadvantage of this approach is that because of its levelwide implementation two or more incompatible systems may be in operation simultaneously. This problem can generate much confusion and anxiety among personnel, especially at the lower levels.

The above three approaches may take different modeling methods when we approach the MBMO implementation through the use of management science. For example, the organizationwide total implementation approach can be viewed as a large-scale modeling approach. A large-scale model encompassing all major components of the organization can be designed and analyzed in order to determine activities that would satisfy important organizational objectives.

The vertical unitwide step implementation is equivalent to modeling for a given unit. A small-scale model for a given unit can be designed to attain major objectives of the unit. The horizontal level-wide step implementation is basically the same as the decomposition approach. Here top management-level headquarters model is designed first, next the second-level divisional models are developed, then the third-level departmental models are formulated, and all level models are connected by organizational constraints and objectives. The decomposition modeling approach allows a neat computational convenience for having smaller divisional models and then ties them to the corporate level model so that the global satisfying can be achieved. In other words, the decomposition approach attempts to achieve the overall organizational objectives by coordinating activities at lower level units.

SUMMARY

This chapter has been devoted to the implementation phase of MBMO. It should be quite clear to the reader that installing an MBMO system in an organization is a complex managerial task. It requires careful assessment of the environmental conditions and planning. Each organization has unique sets of problems, conditions, and capabilities. Thus, a cookbook approach is not appropriate. However, a good review of many ideas, strategies, approaches, and methods discussed in this chapter should provide enough insight and knowledge about the implementation phase of MBMO. An imaginative manager should be able to map out systematic and organized strategies for his or her organization. The very key elements of a successful implementation are organized strategies, effective communication, top-management participation, support of key personnel at various levels, and the management philosophy which encourages self-motivation and involvement.

REFERENCES

Griener, L. "Patterns of Organizational Change." *Harvard Business Review* 45(May-June 1967): 119-30.

Lasagna, J.B. "Make Your MBO Pragmatic." *Harvard Business Review* 49 (November-December 1971): 63-69.

Lewin, K. "Group Decision and Social Change." In *Readings in Social Psychology*, edited by T.H. Newcomb and E.L. Hartley, pp. 340-44. New York: Holt, Rinehart & Winston, 1947.

Lubans, V.A., and Edgar, J.M. *Policing by Objectives*. Hartford, Conn.: Social Development Corp., 1979.

McConkey, D.D. *How to Manage by Results*. New York: American Management Association, 1965.

Morrisey, G.L. *Management by Objectives and Results in the Public Sector*. Reading, Mass.: Addison-Wesley, 1976.

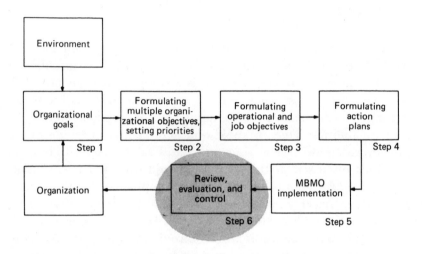

Environment

Organizational goals — Step 1

Formulating multiple organizational objectives, setting priorities — Step 2

Formulating operational and job objectives — Step 3

Formulating action plans — Step 4

Organization

Review, evaluation, and control — Step 6

MBMO implementation — Step 5

8

Review, Evaluation, and Control

Controlling is an important management function which is concerned with "getting things done in a proper way." In other words, control is a process that tries to ensure that objectives are achieved in the most effective way. However, in order to control the MBMO system properly, there should be a review and evaluation process to judge the effectiveness of the entire MBMO system and personnel who run it. Thus, the review and contol process functions as a feedback mechanism and thus closes the MBMO loop. Many management by objectives or results programs are designed without a proper review and control mechanism. Such programs are not only incomplete but they also cannot function effectively without feedback information. It is impossible to achieve a set of desired objectives exactly as planned because of dynamic environmental and organizational factors, uncertainties involved in the situation, unpredictable human attitudes and behaviors, and incomplete information about the system environment.

The principle purpose of the review and control step in MBMO is to provide information about (1) the degree of expected achievement of objectives based on action plans under the changing environment; (2) the efficiency or effectiveness of various components and personnel in the organization; and (3) the magnitude of corrective adjustments and actions required at various levels of the organization and in the MBMO system. The review and control process completes the MBMO loop, as shown in Figure 8.1.

SYSTEM REVIEW

One very important difference between MBMO and traditional management approaches is the organized and systematic way in which progress toward established objectives is reviewed at every level

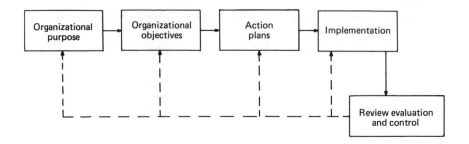

FIGURE 8.1 Review, evaluation, and control in the MBMO system

of the organization. The review process is an integral part of every step of MBMO. For example, the action planning step does not terminate when a set of well thought out activities are determined and scheduled. A continuous review and evaluation of the planned activities in view of changing environmental and organizational factors is essential to keep the action planning step current and effective.

The review for the entire MBMO system must be conducted periodically during the implementation phase in view of new information generated from the actual result of implementation. Also, the final review of the system must take place at the end of the MBMO cycle (planning time horizon) in order to generate information which could be used to make necessary corrective actions for the next planning cycle. The review reveals whether or not certain desired changes or activities are occurring toward objectives. The effectiveness of the planning phase is therefore determined by the information obtained from the review.

TIMELINESS AND COMPREHENSIVENESS OF THE REVIEW

While recognizing the importance of the review process of every major step and component of MBMO, it is difficult to determine how much review is needed. Since the review process represents a significant cost item and requires a great deal of time and effort on the part of managers and staff personnel, it is important to determine a cost-effective review process. We are concerned with two key issues here: (1) timeliness—how often should a review be performed? and (2) magnitude—how comprehensive and elaborate should it be?

In order to make corrective actions as soon as an unexpected change occurs in the environment, we need a constant review system. However, such a proposition for the entire MBMO cycle could be very costly. Thus, the planning group must determine the most cost-effective frequency of interim reviews during the implementation phase. The most widely accepted review cycle is quarterly or monthly, depending upon the nature of the organization. Interim reviews must be frequent enough to monitor all important changes that need to be reflected in the MBMO system, but not cost more than the benefits derived from the corrective actions taken based on the review. In addition to interim system reviews, a final review at the end of a given MBMO cycle is necessary in order to plan for the following cycle.

The comprehensiveness of a review process is very difficult to determine. Perhaps the best way to establish this would be to rely on the experience of other organizations or outside experts. The initial review process should determine a list of key variables and parameters that need to be monitored in order to make necessary changes. For example, for the objective "increase sales by 10 percent during the coming year," we may need to review the following items:

- Sales trends by products, districts, sales people
- Advertising effectiveness
- Allocation patterns of sales force
- Market share analysis
- Analysis of competing products
- Marketing and customer research
- Sales training needs
- New product requirements
- State of and trends in the economy

With the experience obtained from several reviews, the program can be modified, expanded, simplified, or completely overhauled.

The bottom line is of course whether or not the review program generates enough useful information to make corrective actions. Ordinarily, personnel involved in functions related to key result areas can provide a sufficient data base that needs to be reviewed. In more specialized and technical areas, such as research and development, outside experts may be needed to determine the appropriate review program.

INFORMATION THAT MUST BE
OBTAINED FROM THE REVIEW

Any review program must provide information about the progress toward established objectives. If an action plan is not proceding a desired result, the cause should be analyzed and corrective actions taken. Basically, two types of information are needed: quantitative and qualitative. As we discussed in chapter 4, quantitative information is essential to implement any systematic plan based on objective and rational analysis. The review program must generate necessary quantitative data on key objective criteria so that a clear progress evaluation can be made. Qualitative data are also necessary to assess the qualitative objectives. Furthermore, qualitative information complements quantitative data in obtaining a more complete and rounded insight about the effectiveness of action plans.

Once the progress data have been obtained, it can be analyzed quickly as to whether or not a plan is in trouble. If it is indeed in trouble, the possible causes must be analyzed. Several key areas where analysis is required are (1) Are the assumptions made still valid? (2) Have there been any last minute changes to action plans? (3) Has the implementation plan been executed as planned? (4) Are there new developments that affect the desired outcome? Perhaps the most likely occurrence is a combination of some changes in all of the above areas. In such a case, it is extremely difficult to pinpoint causes of the problem.

A new innovative review approach has emerged recently. It is a computer-based interactive analysis approach. Once a general management science model (i.e., a goal programming model) is developed, a solution is derived using a computer. The solution represents the best way to satisfy multiple and sometimes conflicting objectives.

An equally important analysis that is useful for managerial decisions is the effect of changes in environmental and organizational factors (in the form of changing technological coefficients, constraints, and variables), objective levels, priorities, and model assumptions. Perhaps the most prevalent changes would be in objective levels and priorities because of changing environmental conditions and behavioral changes in personnel.

The interactive approach utilizes a conversational monitor system (CMS) which allows the user to interact with the model via a computer terminal (see Lee for a detailed discussion of this sytem and refer to Appendix A for the goal programming approach). The interactive approach points out clearly the impact of certain changes to objective achievements. Thus, it can be used both as a planning tool and a review program.

PLANNING THE REVIEW PROGRAM

An effective review program has to be a part of the MBMO system rather than an after-the-fact effort after the implementation phase. The review planning consists of several elements.

1. *The review design.* In order to design an effective review process, the following analyses are required.
   a) Analysis of projected and actual results—This analysis should reveal the difference, both positive and negative, between the projected results based on action planning and actual results of the implementation.
   b) Trend analysis—This analysis provides general information about where certain activities or objectives would be if the organization maintains the status quo. This information provides the lower bound of the planning for activities.
   c) Comparative analysis—This analysis should indicate where the organization stands in certain objective areas (e.g., profits, sales, research and development, training and development, etc.) as compared to other organizations in the same industry, same product lines, same general size, or same geographical locations.

d) Experimental analysis—This analysis is based on a controlled experiment with a specific unit of the organization concerning the effect of certain programs. The result of the experiment is compared with controlled or nonexperimental units.

2. *The objective criteria.* In order to facilitate objective review, the objective criteria must be measured quantitatively in some way. Certain criteria could be measured directly by quantitative terms, such as increasing total sales in dollars, increasing the market share in percentages, providing contribution to the United Way campaign in dollars, etc. For other objective criteria, quantitative measures can be used only indirectly. For example, the social contribution objective could be measured by such quantitative measures as the number of scholarships provided at a local college, contribution to charity programs, number of hard-core unemployable youths trained by the organization, and the like. There are a number of key measures that are related to organizational objectives. Such measures must be clearly identified and defined for the review program.

3. *Data requirements.* Once the review design and criteria measures are determined, it is necessary to analyze what data are required and how to collect them. Actually, the design and criteria measures will determine the basic data requirement of the review process. Most data required for review are readily available within the organization, such as weekly sales figures, cash flows, payroll, etc. However, certain specific data are available only from special sources, such as industrywide sales, competitors' wage and salary figures, competitors' research and development expenditures, etc. Thus, there is a need for systematic data requirement analysis, including the channels of collection.

4. *Analysis and synthesis of data.* Since raw data are not useful for the review process, the data should be synthesized, classified, or analyzed in such a way that they could be usable for review. For example, weekly sales figures for all individual sales persons during the past year have very little use. However, these data can be classified and analyzed to prepare the following important statistics:

a) Weekly and monthly sales figures by people, sales districts, and products
b) Comparisons with previous years' data
c) Change in market share of products

    d) Change in sales by people, sales districts, and products for the organization

    e) Comparisons with key competitors

    f) Analysis of seasonality in sales

    g) Evaluation of new sales promotion schemes, sales training, and change in sales force

There are a number of quantitative and statistical techniques that can be applied to analyze data. Also, a large number of "canned" computer programs are readily available, such as frequency analysis (percent analysis for various classifications), multiple correlation and regression, cluster analysis, multiple descriminate analysis, factor analysis, cononical analysis, multivariate analysis, etc. If the organization does not have in-house capabilities due to lack of computers or technical skills, a number of external sources could be utilized; for example, a local university or college can provide expert assistance at reasonable or no cost.

5. *Review schedule.* The last element to be discussed in the review plan is the scheduling. The review schedule is a formalized plan as to when interim and final reviews are to be undertaken. This schedule also determines the timing of all other elements of the review plan. For example, if the first quarterly review is planned by March 31, the data collection and data analysis groups must schedule their work accordingly.

Another important consideration here is the review schedule at different levels of the organization. If interim reviews are to be conducted quarterly for the entire organization, lower level units may need to provide review data at more frequent intervals, such as weekly or monthly. The overall review schedule should provide the basis for developing a cascade effect of other required activities in the organization.

EVALUATION OF PERSONNEL PERFORMANCE

MBMO is a systematic management approach. However, it is also a human system. It cannot function properly in spite of all of its systematic features unless the individuals working with the system perform satisfactorily. Organizationwide performance is measured relatively easily by such widely accepted measures as profit figures, market share, earnings per share, return on investment, quality of products, number of employees, turnover rates, social contributions, etc. Personnel performance, while as important as the overall organizational performance, is much more difficult to evaluate. To begin with, there is no complete consensus about what criteria are important. Secondly, some suggested evaluation criteria are highly abstract and elusive, such as creativity, initiative, commitment, attitude, judgment, enthusiasm, and perseverance. Thirdly, there is no standard and objective way to measure these criteria.

MAJOR EVALUATION FACTORS FOR MBMO

Performance evaluation is an important part of any management system, including the MBMO system. Performance evaluation involves two important components: current performance and future potential contribution. Performance evaluation usually does not involve past performance, as we assume that the past contribution was already properly evaluated. Concerning current performance, the evaluation of current contributions and achievements should be based on not only the individual's accomplishment of specific objectives, but it should also include performance in other areas of job responsibility as well.

Evaluation of the individual's future potential contribution usually involves an analysis of certain personal characteristics that have been identified as important predictors of career success and advancement in the organization. Some important characteristics are those closely related to managerial abilities. Several important evaluation factors are as follows:

1. *Accomplishment of objectives.* Perhaps the most visible, quantifiable, and tangible factor for performance evaluation is the individual's accomplishments of specific objectives. In the short run, the result-oriented performance evaluation may result in less than desirable consequences. For example, the accomplished results may be due to others' contribution, luck, given circumstances, or a negative incentive system such as threat or harsh treatment of subordinates. Nevertheless, a performance evaluation based on tangible results is perhaps the most important factor in the long run.

2. *Managerial performance*. Managerial performance involves the way certain results are obtained through people and the potential of future accomplishments. Thus, it should include the system of resource allocation, policies and procedure for work activities, recruiting, training, motivating subordinates, and planning for future activities.

3. *Personal characteristics*. The above two factors are directly related to current work performance. In order to assess the individual's potential for success and advancement in the organization, certain personal characteristics need to be evaluated. In addition to clearly established qualifications and demographics such as education, age, work experience, professional achievements, etc., personal characteristics such as personality, analytical abilities and skills, special aptitudes, etc., must be evaluated in order to assess the potential success of the individual in the organization.

PERFORMANCE EVALUATION METHODS

Perhaps the most widely used performance evaluation method is the appraisal by the immediate superior. The person who supervises an individual on a day-to-day basis should have the most intimate knowledge about the individual's contribution. However, an evaluation method solely based on the immediate superior's appraisal may overemphasize immediate results, develop a halo effect of the superior's personal management style, and ignore other important factors such as potential for advancement and fulfillment of the individual's personal goals.

Many progressive organizations have introduced other supplementary evaluation methods such as self-evaluation, peer ratings, and evaluation by the second level higher superior. These methods may not yield as tangible or concrete evaluations as the immediate superior system; however, additional evaluation methods, including assessment centers, can provide new information about the individual's potential, personal goals, interpersonal relationships, and possible role conflicts on the job. Such information, if properly collected and used, can make the performance evaluation system much more effective.

THE EVALUATION FEEDBACK SYSTEM

The feedback of personnel performance evaluation can be a powerful tool for employee motivation. The evaluation system should be objective oriented, as a part of the MBMO system. The basic purpose of the performance appraisal system should be to help the individual to accomplish specified objectives by removing any obstacles currently in existence. Therefore, the performance evaluation reviewer must be a specially trained person who can provide specific, concrete, and constructive feedback. Empirical studies have shown that criticism or praise alone has very little impact on achievement of results. The most positive results have been achieved through both the superior and the subordinate setting specific objectives.

SOME KEY RELATIONSHIPS

Performance evaluation is a complex topic in itself and a thorough discussion is beyond the scope of this book. However, it should be recognized here that an appraisal system cannot exist in a vacuum. It has key interrelationships with other important components of the organization and its processes. For example, an effective evaluation system requires a direct relationship with the organizational reward-punishment sytem. Desired behaviors or proven contributions must be properly rewarded, while undesirable behaviors should be duly discouraged.

Some key relationships required are shown in Figure 8.2. The performance evaluation system must be closely related to the following systems:

1. Compensation systems
   wage and salary administration
   incentive systems
   fringe benefits
2. Training and development programs
3. Career and manpower planning
4. Advancement and separation policies

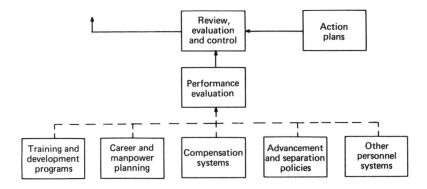

FIGURE 8.2 Performance evaluation and other mangement systems

CONTROL STRATEGIES

CONTROL ELEMENTS

As we discussed earlier, the MBMO system requires periodic system reviews and personnel evaluation in order to analyze the progress toward previously established objectives. This control process should be oriented toward problem solving and taking corrective actions. Since there are numerous factors that offset the achievement of objectives, it is difficult to determine just where the control emphasis should be placed. There are several key elements that need to be considered for control.

The first element is the MBMO system itself. It is quite possible that problems arise because of an ill-prepared system. The second element would be resources (time, manpower, materials, physical facilities, etc.). If necessary resources are not properly allocated at the right time, objectives will not be achieved as desired. The third element is the "principle of the critical few" which we discussed previously in this book. There are always a critical few which present problems. For example, a small number of employees who produce the largest number of defects, accidents, delays, customer complaints, and law suits; a small number of operations that tend to produce the most frequent bottlenecks; certain time periods of the day that employees tend to have the greatest number of accidents; and the like.

Figure 8.3 presents a possible cross-check form which could be used for control purposes. This form is a rudimental approach to identify several key factors that could go wrong in the system. However, the control system usually becomes more systematic as the MBMO system is implemented over several cycles and personnel involved gain experience. Also, an interactive computer-based monitor system can be utilized in flagging certain problem areas where expected progress or performance is not accomplished.

CONTROL CHECK POINTS

In order to monitor the progress toward established objectives, three key check points are essential.

1. *Projection.* The desired objective is usually far above the current state of affairs. For example, an objective "to achieve the total annual sales of $2 million during the next year" may represent $500,000 more than the current year's total sales figure. In order

Elements	Critical Few Items	Possible Actions

System
  What
  Where
  When
  By whom
  How
  Why		

Resources
  Time
  Personnel
  Materials
  Physical facilities
  Financial
  Others		

FIGURE 8.3 Control cross-check form

to increase the sales figure by $500,000 during the next year, certain projections can be developed as shown below:

a) sales increase projections by sales districts

b) sales increase projections by products

c) sales increase projections by monthly and weekly

d) sales increase projections by individuals

e) marketing support activity projections

These projections should provide at least general information about what type of progress will be necessary during the next year in various areas in order to achieve the specified objective.

2. *Performance Standards.* Once the necessary projections are completed, the next step is to establish effective performance standards for departments, work units, and individuals. The performance standard represents a measuring yardstick for effective work efforts toward achieving established objectives. Obviously the standards cannot be established arbitrarily. A joint effort and mutual agreement is necessary between the superior and the subordinate. Since performance standards are developed to indicate successful performance toward achieving objectives, they should be as unbiased, measurable, and concrete as possible. Some qualitative standards, such as innovations, research and development, self-development of managerial skills, etc., may need surrogate quantitative measures as shown below:

Innovations

- number of new ideas suggested

- number of new innovations actually implemented

- estimated cost savings due to innovations

- estimated profit potential of innovations to products

Research and Development

- number of new patents applied

- number of scientific journal articles published by the R&D staff

- number of new systems implemented

- number of new products introduced

- estimated dollar value of new products and systems

Self-development
- number of programs participated in
- number of courses taken and credits earned
- degrees earned
- publication in professional journals or periodicals
- participation in professional conferences
- subordinate reactions—complaints, praise, etc.
- superior and peer reactions—complaints, praise, etc.

3. *Bench Marks*. Once projections and performance standards are established, a clearly defined bench mark must be determined based on realistic scheduling. For example, in order to increase the total annual sales by $500,000 during the next year, the sales increase projection may require $125,000 increase in every quarter. Then, the bench marks can be established for the organization, sales districts, work units, and individuals. These bench marks can serve as intermediate objectives as well as interim hurdles that could flag warning signs when they are not accomplished.

CAUSES OF VARIANCE

Corrective actions are necessary only when actual results do not measure up to the standards and bench marks. Whenever such a variance from the planned performance occurs, it would be caused by one of two primary reasons.

First, internal uncertainties. We live in a dynamic environment where things change constantly. There is a general theory of average or regression which contends that the natural phenomenon tends to regress to the middle. Thus, we may have a general idea about average figures for certain activities within the organization such as accidents, defects, human errors, equipment breakdowns, absenteeism, deaths, etc. However, we do not know when variances from the average will occur in these activities. We may judiciously use historical data and attempt to predict the most likely occurrences of such variances. However, whenever variances do occur due to uncertainties, corrective actions would be needed.

Second, unexpected external events. The organization functions in the environment where unexpected events occur frequently that are beyond the control of the organization. Some good examples would be the oil embargo by oil-producing countries in 1974, the Iranian situation during 1979-80, the Russian adventure in Afghanistan, the economic recession of 1980, etc. Additionally, there could be certain natural disasters, death of a national leader, unexpected government economic policy shifts, a strike by labor unions, discovery of an alternative energy source, etc. When such events occur, the organization may be forced to take corrective actions.

INFORMATION SOURCES FOR CONTROL

There exists a general information explosion. Once we heard a top manager of an organization complain that "it used to take three months to get the lousy quarterly sales figures; now it takes only a couple of hours to get it but it requires three months to read it." However, the abundance of information readily available is not usually the right type of information or it is not in the right format. In this section we shall discuss the most useful information sources for controlling the MBMO system.

First, *computer output*. Almost every organization utilizes a computer-based report system for certain activities (payroll, accounting, sales, production, inventories, etc.). Such information printed out as computer output could be a good source of information to take corrective actions.

Second, *simple figures*. Many managers favor simple visual aids using block diagrams, GANTT time charts, histograms, etc., that summarize some loosely available data such as computer output. Simple visual figures can be prepared by office staff with a limited amount of effort and time. These figures can highlight problem areas that require corrective action without any sophisticated analysis.

Third, *technical reports*. Certain raw data or visual aids have very limited use for analytical purposes. Thus, there is a need to develop technical reports which utilize statistical analysis, management science modeling approaches, or computer-based simulations. For example, if a production manager would like to find the causes of rapidly rising inventory levels, a specially prepared technical report would be required. Many organizations usually have enough professional staff to prepare such reports. Otherwise outside experts could be employed to analyze the available information through sophisticated but very useful techniques. With the availability of many canned computer programs for various analyses, it is no longer a monumental effort to develop a comprehensive statistical report for such activities as production, sales, cash flows, etc.

Fourth, *written special reports*. Although many narrative reports may be useless for controlling purposes, certain special reports prepared by qualified personnel about important current events may be extremely valuable. For example, a special report on "The Prime Rate Trend and Capital Investment Opportunities" prepared by a corporate economist could be a valuable source of information for taking corrective actions. Such special reports could be initiated either by the staff or the concerned manager. However, staff personnel should be given the responsibility to assess any current or expected events that have important implications to the organization and make periodic reports to the manager.

Fifth, *periodic reviews.* It is extremely important to review progress toward set objectives on a regular basis. Such a periodic review could take several different forms: staff reviews, superior-subordinate reviews, committee reviews, and management team reviews. Although each type of review has its own unique purposes, the general goal is to ascertain that timely corrective actions are taken when problems arise in the MBMO system.

CORRECTIVE ACTION ALTERNATIVES

Once projections, standards, and bench marks are clearly established and information sources for control are explored, then corrective action options (or any combinations of them) should be analyzed. Basically, there are three alternatives that could be explored.

First, *individual self-correction*. One widely accepted management principle is that the best place to exercise control is at the point where actions take place. Thus, the individual who is closest to the actual work performance has the best knowledge as to how and what corrective actions must be taken.

Second, *operational correction.* This corrective action takes place at the lower managerial level. When certain variances or problems are identified, the manager can quickly take corrective actions either personally or see to it that such actions are carried out by designated personnel. For example, an inventory manager may call a vendor and expedite the delivery of an out of stock item. The management science director may personally develop a computer simulation model as the deadline approaches. Or the personnel manager may personally meet with union officials about a certain employee grievance. Operational correction is often a quick and simple control device. As a matter of fact, many managers are eager to look into operational actions. However, rescuing the situation tends to create bad work habits in the organization. Individual employees may develop a tendency to rely on the manager's last minute rescue, and, on the other hand, the manager may concentrate on operations while neglecting managerial functions.

Third, *managerial correction.* The highest level control device is the corrective action taken by management. Actions at this level involve the basic system configurations, broad organizational purpose, long-range goals, organizational objectives, and major management support systems (such as personnel, compensation plans, training and development, career and manpower planning, and the like).

CONTROL STEPS

The control process in MBMO requires certain typical steps. Whether or not the entire sequence of steps would be required depends upon the organization, the type of variances or problems encountered, the magnitude of identified problems, etc. The typical sequence of control steps is as follows:

1. *Identify problems.* This step involves not only identifying variances and magnitude of problems but also analyzing the causes of problems. It includes potential future problems as well as current ones.
2. *Remove obstacles.* Sometimes the primary reasons for not being able to achieve a set of objectives are due to certain ob-

stacles. The corrective actions required would be to obtain necessary resources or approvals to remove such obstacles.

3. *Take corrective actions.* Once the cause of the problem has been identified, corrective actions (either one action alternative or a combination of alternatives) should be taken. The steps and magnitude of corrective actions would vary depending upon the nature of the problem and the action alternative selected (self-corrections, operational corrections, or managerial corrections). Some of the possible actions would be:

- change work procedures and policies
- adjust individual or work unit objectives
- change implementation strategies
- revise divisional and organizational objectives
- adjust organizational purpose, long-range planning, and strategic planning
- establish new objective levels
- review personnel performance
- take appropriate actions based on performance evaluations

SUMMARY

The review, evaluation, and control process represents the last phase of the MBMO system. It is designed to close the loop so that the MBMO system becomes a self-contained process through which a set of desired objectives are properly achieved.

The review, evaluation, and control process is a relatively unpleasant part of MBMO, and any system for that matter. People tend to have negative perceptions about being evaluated, appraising others' performance, and then taking corrective actions. However, control should not have such a negative connotation. It does not mean oppression, demanding compliance or obedience, and ramming certain rules down peoples' throats. It does mean getting things accomplished in a proper and organized manner. It should produce positive feedback, challenge, and new aspirations for future endeavors.

REFERENCES

Hatry, H., et al. *Practical Program Evaluation for State and Local Government Officials*. Washington: The Urban Institute, 1973.

Lee, S.M. *Goal Programming Methods for Mutliple Objective Integer Programs*. Atlanta: American Institute of Industrial Engineers, OR Monograph 2, 1979.

Lee, S.M., and Moore, L.J. *Introduction to Decision Science*. New York: Petrocelli/Charter, 1975.

Morrisey, G.L. *Management by Objectives and Results in the Public Sector*. Reading, Mass.: Addison-Wesley, 1976.

Raia, A.P. *Managing by Objectives*, Glenview, Ill.: Scott, Foresman, 1974.

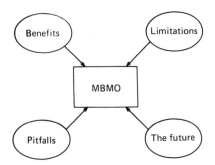

Part III: The Future of
MBMO

MBMO is not MBO with one more word added to it. It is an organized approach to integrate various management systems to achieve a set of multiple organizational objectives in a satisfying manner. This part presents chapter 9 which is devoted to a discussion of benefits, limitations, systematic approaches, and the future of MBMO.

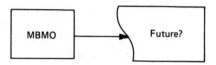

9

The Future of MBMO

Management by multiple objectives is not a new name for MBO. Nor is it an MBO approach with few other things thrown in. Rather, MBMO is a modern management approach which systematically integrates various components and functions of management so as to achieve *multiple* organizational objectives in the most effective way.

It has been generally recognized that organizations, whether business firms, government agencies, or nonprofit organizations, have multiple conflicting objectives, and, further, that management of multiple objectives is not simply an aggregation of systems for management of simple objectives. The magnitude, complexity and implications of MBMO represent exponential effects of interactions and conflicts among multiple objectives. We have discussed various components of MBMO that require extensive modifications or changes from the traditional MBO system.

MBMO is basically a new way to look at management systems. It has borrowed heavily from systems analysis, management science, computer science, managerial economics, and decision sciences. In this chapter we shall discuss the benefits, limitations, possible pitfalls to avoid, and the future of MBMO.

BENEFITS OF MBMO

As we discussed in chapter 1, the basic concept of traditional MBO has been accepted as a more systematic way to evaluate personnel performance. It has also been regarded as a means to more participative management. After the concept became more popular and organizations gained experience with the system through actual applications, it gained acceptance as a good planning process. But it did not provide a way to deal with multiple and conflicting objectives. MBMO's greatest potential is as an integrated management system for improving organizational performance and personnel satisfaction on the job. Some potential benefits of MBMO are discussed below.

ORGANIZATIONAL BENEFITS

1. *Clarification of the organizational purpose and long-range goals.* Implementation of MBMO requires that the organization's mission or purpose, long-range goals, and broad objectives be clearly established. The basic direction, guidelines, and paths are provided for the organization and its members. Consequently, there is less chance that inappropriate, counterproductive, and wasteful activities will occur in the organization.

2. *Analysis of multiple objectives.* Application of the MBMO system accommodates formulation, analysis, and evaluation of multiple organizational objectives. Some of these objectives may be incompatible, competitive, or incommensurable. Thus, there is a need to evaluate their trade-offs and for procedures to resolve conflicts. Analyzing implications, both in economic and noneconomic terms, of objective conflicts and trade-offs provides important information for management decision making.

3. *Better planning.* Planning involves looking ahead toward desired consequences and taking proactive steps in order to achieve objectives. In the MBMO system, planning is imbedded throughout the process. Thus, planning is built into the strategic, tactical, and operational frameworks, and has become a part of the everyday managerial process. The overwhelming emphasis on planning allows the organization to be proactive, avoid crisis management, and utilize time in the most effective way.

4. *Management by exception rather than by crisis.* Because the MBMO system is self-contained, it allows an organization to manage by exception rather than by crisis. Managers and personnel have clearly established targets, schedules, a list of potential problems, and work procedures. They can be more autonomous and manage their own activities. Therefore, they can settle back and need not panic on the job.

5. *Setting proper priorities for objectives.* Since multiple conflicting objectives complete for limited resources, there is a need to assign proper priorities so that resources are directed to important organizational objectives. Analysis of multiple objectives in terms of their cost-effectiveness, appropriate objective levels, and trade-offs enables the organization to set proper priorities for objectives. This important component has been generally neglected in the traditional MBO approach.

6. *Directing resources to important objectives.* In almost any organization, resources required to achieve aspirations or desired objectives usually exceed the available resources. Thus, resources must be used effectively to achieve important objectives. The multiple objectives approach of MBMO—based on clearly established objectives, measurement criteria, priorities, cost-effectiveness, and trade-off analysis—allows the organization to devise work activities in such a way as to best achieve desired objectives. Incongruent or wasteful activities have minimal chance of being left unchecked. Consequently, resources are directed effectively to important objectives.

7. *Clearly established standards for control.* As discussed in chapter 8, objectives cannot be approached without clearly established standards. In MBMO, managers have well-defined objectives and standards that can be used to control work activities and measure performance of subordinates. These standards provide guidelines, directions, and constraints that are clear to all members of the organization.

8. *Equitable compensation programs.* The objectives approach makes it possible to establish more equitable compensation programs based on data obtained from the review and evaluation process. The organization has a more distinct and concrete basis to discriminate producers from nonproducers. This allows a merit-based equitable compensation program to be established.

9. *Improved employee motivation.* Many empirical studies (especially the General Electric study by Meyer et al.) clearly indicate that objectives-based management systems tend to improve performance and employee motivation when fair performance evaluations exist. The management literature generally suggests that managers have the highest level of achievement needs among all occupational groups. It follows, then, that people with high levels of achievement needs tend to derive job satisfaction from working against the chal-

lenge of established standards and objectives. Thus, the MBMO system provides more opportunity to managers and others with high achievement needs to gain a sense of achievement.

Another important source of an improved employee motivation is the knowledge of how an individual's work efforts are related to overall organizational objectives. The MBMO system provides clear information about interactions and interrelations among individuals and work units that are directed toward organizational goals. This information provides individuals with renewed self-esteem, organizational commitment, and self-concept that all lead to an improved motivation.

10. *Better communication.* Communication is the MBMO catalyst. Organizational objectives, long-range planning, divisional objectives, action planning, review and evaluation, etc., cannot be carried out without close vertical and horizontal communications. The improved communication aids employee morale and provides the employee better insights about the organization. Thus, better communication serves as a common denominator for the employees' unified efforts toward organizational objectives.

11. *Improved organizational structures and information systems.* Since the MBMO system requires clearly established work activities, standards, measures, and information needs, it provides the organization with the means to develop new and more effective organizational structures and management information systems. Under an effective MBMO system, more decentralization of managerial responsibilities is possible. Thus, the traditional span of control and the top-down information system can be modified.

12. *More effective budgeting systems.* Since the MBMO system can be tied with the budgeting process, an objectives-based budgeting process can be established. Such well known budgeting systems as the planning-programming-budgeting system (PPBS) and zero-base budgeting (ZBB) can be employed. Since the budgeting process is tied to objectives and action planning, more effective resource allocation decisions could be made.

13. *Improved planning and development of human resources.* MBMO is based on planning. Planning for objectives and future activities can provide more accurate information about human resource needs. Thus, it provides opportunities to program better manpower

and career planning, training and development, and overall human resources management, including succession planning.

14. *Improved performance evaluation system.* Performance evaluation systems based on personality or attributes (characteristics) have many difficulties, as we discussed in chapter 8. The MBMO system allows result-based performance evaluations. Thus, in the long run, an improved performance evaluation system can be established.

15. *Identification of trouble spots and potential problems.* MBMO requires periodic and end-of-the-cycle reviews and evaluations for control. This process can help identify current trouble spots and potential future problem areas. Thus, direct or proactive corrective actions can be taken to avoid or minimize the impact of such problems.

16. *Integration of management systems.* MBMO is a global system for the organization. It involves many subsystems, functions, resources, and coordination. Therefore, the system attempts to achieve a satisfying global solution (i.e., trying to achieve multiple organizational objectives as closely as possible based on their priorities) rather than to find suboptimal solutions (i.e., attempting to find the best solution for each subsystem). The global satisfying approach allows the organization to integrate its various components in the most effective way. Integration of management systems is perhaps the most important feature of the MBMO system.

BENEFITS TO INDIVIDUALS

1. *Clear job responsibilities.* Many organizations have job descriptions and organization charts. However, they are usually quite vague, outdated, poorly developed, or not informative about actual job responsibilities. The MBMO system clearly defines work responsibilities, interactions, evaluations procedures, thus reducing role conflicts and ambiguity for members of the organization.

2. *More work autonomy.* Because of clearly established objectives, criteria, work standards, and responsibilities, individuals can be given greater work autonomy. They can exercise their own creativity,

imagination, and innovations in carrying out their responsibilities toward the established standards. It forces both managers and employees to think in terms of outputs, rather than inputs.

3. *Greater work satisfaction.* The MBMO system provides many positive and intrinsic values to the individual, among them better vertical and horizontal communication, more objective and equitable performance evaluation systems, better compensation systems, a better insight about the overall organizational operations, challenge of meeting standards and objectives, work autonomy, etc. These factors lead to greater work satisfaction.

4. *Self-improvement and development.* The MBMO system identifies weaknesses and development needs of human resources. Although such evaluations may be discomforting initially, if properly administered the system can provide individuals with opportunities to identify their own weaknesses and develop their own capabilities.

LIMITATIONS OF MBMO

We have discussed a number of advantages of MBMO, many of which can quickly become disadvantages or liabilities if the system is not implemented and/or managed properly. As a matter of fact, some consulting fims contend that they spend more time taking MBO out than putting it in. We shall examine several important weaknesses or limitations of MBMO.

First, MBMO requires effort, time, and competence. Implementation of MBMO is a major organizational undertaking. In order to introduce the MBMO system, an organization must invest a considerable amount of effort, time, and resources. Furthermore, the system requires certain levels of human skill and competence. Many organizations believe they simply cannot afford to make the required investment in planning, formulating objectives, developing action plans, educating the staff and key managers, training people for necessary skills, and then actually implementing the system. However, perhaps the opposite would be true—they cannot afford *not* to make such investments.

Second, decisions are sometimes based on simplification and abstraction. MBMO emphasizes systematic approaches based on quantitative data, quantified objectives, systematic analysis of alternatives using models whenever possible, and determination of priorities for multiple objectives. In the process, decisions must be made based on available data, and assumptions must be made in modeling as well as on the validity of certain systematic approaches. For example, a properly implemented science model is only a good representation of the real problem—it is much more abstract and simpler than the real problem. The model may represent only about 75 percent of the actual relationships among components. Thus, a decision based on the result of the model may cover only about 75 percent of the factors. The same type of decision making may prevail for data analysis, objective formulation, and priority setting. Such a decision-making approach is especially necessary during the first cycle of MBMO. Once reliable data bases have been established, the decision making based on quantitative approaches will become more reliable.

Third, MBMO has appreciable paper work and meetings. MBMO requires modern management technologies such as management science, computers, systems science, and up-to-date managerial skills. In order to collect required data, communicate properly, and transmit generated information, an appreciable amount of paper work and a large number of meetings may be necessary—at least, initially. Action-minded executives may quickly become disillusioned with this aspect of MBMO, and regard the system as a good game of esoteric lanaguage and quantitative nonsense. Without careful planning and control, the MBMO system (like any other) can in fact turn into a paper-shuffling process with no practical value to the organization.

Fourth, MBMO does not answer ethical issues. As a management system which attempts to achieve established organizational objectives in an effective way, MBMO does not control or question whether established objectives are ethical or socially moral or desirable. This critical issue must be controlled outside the MBMO system.

Fifth, systematic analysis is not always feasible. MBMO is extremely difficult to implement when quantification is complex and difficult to apply. This is especially true for nonprofit organizations, educational institutions, and government agencies. Much progress has been made in quantifying surrogate and related objectives when it is difficult or almost impossible to quantify an objective. Many qualitative objectives are still extremely difficult to analyze; however, with better data bases and new management technologies, we have made good progress toward more systematic ways to analyze such objectives.

AVOIDING MBMO PITFALLS

Development and implementation of MBMO are difficult—many things require time, resources, human talents, and coordinated efforts. Some organizations may plunge into MBMO without proper planning and face the worst kind of organizational chaos. Pitfalls that should be avoided for successful introduction of the MBMO system include the ones below:

1. *Believing MBMO is a management panacea.* Although MBMO is a management system with great potential for achieving objectives and employee satisfaction, it is not a panacea for management ills such as incompetency, dishonesty, immorality, organizational politics, and poor human relations. MBMO should not be made the scapegoat for organizational failures that are due to inherent management weaknesses.

2. *Questioning the compatibility between MBMO and human values.* Some managers believe that being objective or analytical in managing an organization destroys human values. Development of quantified objectives, objective criteria, work standards, and evaluation measures is sometimes believed to transform human efforts into impersonal activity. However, empirical studies have shown that MBMO is not only compatible with the humanistic approach to management but it tends to enhance employee work satisfaction. MBMO gives individuals a sense of accomplishment, self-control, a challenge to meet established standards and aspiration levels, and rewards for achievements. It is false to assume that MBMO is contradictory to humanistic management.

3. *Attempting to implement MBMO in haste.* Some organizations may be so attracted to the MBMO system that they want to implement the system overnight without proper preparations. Such an implementation can result in the so-called "how to fail with MBMO without really trying." In most organizations approximately one to four years would be necessary to plan and fully implement the

system. Also, the system may need a test implementation of about one year before full-scale operation.

4. *Enforcing a strict top-down system or unrealistic objectives.* The MBMO system requires active participation by top-level managers. They should provide an overall organizational purpose, direction, and organizational objectives. A strict dictatorial type top-down management approach can quickly destroy MBMO, as employees will view the system as a heavy-handed control system. Furthermore, such one-way management style tends to demand and force unrealistic objectives on subordinates. This would ensure a quick death of MBMO in any organization.

5. *Creating a monster bureaucracy.* The integrated MBMO system, with a network of complex communication systems, interactions among subunits, a mass of analytical procedures and review and evaluations, could easily create a monster bureaucracy. The system could become so overwhelmingly large that it might run people instead of people running the system. The system can generate enormous amounts of paper work, detailed forms and work procedures, and the general trend of emphasizing the means rather than the end results. Such bureaucracy can easily destroy people's creativity, imagination, and enthusiasm, as well as organizational flexibility.

6. *Attempting to quantify the entire management system.* Quantification is one of the key elements of MBMO. However, trying to quantify everything in the organization could distort the picture and the system may be based on fabricated data. For an effective MBMO system, the efforts to quantify certain data should continue. However, it should also be recognized that qualitative data should be dealt with differently.

7. *Attempting to find a shortcut implementation.* Some organizations may try to implement MBMO by taking a shortcut. For example, an organization may try to implement the system while omitting one or more of the following important components:

- Organizational purpose
- Long-range goals and strategic planning
- Organizational objectives
- Operational objectives
- Action planning

- Review, evaluation, and control
- Training and development, compensation systems, career and manpower planning, etc.
- Systematic analysis of multiple objectives based on modern management technology
- Implementation plans

When some of the above essential elements are omitted in order to speed up the implementation, the MBMO system will most likely fail. That does not mean that an organization cannot initiate some management programs without adopting a full MBMO system. For example, management can initiate a long-range planning process, systematic analysis of alternatives, or a computer-based information system. However, a full MBMO system requires all supplying components.

8. *Assigning responsibilities without corresponding authority.* Once an individual is assigned with certain objectives, it is essential that the person be given the proper authority to fulfill responsibilities. Otherwise, the individual is put into an impossible situation, being responsible for things over which he or she has no control.

9. *Attempting to use MBMO primarily as a performance appraisal system.* MBMO is an integrated management system; performance appraisal of individuals is only one supporting by-product. When top management attempts to implement MBMO primarily as a performance appraisal system, emphasis is placed in the wrong place and MBMO will not generate the desired consequences. Employees will soon regard the system as a control device and will develop schemes to beat the system.

10. *Lack of proper organizational health for implementation.* Implementing MBMO is a drastic change for most organizations that requires a great deal of effort, time, resources, and planning. Consequently, increased stress may temporarily be placed on members of the organization. Therefore, the organization must be in good managerial health. For example, if top management does not believe in participative management, if the organization has had a long history of poor human relations, or if it has constant political infighting among several factions, it most likely will not be able to bear

the stress and develop a workable MBMO system. Thus, a reasonable organizational health level is a prerequisite for a successful implementation of MBMO.

THE FUTURE OF MBMO

MBMO is a modern management system based on the belief that the organization is most effective when important objectives are planned and pursued in an organized manner. The system promotes not only greater organizational performance but also greater personal satisfaction on the part of organizational members. If MBMO works as it should, an organization and its members can become masters of their own destinies.

Some of the primary reasons for frequent failures of the traditional MBO system have been (1) lack of systematic analysis for alternatives; (2) neglect of multiple conflicting objectives; (3) inadequate methodologies to analyze and integrate system components; (4) greater emphasis of the process itself (e.g., filling out the forms correctly) rather than the desired results; and (5) greater emphasis on performance evaluation and control rather than on the entire system effectiveness. The MBMO system attempts to alleviate these problems.

CHANGING NEEDS AND CHARACTERISTICS OF PEOPLE

We believe the future of management practice will be in the direction of MBMO because of rapidly changing environmental factors. Perhaps the most important of these factors is the changing needs and characteristics of human resources in organizations—people are better educated today and they expect a great deal more from their work than simply pay. Organizations must provide its members with opportunities to achieve their higher dimensional needs such as recognition of individual contributions, feeling of accomplishment, sense of challenge in utilizing one's abilities, potential for per-

sonal growth and development, and sense of self-actualization. The
MBMO system is better suited to meeting such human needs.

The MBMO system for a given organization must be custom built
so that it will suit the organization's unique characteristics. With
the great progress in behavioral sciences during the past two decades,
we believe organizations can implement the MBMO system in such
a way that changing human needs can be met while achieving organizational objectives. MBMO promotes employees' self-control
as the basic form of management. Individual employees will have
greater freedom to decide their own fate, both within the organization and their profession. Thus, we see an increasing popularity
and implementation of MBMO in the future.

CHANGING ENVIRONMENTAL FACTORS

Many difficult social, political, technological, legal, and economic
problems lie ahead for future managers. We have experienced extremely difficult energy problems, a shortage of key raw materials,
exorbitant inflation and unemployment rates, weak dollars abroad,
increasing government regulations, and a stronger voice by consum-
ers. All of these changing environmental factors affect management
functions. It is becoming increasingly difficult to produce desirable
levels of profits, return on investment, and productivity.

The basic concern of management in the future will be to achieve
difficult objectives within the constraints of rapidly changing environmental conditions. The role of planning, forecasting, and analyzing important external and internal factors for organizational success will further increase in the future. The MBMO system promotes
and is based on such adaptive control mechanisms where objectives
are sought based on planning and analysis.

DELEGATION OF MANAGEMENT FUNCTIONS

There is a general tendency to delegate more managerial authority
and responsibility to lower levels in large organizations. With the
increasing size of many corporations, government agencies, and nonprofit institutions, the need to manage by strategic business units,

profit centers, or activity centers is evident. The MBMO system is an effective management approach to coordinate functions of various decentralized subunits toward organizational objectives.

TECHNICAL PROGRESS

In order to analyze the ever increasing complexity of management problems, we need more advanced data collection and decision support techniques. Indeed, we have seen many important technical advances during the past twenty years. First, a number of powerful new techniques and concepts have been developed to solve complex decision problems. For example, goal programming (see Appendix A), multiple criteria linear programming, stochastic network simulation techniques, heuristics, artificial intelligence, and many computer-based interactive systems have been developed for decision analysis.

We have also seen an expanded use of many existing techniques. For example, there has been such improvement in the efficiency of linear programming, inventory models, MRP (materials requirement planning), queuing models, etc., that they can be applied to very large-scale real-world problems. We believe a continuous refinement and expansion of existing management science techniques will clearly lead to more extensive application to real-world problems.

Such technical progress has a profound implication on MBMO. Availability of practical mangement science techniques allows management to incorporate them, with relative ease, in the MBMO process. For example, the interactive goal programming approach can be imbedded in the MBMO system so that a systematic analysis of multiple objectives based on priorities could be implemented on the computer in order to generate relevant information. Thus, development and implementation of MBMO will be much more effective with continued technical progress in the future.

TECHNOLOGICAL PROGRESS

Technological progress provides the necessary means to perform a systematic analysis. However, actual applications of analytical techniques to complex real-world situations require the use of electronic computers. The remarkable progress in computer technology, both in hardware and software areas, has allowed a greater sophistication of decision models. Already, the time-sharing method and microcomputers have brought dramatic changes in modeling.

With the convenience and ready availability of computing facilities, a continuous monitoring of the decision system is possible. Also, easier access to computers at all levels of the organization certainly provides increased opportunities for people to utilize the modeling concept and analytical techniques. With the progress in computer technology, many repetitive-type operations can be handled by the computer. Another important advance in computer technology that has had a significant impact on the application of analytical techniques is the standardization of various methods (e.g., statistical and management science techniques) in the form of software packages.

Technological advance in the area of computers will have a profound impact on MBMO. Routine data collection, storage, analysis, and management control can be computerized. Thus, MBMO systems will be designed and implemented more easily in the future with the availability of advanced computer facilities.

IMPROVEMENT OF TOP-MANAGEMENT ABILITIES

Many top management personnel—the chief executives or chief operating officers—are well known for their primary concern with immediate problems and short-run objectives. For example, some top executives are generally more interested in this year's profit or sales figures rather than the organization's long-term prosperity. However, we believe the top managers are beginning to recognize the value of strategic and long-range planning plus long-term objectives. Such trends will definitely provide a strong stimulus for the use of MBMO in the future. The top-down direction in terms of long-term organizational goals, policies, and strategic planning is the very foundation of MBMO.

MBMO is likely to make the greatest contribution, therefore, to the already well managed, healthy organization, the organization willing to go that "extra mile" to be the leader in its industry.

REFERENCES

Atkinson, J.W., and Feather, N.T., eds. *A Theory of Achievement Motivation.* New York: Wiley, 1966.

Carroll, S.J., and Tosi, H.L. *Management by Objectives.* New York: Macmillan, 1973.

Harvey, L.J. *Managing Colleges and Universities by Objectives.* Wheaton, Ill.: Ireland Educational Corp., 1976.

Lee, S.M., and Moore, L.J. *Introduction to Decision Science.* New York: Petrocelli/Charter, 1975.

Meyer, H.H., Kay, E., and French, J.R.P. "Split Roles in Performance Appraisal." *Harvard Business Review* 43(1965): 123-29.

Odiorne, G.S. *MBO II: A System of Managerial Leadership for the 80's.* Belmont, Calif.: Fearon Pitman, 1979.

Appendices

A. The Concept of Goal Programming for MBMO

One of the most promising techniques for multiple objective decision making is goal programming. Goal programming is a powerful tool which draws upon the highly developed and tested technique of linear programming, but provides a simultaneous solution to a complex system of competing objectives. Goal programming can handle decision problems having a single goal with multiple subgoals.

Often goals set by management compete for scarce resources. Furthermore, these goals may be incommensurable. Thus there is a need to establish a hierarchy of importance among these conflicting goals so that low-order goals are satisfied or have reached the point beyond which no further improvements are desirable, as clearly shown by the MBMO system. If management can provide an ordinal ranking of goals in terms of their contributions or importance to the organization and if all relationships of the model are linear, the problem can be solved by goal programming.

In goal programming, instead of attempting to maximize or minimize the objective criterion directly, as in linear programming, the deviations between goals and what can be achieved within the given set of constraints are minimized. In the simplex algorithm of linear programming such deviations are called slack variables. These variables take on a new significance in goal programming. The deviational variable is represented in two dimensions, both positive and negative deviations from each subgoal or goal. The objective function then becomes the minimization of these deviations based on the relative importance or priority assigned to them.

The solution of any linear programming problem is based on a cardinal value such as profit or cost. The distinguishing characteristic of goal programming is that it allows for an ordinal solution. The decision maker may be unable to obtain information about the value or cost of a goal or a subgoal, but often can determine its upper or lower limits. Usually, the decision maker can determine the priority of the desired attainment of each goal or subgoal and rank the priorities in an ordinal sequence. Obviously, it is not possible to achieve every goal to the extent desired. Thus, with or without goal programming, the decision maker attaches a certain priority to the achievement of a particular goal. The true value of goal programming, therefore, is its contribution to the solution of decision problems involving multiple and conflicting goals according to management's priority structure.

Goal programming has been applied to a wide range of planning, resource allocation, policy analysis, and functional management problems. The first application study was for advertising media planning. However, the first real-world application was in the area of manpower planning. Subsequently, goal programming was applied to aggregate production planning, transportation logistics, academic resource planning, hospital administration, marketing planning, capital budgeting, portfolio selection, municipal economic planning, resource allocation for environmental protection, and many other managerial problems.

THE GOAL PROGRAMMING MODEL

Goal programming is a linear mathematical model in which the optimum attainment of multiple goals is sought within the given decision environment. The decision environment determines the basic components of the model, namely, the decision variables, constraints, and the objective function.

Let us now consider the goal programming model through a simple illustration. Goal programming involving a simple goal with multiple subgoals will be discussed first, followed by an analysis of multiple goals.

SINGLE GOAL WITH MULTIPLE SUBGOALS

A furniture manufacturer produces two products, desks and tables. The unit profit is $80 for a desk and $40 for a table. The goal of the plant manager is to earn a total profit of exactly $640 in the next week.

We can interpret the profit goal in terms of subgoals, which are sales volumes of desks and tables. Then a goal programming model can be formulated as follows:

Minimize

$$Z = d_1^- + d_1^+$$

subject to

$$\$80X_1 + \$40X_2 + d_1^- - d_1^+ = \$640$$
$$X_1, X_2, d_1^-, d_1^+ \geqslant 0$$

where

X_1 = number of desks sold
X_2 = number of tables sold
d_1^- = underachievement of the profit goal of $640
d_1^+ = overachievement of the profit goal of $640

If the profit goal is not completely achieved, then obviously the slack in the profit goal will be expressed by d_1^-, which represents the underachievement of the goal (or negative deviation from the goal). On the other hand, if the solution shows a profit in excess of $640, the d_1^+ will show some value. If the profit goal of $640 is achieved exactly, both d_1^- and d_1^+ will be zero. It should be noted that d_1^- and d_1^+ are complementary. If d_1^- takes a nonzero value, d_1^+ will be zero, and vice versa. Since at least one of the deviational variables will always be zero, $d_1^- \times d_1^+ = 0$. In the above example, there are an infinite number of combinations of X_1 and X_2 that will achieve the goal. The solution will be any linear combination of X_1 and X_2 between the two points ($X_1 = 8$, $X_2 = 0$) and $X_1 = 0$, $X_2 = 16$). This straight line is exactly the isoprofit function when total profit is $640.

In the above example we did not have any model constraints. Now let us suppose that in addition to the profit goal constraint considered, the following two constraints are imposed. The marketing department reports that the maximum number of desks that can be sold in a week is six. The maximum number of tables that can be sold is eight.

Now the new goal programming model can be presented in the following way:

Minimize

$$Z = d_1^- + d_1^+$$

subject to

$$\$80X_1 + \$40X_2 + d_1^- - d_1^+ = \$640$$
$$X_1 \leqslant 6$$
$$X_2 \leqslant 8$$
$$X_1, X_2, d_1^-, d_1^+ \geqslant 0$$

The solution to the above problem can be easily calculated on the back of an envelope. The solution is $X_1 = 6$ and $X_2 = 4$. With this solution the deviational variables d_1^- and d_1^+ will both be zero. The plant manager's profit goal can be achieved under the new constraints imposed on the subgoals.

ANALYSIS OF MULTIPLE GOALS

The model illustrated above can be extended to handle cases of multiple goals. Let us assume that these goals are conflicting and incommensurable.

The manager from the furniture manufacturer case illustrated above desires to achieve a weekly profit as close to $640 as possible. The manager also wants to achieve sales volume for desks and tables close to six and to four, respectively. The manager's decision problem can be formulated as a goal programming model as follows:

Minimize

$$Z = d_1^- + d_2^- + d_3^- + d_1^+$$

subject to

$$\$80X_1 + \$40X_2 + d_1{}^- - d_1{}^+ = \$640$$
$$X_1 + d_2{}^- = 6$$
$$X_2 + d_3{}^- = 4$$

where $d_2{}^-$ and $d_3{}^-$ represent underachievements of sales volume for desks and tables, respectively. It should be noted that $d_2{}^+$ and $d_3{}^+$ are not included in the second and third constraints, since the sales goals are given as the maximum possible sales volume. The solution to this problem can be found by a simple examination of the problem: If $X_1 = 6$, and $X_2 = 4$, all goals will be completely attained. Therefore, $d_1{}^- = d_2{}^- = d_3{}^- = d_1{}^+ = 0$.

RANKING AND WEIGHTING OF MULTIPLE GOALS

In the above example we had a case in which all goals are achieved simultaneously within the given constraints. However, in a real decision environment this is rarely the case. Quite often, most goals are competitive in terms of need for scarce resources. In the presence of incompatible multiple goals the manager needs to exercise judgment about the importance of the individual goals. In other words, the most important goal must be achieved to the extent desired before the next goal is considered.

Goals of the decision maker may simply be meeting a certain set of constraints. For example, the manager may set a goal concerning a stable employment level in the plant, which is simply a part of the production constraint. Or the goal may be an entirely separate function from the constraints of the system. If that is the case, the goal constraint must be generated in the model. The decision maker must analyze the system and investigate whether all of his or her goals are expressed in the goal programming model. When all constraints and goals are completely identified in the model, the decision maker must analyze each goal in terms of whether over- or underachievement of the goal is satisfactory or not. Based on this analysis he or she can assign deviational variables to the regular and/or goal constraints. If overachievement is acceptable, positive deviation from the goal can be eliminated from the objective function. On the other hand, if underachievement of a certain goal is acceptable, negative deviation should not be included in the objective function. If the exact achievement of the goal is desired, both negative and positive deviations must be represented in the objective function.

In order to achieve the ordinal solution—that is, to achieve the goals according to their importance—negative and/or positive deviations about the goal must be ranked according to the "preemptive" priority factors. In this way the low-order goals are considered only after high-order goals are achieved as desired. If there are goals in several ranks of importance, the preemptive priority factor p_k ($k = 1$, $2, \ldots, k$) should be assigned to the negative and/or positive deviational variables. The preemptive priority factors have the relationship of $p_1 \ggg p_2 \ggg p_3 \cdots p_k \ggg p_{k+1}$, where $\ggg$ means "very much greater than." The priority relationship implies that multiplication by n, however large it may be, cannot make the lower level goal as important as the higher goal. It is, of course, possible to refine goals even further by means of decomposing (subdividing) the deviational variables. To do this, additional constraints and additional priority factors may be required.

One more step to be considered in the goal programming model formulation is the weighting of deviational variables at the same priority level. For example, if the sales goal involves two different products there will be two deviational variables with the same priority factor. The criterion to be used in determining the differential weights of deviational variables is the minimization of the opportunity cost or regret. This implies that the coefficient of regret, which is always positive, should be assigned to the individual deviational variable with the identical p_k factor. The coefficient of regret simply represents the relative amount of unsatisfactory deviation from the goal. Therefore, deviational variables on the same priority level must be commensurable, although deviations that are on different priority levels need not be commensurable.

Consider the following modified case of the illustration given in the previous examples. Production of either a desk or a table requires one hour of production capacity in the plant. The plant has a normal maximum production capacity of 10 hours/week. Because of the limited sales capacity, the maximum number of desks and tables that can be sold are six and eight per week, respectively. The unit profit for a desk is \$80 and for a table \$40.

The plant manager has set the following goals, arranged in order of importance:

1. Avoid any underutilization of production capacity (providing job security to the plant employees).
2. Sell as many desks and tables as possible. Since the unit profit from the sale of a desk is twice the amount of profit from a table, the manager has twice as much desire to achieve the sales goal for desks as for tables.
3. Minimize overtime operation of the plant as much as possible.

In the above example, the plant manager is to make a decision that will achieve the goals as closely as possible with minimum sacrifice. Since overtime operation is allowed in this example, production of desk and tables may take more than the normal production capacity of 10 hours. Therefore, the operational capacity can be expressed as

$$X_1 + X_2 + d_1^- - d_1^+ = 10$$

where

X_1 = number of desks to be produced
X_2 = number of tables to be produced
d_1^- = idle (underutilization of) production capacity
d_1^+ = overtime operation

Accordingly, the sales capacity constraints can be written as

$$X_1 + d_2^- = 6$$
$$X_2 + d_3^- = 8$$

where

d_2^- = underachievement of sales goal for desks
d_3^- = underachievement of sales goal for tables

It should be noted that d_2^+ and d_3^+ are not in the equation, since the sales goals given are the maximum possible sales volume.

In addition to the variables and constraints stated above, the following preemptive priority factors are to be defined:

P_1 : The highest priority, assigned by management to the underutilization of product capacity (i.e., d_1^-).

P_2: The second priority factor, assigned to the underutilization of sales capacity (i.e., d_2^- and d_3^-). However, management puts twice the importance of d_2^- as that on d_3^- in accordance with respective profit figures for desks and tables.

P_3: The lowest priority factor, assigned to overtime in the production capacity (i.e., d_1^+).

Now the complete model can be formulated. The objective is the minimization of deviation from goals. The deviant variable associated with the highest preemptive priority must be minimized to the fullest possible extent. When no further improvement is desirable or possible in the highest goal, then the deviations associated with the next highest priority factor will be minimized. The model can be expressed as:
Minimize

$$Z = P_1 d_1^- + 2P_2 d_2^- + P_2 d_3^- + P_3 d_1^+$$

subject to

$$X_1 + X_2 + d_1^- - d_1^+ = 10$$
$$X_1 + d_2^- = 6$$
$$X_2 + d_3^- = 8$$
$$X_1, X_2, d_1^-, d_2^-, d_3^-, d_1^+ \geqslant 0$$

From a simple investigation of the model we can derive the following optimal solution: $X_1 = 6, X_2 = 8, d_1^- = d_2^- = d_3^- = 0, d_1^+ = 4$. The first two goals are completely attained, but the third goal is only partially achieved, since the overtime operation could not be minimized to zero. This result is due to the direct conflict between the second (sales) goal and the third (minimization of overtime) goal. This kind of result reflects the everyday problem experienced in business when there are several conflicting goals.

Now the general goal programming model can be presented as:
Minimize

$$Z = \sum_{k=1}^{K} \sum_{i=1}^{m} p_k (w_i^- d_i^- + w_i^+ d_i^+)$$

subject to

$$\sum_{j=1}^{n} a_{ij} X_j + d_i^- - d_i^+ = b_i \quad (i = 1, \ldots, m)$$

$$X_j, d_i^-, d_i^+ \geqslant 0$$

In this model, P_k is the preemptive priority factor assigned to goal k; w_i^- and w_i^+ are numerical weights assigned to the deviations of goal i at a given priority level; d_i^- and d_i^+ are the negative and positive deviations, respectively; a_{ij} is the technological coefficient of X_j in goal i; and b_i is the right-hand side value of goal i.

MODIFIED SIMPLEX METHOD OF GOAL PROGRAMMING

In general, the goal programming model is a linear mathematical model in which the optimum attainment of objectives is sought within the given decision environment. The decision environment determines the basic components of the model, namely, the constraints (system and goal), decision variables, and the objective function. A goal programming model can perform three types of analysis: (1) it determines the input (resource) requirements to achieve a set of goals; (2) it determines the degree of attainment of defined goals with given resources; and (3) it provides the optimum solution under the varying inputs and priority structures of goals.

The system constraints represent the absolute restrictions imposed by the decision environment on the model. For example, there are only seven days in a week (time constraint); the production capacity in a short run is limited to certain available hours (manpower constraint); the production should be limited to demand and storage capacity (physical constraint). The system constraints must be satisfied before any of the goal constraints can be considered.

The goal constraints represent those functions that present desired levels of certain measurements. For example, desired level of pollution control, desired level of profit, desired diversification of investments among various available alternatives, and desired market share fore each product, are good illustrations of goal constraints. In order to achieve the ordinal solution, negative and/or positive deviations about the goal must be minimized based on the preemptive priority weights assigned to them. Thus the low-order goals are sought only after the higher order goals are fully attained as desired ($P_k \ggg P_{k+1}$). When there are multiple goals at a given priority level, differential weights (w_i) are assigned based on the numerical opportunity costs.

The most widely used solution method of goal programming is the modified simplex method. Those who are not familiar with goal programming should consult the references at the end of chapter 6.

INTERACTIVE APPROACH TO GOAL PROGRAMMING

One of the primary characteristics of the application of goal programming is the concept of an ordinal solution based on preemptive priority weights which are assigned to multiple conflicting objectives. It is necessary to analyze the trade-offs among the objectives when their priority structure is changed due to a changing decision environment. If a goal programming model uses numerical weights instead of preemptive priority weights, an ordinary sensitivity analysis can be easily performed. However, the ordinal solution approach based on the preemptive priorities makes it difficult to analyze the trade-offs among the goals in the conventional sensitivity analysis fashion.

An equally important analysis that is useful for managerial decisions is the effect of changes in goal levels (b_i) and technological coefficients (a_{ij}), addition or deletion of constraints, and addition or deletion of decision variables. Perhaps the most prevalent changes would be in goal levels because of changing environmental conditions and technological coefficients due to technical improvements and behavioral changes of personnel.

Perhaps the best way to analyze changes to the system under analysis would be an interactive mode where the decision maker and the goal programming model interact via a computer terminal. The interactive approach proposed here can perform an on-line analysis of the effect of changes in model parameters as well as a complete sensitivity analysis of the optimal solution. The interactive goal programming approach provides a systematic process in which the decision maker seeks the most satisfactory solution. The process allows the decision maker to reformulate the model and compare the solutions systematically in terms of their achievement of multiple objectives.

The interactive system is installed on an IBM 370-158 and consists of a control program (CP) and the conversational monitor system (CMS). The system allows the user to create and edit files (programs, problems, etc.) and to execute programs conversationally. The interactive goal programming is based on the modified simplex method of Lee. Consequently, once the preliminary logon procedure is completed, the input formal is exactly the same as the regular goal programming input required by Lee's program.

B. An Application Example of Goal Programming

The action planning phase of MBMO can be an extremely complex process when we attempt to achieve a set of multiple and conflicting objectives. A stepwise "one objective at a time" approach has very limited value because the goal conflict presents trade-off situations. Perhaps the most pragmatic and widely applied management science technique to handle multiple objective decision problems is goal programming. In this appendix, a relatively simple capital budgeting problem will be analyzed by zero-one goal programming approach. Readers interested in learning more about the goal programming approach should consult the first two references at the end of chapter 6.

A CAPITAL BUDGETING PROBLEM WITH MULTIPLE OBJECTIVES

A chemical firm is currently considering 14 investment opportunities. The problem is a case of capital budgeting under a capital rationing situation where there are multiple conflicting objectives. Furthermore, investment projects under consideration are indivisible. Thus, the problem requires a zero-one solution.

Table B.1 presents the pertinent information about the firm's current operations and estimated consequences of the investment projects. It is assumed that the medium-run goals concerning sales level are for time periods 4 to 6, and the long-run goals concerning the market share are for periods 7 to 9. Consequently, all short-run goals are for time periods 1, 2, and 3.

TABLE B.1 Summary of Investment Projects and Current Operations

Projects i	ICO	NPV	NCF$_j$			PAT$_j$			MMN	SAL$_j$			MKT$_j$		
			$j=1$	$j=2$	$j=3$	$j=1$	$j=2$	$j=3$		$j=4$	$j=5$	$j=6$	$j=7$	$j=8$	$j=9$
1	$375	$215	$77.0	$133.8	$175.7	$56	$115	$149	31	$250	$165	$120	.300%	.250%	.250%
2	350	150	60.0	95.6	131.8	46	75	111	29	110	140	170	.500	.500	.500
3	100	40	27.5	41.5	58.6	7	21	38	20	60	0	0	.0	.0	.0
4	380	280	22.0	32.1	58.6	2	5.5	18	32	300	450	530	1.000	1.000	1.000
5	500	365	38.5	64.2	117.1	15	32.5	65	42	420	695	1000	1.700	1.900	2.100
6	440	220	60.5	69.9	80.5	20	28.5	40	37	220	300	360	.700	.850	1.100
7	330	115	27.5	35.1	51.2	5	11	22	27	250	330	380	1.000	1.150	1.300
8	150	65	33.0	41.5	51.2	10	20	30	21	130	160	190	.400	.150	.100
9	210	95	27.5	41.5	58.6	10	25	40	17	200	230	160	.500	.450	.400
10	600	475	5.5	13.0	29.3	0	2.5	5	50	100	170	330	1.600	2.500	3.200
11	450	315	5.5	9.7	14.6	0	0	5	37	55	107.5	190	2.000	2.550	2.900
12	260	170	5.5	9.7	14.6	0	0	0	21	55	70	140	1.800	2.100	2.400
13*	270	120	27.5	51.1	80.5	10	27.5	50	30	220	285	355	.200	.100	.100
14**	290	140	27.5	51.1	80.5	15	15	30	26	160	160	160	.400	.525	.600
Current Operations	–	–	303.0	350.0	403.0	150	172.5	198	–	1174	1361	1579	4.280	4.970	5.760

$ = 1,000

*pollution control project for plant improvement
**pollution contol project for the installation of a new system

ICO = initial cash outflow of each project
NPV = net present value of each project
NCF$_j$ = net cash flow in period j for each project
PAT$_j$ = after-tax profit contribution in period j for each project
MMN = management manpower needs for each project
SAL$_j$ = sales contribution in period j for each project
MKT$_j$ = market share contribution in period j for each project

ANSWER

$$NCF_j \qquad j=1 \ \ j=2 \ \ j=3$$
$$PAT_j \qquad j=1 \ \ j=2 \ \ j=3$$
$$SAL_j \qquad j=4 \ \ j=5 \ \ j=6$$
$$MKT_j \qquad j=7 \ \ j=8 \ \ j=9$$

etc.

DECISION VARIABLES

Decision variables are 14 potential projects as shown below.

X_i = Project i (i = 1, 2, . . . , 14)
X_i = 1 when project i is accepted
X_i = 0 when project i is rejected

MANAGEMENT GOALS AND PRIORITIES

Management has provided the following goals in the order of their importance:

P_1: The most important goal of management is to accept one of the two mutually exclusive antipollution projects (either X_{13} or X_{14}).

P_2: The second goal is to limit the total investment expenditure to the allocated budget of \$1,400 (in \$1,000).

P_3: The third goal is to limit the total management manpower needs of the new investment project to 130.

P_4: The fourth goal of management is to achieve adequate levels of net cash flow during the first three periods. The desired aggregate net cash flows during the periods are: period 1 = \$450, period 2 = \$589, and period 3 = \$772 (growth rate of 31 percent). The expected cash flows from the current operations during the same periods are \$303, \$350, and \$403, respectively. Consequently, the desired net cash flows from the investment project during the first three periods are \$147, \$239, and \$369, respectively. It is assumed that all funds not allocated to new projects will be employed in short-term money market instruments yielding 10 percent on an after-tax basis and coming due at the end of the first period. Thus, the net cash flow goal constraint for period 1 can be formulated in the following manner:

$$(1400 - \sum_{i=1}^{14} ICO_i X_i)1.10 + \sum_{i=1}^{14} NCF_{i1} X_i + d^- - d^+ = 147$$

P_5: The fifth goal is to secure satisfactory levels of profit after tax during the three periods. The desired aggregate profits after tax are: period 1 = \$220, period 2 = \$308, and period 3 = \$431 (growth rate of 40 percent). The expected PATs from ongoing operations during the same periods are \$150, \$172.5, and \$198, respectively. Again, it is assumed that all funds not allocated to new projects will be employed in short-term money market instruments yielding 10 percent on an after-tax basis and coming due at the end of the first period.

P_6: The sixth goal of the firm is to achieve satisfactory medium-range sales levels during periods 4, 5, and 6. While the firm has confidence in its cash flow and profit forecasts in the early time periods of a project's life, the accuracy of forecasts beyond the short run diminishes at an increasing rate. Consequently, management attempts to use the sales goal as a surrogate as they feel more confident in the forecasts of sales than either cash flows or profits during the medium-run periods. The desired aggregate sales levels are: period 4 = \$2100, period 5 = \$2604, and period 6 = \$3229 (growth rate of 24 percent). The expected sales from ongoing operations during the same period are \$1174, \$1361, and \$1579, respectively.

P_7: The seventh goal of management is to achieve a desired market share from the current capital budget in the long run. The goal level is in terms of the percentage market share from projects accepted under the current capital budget and ongoing operations. The desired aggregate market share during the periods 7 through 9 is period 7 = 10.0 percent, period 8 = 11.9 percent, and period 9 = 14.16 percent (growth rate of 19 percent). The expected market share from the ongoing operations is 4.28 percent, 4.97 percent, and 5.76 percent during the same periods.

P_8: The last goal of management is to maximize the net present value of the selected projects.

SYSTEM CONSTRAINTS

The zero-one requirement for the decision variables (investment projects) is automatically taken care of by the enumeration procedure of the zero-one goal programming approach. The mutually exclusive pollution control projects (X_{13} and X_{14}), one of which must be accepted to meet federal guidelines, can also be easily handled by the zero-one goal programming algorithm as a regular goal constraint. However, the ordinary goal programming formulation requires two separate runs with the combination of ($X_{13} = 1, X_{14} = 0$), and ($X_{13} = 0, X_{14} = 1$), and cannot handle the problem of indivisibility of projects.

MODEL CONSTRAINTS

System Constraints

$$X_i + d_i^- - d_i^+ = 1.0 \ (i = 1, \ldots, 12)$$

Government Regulations or Standards Constraint

$$X_{13} + X_{14} + d_{13}^- - d_{13}^+ = 1.0$$

Budget Ceiling Goal

$$375X_1 + 350X_2 + 100X_3 + 380X_4 + 500X_5 + 400X_6 + 330X_7$$
$$+ 150X_8 + 210X_9 + 600X_{10} + 450X_{11} + 260X_{12} + 270X_{13} + 290X_{14}$$
$$+ d_{15}^- - d_{15}^+ = 1400$$

Management Manpower Needs Goal

$$31X_1 + 29X_2 + 20X_3 + 32X_4 + 42X_5 + 37X_6 + 27X_7 + 21X_8$$
$$+ 17X_9 + 50X_{10} + 37X_{11} + 21X_{12} + 30X_{13} + 26X_{14} + d_{16}^- - d_{16}^+$$
$$= 130$$

Net Cash Flow Goal

$$- 335.5X_1 - 319.0X_2 - 82.5X_3 - 396.0X_4 - 511.0X_5 - 423.5X_6$$
$$- 335.5X_7 - 132.0X_8 - 203.5X_9 - 654.5X_{10} - 489.5X_{11} - 280.5X_{12}$$
$$- 269.5X_{13} - 291.5X_{14} + d_{17}^- - d_{17}^+ = - 1393.0$$

$$133.8X_1 + 95.6X_2 + 41.5X_3 + 32.1X_4 + 64.2X_5 + 69.9X_6$$
$$+ 35.1X_7 + 41.5X_8 + 41.5X_9 + 13.0X_{10} + 9.7X_{11} + 9.7X_{12}$$
$$+ 51.1X_{13} + 51.1X_{14} + d_{18}^- - d_{18}^+ = 239.0$$

$$175.7X_1 + 131.8X_2 + 58.6X_3 + 58.6X_4 + 117.1X_5 + 80.5X_6$$
$$+ 51.2X_7 + 51.2X_8 + 58.6X_9 + 29.3X_{10} + 14.6X_{11} + 14.6X_{12}$$
$$+ 80.5X_{13} + 80.5X_{14} + d_{19}^- - d_{19}^+ = 369.0$$

Profit After-Tax Goal

$$18.5X_1 + 11.0X_2 - 3.0X_3 - 36.0X_4 - 35.0X_5 - 24.0X_6 - 28.0X_7$$
$$- 5.0X_8 - 11.0X_9 - 60.0X_{10} - 45.0X_{11} - 26.0X_{12} - 17.0X_{13} - 24.0X_{14}$$
$$+ d_{20}^- - d_{20}^+ = 70.0$$

$$115.0X_1 + 75.0X_2 + 21.0X_3 + 5.5X_4 + 32.5X_5 + 28.5X_6$$
$$+ 11.0X_7 + 20.0X_8 + 25.0X_9 + 2.5X_{10} + 0.0X_{11} + 0.0X_{12} + 27.5X_{13}$$
$$+ 15.0X_{14} + d_{21}^- - d_{21}^+ = 135.0$$

$$149X_1 + 111X_2 + 38X_3 + 18X_4 + 65X_5 + 40X_6 + 22X_7$$
$$+ 30X_8 + 40X_9 + 5X_{11} + 0X_{12} + 50X_{13} + 30X_{14} + d_{22}^- - d_{22}^+$$
$$= 233.0$$

Sales Level Goal

$$250X_1 + 110X_2 + 60X_3 + 300X_4 + 420X_5 + 220X_6 + 250X_7$$
$$+ 130X_8 + 200X_9 + 100X_{10} + 55X_{11} + 55X_{12} + 220X_{13} + 160X_{14}$$
$$+ d_{23}^- - d_{23}^+ = 926$$

$$165.0X_1 + 140.0X_2 + 0.0X_3 + 450.0X_4 + 695.0X_5 + 300.0X_6$$
$$+ 330.0X_7 + 160.0X_8 + 230.0X_9 + 170.0X_{10} + 107.5X_{11} + 70.0X_{12}$$
$$+ 285.0X_{13} + 160.0X_{14} + d_{24}^- - d_{24}^+ = 1243$$

$$120X_1 + 170X_2 + 0X_3 + 530X_4 + 1000X_5 + 360X_6 + 380X_7$$
$$+ 190X_8 + 160X_9 + 330X_{10} + 190X_{11} + 140X_{12} + 355X_{13} + 160X_{14}$$
$$+ d_{25}^- - d_{25}^+ = 1650$$

Market Share Goal

$$0.30X_1 + 0.50X_2 + 0.00X_3 + 1.00X_4 + 1.70X_5 + 0.70X_6$$
$$+ 1.00X_7 + 0.40X_8 + 0.50X_9 + 1.60X_{10} + 2.00X_{11} + 1.80X_{12}$$
$$+ 0.20X_{13} + 0.40X_{14} + d_{26}^- - d_{26}^+ = 5.72$$

$$0.250X_1 + 0.500X_2 + 0.000X_3 + 1.000X_4 + 1.900X_5$$
$$+ 0.850X_6 + 1.150X_7 + 0.150X_8 + 0.450X_9 + 2.500X_{10} + 2.550X_{11}$$
$$+ 2.100X_{12} + 0.100X_{13} + 0.525X_{14} + d_{27}^- - d_{27}^+ = 6.935$$

$$0.250X_1 + 0.500X_2 + 0.000X_3 + 1.000X_4 + 2.100X_5$$
$$+ 1.100X_6 + 1.300X_7 + 0.100X_8 + 0.400X_9 + 3.200X_{10} + 2.900X_{11}$$
$$+ 2.400X_{12} + 0.000X_{13} + 0.600X_{14} + d_{28}^- - d_{28}^+ = 8.402$$

Maximize Net Present Value

$$215X_1 + 150X_2 + 40X_3 + 280X_4 + 365X_5 + 220X_6 + 115X_7$$
$$+ 65X_8 + 95X_9 + 475X_{10} + 315X_{11} + 170X_{12} + 120X_{13} + 140X_{14}$$
$$+ d_{29}^- - d_{29}^+ = 1000000$$

Objective Function

Minimize
$$Z = P_0 \sum_{i=1}^{12} d_i^+ + P_1(d_{13}^- + d_{13}^+ + d_{14}^- + d_{14}^+) + P_2 d_{15}^+ + P_3 d_{16}^+$$
$$+ P_4(.90909d_{17}^- + .82645d_{18}^- + .75131d_{19}^-) + P_5 \sum_{i=20}^{22} d_i^-$$
$$+ P_6 \sum_{i=23}^{25} d_i^- + P_7 \sum_{i=26}^{28} d_i^- + P_8 d_{29}^-$$

MODEL RESULTS AND DISCUSSION

GOAL PROGRAMMING MODEL 1

In this model, the mutually exclusive pollution control projects X_{13} and X_{14} are given values of 1 and 0, respectively. In other words, project 13 is accepted and project 14 rejected. The results of the model are:

Variables

$X_1 = 0.697$
$X_3 = 0.174$
$X_5 = 1.000$
$X_8 = 0.455$
$X_{11} = 0.047$
$X_{12} = 1.000$
$X_{13} = 1.000$

all other $X_i = 0$

GOAL ATTAINMENT MODEL 1

P_1: completely attained. Project X_{13} is accepted for pollution control.

P_2: completely attained. The total amount of funds allocated to the projects was \$1,398.46, \$1.54 below the budget ceiling.

P_3: completely attained. The total management manpower utilized was 129.41, 0.59 below the maximum ceiling of 130.

P_4: completely attained. The net cash flows for the first three periods were:

period	desired level	actual level
1	\$147.00	\$147.00
2	239.00	244.94
3	369.00	369.00

There was a slight overachievement in period 2.

P_5: completely attained. The profits after tax for the first three periods were:

period	desired level	actual level
1	\$ 70.00	\$ 70.00
2	135.50	153.00
3	233.00	239.48

There were overachievements in periods 2 and 3.

P_6: completely attained. The sales levels during periods 4, 5, and 6 were projected as:

period	desired level	projected level
4	\$ 926.00	\$ 941.65
5	1243.00	1243.00
6	1650.00	1674.13

There were overachievements in periods 4 and 6.

P_7: not completely attained (unattained portion = 3.445). The market shares resulting from the projects during periods 7, 8, and 9 were:

period	desired level	projected level
7	5.720%	4.185%
8	6.935	4.462
9	8.402	4.856

There was considerable degree of underattainment in each period. The primary reason for this result is that there exists conflict between these three goals and higher order goals, namely, acceptance of the mutually exclusive projects ($X_{13} = 1$, $X_{14} = 0$), the cash flow goals (P_3), and the sales goals (P_5). A more complete sensitivity analysis of the trade-offs among the conflicting goals can be made from the modified simplex solution.

P_8: not completely attained as expected. In order to attain higher order goals, the maximum net present value attained was $857.06. The basic goal conflicts exist between this goal and P_4, P_6, and P_7.

GOAL PROGRAMMING MODEL 2

In this model, the mutually exclusive pollution control projects X_{13} and X_{14} are given values of 0 and 1, respectively. Thus, project 13 is rejected and project 14 is fully accepted.

Variable
$X_1 = 0.536$
$X_2 = 0.204$
$X_4 = 0.307$
$X_5 = 1.000$
$X_8 = 1.000$
$X_{12} = 0.273$
$X_{14} = 1.000$
all other $X_i = 0$

GOAL ATTAINMENT MODEL 2

This model also yielded complete attainment of the first six goals (P_1 through P_6). However, the unattainments of P_7 and P_8 are higher for this model than for model 1. For example, the degree of goal attainments for P_7 and P_8 were:

P_7: market share goals (unattained portion = 4.489).

period	desired level	projected level
7	4.720%	3.551%
8	6.935	3.691
9	8.402	3.998

P_8: net present value attained = \$849.00.

Consequently, we can easily conclude that goal programming model 1 yields a superior result. Thus, if the indivisibility requirement is not enforced, project 13 should be accepted and project 14 be rejected.

GOAL PROGRAMMING MODEL 3
(ZERO-ONE GOAL PROGRAMMING MODEL)

This model is based on the implicit enumerative zero-one goal programming algorithm. The results are:

Variables

X_2 = 1.000

X_5 = 1.000

X_9 = 1.000

X_{13} = 1.000

all other X_i = 0

GOAL ATTAINMENT MODEL 3

The zero-one model yielded complete attainment of the first six goals (P_1 through P_6). However, the levels of goal attainment for P_7 and P_8 goals were inferior to that of the first two models. The degree of goal attainments for P_7 and P_8 were:

P_7: market share goals (unattained portion = 5.579).

period	desired level	projected level
7	5.720%	2.900%
8	6.935	2.950
9	8.402	3.000

P_8: net present value attained = $730.00

The above solution is based on not only the indivisibility require-ments for the projects but also the multiple conflicting objectives considered in the capital rationing problem. Since the imposition of the indivisibility requirements of the projects can only further reduce the solution space for the problem, the zero-one solution is expected to be less satisfactory than that of a regular goal program-ming model. Then, the cost of indivisibility of projects will be simply the difference in the goal attainments of model 1 and zero-one model as shown below.

Model 1		*Zero–One Model*	
P_1 to P_6 completely attained		P_1 to P_6 completely attained	
P_7:		P_7:	
period	market share	period	market share
7	4.185%	7	2.900%
8	4.462	8	2.950
9	4.856	9	3.000
P_8: NPV = $857.06		P_8: NPV = $730.00	

This study is intended to demonstrate that a capital budgeting model which permits the incorporation of management's priority for multiple objectives and indivisibility requirement to projects would be a significant contribution. In fact, it is the only way of solving the real problem where the investments *are* actually indivisible. The zero-one goal programming model presented in this study permits solution, under these conditions, with relative ease and speed. Once the data for the potential list of projects has been entered, simple changes in model parameters (priority structure, goal levels, or technological coefficients) can be easily facilitated resulting in sensitivity insights into the model.

Index